Other books by Randy Alcorn

If God Is Good...

Faith *in the* Midst *of* Suffering *and* Evil

RANDY ALCORN

MULTNOMAH
BOOKS

IF GOD IS GOOD
PUBLISHED BY MULTNOMAH BOOKS
12265 Oracle Boulevard, Suite 200
Colorado Springs, Colorado 80921

All Scripture quotations, unless otherwise indicated, are taken from the Holy Bible, New International Version®. NIV®. Copyright © 1973, 1978, 1984 by International Bible Society. Used by permission of Zondervan Publishing House. All rights reserved. Scripture quotations marked (ESV) are taken from The Holy Bible, English Standard Version, copyright © 2001 by Crossway Bibles, a division of Good News Publishers. Used by permission. All rights reserved. Scripture quotations marked (MSG) are taken from The Message by Eugene H. Peterson. Copyright © 1993, 1994, 1995, 1996, 2000, 2001, 2002. Used by permission of NavPress Publishing Group. All rights reserved. Scripture quotations marked (KJV) are taken from the King James Version. Scripture quotations marked (NASB) are taken from the New American Standard Bible®. © Copyright The Lockman Foundation 1960, 1962, 1963, 1968, 1971, 1972, 1973, 1975, 1977. Used by permission. (www.Lockman.org). Scripture quotations marked (NKJV) are taken from the New King James Version®. Copyright © 1982 by Thomas Nelson Inc. Used by permission. All rights reserved. Scripture quotations marked (NLT) are taken from the Holy Bible, New Living Translation, copyright © 1996, 2004. Used by permission of Tyndale House Publishers Inc., Wheaton, Illinois 60189. All rights reserved. Scripture quotations marked (RSV) are taken from the Revised Standard Version of the Bible, copyright © 1952 [2nd edition, 1971] by the Division of Christian Education of the National Council of the Churches of Christ in the USA. Used by permission. All rights reserved. Scripture quotations marked (Phillips) are taken from The New Testament in Modern English, Revised Edition © 1972 by J. B. Phillips. Copyright renewed © 1986, 1988 by Vera M. Phillips. Scripture quotations marked (Moffatt) are taken from The Bible: James Moffatt Translation by James A. R. Moffatt. Copyright © 1954 by James A. R. Moffatt. Harper Collins Inc. and Hodder and Stoughton Ltd.

Italics in Scripture quotations reflect the author's added emphasis, except in The Message.

ISBN 978-1-60142-132-6
ISBN 978-1-60142-254-5 (electronic)

Published in the United States by WaterBrook Multnomah, an imprint of the Crown Publishing Group, a division of Random House Inc., New York.

MULTNOMAH and its mountain colophon are registered trademarks of Random House Inc.
Library of Congress Cataloging-in-Publication Data
Alcorn, Randy C.
   If God is good : faith in the midst of suffering and evil / Randy Alcorn.—1st ed.
      p. cm.
Includes bibliographical references (p.   ).
   ISBN 978-1-60142-132-6—ISBN 978-1-60142-254-5 (electronic) 1. Theodicy. I. Title.
   BT160.A42 2009
   231'.8—dc22

                                    2009021787

Printed in the United States of America
2009— First Edition

10 9 8 7 6 5 4 3 2 1

SPECIAL SALES
Most WaterBrook Multnomah books are available at special quantity discounts when purchased in bulk by corporations, organizations, and special-interest groups. Custom imprinting or excerpting can also be done to fit special needs. For information, please e-mail SpecialMarkets@WaterBrookMultnomah.com or call 1-800-603-7051.

This book is dedicated to:

Jim Harrell, Joni Eareckson Tada,
John and Patti Franklin, David O'Brien,
Sarah Thebarge, Scott and Janet Willis, Mona Krueger,
Robert Rogers, Ron and Carol and Connie Speer, Darrell Scott,
Roger and Carole Huntington, David and Nancy Guthrie, Carol Hardin,
Dan and Suzanne Maust, Daniel and Minnie Broas, Josef Tson,
John and Ann Stump, Jerry Tobias, Val Shean, Elisabeth Elliot,
Emmanuel Ndikumana, Randy and Joanie Butler, Kimberly Smith,
John and Carolyn Kohlenberger, Steve and Ginny Saint, Ethel Herr,
and a number of friends who must remain anonymous,
but who are well known by God;
as well as countless missionaries, martyrs,
and ordinary Christians throughout history
and around the world today,
faithful sufferers
whose extraordinary stories touch my heart
and prompt me to worship the God of goodness
who forever answers our cries with Jesus.

One hundred percent of the royalties from this book
will be given to promote good, oppose evil,
and relieve suffering around the world.

Contents

Section 1
Understanding the Problem of Evil and Suffering

Section 2
Understanding Evil: Its Origins, Nature, and Consequences

Section 3
Problems for Non-Theists: Moral Standards, Goodness, and Extreme Evil

Contents

Section 4
Proposed Solutions to the Problem of Evil and Suffering: Limiting God's Attributes

Section 5
Evil and Suffering in the Great Drama of Christ's Redemptive Work

Section 6
Divine Sovereignty and Meaningful Human Choice: Accounting for Evil and Suffering

Section 7
The Two Eternal Solutions to the Problem of Evil: Heaven and Hell

Section 8
God's Allowance and Restraint of Evil and Suffering

Section 9
Evil and Suffering Used for God's Glory

Section 10
Why Does God Allow Suffering?

Section 11
Living Meaningfully in Suffering

Acknowledgments

I couldn't have written *If God Is Good* without God graciously sending me many people whose insights and practical help proved vital.

Above all, I'm grateful to Doreen Button, a skilled editor, staff member, and friend, who looked over every line, most of them multiple times, from the manuscript's early stages. Doreen, you were God's gift to me in this project.

Shel Arensen—missionary, writer, editor, and friend—brought his own skills and insights to portions of the book. Thank you, my brother.

Steve Halliday skillfully edited the submitted draft, with keen eye and insight. Ken Petersen, Multnomah's publisher, believed in this book and also read through the entire manuscript, looking for areas to improve. Thank you, brothers, for your investment in this project.

Doug Gabbert originally encouraged me to write on this subject, and Brian Thomasson and Dudley Delffs were in on the early discussions. Sarah Thebarge and Tim Newcomb tracked down source material for me, and commented on portions of the manuscript. Wendy Jeffries edited some of the stories and Sandi Swanson combed through books for me. Thanks to Pam Shoup for carefully managing the manuscript, and Holly Briscoe for her detailed copyediting and fact-checking.

Many scholars and friends critiqued portions of the manuscript, including Andy Naselli, Justin Taylor, Chris Franklin, Wayne Grudem, Larry Waters, Larry Gadbaugh, Doug Gresham, Keith Krell, Roy Peterson, and Scott Lindsey. Thanks to all who were willing to see the manuscript at its worst in order to help bring it to its best. I'm grateful to the men who spent a day with me discussing the problem of evil and suffering in a theological roundtable: Paul Metzger, John Terveen, Gerry Breshears, Steve Keels, and my sons-in-law Dan Stump and Dan Franklin. Gerry, I'm also in your debt for your extensive comments on the manuscript.

I interviewed and exchanged correspondence with many people who shared their stories and perspectives, including these: Randy Butler, John and Patti Franklin, John Kohlenberger, Scott and Janet Willis, Georgene Rice, Joni Eareckson Tada, Erin Seymour, Dan Maust, Robert Rogers, Darrell Scott, Mona Krueger, Kimberly Smith, Jerry and Candis Bingham, Darryl Burkholder, Bob and Pam Tebow, Josef Tson, Ron and Carol Speer, David and Nancy Guthrie, Craig and Kristina Glazier, Jim Harrell, Claudia Burrows, Emmanuel Ndikumana, Minnie Broas, Penny Hunter, Jerry Tobias, Bryant Young, Greg Laurie, and Denny and Claire Hartford. Thanks also to Mark Crumley and Don Pape.

There are many with whom I discussed the book's issues, and who gave me helpful input and stories, including my dear friends Steve Keels (some of whose insights were surprisingly good), Stu Weber, Tony Cimmarrusti, and Diane Meyer, as well as Chris Mitchell, Rick Campbell, Kirk Cameron, Doug Nichols, Todd DuBord, Jay Echternach, Jim Swanson, and Joe Gibbs.

I'm grateful for my fellow novelists who are part of ChiLibris and who offered their stories and insights: Angela Hunt, Janelle Schneider, Athol Dickson, Linda Hall, Robin Lee Hatcher, Ethel Herr, Stephanie Higgins, Lissa Halls Johnson, Lois Walfrid Johnson, Nancy Mehl, Gayle Roper, and Patti Hickman.

I want to thank Multnomah and WaterBrook staff, including but not limited to Tiffany Lauer Walker, Melissa Sturgess, Lori Addicott, Joel Ruse, Liz Johnson, Sara Selkirk, and Leah McMahan Apineru.

I could never carve out time to write if not for the servant-hearted efforts of the wonderful staff of Eternal Perspective Ministries, including Kathy Norquist, Bonnie Hiestand, Janet Albers, Linda Jeffries, Stephanie Anderson, Sharon Misenhimer, Catherine Simons, and Dwight Myers. (Kathy made manuscript corrections and Bonnie typed a great deal of my research.)

I owe a great deal to the EPM Prayer Partners who upheld me before God's throne in the most difficult days of writing this book. You know who you are, and God does too—if he uses this book for his glory, if he touches lives through it for eternal purposes, then he will reward you for your vital part.

Several people were generous in letting me use their cabins during the writing, including Mark and Debbie Eisenzimmer, Steve and Kathy Peil, and Ron and Karen Russell. Thanks also to Charles Steynor and the staff of Ecola Creek Lodge. And special thanks to our dear friends Carlos and Gena Norris, with whom we spent a wonderful rejuvenating week on the ranch immediately following the book's finish.

More than anyone, I want to thank my precious wife, Nanci, my life's partner and soul mate, who discussed countless aspects of this project with me, and brought great insights, encouragement, and continuous laughter. Thanks to our precious daughters, Karina and Angela, who along with their husbands, our sons, are God's gifts to us. Finally, I'm grateful to our grandsons, Jake and Ty Stump, and Matt and Jack Franklin, who brought incredible joy as they often charged through my office door yelling, *"Pops, we're here!"*

Above all, my heartfelt thanks to the only Answer to evil and suffering who is bigger than the questions: Jesus Christ, my Savior, Lord, and closest friend.

"What is the meaning of it, Watson?" said Holmes
solemnly as he laid down the paper. "What object is
served by this circle of misery and violence and fear? It
must tend to some end, or else our universe is ruled by
chance, which is unthinkable. But what end? There is the
great standing perennial problem to which human reason
is as far from an answer as ever."
—SIR ARTHUR CONAN DOYLE, *The Adventure of the
Cardboard Box*

Introduction

I came to know my friend Jim Harrell after he read my book *Heaven*. We talked on the phone, exchanged e-mails, and quickly connected at a heart level. Jim, a successful businessman, strong and athletic for most of his life, told me he really looked forward to reading this book. He asked me for the first draft, which I happily sent him.

Jim contracted ALS, Lou Gehrig's disease, in 2003. Yet he has called the last six years of his life the most significant. In his last dictated e-mail, he told me he now has no ability to move from his neck downward. While his body has deteriorated and he's lost normal functions, one after another, Jim has touched more people (and been touched more by God) than at any other time of his life.

While writing this book I drew on Jim's wisdom, as well as that of many other sufferers.

During the two years it has taken me to research and write this book, many people have asked about the project. I expected that my answer, containing the words *evil* and *suffering,* would prompt a quick change of subject. Most, however, expressed keen interest and asked penetrating questions. Several launched into their own stories, as if having received permission to uncork the bottle.

What, after all, is more universal to human experience than suffering? And what is more important than the perspective we bring to it?

How we answer this book's central question will radically affect how we see God and the world around us.

We may want to turn away from world suffering and refuse to reflect on the significance of our own pain; we just want it to go away. But despite the superficiality of

1

our culture, we remain God's image-bearers—thinking and caring people, wired to ask questions and seek answers.

No question looms larger than the central question of this book: If God is good...*why all this evil and suffering?* If God loves us, how can he justify allowing (or sending) the sometimes overwhelming difficulties we face?

Does this great question interest you? If so, I invite you to join me on a journey of discovery.

While traveling this long road, I found something surprising: the journey was not only rewarding, but fascinating, enlightening, and at times downright enjoyable. I know it sounds counterintuitive—shouldn't it *depress* someone to meditate on evil and suffering? In fact, I'd already seen enough evil and suffering to feel deeply troubled. What I needed was *perspective.* Instead of being disheartened, I'm encouraged.

In this process, I've taken the most pleasure in focusing on God, exploring his attributes of goodness, love, holiness, justice, patience, grace, and mercy. While my journey hasn't unearthed easy answers, I'm astonished at how much insight Scripture offers.

Seeking answers to this question should turn us toward Jesus in a fresh way.

In looking for answers, I've beheld a God who says, "I have indeed seen the misery of my people in Egypt. I have heard them crying out because of their slave drivers, and I am concerned about their suffering" (Exodus 3:7). I've found great comfort in hearing God speak of a time when he could bear his people's misery no longer (see Judges 10:16). I revel in God's emphatic promise that he will make a New Earth where he will come down to live with us, and on which "he will wipe every tear from their eyes. There will be no more death or mourning or crying or pain" (Revelation 21:4). Above all, in this process, I've seen Jesus.

The first physician to die of the AIDS virus in the United Kingdom was a young Christian. He contracted the disease while conducting medical research in Zimbabwe. In the last days of his life he struggled to express himself to his wife. Near the end, he couldn't talk, and had only enough strength to write the letter *J*. She ran through her mental dictionary, saying various words beginning with J. None was right. Finally she said, "Jesus?"

He nodded. Yes, Jesus.[1]

Jesus filled his thoughts. That's all he wanted to say. That's all his wife needed to hear.

In my research and writing, my thoughts too kept coming back to Jesus. What better place?

Often God has wiped away my own tears as I've contemplated potentially faith-jarring situations. I've been left not in despair, but with great hope that defies description and a peace that transcends understanding (see Philippians 4:7).

This journey has stretched my trust in God and his purposes, and I have emerged better prepared to face suffering and help others because of it. I feel I have much more to offer believers in Christ who may be questioning their faith, as well as unbelievers who consider the problem of evil and suffering their single greatest obstacle to faith.

If you stay with this book until the end, I feel certain you'll be better for it. I believe God will reward you, as he has me, not only with much-needed perspective, but with deep-rooted peace and joy, and renewed perseverance.

We each bring our own burdens on the journey.

If abuse, rape, desertion, paralysis, debilitating disease, or the loss of a loved one has devastated you, then this issue isn't theoretical, philosophical, or theological. It's deeply personal. Logical arguments won't satisfy you; in fact, they might offend you. You need help with the *emotional* problem of evil, not merely the *logical* problem of evil.

Though I write personally, from the heart, and tell stories of great courage and perspective, I must also present a case from Scripture and appeal to logic. But remember this: you are a whole person, and the path to your heart travels through your mind. Truth matters. To touch us at the heart level—and to keep touching us over days, months, years, and decades—truth must work its way into our *minds*.

By all means, speak with a friend and perhaps a pastor or counselor. But in the process don't seek comfort by ignoring truth. When you try to soothe your feelings without bothering to think deeply about ideas, you are asking to be manipulated. Quick-fix feelings won't sustain you over the long haul. On the other hand, deeply rooted beliefs—specifically a worldview grounded in Scripture—will allow you to persevere and hold on to a faith built on the solid rock of God's truth.

In writing his magnificent story of redemption, God has revealed truths about himself, us, the world, goodness, evil, suffering, and Heaven and Hell. (I capitalize those terms as proper nouns throughout the book, since they are actual places, like New England or Saturn.) Those truths God reveals to us teem with life. The blood of man and God flows through them. God speaks with passion, not indifference; he utters fascinating words, not dull ones. To come to grips with the problem of evil and suffering, you must do more than hear heart-wrenching stories about suffering people. You must hear God's truth to help you interpret those stories.

Maybe you're holding on to years of bitterness and depression. You blame someone for your suffering—and that someone may be God. You will not find relief unless you gain perspective.

Or perhaps you fear that any attempt to "gain perspective" will deny or minimize your suffering, or that of others. I promise you, the Bible doesn't minimize suffering or gloss over it, and neither will I.

At times, each of us must snuggle into our Father's arms, like children, and there receive the comfort we need. Joni Eareckson Tada and Steve Estes write,

> God, like a father, doesn't just give advice. He gives himself. He becomes the husband to the grieving widow (Isaiah 54:5). He becomes the comforter to the barren woman (Isaiah 54:1). He becomes the father of the orphaned (Psalm 10:14). He becomes the bridegroom to the single person (Isaiah 62:5). He is the healer to the sick (Exodus 15:26). He is the wonderful counselor to the confused and depressed (Isaiah 9:6).[2]

The faith that can't be shaken is the faith that has been shaken.

God tells us that trials in which evil and suffering come upon us "have come so that your faith—of greater worth than gold, which perishes even though refined by fire—may be proved genuine and may result in praise, glory and honor when Jesus Christ is revealed" (1 Peter 1:7).

Alice Gray writes of sitting at a restaurant, talking with a friend about painful challenges in their lives. They frequently mentioned the Lord.

Alice noticed a young woman at the next table with a radiant, joyful face. The young woman smiled and said she'd overheard their conversation. Speaking softly, she encouraged Alice and Marlene that God understood and cared about their heartaches, and nothing could separate them from God's love.

Alice continued talking with Marlene but realized something was different. The young woman's words had refreshed them. When the smiling woman got up to leave, Alice saw that she wore bulky shoes, carried a walking stick, and moved with a severe limp.

The waitress told Alice this woman had been in a near-fatal automobile accident the year before. She'd been in and out of the hospital and rehabilitation. Her husband divorced her, their home had been sold, and she'd just moved into her own apartment. She used public transportation because she couldn't drive. She'd been unable to find a job.

Alice sat stunned. She said, "This young woman's conversation had been filled with delights of the Lord. There had been no weariness about her. She had encouraged us with words of praise and promise. Meeting her that day, we never would have suspected that storms were raging in her life. Even as she stepped outside into the cold winter wind, she seemed to carry God's warm shelter of hope with her."[3]

God's Word is central to gaining an eternal perspective.

In times of crisis we try to make sense of life. We crave perspective for our minds and relief for our hearts. We need our worldview realigned by God's inspired Word: "All Scripture is God-breathed and is useful for teaching, rebuking, correcting and training in righteousness" (2 Timothy 3:16).

I quote Scripture frequently in this book because God promises that his Word "will not return to me empty, but will accomplish what I desire and achieve the purpose for which I sent it" (Isaiah 55:11). God never makes such a promise about my words or your words. I want this book to accomplish God's purpose—and that will happen only if it remains faithful to his words.

This book won't work magic or make your problems disappear. But I hope God will use it to help you, regardless of the difficulties you face. He offers us profound, moving, and surprising insights that can feed our minds, warm our hearts, and give us the strength to face a world that is not what it once was, or what it one day will be. I pray that readers of *If God Is Good* will not only find help for themselves, but life-changing insights to share with others—believers and unbelievers, family and friends and neighbors and co-workers—in their time of greatest need.

Notes

1. Sinclair B. Ferguson, *Deserted by God?* (Grand Rapids, MI: Baker Books, 1993), 51.
2. Joni Eareckson Tada and Steven Estes, *When God Weeps* (Grand Rapids, MI: Zondervan, 1997), 125.
3. Alice Gray, *Treasures for Women Who Hope* (Nashville: Thomas Nelson, 2005), 11–12.

Understanding the Problem of Evil and Suffering

1

Why Is the Problem of Evil and Suffering So Important?

The problem of evil and suffering moves from the philosophical to the personal in a moment of time.

During my research I read all sorts of books—philosophical, theological, practical, and personal. It's one thing to talk about evil and suffering philosophically; it's another to live with it. Philosophy professor Peter van Inwagen wrote,

> Angels may weep because the world is filled with suffering. A human
> being weeps because his daughter, she and not another, has died of
> leukemia this very night, or because her village, the only world she knows,
> is burning and the mutilated bodies of her husband and her son lie at her
> feet.[1]

Three weeks after his thirty-three-year-old son, Christopher, died in a car crash, pastor and evangelist Greg Laurie addressed a crowd of twenty-nine thousand at Angel Stadium in Anaheim, California. "I've talked about Heaven my whole life," Laurie said, "and I've given many messages on life after death. I've counseled many people who have lost a loved one, and I thought I knew a little bit about it. But I have to say that when it happens to you, it's a whole new world." The day his son died, he told the crowd, was "the hardest day of my life."[2]

When I spoke with Greg ten months later, his faith was strong, but his profound sense of loss remained. Pain is always local. It has a face and a name. And sometimes, for now, it doesn't go away.

The American response to the terrorist attacks on September 11, 2001, demonstrated that large-scale evil and suffering usually remain distant from us.

In Sudan, millions, including children, have been murdered, raped, and enslaved. The 2004 Asian tsunami killed more than 280,000 people. Malaria causes more than two million fatalities annually, the majority of them African children. Around the world, some 26,500 children die every day; eighteen every minute.

The loss of American lives in the terrorist attacks of September 11, 2001, numbered 2,973—horrible indeed, yet a small fraction of the terror and loss of life faced daily around the world. The death toll in the 1994 Rwandan genocide, for example, amounted to more than *two* World Trade Center disasters *every day for one hundred days straight.* Americans discovered in one day what much of the world already knew—violent death comes quickly, hits hard, and can be unspeakably dreadful.

If we open our eyes, we'll see the problem of evil and suffering even when it doesn't touch us directly.

A friend of ours spoke at a Christian gathering. On her way back to her car, someone raped her. She became pregnant and gave birth to her first child. Because racial differences would have made it clear her husband hadn't fathered the baby, the couple placed the infant for adoption. Since then, they've been unable to conceive another child. Her lifelong dream of raising children remains unfulfilled.

I once had to tell a wife, son, and daughter that their husband and father had died on a hunting trip. I still remember the anguished face of the little girl, then hearing her wail, "Not Daddy, no, not Daddy!"

Years ago I had to tell my mother that her only brother had been murdered with a meat cleaver.

A Christian woman tipped over on her riding lawn mower and fell into a pond. The machine landed on top of her, pinning her to the bottom and drowning her. Such a bizarre death prompted some to ask, "Why, God?" and "Why like this?"

After his wife died, in great pain C. S. Lewis realized, "If I had really cared, as I thought I did, about the sorrows of the world, I should not have been so overwhelmed when my own sorrow came."[3]

Our own suffering is often our wake-up call. But even if you aren't now facing it, look around and you'll see many who are.

WHY TALK ABOUT THE PROBLEM?

More people point to the problem of evil and suffering as their reason for not believing in God than any other—it is not merely *a* problem, it is *the* problem.

A Barna poll asked, "If you could ask God only one question and you knew he would give you an answer, what would you ask?" The most common response was, "Why is there pain and suffering in the world?"[4]

John Stott says,

> The fact of suffering undoubtedly constitutes the single greatest challenge
> to the Christian faith, and has been in every generation. Its distribution
> and degree appear to be entirely random and therefore unfair. Sensitive
> spirits ask if it can possibly be reconciled with God's justice and love.[5]

Richard Swinburne, writing in the *Oxford Companion to Philosophy,* says the problem of evil is *"the most powerful objection to traditional theism."*[6]

Ronald Nash writes, "Objections to theism come and go.... But every philosopher I know believes that the most serious challenge to theism was, is, and will continue to be the problem of evil."[7]

You will not get far in a conversation with someone who rejects the Christian faith before the problem of evil is raised. Pulled out like the ultimate trump card, it's supposed to silence believers and prove that the all-good and all-powerful God of the Bible doesn't exist.

The problem of evil is atheism's cornerstone.

German playwright Georg Büchner (1813–37) called the problem of evil "the rock of atheism." Atheists point to the problem of evil as proof that the God of the Bible doesn't exist. Every day the ancient argument gets raised in college philosophy classes, coffee shops, dinner discussions, e-mail exchanges, blogs, talk shows, and best-selling books.

Atheists write page after page about evil and suffering. The problem of evil never strays far from their view; it intrudes upon chapters with vastly different subjects. It's one of the central reasons Sam Harris writes, "Atheism is not a philosophy; it is not even a view of the world; it is simply an admission of the obvious."[8] Harris then scolds Christians, saying about intelligent people (such as himself), "We stand dumbstruck by *you*—by your denial of tangible reality, by the suffering you create in service to your religious myths, and by your attachment to an imaginary God."[9] (At least we know what he's thinking!)

Many suppose that scientific evidence is the cornerstone of atheism. But the famous one-time champion of atheism, Britain's Anthony Flew, renounced his atheism due to the complexity of the universe and his belief in the overwhelming evidence for intelligent design. After examining Richard Dawkins's reasoning in *The God Delusion*—that the origin of life can be attributed to a "lucky chance"—Flew said, "If that's the best argument you have, then the game is over." However, although he abandoned his atheism, Flew did not convert to the Christian faith, but to deism. Why? Flew could not get past the problem of evil. He believes that God must have created the universe, then abandoned it.

A faith that leaves us unprepared for suffering is a false faith that deserves to be lost.

A lot of bad theology inevitably surfaces when we face suffering. John Piper writes, "Wimpy worldviews make wimpy Christians. And wimpy Christians won't survive the days ahead."[10]

Auschwitz survivor Viktor Frankl wrote, "Just as the small fire is extinguished by the storm whereas a large fire is enhanced by it, likewise a weak faith is weakened by predicaments and catastrophes whereas a strong faith is strengthened by them."[11] When people lose their faith because of suffering, it's usually a weak or nominal faith that doesn't account for or prepare them for evil and suffering. I believe that any faith not based on the truth needs to be lost. The sooner, the better.

Believing God exists is not the same as trusting the God who exists. A nominal Christian often discovers in suffering that his faith has been in his church, denomination, or family tradition, but not Christ. As he faces evil and suffering, he may lose his faith. But that's actually a good thing. I have sympathy for people who lose their faith, but any faith lost in suffering wasn't a faith worth keeping. (Genuine faith will be tested; false faith will be lost.)

If you base your faith on lack of affliction, your faith lives on the brink of extinction and will fall apart because of a frightening diagnosis or a shattering phone call. Token faith will not survive suffering, nor should it.

Suffering and evil exert a force that either pushes us away from God or pulls us toward him. I know a man who lost his faith after facing terrible evil, suffering, and injustice. My heart breaks for him, and I pray that my family and I will never suffer what he did. But if personal suffering gives sufficient evidence that God doesn't exist, then surely I shouldn't wait until *I* suffer to conclude he's a myth. If *my* suffering would one day justify denying God, then I should deny him now in light of *other* people's suffering.

The devastation of tragedy feels just as real for people whose faith endures suffering. But because they know that others have suffered and learned to trust God anyway, they can apply that trust to God as they face their own disasters. Because they do not place their hope for health and abundance and secure relationships in this life, but in an eternal life to come, their hope remains firm regardless of what happens.

Losing your faith may be God's gift to you. Only when you jettison ungrounded and untrue faith can you replace it with valid faith in the true God—faith that can pass, and even find strength in, the most formidable of life's tests.

In her moving book *The Year of Magical Thinking,* Joan Didion writes about the sudden, unexpected death of her husband. As I read, my heart broke not only for what happened to her, but for the first six words of the book's concluding sentence: "No eye is on the sparrow."[12]

Didion apparently means that so far as she can tell, there is no God, or at least, no God who cares and watches over us. She's most likely a normal hurting person who needs men and women around her who can see God in the midst of their suffering, so they might help her see him in hers.

Suffering will come; we owe it to God, ourselves, and those around us to prepare for it.

Live long enough and you *will* suffer. In this life, the only way to avoid suffering is to die.

Bethany Hamilton grew up surfing on the island of Kauai, Hawaii. At age five she chose to follow Jesus. When she was thirteen, a fourteen-foot tiger shark attacked her, severing one of her arms. Bethany returned to surfing one month later. A year later, despite her disability, she won her first national title.

Bethany says, "It was Jesus Christ who gave me peace when I got attacked by the shark.... And it was what God had taught me growing up that helped me overcome my fears...to get back into the water to keep surfing."

She continues, "My mom and I were praying before the shark attack that God would use me. Well, to me, 1 Timothy 1:12 kind of tells me that God considered me faithful enough to appoint me to his service. I just want to say that no matter who you are, God can use you even if you think you're not the kind of person that can be used. You might think: why would God use me? That's what I thought.... I was like thirteen and there God goes using me!"[13]

Bethany and her parents had given careful thought to the God they served and his sovereign purposes. Obviously not every tragedy leads to winning a national title, but Bethany began where all of us can, by trusting God; in her case, with a support system of people having an eternal perspective. Hence, she was prepared to face suffering when it came, and to emerge stronger.

Unfortunately, most evangelical churches—whether traditional, liturgical, or emergent—have failed to teach people to think biblically about the realities of evil and suffering. A pastor's daughter told me, "I was never taught the Christian life was going to be difficult. I've discovered it is, and I wasn't ready."

A young woman battling cancer wrote me, "I was surprised that when it happened, it was hard and it hurt and I was sad and I couldn't find anything good or redeeming about my losses. I never expected that a Christian who had access to God could feel so empty and alone."

Our failure to teach a biblical theology of suffering leaves Christians unprepared for harsh realities. It also leaves our children vulnerable to history, philosophy, and global studies classes that raise the problems of evil and suffering while denying the Christian worldview. Since the question *will* be raised, shouldn't Christian parents and churches raise it first and take people to Scripture to see what God says about it?

Most of us don't give focused thought to evil and suffering until we experience them. This forces us to formulate perspective on the fly, at a time when our thinking is muddled and we're exhausted and consumed by pressing issues. Readers who have "been there" will attest that it's far better to think through suffering in advance.

Sometimes sufferers reach out for answers to those woefully unprepared. A physician's assistant friend of ours wrote,

When I was admitted to the hospital in sepsis with a 50/50 chance of survival, I asked the chaplain how we could believe that God is love, when this felt like the antithesis of love. I said I wouldn't inflict this much suffering on someone I hated, let alone someone I loved. She told me she would "look it up," then left my room and never came back. I posed the same question to the social worker who came to visit me a few days later. She told me that God's like a giant and we're like little ants, and sometimes He accidentally steps on our ant hills and some of us get hurt. She said our suffering is random and God's probably not even aware of it.

Pastor James Montgomery Boice had a clearer perspective. In May 2000, he stood before his Philadelphia church and explained that he'd been diagnosed with liver cancer:

> Should you pray for a miracle? Well, you're free to do that, of course. My general impression is that the God who is able to do miracles—and He certainly can—is also able to keep you from getting the problem in the first place. So although miracles do happen, they're rare by definition.…
> Above all, I would say pray for the glory of God. If you think of God glorifying Himself in history and you say, where in all of history has God most glorified Himself? He did it at the cross of Jesus Christ, and it wasn't by delivering Jesus from the cross, though He could have.…
>   God is in charge. When things like this come into our lives, they are not accidental. It's not as if God somehow forgot what was going on, and something bad slipped by.… God is not only the one who is in charge; God is also good. Everything He does is good.… If God does something in your life, would you change it? If you'd change it, you'd make it worse. It wouldn't be as good.[14]

Eight weeks later, having taught his people first how to live and then how to die, Pastor Boice departed this world to "be with Christ, which is better by far" (Philippians 1:23).

On the other side of death, the Bible promises that all who know him will fall into the open arms of a holy, loving, and gracious God—the greatest miracle, the answer to the problem of evil and suffering. He promises us an eternal kingdom on the New Earth, where he says of those who come to trust him in this present world of evil and suffering, "They will be his people, and God himself will be with them and be their God. He will wipe every tear from their eyes. There will be no more death or mourning or crying or pain" (Revelation 21:3–4).

Notes

1. Peter van Inwagen, ed., *Christian Faith and the Problem of Evil* (Grand Rapids, MI: Eerdmans, 2004), xii.
2. Paul Asay, "Continuing Harvest," *Christianity Today*, October 2008, 17–18.
3. C. S. Lewis, *A Grief Observed* (Whitstable, Kent, UK: Whitstable Litho, 1966), 31.
4. Lee Strobel, *The Case for Faith* (Grand Rapids, MI: Zondervan, 2000), 29.
5. John R. W. Stott, *The Cross of Christ* (Downers Grove, IL: InterVarsity, 1986), 311.
6. Richard Swinburne, quoted in *Oxford Companion to Philosophy*, ed. Ted Honderich (Oxford, UK: Oxford University Press, 1995), 255.

7. Ronald H. Nash, *Faith and Reason* (Grand Rapids, MI: Zondervan, 1988), 177.
8. Sam Harris, *Letter to a Christian Nation* (New York: Knopf, 2006), 51.
9. Harris, *Letter,* 91.
10. John Piper, *Spectacular Sins* (Wheaton, IL: Good News, 2008), 57.
11. Viktor E. Frankl, *The Unconscious God* (New York: Simon & Schuster, 1975), 16.
12. Joan Didion, *The Year of Magical Thinking* (New York: Knopf, 2005), 190.
13. "Bethany Hamilton–soul surfer," www.bethanyhamilton.com.
14. James Boice (sermon, Tenth Presbyterian Church, Philadelphia, PA, May 7, 2000), www.seegod.org/boice_example.htm (accessed May 2, 2009).

2

What Is the Problem of Evil
and Suffering?

The last line of Robert Browning's poem "The Year's at the Spring," reads, "God's in his heaven—All's right with the world!"

A beautiful sentiment—but the words ring hollow, don't they?

I don't begrudge Browning his moment of tranquility, but not since evil invaded this world (recorded in the Bible's third chapter) has all been right with the world. And not until the final judgment (recorded in the Bible's third-to-last chapter) will all be right again.

While teaching a seminary course on the theology of Heaven, I met Randy Butler, a pastor, who told us about his teenage son's death three months earlier. Randy took the class on Heaven so he'd understand what Kevin, who was both his son and best friend, was experiencing.

After the class Randy said, "For twenty years, God gave me a perfect life, family, and ministry. Then Kevin died, and nearly every morning, for three or four months, I screamed questions at him. I asked, 'What were you thinking?' And, 'Is this the best you can do for me?' And finally, 'Do you really expect me to show up every Sunday and tell everyone how great you are?' In the silence I began to hear the voice of God…then, without any announcement, when I became silent, God spoke to my soul. He had an answer for each of my three questions."

Had Randy not been painfully honest with God, he might never have come to such an understanding. He might never have realized that he was not the first father to watch his son die. God had endured the same thing—so, better than anyone in the universe, God understood the pain.

We live between Genesis 3 and Revelation 20, between Eden and the New Earth. Things are *not* all right with the world. But does that mean God is *not* in his Heaven, after all? This is the enormous question the problem of evil poses.

As we'll see, people have stated the problem in various ways, with different nuances. I'll phrase it this way:

> If God is all good, then he would want to prevent evil and suffering. If he is all knowing, then he would know how to prevent it. If God is all powerful, then he is able to prevent it. And yet…a great deal of evil and suffering exists. Why?

THE PROBLEM'S LONG HISTORY

Philosophers throughout the ages have pondered the problem of evil and suffering.

Three centuries before Christ, the Greek philosopher Epicurus asked, "Whence evil—if there be a God?" In 1776, skeptic David Hume asked a series of questions about God:

> Is he willing to prevent evil, but not able? then is he impotent. Is he able, but not willing? then is he malevolent. Is he both able and willing? whence then is evil?…
>
> Why is there any misery at all in the world? Not by chance surely. From some cause then. Is it from the intention of the Deity? But he is perfectly benevolent. Is it contrary to his intention? But he is almighty. Nothing can shake the solidity of this reasoning, so short, so clear, so decisive.[1]

Modern atheists take the same approach. George Smith states in *Atheism: The Case Against God,* "The problem of evil is this:… If God knows there is evil but cannot prevent it, he is not omnipotent. If God knows there is evil and can prevent it but desires not to, he is not omnibenevolent."[2]

Recently I received this e-mail: "I have family members who tell me it is evil and suffering that keeps them from seeing God as good; or if he's good, they say he must not be powerful enough or interested enough to do something about it." Neither the writer of the note nor his family members claim to be philosophers. Nonetheless, they wrestle with exactly the same question: why would a good and all-powerful God permit evil and suffering?

This problem crosses all barriers of time and culture.

The ancients never had to deal with nuclear weapons, but they did face plagues, invading armies, floods, and earthquakes without the benefit of even aspirin or penicillin. In 1651 Thomas Hobbes spoke of the natural human condition as "solitary, poor, nasty, brutish, and short." Their knowledge of suffering may have been greater than ours.

A book on my shelf written in France 140 years ago, *The Problem of Evil* by Ernest Naville,[3] could have been written this year in America. Page after page the basic issues remain the same; only the illustrations have changed. Every generation in history, every place in the world can fill in the stories—and even many of those sound remarkably similar. When it comes to evil and suffering, the more things change, the more they stay the same.

The problem of evil is a central theme in human storytelling.

Many books of the Bible address the problem of evil, as did Epicurus, Augustine, Aquinas, Luther, Voltaire, Hume, and Jung.

In fiction, Homer, Milton, Mary Shelley, Shakespeare, Tolstoy, and Flannery O'Connor all raised it. Dostoevsky dealt with it powerfully in *The Brothers Karamazov.* Countless contemporary novelists, myself included, have woven it into their stories. In Sir Arthur Conan Doyle's *The Adventure of the Cardboard Box,* Sherlock Holmes wrestles with the problem of evil:

> "What is the meaning of it, Watson?" said Holmes solemnly as he laid down the paper. "What object is served by this circle of misery and violence and fear? It must tend to some end, or else our universe is ruled by chance, which is unthinkable. But what end? There is the great standing perennial problem to which human reason is as far from an answer as ever."[4]

Even the world's greatest fictional detective couldn't solve the mystery of evil.

Christians made the problem of evil a central area of study long before the birth of modern atheism, and in every generation God's people have tackled it.

To hear some modern atheists talk, you'd think they originated the idea that evil's existence serves as an argument against God. But history shows that those who *did* believe in God addressed the problem of evil much more carefully than those who did *not.*

Evil's reality, quantity, and extremes have long perplexed Christians. Why does God permit evil? And why so much? And why in its most hideous forms?

Dostoevsky, one of history's greatest novelists, put the following words in the mouth of his character Ivan Karamazov as he challenged his Christian brother Alyosha about the problem of evil:

> "Tell me frankly, I appeal to you—answer me: imagine that it is you your-self who are erecting the edifice of human destiny with the aim of making men happy in the end, of giving them peace and contentment at last, but that to do that it is absolutely necessary, and indeed quite inevitable, to torture to death only one tiny creature, the little girl who beat her breast with her little fist, and to found the edifice on her unavenged tears—would you consent to be the architect on those conditions? Tell me and do not lie!"
>
> "No, I wouldn't consent," said Alyosha softly.[5]

As a committed Christian, Dostoevsky's worldview allowed him to grasp and express this difficult issue at its deepest level.

The problem of evil has found a prominent voice in what may seem the most unlikely place...the Bible.

No other book asks so bluntly, passionately, and frequently why God permits evil and why evil people sometimes thrive while the righteous suffer.

Why, God's people have wondered, would a sovereign and loving God not immediately rid the universe of evil? People and prophets alike ask, "How long, O LORD?" (see, for example, Psalm 6:3; 13:1; Habakkuk 1:2).

Remarkably, not just God's saints on Earth, but martyrs in Heaven—morally perfect but still finite—cry out, "How long, Sovereign Lord?" (Revelation 6:10). The books of Job and Ecclesiastes both raise the problem of evil and the apparent randomness of life.

If atheists would read Scripture, they'd find their best arguments articulated there.

Barely have the first two chapters of the Bible described the original creation, saying, "God saw all that he had made, and it was very good" before a terrible shadow falls—evil and suffering burst into the world. Scripture deals with evil's origin, nature, and consequences. Six hundred times specific terms for *evil* appear, with thousands of other references to sin and wickedness, detailing particular sins from idolatry and child-killing to gossip, gluttony, and fornication.

Adam and Eve's fall, Cain's murder of Abel, Noah's flood, the tower of Babel, the patriarchs' sins, Job's tragedies, Egypt's oppression of Israel, David's psalms of lament, Israel's rebellion and exile, the suffering of the prophets, and the long, lonely wait for Messiah—it goes on relentlessly, so that when Jesus finally comes as the Lamb of God, he comes not a moment too soon. And when he returns as the Lion, again it will be not a moment too soon—nor too late.

The problem of evil lies at the very heart of the biblical account and serves as the crux of the unfolding drama of redemption. The first act of human evil moved God to bring decisive judgment while simultaneously unveiling his master plan. To complete our redemption—as well as that of the entire fallen creation—he sets in motion his strategy of incarnation, atoning death, resurrection, and ultimate return.

The Bible never sugarcoats evil. Jesus called an entire generation "evil" (Matthew 12:39, KJV). We are to pray, "Deliver us from evil" (Matthew 6:13, KJV), not simply, "Help us face tough times." Scripture tells us, "Do not be overcome by evil, but overcome evil with good" (Romans 12:21). One day the Judge will say, "Away from me, all you evildoers!" (Luke 13:27).

The Christian worldview concerning this central problem is utterly unique. When compared to other belief systems, it is singularly profound, satisfying, and comforting. In fact, in the end, I'm convinced the Christian worldview is the only one that adequately deals with evil and suffering.

The fact that the Bible raises the problem of evil gives us full permission to do so.

The Old Testament prophet Habakkuk cried out to God,

> How long, O LORD, must I call for help,
>   but you do not listen?
> Or cry out to you, "Violence!"
>   but you do not save?
> Why do you make me look at injustice?
>   Why do you tolerate wrong? (1:2–3)

The book of Psalms brims with honest questions to God about evil and suffering and asks why God doesn't intervene:

> Why, O LORD, do you stand far away?
> Why do you hide yourself in times of trouble? (10:1, ESV)

I say to God, my rock:
    "Why have you forgotten me?
Why do I go mourning
    because of the oppression of the enemy?" (42:9, ESV)

Awake! Why are you sleeping, O LORD?
    Rouse yourself! Do not reject us forever!
Why do you hide your face?
    Why do you forget our affliction and oppression? (44:23–24, ESV)

By including these and many other laments in his inspired Word, God graciously invites our cries, so long as we remain willing to listen to his response.

Some perspectives can give great help in dealing with the problem, but none bring neat and tidy solutions.

Joni Eareckson Tada, reflecting on forty years in a wheelchair, told me, "I've learned that suffering is messier than I once thought."

One blogger thought everything through, he said, and had come up with *the* answer to the problem of evil. Despite his sincerity, the writer said nothing original and proposed a hodgepodge of insights, some valid, others naive or senseless. He honestly thought he'd solved the problem of the ages, drawing from little more than a philosophy class lecture, a coffee shop discussion, and a Wikipedia article.

I've read books by atheists and Holocaust survivors, and have interviewed dozens of men and women who have endured extreme evil and suffering. The more I've done so, the more I've asked God to give me wisdom—and I've discovered that wisdom begins with the humility to say there's a great deal I don't understand.

If I thought I had no helpful perspectives on the problem, it would be pointless for me to write this book. If I imagined I had all the answers neatly lined up, it would be pointless for you to read it.

Someone told me the story of a teenager who didn't want to be seen in public with her mother, because her mother's arms were terribly disfigured. One day when her mother took her shopping and reached out her hand, a clerk looked horrified. Later, crying, the girl told her mother how embarrassed she was.

Understandably hurt, the mother waited an hour before going to her daughter's room to tell her, for the first time, what had happened.

"When you were a baby, I woke up to a burning house. Your room was an inferno. Flames were everywhere. I could have gotten out the front door, but I decided I'd rather die with you than leave you to die alone. I ran through the fire and wrapped my arms around you. Then I went back through the flames, my arms on fire. When I got outside on the lawn, the pain was agonizing, but when I looked at you, all I could do was rejoice that the flames hadn't touched you."

Stunned, the girl looked at her mother through new eyes. Weeping in shame and gratitude, she kissed her mother's marred hands and arms.

May we learn to see the problem of evil and suffering through new eyes.

Notes

1. David Hume, *Dialogues Concerning Natural Religion* (London: William Blackwood, 1907), 134, 140.
2. George H. Smith, *Atheism: The Case Against God* (New York: Prometheus Books, 1989).
3. Ernest Naville, *The Problem of Evil*, trans. John P. Lacroix (New York: Carlton and Lanahan, 1871).
4. Sir Arthur Conan Doyle, *The Adventure of the Cardboard Box*, (Whitefish, MT: Kessinger, 2004), 22.
5. Fyodor Dostoevsky, *The Brothers Karamazov*, trans. Constance Garnett (New York: Modern Library, 1950), bk. 5, chap. 4.

3

What Is Evil, and How Does It Differ from Suffering?

Understanding Evil

God wants the difference between good and evil to remain clear.

In every place and time, some people switch price tags so what's valuable looks worthless and what's cheap demands a high price. It's bad enough to do evil and abstain from good. But God condemns the moral sleight of hand by which we confuse good and evil: "Woe to those who call evil good and good evil, who put darkness for light and light for darkness, who put bitter for sweet and sweet for bitter" (Isaiah 5:20).

God calls upon his people to embrace good and reject evil (see Amos 5:14–15; Romans 16:19; 1 Peter 3:11; 3 John 11). God says, "Hate what is evil; cling to what is good" (Romans 12:9). All these passages presume we know the difference between good and evil. But in a culture that so often switches the price tags, this doesn't come naturally. We must regularly withdraw to Scripture and ask God's Spirit to train our minds and consciences to recognize what's truly good and what's truly evil. Speaking of learning and obeying biblical teaching, God says, "But solid food is for the mature, who by constant use have trained themselves to distinguish good from evil" (Hebrews 5:14).

Evil, in its essence, refuses to accept God as God and puts someone or something else in his place.
Most people today understand evil as anything that harms others. The more harm done, the more evil the action.

Cornelius Plantinga named his book about sin after a line from the movie *Grand Canyon*: "Not the way it's supposed to be." Evil is exactly that—a fundamental and troubling departure from goodness. The Bible uses the word *evil* to describe anything that violates God's moral will. The first human evil occurred when Eve and Adam disobeyed God. From that original sin—a moral evil— came the consequence of suffering. Although suffering results from moral evil, it is distinguishable from it, just as an injury caused by drunken driving isn't synonymous with the offense.

Evil could be defined as "the refusal to accept the true God as God." True evil elevates itself or another to replace God. For this very reason, the Bible treats idolatry as the ultimate sin, since it worships as God what is *not* God.

Any attempt to liberate ourselves from God's standards constitutes rebellion against God. In replacing his standards with our own, we not only deny God but affirm ourselves as God. Evil is always an attempted coup, an effort to usurp God's throne.

Psalm 2 describes earthly kings standing against God and his anointed one and declaring, "Let us break their chains." God scoffs at them and replies that he has installed his king on Zion—and they have no hope of conquering his Chosen One (see 2:2–6).

Evildoers not only reject God's law and create their own; they attempt to take the moral high ground by calling God's standards "unloving," "intolerant," and "evil."

Moral evil comes in two forms—blatant evil that admits its hatred for goodness, and subtle evil that professes to love goodness while violating it.

Some view evil as the absence of good.

The logic goes like this: There is no such thing as cold, only lower degrees of heat (or the complete lack of it). Darkness is not the opposite of light, but the absence of light. Death is not the opposite of life, but its privation. A cloth can exist without a hole, but that hole cannot exist without the cloth. Good can, did, and will exist without evil. But evil cannot exist without the good it opposes. A shadow is nothing but the obstruction of light—no light, no shadow. Augustine said, "Evil has no positive nature; but the loss of good has received the name 'evil.'"[1]

New Testament vocabulary sometimes supports this concept, commonly using the Greek "alpha privative" (the single letter α at the beginning of words) to negate words referring to goodness. We see it in words such as *un*righteous, *un*just, *un*godly, law*less,* and god*less.* These suggest that we best understand evil as a departure from God's goodness. However, while this definition contains helpful insights, it doesn't go far enough.

More than merely the absence of good, evil is the corruption of good.

The Holocaust was not "nothing." The Killing Fields were not "nothing." The 9/11 attacks were not "nothing." All were real horrors, down to every emaciated corpse, bullet-riddled body, and person jumping out a window.

Perhaps we could better conceive of evil as a parasite on God's good creation, since a parasite is something substantial. Without the living organism it uses as a host, the parasite cannot exist. Likewise, cancer thrives on, consumes, and ultimately kills healthy, living cells. As metal does not need rust, but rust needs metal, so good doesn't need evil, but evil needs good.

Grace and forgiveness, both expressions of God's eternal character, are moral goods, but without evil they wouldn't have become clearly evident. Father, Son, and Holy Spirit don't need compassion, mercy, grace, or forgiveness. These qualities could only be fully expressed to finite and fallen creatures.

God is accomplishing his redemptive work in our lives, and will one day conquer evil and eliminate suffering "so that in the coming ages he might show the immeasurable riches of his grace in kindness toward us in Christ Jesus" (Ephesians 2:7, ESV).

Some of God's virtues will forever capture the spotlight that, without evil and suffering's temporary hold on us, never would have taken the stage.

PRIMARY AND SECONDARY EVIL

Scripture portrays moral evils of rebelling against God, and natural evils including disease and disasters.

Child abuse is evil, demonstrated by the harm it inflicts on the innocent victim. We consider cancer and earthquakes evils because they bring suffering. While the evils of cancer and earthquakes differ from the moral evil of rebellion against God, the two are related. Human rebellion led God to curse the earth, which brought severe physical consequences.

While often called "natural" evils, diseases and disasters are in another sense unnatural in that they result from evil, an unnatural condition.

The immoral things we do are *primary* evils, while the consequences we suffer are *secondary* evils.

Disobeying God, inseparable from the failure to trust God, was the original evil. From that sin—a *moral* evil—came the consequence of suffering. So suffering follows evil as a caboose follows an engine. Scripture sometimes refers to calamities and tragic events as evils. To distinguish these, we can call moral evil *primary* evil and suffering *secondary* evil.

"But just as every good promise of the LORD your God has come true, so the LORD will bring on you all the evil he has threatened, until he has destroyed you from this good land he has given you" (Joshua 23:15). Note that the "evil" mentioned here is not moral evil. Rather, it's a holy God bringing judgment upon guilty people.

In some cases God builds punishments into moral evils. Paul says of those committing sexual sins that they "received in themselves the due penalty for their perversion" (Romans 1:27).

Secondary evils point to primary evil, reminding us that humanity, guilty of sin, deserves suffering.

Secondary evil, the direct and indirect consequences of primary evil, provokes our indignation. Why do innocent people suffer? God hates the primary evils we commit, while we hate the secondary evils (consequences) God determines or permits.

As humans, however, we all stand guilty. Although many secondary evils befall us even when we have not directly committed a sin that causes them, we would not have to deal with secondary evils if we didn't belong to a sinful race. Short-term suffering serves as a warning and foretaste of eternal suffering. Without a taste of Hell, we would not see its horrors nor feel much motivation to do everything possible to avoid it. Hence, the secondary evil of suffering can get our attention and prompt us to repent of our primary moral evil.

Scripture sometimes speaks of primary and secondary evils in the same context, explaining how God uses secondary evils as judgments that may produce ultimate good.

Jeremiah 11:17 uses the same Hebrew word for evil *(ra)* in both the primary sense (moral evil) and the secondary sense (adverse consequences of moral evil): "The LORD of hosts, who planted you, has pronounced *evil* against you because of the *evil* of the house of Israel and of the house of Judah, which they have done to provoke Me by offering up sacrifices to Baal" (NASB).

Other versions, including the ESV and NIV, translate the first use of *ra* as "disaster." Are these scholars wrong to render it *disaster* instead of *evil*? I don't think so. The translators correctly recognize that the "evil" God brings is a consequence—a judgment upon Israel's actions—*not* a moral evil, as is the evil committed by Israel. God is righteous and just in bringing this disaster.

For good reason, most translators normally render *ra* as "evil" when used of people disobeying God, but "disaster" or "calamity" when used of God bringing judgment on sinful people. The original Hebrew readers, knowing the elasticity of the word, could contextually discern the difference in meaning. But the English word *evil* is for most a synonym for moral wickedness, making it a narrower word than the Hebrew *ra*. (There can be righteous *ra* but not righteous *evil*.)

In Jeremiah 32 the prophet speaks of God giving the land to Israel: "They came in and took possession of it, but they did not obey you or follow your law; they did not do what you commanded them to do. So you brought all this disaster upon them" (verse 23). The word translated "disaster" is again *ra*. Israel brought the sin; God righteously brought sin's disastrous consequences.

After promising judgment, God also promised he would bring good to his people—good that ultimately would outweigh the evil. Note the repetition of the word "good" in the following. God says,

> They will be my people, and I will be their God. I will give them single-ness of heart and action, so that they will always fear me *for their own good* and *the good of their children* after them. I will make an everlasting covenant with them: I will *never stop doing good* to them, and I will inspire them to fear me, so that they will never turn away from me. *I will rejoice in doing them good* and will assuredly plant them in this land with all my heart and soul. (Jeremiah 32:38–41)

God's people endure *temporary* judgments for their sin. But God makes an "everlasting covenant," promising, *"I will never stop doing good to them."*

Evils, whether moral or natural, will not have the final say. God will replace both with everlasting good.

The passage continues, "For thus says the LORD: Just as I have brought all this great disaster upon this people, so I will bring upon them all the good that I promise them" (verse 42, ESV).

Howard Hendricks tells of visiting a leprosy center in India. The morning he arrived, the residents were gathered for a praise service. One of the women with leprosy hobbled to the platform. Hendricks said that even though she was partially blind and badly disfigured, she was one of the most beautiful women he'd ever seen.

Raising both of her nearly fingerless hands toward Heaven, she said in a clear voice, "I want to praise God that I am a leper because it was through my leprosy that I came to know Jesus Christ as my Savior. And I would rather be a leper who knows Christ than be completely whole and a stranger to His grace."[2]

The surgeon inflicts suffering on the patient and the parent disciplines the child, but they do good, not evil. Likewise, God can permit and even bring suffering upon his children without being morally evil. God hates moral evil and is committed to utterly destroying it. Yet for now he allows evil and suffering, and can providentially use them for his own good purposes.

Notes

1. Augustine, *The City of God*, bk. 11, chap. 9, www.newadvent.org/fathers/ 120111.htm.
2. Alice Gray, *Treasures for Women Who Hope* (Nashville: Thomas Nelson, 2005), 71-72.

4

What Are Some Possible Responses to the Problem of Evil and Suffering?

Raised in a Christian home, Jeremy was bitter toward God because both his parents had been born with cerebral palsy. He broke his father's heart when, as a young man, Jeremy told him he would never worship a God who had done this to his parents.

Jeremy's life became a train wreck of drugs and alcohol. He went through rehabilitation centers and two separations from his wife, who prayed twenty-seven years for her husband to trust Christ.

Arrested for drunk driving, Jeremy finally broke. He yielded his life to Jesus and immediately felt the bitterness lift.

After nearly three decades of pain in her marriage, Jeremy's wife, Sarah, wrote, "I am here to tell you I would not have the relationship with God that I have if I had not suffered deeply. God revealed treasures to me that can only be found, I believe, in the darkness."

Sarah comes to the problem of evil from a distinct worldview. But there are other views. Each attempts to answer the question, "How can we reconcile evil and suffering with a God who is all-good, all-powerful, and all-knowing?" I will present and comment briefly on six answers, returning later to develop several of them.

THE PROBLEM SEEN FROM SIX WORLDVIEWS

1. There is no evil and suffering.
Some pantheistic religions, often related to Hinduism, essentially deny the existence of suffering and evil. It's unreal, an illusion.

Others question evil's reality or define it vaguely. Eckhart Tolle comments, "If evil has any reality…it has a relative, not an absolute, reality." He relates evil to denying "my intrinsic oneness" with all others.[1]

Pantheists believe that everything is god. God is nature and nature is god. The things we call "evil" are only imperfections in our view of reality that progressive self-realization and self-improvement can remove.

It's hard to imagine how anyone who looks evil in the face can seriously maintain it's not real. One day I sat on a plane next to a young man, an intelligent college graduate, who told me he believed evil doesn't exist.

"If there's no such thing as evil," I said, "then the Holocaust wasn't evil. Is that what you believe?"

He grimaced, then finally, stammering, said, "Well, I guess the Holocaust was a mistake." I suggested to him that in his heart he must know it was something far worse.

Some worldviews, including Christian Science, argue that suffering doesn't exist. The irrationality of this worldview is illustrated by a boy who visits his family's Christian Science practitioner to ask him to pray for his very sick father. The practitioner replies, "Son, your father only *thinks* he's sick. Tell him to have faith and believe he's not sick, but well."

The boy did so. The practitioner sees him the next day and asks, "How's your father?"

The boy answers, "Now he thinks he's dead."

Endless newspaper accounts detail evil and suffering, but I have never read one more theologically charged than a story with the headline "Two Minneapolis Teens Charged with Murdering Mother, 10-Year-Old Son." The article says of the two murders a sixteen- and a seventeen-year-old committed:

> The crime…was as savage as it was senseless.
>
> Minneapolis police detectives said that in the just-the-facts world they inhabit, they will probably never hear a good explanation for the rage and violence shown in last week's brutal killings of Katricia Latrice Daniels, 36, and her 10-year-old son, Robert Shepard.
>
> "I think what you're confronted with is that age-old problem of evil," said Lt. Amelia Huffman, chief of the homicide unit, after murder charges were filed Tuesday against the two teens. "We certainly see the consequences of it."
>
> Asked about a motive for the crime, Huffman answered: "I don't think that that's a question that any of us can really answer. That's really a

question for a theologian or a psychologist. There's no sufficient answer to that question that would explain what happened to these two victims. These were very monstrous crimes."[2]

What accounts for a sixteen- and a seventeen-year-old committing such vile offenses? This homicide chief rightly referred to "that age-old problem of evil."

2. There is no God.

David Hume and Bertrand Russell offered this solution, as do the currently popular atheists, including Christopher Hitchens, author of *God Is Not Great.*

Atheist Andrea Weisberger concludes in her book *Suffering Belief,* "None can account for the tremendous amount of suffering in a world in which an allegedly omnipotent, omniscient and wholly good God reigns.... The conclusion to which we are drawn, therefore, is that the existence of such a God is implausible."[3]

Implausible does not mean impossible; but her conclusion echoes that of many other philosophers, who see belief in God, at least the Christian God who is good and caring and personal, as irrational.

3. God has limited goodness.

Second-century Gnostics thought the world's evil proceeded from God's own being. Hence, they had no "problem of evil."

Nietzsche's *Thus Spake Zarathustra* portrays God as the creator of both good and evil. Such a God is the source not only of truth, but also of lies.

Richard Dawkins, author of *The God Delusion,* says it is as easy to imagine an evil God as a good one. In fact, he considers the God of the Old Testament an evil deity.[4]

Archibald MacLeish's Pulitzer Prize–winning play *J. B.* argues, "If God is God, he is not good; if God is good, he is not God."

In *The Problem of Pain,* C. S. Lewis described how he viewed God's goodness prior to becoming a Christian:

Not many years ago when I was an atheist, if anyone had asked me, "Why do you not believe in God?" my reply would have run something like this: "Look at the universe we live in."... History is largely a record of crime, war, disease, and terror.... But all civilizations pass away and, even while they remain, inflict peculiar sufferings of their own.... Every race that comes into being in any part of the universe is doomed; for the universe, they tell us, is running down.... All stories will come to nothing:

all life will turn out in the end to have been a transitory and senseless contortion upon the idiotic face of infinite matter. If you ask me to believe that this is the work of a benevolent and omnipotent spirit, I reply that all the evidence points in the opposite direction. Either there is no spirit behind the universe, or else a spirit indifferent to good and evil, or else an evil spirit.[5]

Atheist James Wood, looking at the evil and suffering in the world, writes in the *New Yorker,* "Twenty-five years ago…I decided that if God existed, which I strongly doubted, then this entity was neither describable nor cherishable but was a vaporous, quite possibly malign force."[6]

4. God has limited power.

If more than one god exists, then divine power is divided and cannot reside in a single God. Hence, in the worldview of polytheism, no god can be all powerful. The gods of ancient Greece, including Zeus and Apollo, possessed great power but were far from omnipotent.

Zoroastrianism, an ancient religion, teaches dualism. It sees the universe as a cosmic battleground between two equal opposites, personalized in two gods, one good and one evil. Ahura Mazda is the good god, creator of all good. Ahriman is the bad god, creator of all evil. Ahura Mazda created life and love, Ahriman death and hate. Since Ahura Mazda is not all powerful, one cannot blame him for evil. He does the best he can (and you have to love him for it), but that scoundrel Ahriman lies outside his control.

While this provides a tidy resolution to the problem of evil, it utterly contradicts Scripture, which affirms one and only one God, who has all power.

More subtle forms of dualism exist, even among Christians. Some believe that though God may win in the end, Satan has so much power and brings so much suffering and evil that God simply cannot stop him, at least for now.

Some see dualism as a single impersonal force, such as in the *Star Wars* movies, where the Force has both a light and a dark side. Who will win in the end? No one can say for sure.

Process theology conceives of God as always evolving. God supposedly emerges and grows with the universe. He is powerful, but not all powerful. Think of him as a conductor limited by an orchestra's skills. He can lead, but he can't control.

One of the most influential books in the last half of the twentieth century was Rabbi Harold Kushner's *New York Times* bestseller *When Bad Things Happen to*

Good People. After watching his son die from a rare disease, Kushner concluded God is all good but not all powerful. He wrote, "It is too difficult even for God to keep cruelty and chaos from claiming their innocent victims."[7]

5. God has limited knowledge.

In the last twenty years some Christians, called open theists, have denied that God has moral responsibility for the bad things that happen because he doesn't know they will happen. If he did know, he would stop them, since he's all loving.

Open theists believe that God's love overshadows all else, but they believe human free will has sufficient power to thwart God's loving plan.

Clark Pinnock says, "Decisions not yet made do not exist anywhere to be known even by God. They are potential—yet to be realized but not yet actual. God can predict a great deal of what we will choose to do, but not all of it, because some of it remains hidden in the mystery of human freedom.... The God of the Bible displays an openness to the future that the traditional view of omniscience simply cannot accommodate."[8]

Open theists often emphasize that God takes risks. Furthermore, because he has limited information, he can make errors in judgment; and when he realizes he's done so, he changes his mind.

Open theists will object to my categorization of their position as "God is not all knowing," since they say God knows everything that can be known. Future events, however, *cannot* be known, even to God, they say, and hence they claim to believe in God's "dynamic omniscience." Regardless of the terminology, they believe that much of the future remains opaque to God, and on that basis they argue that he is more loving and bears less responsibility for the world's evil and suffering.

6. God is all good, all powerful, and all knowing; he hates evil and will ultimately judge evildoers, and remove evil and suffering after accomplishing a greater, eternal good.

The Bible confirms evil's existence and considers all of God's attributes as infinite. Joni Eareckson Tada writes, "God permits what he hates to accomplish that which he loves."[9] Evil is never good, yet God can use any evil to accomplish good and sovereign purposes.

Through the redemptive suffering of Christ—in which he took all human evils on himself—and through his triumph over evil and death, God has done everything necessary to defeat evil. One day he will carry out his final redemptive work: "He will swallow up death forever. The Sovereign LORD will wipe away the tears from all faces; he will remove the disgrace of his people from all the earth. The LORD has spoken" (Isaiah 25:8).

We live in a post-Christian era. Among Westerners, especially, the Christian worldview is increasingly unpopular. Non-Christian worldviews are winning the public relations war, replacing Christianity's seemingly old and repressive way of thinking with more positive, progressive, and inclusive ideologies. People suppose the Christian faith has been tried and found wanting, when in fact, to paraphrase G. K. Chesterton, they have been repeatedly told it's wanting and therefore have never tried it.

The fact that there are fewer nominal Christians today is good. It's better for people to deny the Christian faith outright than to profess it in weak and shallow ways. Many have become immune to Christianity by contracting a mild and unbiblical form of it. Some find, as C. S. Lewis did, that after getting far enough away from a false Christianity, they can see with fresh eyes what true Christianity is—a dynamic and persuasive competitor in the marketplace of ideas.

Having grown up in a non-Christian home, and still vividly remembering my unbelief as a young teenager, I'm convinced that Christianity's explanation of why evil and suffering exist beats that of any other worldview. Its explanation of why we can expect God to forever deliver his redeemed people from evil and suffering is better still. The answers revealed in Scripture not only account for how the world is, they offer the greatest hope for where the world is headed.

How does your own worldview stack up against the real world around you? Does it credibly explain the way things are and offer persuasive reasons for believing in a hopeful future? Or do you need to revise or abandon it in order to embrace the biblical worldview because it better explains your condition and that of the world around you?

THE PERSPECTIVE WE NEED TO ADDRESS THE PROBLEM

We should bring an accurate view of God to this issue, magnifying and glorifying him, not diminishing him.
Besides the irrational solution that evil and suffering do not exist, and the atheistic solution that God does not exist, the most popular ways of addressing the problem of evil minimize one or more of God's attributes, especially his power, knowledge, or goodness. In contrast, the Bible never shrinks God but always magnifies him:

> For the LORD your God is God of gods and Lord of lords, the great God, mighty and awesome. (Deuteronomy 10:17)

Oh, praise the greatness of our God! (Deuteronomy 32:3)

Yours, O LORD, is the greatness and the power and the glory and the majesty and the splendor, for everything in heaven and earth is yours. Yours, O LORD, is the kingdom; you are exalted as head over all. (1 Chronicles 29:11)

And Mary said, "My soul magnifies the Lord." (Luke 1:46, ESV)

To glorify and magnify God is not to make more of him than he is; that's impossible. Rather, it's to affirm his greatness, attempting to do justice to his infinite majesty and power and wisdom and love, even though inevitably we'll fall short.

To address good and evil without gazing upon God is fruitless. Good flows from the life connected to God. Evil flows from the life alienated from God.

"Anyone who does what is good is from God. Anyone who does what is evil has not seen God" (3 John 11). To embrace good and turn from evil, we must see God *as he really is.* We must not simply believe in God, but believe *what is true about God.* Diminishing God not only fails to solve theological problems, it dishonors him and becomes idolatry. When we see God as he is, we will see ourselves as we are, leaving him in his rightful place and us in ours.

As a young Christian I read and reread A. W. Tozer's *The Knowledge of the Holy.* What Tozer says in the book's first chapter sheds light on how to, and how not to, approach the problem of evil:

What comes into our minds when we think about God is the most important thing about us. The most portentous fact about any man is not what he at a given time may say or do, but what he in his deep heart conceives God to be like. . . .

That our idea of God corresponds as nearly as possible to the true being of God is of immense importance to us. Compared with our actual thoughts about Him, our creedal statements are of little consequence.

The idolatrous heart assumes that God is other than He is—in itself a monstrous sin—and substitutes for the true God one made after its own likeness. Always this god will conform to the image of the one who created it... A god begotten in the shadows of a fallen heart will quite naturally be no true likeness of the true God. . . .

> Before the Christian Church goes into eclipse anywhere there must
> first be a corrupting of her simple basic theology. She simply gets a wrong
> answer to the question, "What is God like?" and goes on from there.[10]

Tozer prophetically warns against any modern solution to the problem of evil
and suffering which minimizes or redefines God's attributes (inevitably creating
far greater problems).

A friend wrestled with the problem of evil after a terrible accident. He concluded that we err whenever we speak of only two or three attributes of God in
relation to the problem of evil. He meant that we must bring *all* of God's attributes to the table.

If we see God only in terms of his love, mercy, and compassion, we will not
envision the true God, but only an idol of our own imagination—and that is precisely what we see in the airbrushed God of various modern solutions to the problem of evil.

Many imagine that if we believe in God and serve him, we earn status with God so he won't let serious harm befall us.

Robert Rogers's entire family drowned in a 2003 Kansas flash flood. In a moment
he lost his beloved wife and all four of his children. This Christ-centered family
went to church, tithed, read the Bible, and prayed together. After the disaster,
Robert entered a dark world of Job-like suffering.

Sufferers have told me, "We did everything right. We attended church and
gave our money to missions—and then God did this to us. I don't get it." At
times like these our faith gets exposed as an insurance policy in which we pay our
premiums to protect us from harm.

Shortly after I became a Christian, my close friend, Greg, died in a horrible
accident. I felt devastated, partly because I believed God wouldn't permit such a
thing. After all, Greg and I both had deep commitments to Christ. Didn't that
mean he'd spare us?

A man whose wife was murdered told me, "We thought we were doing everything right. Nothing like this was supposed to happen." He felt overwhelming
pain, understandably. But—and I say this gently—he had misguided expectations. Where does God promise us that by making good, godly choices we'll avoid
suffering?

Janet Willis told me she sometimes used to think, *I want to stay close to God
so nothing bad happens.* When her van crashed on a Wisconsin freeway and six of

her children died, she drew close to God because she needed him. Now he became not a means to prevent harm, but her only way to survive.

We need only read Scripture, look around us, or live long enough in order to learn that *trusting God doesn't ward off all evil and suffering.*

He never said it would.

We must form our perspective from God's Word, not popular culture.

We live in an era when popular culture, despite its shallowness, has a far-reaching influence on the average person's worldview. This entertainment-driven and self-gratification-obsessed blend of pop psychology, pop philosophy, and pop theology has become its own worldview. Never have people needed to hear the biblical worldview more—and perhaps never have they been more culturally conditioned to dismiss it.

"If your law had not been my delight," said David, "I would have perished in my affliction" (Psalm 119:92). While the Bible provides answers, it is also a source of great personal perspective and comfort.

Martin Niemöller, a courageous German pastor, spent years in a concentration camp because he spoke out against the ungodly influence that Adolf Hitler's regime exerted on the German church. Niemöller later said about the Bible,

> What did this book mean to me during the long and weary years of solitary confinement and then for the last four years at Dachau? The Word of God was simply everything to me—comfort and strength, guidance and hope, master of my days and companion of my nights, the bread which kept me from starvation and the water of life that refreshed my soul.[11]

Darrell Scott's daughter Rachel was the first to die in 1999's Columbine school shootings. I asked Darrell what we should do to prepare for evil and suffering. Without hesitation he said, "Become a student of God's Word."

Darrell's view of God already had a firm place in his heart when Rachel died. He trusted from the first that God had a purpose. While this did not remove his pain, it did provide solid footing from which he could move forward, trusting God instead of resenting him.

In my experience, most Christians lack grounding in God's attributes, including his sovereignty, omnipotence, omniscience, justice, and patience. We dare not wait for the time of crisis to learn perspective! "Don't be content to be hand-fed by others," Darrell said. "Do your own reading and study, devour good books, talk about the things of God."

Before I became a scuba diver, I learned in a classroom how to use the equipment. My friend Don Maxwell and I studied and discussed the manual at length, then took the test. Obviously, the underwater world differed considerably from our classroom or Don's living room. But what we learned outside the water gave us a great head start in coping with real-life underwater challenges.

Studying about evil and suffering doesn't equal facing it, but the study and discussion can go a long way in preparing us for it. It will provide a reservoir of perspective from which we can draw. It will minimize disorientation and panic when we plunge into life's turbulence. This is why I encourage you to meditate on and discuss with others the themes of this book.

We shouldn't wait until suffering comes to start learning about how to face it any more than we should wait until we fall into the water to start learning how to scuba dive.

Notes

1. Eckhart Tolle, *A New Earth* (New York: Penguin Books, 2005), 22.
2. *St. Paul Pioneer Press* (Minnesota), June 18, 2008.
3. Andrea M. Weisberger, *Suffering Belief* (New York: Peter Lang, 1999), 234.
4. The Old Testament itself says something different about God: "He is the Rock, his works are perfect, and all his ways are just. A faithful God who does no wrong, upright and just is he" (Deuteronomy 32:4).
5. C. S. Lewis, *The Problem of Pain* (New York: Macmillan, 1962), 13–15.
6. James Wood, "Holiday in Hellmouth," *New Yorker,* June 2008, www.newyorker.com/arts/critics/books/2008/06/09/080609crbo_books_wood?currentPage=all (accessed May 2, 2009).
7. Harold S. Kushner, *When Bad Things Happen to Good People* (New York: Avon, 1983), 43.
8. Clark H. Pinnock, ed., *The Grace of God, the Will of Man* (Grand Rapids, MI: Zondervan, 1989), 25–26.
9. Joni Eareckson Tada, *Pearls of Great Price: 366 Daily Devotional Readings* (Grand Rapids, MI: Zondervan, 2006), 387.
10. A. W. Tozer, *The Knowledge of the Holy* (San Francisco: HarperOne, 1992), 1–6.
11. Martin Niemöller, quoted in George E. Good, *Living Stones* (Newtownards, Northern Ireland: April Sky Design, 2004), 57.

5

A Closer Look at Central Issues in the Problem of Evil

Gianna Jessen, as a preborn child, survived a botched saline abortion. Gianna says that while the saline solution was burning her alive, "The lack of oxygen to my brain is what caused my gift of cerebral palsy."[1] Upon hearing her call cerebral palsy a "gift," some feel perplexed, but Gianna has had her whole life to think about it.

She doesn't see God as merely "permitting" her suffering or "using" it. She considers her cerebral palsy a gift from God's hand. She doesn't deny that the choices of her mother and the actions of a physician caused her condition and the terrible evil inflicted upon her. And yet, Gianna sees God's hand even in her suffering.

A *theodicy* is an attempt to show that God is just and to argue that he can be sovereign and good despite the world's evil and suffering.
Milton says he wrote *Paradise Lost* to "justify the ways of God to men."[2] In Greek, *theos* means "God," and *dike* means "justice." Google *theodicy* and you will find a dizzying and ever-increasing body of resources on this subject, everything from academic treatises to bloggers sounding off on this age-old problem.

John Feinberg points out that multiple problems of evil can be worded in various ways. Failing to define what problem we're talking about, he says, makes resolution impossible: "It is wrongheaded at a very fundamental level to think that because a given defense or theodicy doesn't solve *every* problem of evil, it doesn't solve *any* problem of evil."[3]

The "problem of evil" is like the "problem of bad weather." Bad weather comes in many forms. Hail destroys crops, snow collapses buildings, rain causes flooding, wind fells trees, lightning causes forest fires, and icy roads facilitate fatal car accidents. This book's treatment of character building doesn't explain the

Holocaust. What I say about meaningful choice doesn't make sense of natural disasters. *It doesn't intend to.*

No single idea or theodicy in this book answers every question. I encourage you to look at the cumulative effect of these arguments, then judge for yourself whether the worldview they represent offers help and insight as you face the problem of evil and suffering.

The argument in the problem of evil, as sometimes stated, is circular.

A circular argument assumes as fact what it attempts to prove. As frequently expressed, the problem of evil assumes that an all-good, all-powerful, and all-knowing God cannot have good reasons for creating a universe in which evil and suffering exist. But shouldn't this assumption require some proof?

We may not understand why a good God would allow terrible suffering. But this merely establishes that if there is a God, we do not know everything he knows. Why should this surprise us?

Suppose we add only one premise to the argument that God is all powerful, all knowing, and all loving, and yet evil exists: *God has a morally sufficient reason for permitting evil.* You may disagree with this premise, but it does *not* contradict the others.

We've all seen people say or do things that we considered unjustifiable. When we later learn why they did them, everything may change. The man who passed us on the freeway, honking his horn, was driving his injured daughter to the hospital. Realizing he had compelling reasons, we say, "I get it now; I misjudged him."

To disprove the God of the Bible exists, someone must demonstrate there can be no moral justification for an all-good, all-powerful, and all-knowing God to allow evil. Has this been proven? No. This doesn't mean the question isn't valid, only that a question is not the same as a proof.

God could create a universe in which he knew people would commit evil and suffer, *if* that was a necessary price to achieve a far greater eternal result.

Believers share common ground with unbelievers. We feel mutual horror at the reality, depth, and duration of human and animal suffering. We share a conviction that this kind of pain is terribly wrong and that it should be made right. In this way, evil and suffering serve as a bridge to the biblical account and its promise of redemption.

Consider two claims of Scripture:

Our present sufferings are not worth comparing with the glory that will be revealed in us. (Romans 8:18)

Our light and momentary troubles are achieving for us an eternal glory that far outweighs them all. (2 Corinthians 4:17)

"Well," a critic might say, "such affirmations reflect the naive idealism of someone insulated from evil and suffering." But in fact, the apostle Paul who made these statements, and he had endured extreme evil and suffering (see 2 Corinthians 11:23–33). He'd suffered through hunger, thirst, cold, imprisonment, murderous mob attacks, and repeated beatings and floggings—five times within an inch of his life. Evildoers had stoned him and put him in constant danger. He described himself as "exposed to death again and again." *This* is what Paul means by "our present sufferings" and "our light and momentary troubles."

Paul insists that our sufferings will result in our greater good—God's people will be better off *eternally* because they suffer *temporarily.* From Paul's perspective, this trade-off will in eternity prove to be a great bargain.

In fact, the argument for the *greater good* may be the strongest biblical case for God permitting evil and suffering. However, it requires trust, since the promised greater good is future and we can't see it in the present. If Paul is right, then by eliminating temporary evil and suffering, God would also eliminate eternal good.

I usually enjoy the research and writing I do, but at times it's very difficult. I do it anyway because I anticipate the reward that could never come without paying the price. In marriage and parenting, exercise and eating habits, study and work and spiritual disciplines, we often make short-term sacrifices in the interests of long-term gain.

In light of this, doesn't it seem logical, or at least *possible,* that a good God could have legitimate reasons for allowing evil and suffering to continue for the present? If so, then the problem of evil, while difficult, is not insurmountable.

Lt. Col. Brian Birdwell was working in the Pentagon on September 11, 2001, when the nose of the hijacked plane which ripped through the walls stopped just yards from where he lay burning and bleeding.

With more than 60 percent of his body blistered and his lungs seared, Birdwell made peace with God and readied himself for the relief of death. "I'm coming to see you," he said to Jesus. But he didn't die. An excruciating six days later, after being told his chance of survival was less than 1 percent, he said a last goodbye to his twelve-year-old son. But he still didn't die.

The next ninety-two days were filled with agonizing treatments, physical therapy, and over thirty-nine surgeries, including facial reconstruction. There is no way, he says, to describe the pain a burn victim experiences in recovery.

During his physical therapy, a pastor told him, "God never wastes our pain." Birdwell disregarded the words at the time. But in 2002, he was asked to visit and encourage a badly burned young man. That experience shaped his future. Retiring from the Army in 2004, Brian, along with his wife, began a ministry to critical-burn survivors, helping them to see beyond their pain to eternal spiritual realities.

Brian says, "An 80-ton 757 came through at 530 miles an hour with 3,000 pounds of jet fuel and I'm still here and the plane isn't," and adds, "You don't survive that because the Army made you tough. You survive it because the Lord's got something else in mind for you."[4]

Suffering reminds us to stop taking life for granted and to contemplate the larger picture. God intends that it draw our attention to life-and-death realities far greater than ourselves.

For those who know Christ, present pleasure foreshadows eternal pleasure: "In your presence there is fullness of joy; at your right hand are pleasures forevermore" (Psalm 16:11, ESV). For those without Christ, present suffering foreshadows eternal suffering where unbelievers "will be thrown outside, into the darkness, where there will be weeping and gnashing of teeth" (Matthew 8:12).

Paul speaks of the vital importance of our future resurrection. He says, "If I fought wild beasts in Ephesus for merely human reasons, what have I gained? If the dead are not raised, 'Let us eat and drink, for tomorrow we die'" (1 Corinthians 15:32).

If we have no eternal future as resurrected people living under the benevolent rule of King Jesus, *then our present sufferings will ultimately be worth nothing*. If we have such a future, however, then no present suffering—regardless of its scope—will prove worthless. In fact, such sufferings are a means to an end: incalculable future goodness.

The dysfunction of the present is the exception, not the rule—a small fraction of our history. Evil, suffering, and death will end forever (see Revelation 21:4). May we learn now what Paul knew: our present sufferings are a brief but important part of a larger plan that one day will prove them all worthwhile.

Notes

1. Gianna Jessen, interview by Hannity and Colmes, *Hannity and Colmes,* Fox, September 15, 2008.

2. John Milton, *Paradise Lost,* bk. 1, line 26.

3. John S. Feinberg, *The Many Faces of Evil* (Wheaton, IL: Crossway Books, 2004), 27.

4. Brian Birdwell, quoted in Fred W. Baker III, "9/11 Survivor Returns to Tell Story of Hope," American Forces Press Service, September 11, 2007, www.defenselink .mil/news/newsarticle.aspx?id=47411 (accessed May 2, 2009).

Understanding Evil:
Its Origins, Nature,
and Consequences

6

Evil's Entry into the Universe: A Rebellion of Angels

Mark 5:1–20 speaks powerfully of an angry, alienated, and lonely man, driven to despair at the hands of evil spirits. This ancient story captures the emptiness and desperation of countless people today.

"This man lived in the tombs, and no one could bind him.... He tore the chains apart and broke the irons on his feet. No one was strong enough to subdue him. Night and day among the tombs and in the hills he would cry out and cut himself with stones."

The man inflicted punishment on himself, as many in our culture do emotionally, and some physically, including cutting themselves.

When Jesus saw him he said, "Come out of this man, you evil spirit!"

Christ addressed one demon who had a legion of demons under him. This lead demon, realizing Christ's authority, begged Jesus to cast them into a herd of pigs. "He gave them permission, and the evil spirits came out and went into the pigs. The herd, about two thousand in number, rushed down the steep bank into the lake and were drowned."

A crowd gathered around Jesus and saw the formerly possessed man "sitting there, dressed and in his right mind." Jesus told him, "Go home to your family and tell them how much the Lord has done for you, and how he has had mercy on you." Mark writes, "So the man went away and began to tell in the Decapolis how much Jesus had done for him. And all the people were amazed."

This story reveals much about demons, people, and Jesus. Demons oppress, attack, and possess people, sometimes empowering them to do evil, always doing them great harm. They prompt people to hurt themselves and inflict evil and suffering on God's image-bearers. Perhaps this is the closest demons can come to avenging God for casting them out of Heaven because of their sin.

Demons recognize Christ's absolute authority over them. Jesus commands them at will, and in loving mercy delivers a man from his miserable life.

This extreme case is relevant to all of us. In cultures where everyone realizes there's a supernatural world, demons make themselves known as false gods to intimidate people, demanding worship and exacting retribution. In modern Western cultures where people routinely deny the supernatural, demons often accomplish their purposes more effectively by flying under the radar and working covertly. If we had eyes to see, we'd realize that all around us, fallen humans become the unwitting tools of evil spirits, harming themselves and others, and living wretched lives, sometimes quietly under the facade of social respectability.

Jesus loves afflicted people and went to the cross to deliver *us*, freeing us from the evil and suffering inflicted upon us by demons and ourselves. In delivering that desperate man, he gives hope to us all, showing us a picture of the total and final deliverance of his people from the powers of evil.

When Jesus rescued him from evil spirits, the man was at last "in his right mind," thinking clearly. Jesus transformed him. The delivered man overflowed with gratitude, as should all who know Christ's grace. To embrace Jesus as our redeemer is to be delivered from considerable evil and suffering now, and eventually from *all* evil and suffering. Jesus liberates us and calls us to testify to others of his mercy and power to defeat evil and relieve suffering.

God created all angels good.

All that God created he called "very good" (Genesis 1:31). Apparently after his creation of the universe, some angels rebelled against God, becoming "the angels who did not keep their positions of authority but abandoned their own home" (Jude 6).

While scholars debate whether it's a reference to Satan, Isaiah 14's account of the evil king of Babylon seems at least suggestive of what happened to Lucifer, who became Satan: "How you have fallen from heaven, O morning star, son of the dawn! You have been cast down to the earth. . . . You said in your heart, 'I will ascend to heaven; I will raise my throne above the stars of God; I will sit enthroned on the mount of assembly, on the utmost heights of the sacred mountain. . . . I will ascend above the tops of the clouds; I will make myself like the Most High" (verses 12–14).

This rebel was cast out, taken down to "the depths of the pit" (verse 15).

The king of Tyre, another evil ruler of his day, is likewise pictured in ways that seem to transcend his humanity, suggesting an allusion to Satan. God says to him,

"You were the model of perfection, full of wisdom and perfect in beauty.... You were anointed as a guardian cherub, for so I ordained you. You were on the holy mount of God.... You were blameless in your ways from the day you were created till wickedness was found in you" (Ezekiel 28:11, 14–15).

Note that God created him "blameless" and only later did he become wicked.

It's misleading to say "God created Satan and demons." Rather, God created Lucifer and other righteous angels, who later chose to rebel against God, and in so doing *became* Satan and demons.

Evil entered the universe through Satan, then the fallen angels.

The great archangel who rebelled against his Creator is called the devil (which means "slanderer") and Satan ("accuser"). Genesis introduces him as a word-master, using persuasive speech to deceive humans. Jesus called him "a liar and the father of lies" and a "murderer from the beginning" (John 8:44). Christ also referred to him as "the evil one" (Matthew 13:19) and "the prince of this world" (John 12:31; 14:30; 16:11).

Elsewhere the Bible calls him "the accuser of our brothers" (Revelation 12:10) and one determined to lead "the whole world astray" (Revelation 12:9). He is "Beelzebub, the prince of demons" (Matthew 12:24).

Revelation depicts him as an enormous red dragon whose "tail swept a third of the stars out of the sky and flung them to the earth" (12:4). Since the Bible often refers to angelic beings as stars, this may suggest that a third of the angels followed Satan in his rebellion against God. The Bible speaks of multitudes of demons (see Luke 8:30).

Satan and the demons dreamed of having authority over themselves and exalting themselves above God. They sinned by desiring to have more power than God appointed to them.

God knew that the angelic beings he created would rebel; their rebellion did not surprise him.

Paul writes, "For by him [Christ] all things were created: things in heaven and on earth, visible and invisible, whether thrones or powers or rulers or authorities; all things were created by him and for him" (Colossians 1:16). These "rulers or authorities" include demonic powers (see Ephesians 6:12).

How can evil demonic rulers have been created for Christ, when God knew they would rebel against him and declare war on his people? The Bible answers that through Jesus' redemptive sacrifice he is able to conquer their evil and display the greatness of his character, including his power and love, assuring unending God-centered joy for his followers.

Though demons hate God and us (and inflict suffering on us while they still can), in the end we'll see that God will have somehow used even them for his glory and our transformation, as we forever manifest his character.

The Bible tells us about the *entry* of evil into the universe, but evil's ultimate *origin* remains a mystery.

How could evil with no prior existence take hold within a perfect being?

We can more easily understand Adam and Eve's fall because an evil being tempted them. But how do we explain Satan's vulnerability to an evil that didn't yet exist? Some suggest evil existed in an embryonic form in the original creation. But surely God wouldn't call his creation "very good" if it harbored evil about to give birth to ruin! Genesis 1–3 clearly shows that evil had no place in Eden; rather, it intruded into a perfect world, foreign to God and his creation.

Then could evil have come into existence *ex nihilo,* out of nothing?

Scripture addresses *when* evil came into being, but not *how.* Deuteronomy 29:29 seems to apply here: "The secret things belong to the LORD our God." God has chosen to remain silent on this question, which may mean something significant. If evil is irrational, how can its point of origin be rationally explained? Perhaps God does not offer any explanation because evil defies explanation. It might make sense to an all-knowing God but no sense at all to us.

Every parent of small children knows that giving no explanation is sometimes better than a partial explanation that misleads little minds. Perhaps, then, we should interpret God's silence about the origin of evil not as a refusal to explain, but as a kindness. Maybe his explanation would, given our limitations, lead us to greater misunderstanding or even heresy.

As our children will one day understand things we don't try to explain now, so one day, in God's presence, we will have the reference points to understand what now remains a mystery.

Immediately after the Fall, God revealed both Satan's and humanity's roles in God's redemptive plan.

God pronounced a punishment on Satan after the devil seduced Adam and Eve to sin. "Cursed are you.... And I will put enmity between you and the woman, and between your offspring and hers; he will crush your head, and you will strike his heel" (Genesis 3:14–15).

At first it looks like two descendants would battle it out: "between your off-spring and hers." But then God says something surprising: "*He* will crush *your* head." Who is "he"? The woman's offspring. Whose is "your" head? The devil's. So Eve's descendant would crush the head of the serpent himself.

Hebrews 2:14 describes the connection between Christ's humanity and Satan's destruction: "Since therefore the children share in flesh and blood, he himself likewise partook of the same things, that through death he might destroy the one who has the power of death, that is, the devil" (ESV). In other words, God became a woman's offspring that he might crush Satan's head. A human would ultimately defeat the one who led humans into sin. To defeat Satan would require God's superior nature, suggesting this man might also be God.

Satan's work is evil and suffering—exactly what the messianic promise of Genesis 3 is said to ultimately defeat. "The reason the Son of God appeared was to destroy the devil's work" (1 John 3:8). From the beginning, God planned that his Son should deal the death blow to Satan, evil, and suffering, to reverse the Curse, redeem a fallen humanity, and repair a broken world.

The Bible says that Jesus, "having disarmed the powers and authorities... made a public spectacle of them, triumphing over them by the cross" (Colossians 2:15). Jesus' triumph ensured Satan's defeat; only the execution of Satan's sentence remains (Revelation 20:10). The devil sits on death row. He lashes out against God's image-bearers, trying to kill God in effigy: "He is filled with fury, because he knows that his time is short" (Revelation 12:12).

Satan is not God's opposite, fighting a cosmic duel with an uncertain outcome.

What's the opposite of light? Darkness. What's the opposite of good? Evil. When asked to name the opposite of God, people often answer, "Satan." But that's false. Michael, the righteous archangel, is Satan's opposite. Satan is finite; God is infinite. God has no equal.

A duel implies a competition with an unknown outcome. That's not at all like the cosmic clash between God and Satan. Their conflict better resembles the undefeated world heavyweight champion (God) taking on a cranky three-year-old (Satan). Consider this great conflict:

> When the thousand years are over, Satan will be released from his prison and
> will go out to deceive the nations...to gather them for battle. In number
> they are like the sand on the seashore. They marched across the breadth of

the earth and surrounded the camp of God's people, the city he loves. But fire came down from heaven and devoured them. (Revelation 20:7–9)

Satan gathers people for battle and they march. But in the end, one side suffers not a single casualty, while the other side has not a single survivor. Fire consumes all the enemies of God. The whole conflict ends before it begins. It's not a battle at all; it's an execution.

Satan and God do not engage in hand-to-hand combat, with Satan sometimes getting the edge. That's not the Bible; that's *Star Wars*. Many of us make Satan too big and God too small.

True, we have not yet reached the time when we no longer suffer casualties. Satan is called the "god of this world" (2 Corinthians 4:4, ESV), "the prince of the power of the air" (Ephesians 2:2, ESV) and one of the "cosmic powers over this present darkness" (Ephesians 6:12, ESV). But Scripture always describes Satan's power in the context of God's absolute sovereignty. Satan remains under God's authority at all times. The devil is nowhere close to being omnipotent, omniscient, omnipresent, or anything like God.

The same goes for demons. Though unclean spirits work to deceive and kill, Jesus maintains authority over them: "He commands even the unclean spirits, and they obey him" (Mark 1:27, ESV).

When Christ commands, the devil himself obeys. The question, then, is, "Why doesn't God once and for all command the devil to stop inflicting evil and suffering on human beings God loves?"

Scripture ascribes to Satan and demons vast power we dare not underestimate.

Satan inflicts evil and suffering on both the world and God's people. He is like "a roaring lion, seeking for someone to devour" (1 Peter 5:8). That describes only part of the picture, however. Satan is a lion, yes, but a lion on God's leash.

Though Satan seeks to devour us, he poses no threat to God. We are no match for Satan, yet we're told, "Submit yourselves, then, to God. Resist the devil, and he will flee from you" (James 4:7). We should never quote the last part of that verse without the first: *Submit yourselves to God.* That alone is the basis upon which we can successfully resist the devil.

Satan, the ultimate evildoer, sometimes disguises his evil as goodness.

Satan often appears as an "angel of light" (2 Corinthians 11:14)—appealing, beautiful, enticing. Yet he always begins with questioning God's Word: "Did God *really* say that?" He whispers to us as he did to Eve: "Question God. Reinterpret God's command. Don't take seriously his warning of death following sin. Don't worry; evil won't have consequences. God is withholding good from you. You don't need God. You can call your own shots."

Satan labors to keep unbelievers from trusting Christ. "The god of this age has blinded the minds of unbelievers, so that they cannot see the light of the gospel of the glory of Christ" (2 Corinthians 4:4). Satan "leads the whole world astray" (Revelation 12:9). He battles those who believe (see Ephesians 6:11). He works to keep us from trusting our Savior. So it should not surprise us when he uses evil and suffering—the very things he specializes in—to get us to question God's goodness, love, power, or knowledge.

Satan can attack our faith only within God's set limits.

Jesus said to Peter, "Satan demanded to have you, that he might sift you like wheat" (Luke 22:31, ESV). The devil sought to destroy Peter's faith, just as he tried to demolish Job's. Ultimately, he failed to succeed with either. Satan could bring into Peter's life only what the all-knowing and all-powerful God gave him permission to bring. God has veto power over Satan. Perhaps one day we'll learn how many times God refused Satan's requests to bring greater temptations and hardships upon us.

God has good reasons for delaying his final judgment against Satan.

Satan will forever pay the price for his evil: "And the devil, who deceived them, was thrown into the lake of burning sulfur," where he "will be tormented day and night for ever and ever" (Revelation 20:10).

Some fallen angels are already "kept in darkness, bound with everlasting chains for judgment on the great Day" (Jude 6). Yet many remain free to inflict harm, tempting and deceiving humans.

John Piper writes, "Satan's fall and ongoing existence are for the glory of Christ. The Son of God, Jesus Christ, will be more highly honored and more deeply appreciated and loved in the end because he defeats Satan not the moment after Satan fell, but through millennia of long-suffering, patience, humility, servanthood, suffering, and decisively through his own death."[1]

God has both the power and the right to destroy Satan and the demons *now*, which would demonstrate his justice. But he wants to display his other attributes as well, among them grace, mercy, and patience.

Every day that God delays his final judgment against Satan is one more day to extend his grace to a needy world. And it is one more day for his kindness in Christ to accomplish in this fallen world the work for which we will be praising him ten million years from now.

Notes

1. John Piper, *Spectacular Sins* (Wheaton, IL: Good News, 2008), 49.

7

Humanity's Evil and the Suffering It Has Caused

I f *God Is Good* contains many stories of people's challenges and triumphs. But there are subjects of doctrinal significance we must be clear on in order to accurately and biblically interpret these experiences. It's tempting to bypass these issues, just as it's tempting to take shortcuts in laying a building's foundation. But for exactly the same reason, we should resist that temptation.

The book of Judges overflows with terrible stories of evil and violence. People keep sinning, God keeps judging them. He sends consequences, and in their desperation they cry out. He delivers them by sending another rescuer. Soon they become self-satisfied and pursue evil again. The cycle goes on and on, until the reader despairs over the abject poverty of the human condition. The book's final sentence offers a penetrating diagnosis of the problem: "In those days there was no king in Israel. Everyone did what was right in his own eyes" (Judges 21:25, ESV).

This passage is profoundly pertinent to us. What's right in *our* eyes is not synonymous with what's right. The King of the universe determines what is right. If we don't recognize him as King, if we refuse to bow to his moral authority, like Israel in the time of the judges, we experience chaos because we trust ourselves to redefine good and evil. The history of the human race, in every culture and time, demonstrates the dire consequences of living life as we prefer rather than as God commands.

EVIL'S EMERGENCE IN HUMANITY

Evil violates the standards that express God's divine character.
For decades a popular television pastor has defined sin as "any act or thought that

robs myself or another human being of his or her self-esteem."[1] Sin is in fact something far greater than that. Sin attacks the spotless character of almighty God. At its root, evil violates God's nature and insults his supremacy. It rejects God and rebels against his authority. Therefore we cannot understand evil without understanding the nature of the one true God.

God's character provides the basis for moral standards: "Be holy because I, the LORD your God, am holy" (Leviticus 19:2). Ungodliness means the failure to conform to God's nature.

Jeffrey Burton Russell writes, "The essence of evil is abuse of a sentient being, a being that can feel pain. It is the pain that matters."[2] But surely it is more than the pain. It is also the value of the being, and the degree to which his honor has been violated.

The Old Testament sacrificial system sent the unmistakable message that a holy God cannot overlook sin which exacts a terrible price. This pointed to the one John the Baptist called "the Lamb of God, who takes away the sin of the world" (John 1:29).

Hebrews 10:4 argues, "It is impossible for the blood of bulls and goats to take away sins." God's standards are so high that only a perfect and infinite sacrifice, which couldn't be less than God himself, can atone for sins against his nature. Combine this with the promise that a descendant of the woman would crush the head of Satan, and reparation demands a Redeemer who is the God-man. Jesus Christ *had to be made like his brothers*...that he might make atonement for the sins of the people" (Hebrews 2:17).

The primary Hebrew and Greek words for "sin" connote "missing the mark" or "falling short": "All have sinned and fall short of the glory of God" (Romans 3:23). Common synonyms for *evil* such as *rebellion, transgression,* and *trespass* all involve overstepping the limits imposed upon creatures by their Creator. Those limits are grounded in God's character, which is expressed in his commandments. To sin is to exalt self and to depreciate the God who created us to live in loving relationship with him.

The first humans, although created sinless, chose to rebel against God.
After God declared his creation "very good," we're told, "And the LORD God commanded the man, 'You are free to eat from any tree in the garden; but you must not eat from the tree of the knowledge of good and evil, for when you eat of it you will surely die'" (Genesis 2:16–17).

Somehow, as the first human couple weighed their alternatives, evil entered their hearts. Adam and Eve rebelled, choosing to violate God's explicit command. They trusted a fallen creature's logic, rather than their Creator's goodness, when he'd given them no reason to doubt him. They ate, the curse fell on them, their pain greatly increased, the earth became a world of hurt, and they forfeited paradise.

Adam and Eve's disobedience did not surprise God or cause him to wring his hands.

A just and merciful God chose a measured punishment for the first human sin: suffering. Had God meted out the full and immediate punishment, the first humans would have died on the spot (see Romans 6:23). In that case, there would have been no redemptive history—no human history at all.

The Fall, the first human tragedy, became the mother of all subsequent ones. We should do nothing to minimize it or to pretend it mattered less than it did. Yet, the Fall did *not* end God's plan for humanity. God would ultimately use evil to accomplish the greater end of redemption in Christ:

> And he *made known to us the mystery of his will according to his good pleasure, which he purposed in Christ,* to be put into effect when the times will have reached their fulfillment—to bring all things in heaven and on earth together under one head, even Christ.
>
> In him we were also chosen, *having been predestined according to the plan of him who works out everything* in conformity with the purpose of his will. (Ephesians 1:9–11)

God could hate evil and yet permit it in order to carry out an astounding, far-reaching redemptive plan in Christ, one that would forever overshadow the evil and sufferings of this present world.

Because the Fall really happened in history, God's Son had to enter history (incarnation), suffer and die in history (redemption), and rise from the grave in history (resurrection).

Romans 5:12–21 assumes that a real Adam and Eve fell in history. Other passages affirm the same (see 1 Corinthians 15:22, 45; 1 Timothy 2:13–14). Paul speaks of Adam as the historical head of humanity in the same way that he speaks of Christ as the new head of redeemed humanity. Adam was no more fictional than Jesus.

In *Genesis in Space and Time,* Francis Schaeffer stressed the importance of not fictionalizing the events of the early chapters of Genesis. Whenever these events are reduced to folk tales, ultimately the gospel gets reduced to fables. If Adam and Eve were not real people and therefore never chose to commit evil, then Christ's redemptive work can also be seen as symbolic rather than historical.

But Adam and Eve appear in biblical genealogies with other historical people (see 1 Chronicles 1:1; Luke 3:37). Christ cited the Genesis account about the first man and woman (see Matthew 19:4–6), showing he believed in the historicity of Adam and Eve. To deny their historicity is to contradict Jesus.

The Three Curses After Humanity's Fall

God's curse upon Satan predicted Christ's redemptive work.

The first curse fell on Satan, who had taken the form of a serpent. As we've seen, although Satan would wound the woman's offspring, that descendant, the Messiah, would crush Satan's head (see Genesis 3:15).

We can view that trouncing of Satan as taking place in the past, in the ministry of Christ and his apostles (see Luke 10:17–20), and in Christ's death and resurrection (see Colossians 2:15). We should also view it as taking place in the future, after the triumphant return of Jesus (see Revelation 20:7). God's people will take part in Christ's success over Satan: "The God of peace will soon crush Satan under your feet" (Romans 16:20).

God's judgment upon Eve increased the intensity of physical, emotional, and relational pain.

God said to Eve, "I will greatly increase your pains in childbearing; with pain you will give birth to children. Your desire will be for your husband, and he will rule over you" (Genesis 3:16).

Increased pain implies already-existing pain. Likely, pain in Eden helped keep its residents aware of the environment; pain, for example, prompted them to pull their hands back from fire. Mild pain apparently stimulated a physical response that aided childbirth. The increase of pain in childbearing may also suggest the difficulty and heartbreak of parenting that would come with the Fall.

Death's entrance into the world would lead to a high rate of infant mortality, miscarriages, and stillbirths. As every parent knows who has suffered the loss of a child, this aspect of the Curse brings unspeakable heaviness. Adam and Eve had known a truly good world, while we still haven't. So when Cain killed Abel, the first parents must have endured haunting memories of paradise lost.

The Curse also disfigured God's gift of marriage. Fallen men misused their strength, not to protect their wives, but turn it against them. Women sought to control their husbands, while men lost interest in becoming the sensitive, servant-leaders God mean them to be.

God's judgment upon Adam addressed the corruption of Earth and the burden of human labor.

God said to Adam, "Cursed is the ground because of you" (Genesis 3:17). The word translated "ground" is the Hebrew *adama,* sometimes rendered "land" or "earth." God entrusted the governance of Earth and its animals to humankind, and when Adam fell, Earth fell on his coattails. The curse upon the earth is a curse upon Adam and his descendants, whom God called to tend the earth.

Growing food became much harder, with weeds getting in the way and a hostile climate creating droughts and famines. Work, designed to fulfill, became difficult and exhausting.

God placed suffering upon humanity as a judgment. Yet mercy surfaces even then. Before God banishes the couple from Eden, he alludes a second time to his redemptive plan. Seeing human misery, "The LORD God made garments of skin for Adam and his wife and clothed them" (Genesis 3:21). Presumably the garments coincided with the first animal sacrifice, foreshadowing God's eventual sacrifice of his Son.

A WORLDVIEW THAT SEES EVIL FOR WHAT IT IS

The Christian worldview's account of evil and suffering is uniquely and profoundly God-centered.

Too many people, Christians included, view the Christian faith in bits and pieces. We should see it as a holistic worldview, a large-scale belief system based on the unfolding of redemptive history.

The Christian worldview concerns far more than the spiritual salvation of individuals. It touches on every aspect of human existence and extends beyond humanity to the very nature of God.

Everyone has a worldview, inconsistent and superficial though it might be. Worldviews invite contemplation and comparison. As I have compared the Christian worldview to others, I have found it both comprehensive and satisfying. I believe the greatest test of any worldview is how it deals with the problem of evil and suffering. And Scripture's redemptive story passes that test with remarkable depth and substance.

But as dozens of books demonstrate, it is easy to make a critical error in evaluating the Christian worldview. Peter Hicks put it this way:

> If we start with a definition that, like the Bible's, accepts the existence of God and roots the concepts of good and evil in him, then our subsequent discussion should consistently operate with that definition and according to that worldview. What we should not do is to start with one definition and then discuss it in the context of the other worldview. In particular, we should not, as Christians, be required to defend our belief in God and at the same time accept that good and evil are to be defined in terms of human happiness.[3]

The Bible starts with God: "*In the beginning God* created the heavens and the earth" (Genesis 1:1). It presents good and evil as determined by God alone—not by human nature or nurture, culture or preferences. We don't decide good and evil based on what we want and don't want, or by what we understand or don't understand. We can choose to do either good or evil, but we have no vote in *establishing* whether something is good or evil.

Unfortunately, when evaluating the problem of evil and suffering, many Christians retreat into a man-centered worldview. Once they do this, subsequent discussion becomes almost pointless. If we accept the argument that the highest value of the universe is short-term human happiness in the form of immediate fulfillment of desires, then *we cannot defend the Christian worldview, because we ourselves have departed from it.*

The Christian worldview is God-centered, not man-centered; and while Scripture shows concern for human happiness, especially eternal happiness, even this bows to God's character revealed, forever exalted, and fully enjoyed in the ages to come (see Ephesians 2:7).

While God assures us that he will one day remove all suffering and sorrow, he will do so as a by-product of his highest purpose for us: "The LORD will be your everlasting light, and your God will be your glory" (Isaiah 60:19). If we come to see the purpose of the universe as God's long-term glory rather than our short-term happiness, then we will undergo a critical paradigm shift in tackling the problem of evil and suffering.

The world has gone terribly wrong.

God is going to fix it.

First, for his eternal glory.

Second, for our eternal good.

Notes

1. Robert H. Schuller, *Self-Esteem: The New Reformation* (Waco, TX: Word, 1982), 14.
2. For development of this interpretation, see Susan Foh, *Women and the Word of God* (Phillipsburg, NJ: Presbyterian and Reformed, 1978).
3. Peter Hicks, *The Message of Evil and Suffering* (Downers Grove, IL: InterVarsity, 2007), 112.

8

Inherited Sin and Our Sin Nature

In 1750, at age twenty-five, John Newton commanded an English slave ship. He anchored off the African coast, purchasing natives taken captive by rival tribes. The slave traders bartered to get the finest specimens, offering alcohol, cloth, and weapons. Newton's men took the terrified slaves aboard and chained them below decks in two-foot-high pens to prevent suicides. As many as six hundred lay side by side like fireplace logs, row after row. There were no toilet facilities or ventilation. The stench was indescribable.

Newton's ship had not only chains, but neck collars, handcuffs, and thumbscrews, a torture device. They sailed from Africa to the Caribbean, selling the slaves for molasses, rum, and other valuables.

Like other captains, Newton allowed his crew to rape female slaves, as Newton did himself. Sometimes a quarter of the slaves died on the journey, sometimes more. Newton blasphemed God and engaged in brutality and immorality. He prided himself on being incorrigible.

As a young crewman, when his ship nearly sank, Newton professed Christ. But he spent years committing evil before he experienced a true conversion. He left the slave trade and felt increasing remorse for what he'd done. For the last half of his life he pastored a church near London, where he preached the gospel, taught the Scriptures, and eventually spoke against the slave trade, encouraging young parliamentarian William Wilberforce in his battle to outlaw slavery.

At age eighty-two, shortly before his death, a physically blind and spiritually sighted John Newton said, "My memory is nearly gone, but I remember two things: That I am a great sinner, and that Christ is a great Saviour."[1]

Newton's tombstone reads, "John Newton...once an infidel...was, by the rich mercy of our Lord and Saviour Jesus Christ, preserved, restored, pardoned, and appointed to preach the faith he had long labored to destroy."

Newton wrote hundreds of hymns, the most famous of which is the most popular song among many African Christians throughout the world:

Amazing grace! How sweet the sound
That saved a wretch like me,
I once was lost, but now am found,
Was blind, but now I see.

Newton's claim to wretchedness wasn't hyperbole; he clearly saw the evil in himself, an evil that remains better hidden in many. While Newton may appear an extreme case, the Bible teaches that all of us are evil-lovers and evildoers, blind wretches in desperate need of God's transforming grace.

J. I. Packer wrote what we need to keep in mind in the next few chapters:

The subject of sin is vital knowledge. To say that our first need in life is to learn about sin may sound strange, but in the sense intended it is profoundly true. If you have not learned about sin, you cannot understand yourself, or your fellow-men, or the world you live in, or the Christian faith. And you will not be able to make head or tail of the Bible. For the Bible is an exposition of God's answer to the problem of human sin and unless you have that problem clearly before you, you will keep missing the point of what it says.[2]

The Semantics of the Sin Nature and Total Depravity

The *sin nature* refers to our fallen state that distrusts, dishonors, and rejects God.

Scripture emphatically declares our sin nature:

The heart is deceitful above all things
    and beyond cure. (Jeremiah 17:9)

"There is no one righteous, not even one.…
All have turned away,
    they have together become worthless;
there is no one who does good,
    not even one."
"Their throats are open graves;
    their tongues practice deceit."
"The poison of vipers is on their lips."
    "Their mouths are full of cursing and bitterness."

"Their feet are swift to shed blood...."

"There is no fear of God before their eyes." (Romans 3:10–18)

All have sinned and fall short of the glory of God. (Romans 3:23)

"If we claim to be without sin, we deceive ourselves and the truth is not in us" (1 John 1:8). Before Christ redeemed us, "All of us also lived among them [those disobedient to God] at one time, gratifying the cravings of our sinful nature and following its desires and thoughts. Like the rest, we were by nature objects of wrath" (Ephesians 2:3). Unredeemed human beings "are darkened in their understanding and separated from the life of God because of the ignorance that is in them due to the hardening of their hearts" (Ephesians 4:18).

The sin nature compels us to love ourselves. In our reckless pursuit of self-gratification, we impose upon ourselves gnawing emptiness rather than the joy and contentment that comes in loving God and others.

Though we naturally resist the biblical revelation about our sin natures, we find freedom when we recognize its reality. C. S. Lewis wrote,

> It is the high-minded unbeliever, desperately trying in the teeth of repeated disillusions to retain his "faith in human nature" who is really sad.... We actually are, at present, creatures whose character must be, in some respects, a horror to God, as it is, when we really see it, a horror to ourselves. This I believe to be a fact: and I notice that the holier a man is, the more fully he is aware of that fact.[3]

To view evil accurately, we must see it above all as an outrageous offense against God.

We tend to minimize our sin because we fail to see its real object. When we hurt those we love, we become aware of our sin. Their pain reflects our evil back to us, like a mirror. But because we do not see God and see how our sin hurts *him*, we don't see either the frequency or the gravity of our offenses. We imagine our sin has no effect on him.

We couldn't be more wrong.

After coming to terms with his adultery with Bathsheba and his part in the murder of Uriah, her husband, David confesses his sin, then says something surprising: "I know my transgressions, and my sin is always before me. *Against you, you only, have I sinned* and done what is evil in your sight" (Psalm 51:3–4).

David rightly recognizes the very definition of sin: Whatever is "evil in [God's] sight." But David sinned against his friend, his family, and his nation. Why then does he say, "Against you, you *only*, have I sinned"?

I think David is correcting in himself the tendency we all have—to limit our sorrow to the hurt we've inflicted on human beings. No doubt he had agonized over his betrayal of loyal Uriah, a man who would have gladly died for his king's honor. David probably caught himself mourning more over what he had done to others than what he had done to God.

Pastors who have committed adultery often feel profoundly the consequences of their evil as they see the faces of their wives, children, friends, fellow pastors, and congregations. They may feel deep sorrow for the hurt they've brought. But sometimes they fail to see their primary sin against God. And when we fail to see that we have sinned against God above all—the One who has maximum worthiness—then no matter how bad we feel about what we've done to others, we will inevitably minimize our sin.

The depth of pain that others suffer because of our sins should point us to the depth of our evil before God almighty. All sin is against God, from the first one in Eden to the last one in history. The man who commits adultery does not trespass against only his wife and children. He violates the standards of the God before whom angels cry out, "Holy, holy, holy." Repentance without recognizing our offense against God is not repentance.

Our sin natures mean that, generally, "Be yourself" is not good advice.

We grasp the horror of human evil only when we focus on God's standards and on the atonement necessary to satisfy them.

Anything that violates God's nature is evil. Sin is not merely a minor deviation from a negotiable standard. It is, in the eyes of a holy God and the holy angels who serve him, a despicable aberration from God's nature.

The clearest indication of our evil's depth is what it cost to redeem us. Some talk as if God's bighearted love for us is sufficient to save us. But the problem of how to reconcile evil people with a God who hates evil is the greatest problem of history. It calls for no less than the greatest solution ever devised, one so radical as to be nearly unthinkable, and to offend the sensibilities of countless people throughout history.

Since evil offends God's nature, the true test of good and evil is how God sees it. Simply serving our desired ends does not make something good; neither does causing our unhappiness make something evil.

So many human cultures agree on basic issues of right and wrong because, as his image-bearers, our consciences can give us insight (see Romans 2:15). But as finite and fallen creatures, our consciences can be misguided and weak (see 1 Corinthians 4:4; 8:7), and even seared and corrupted (see 1 Timothy 4:2; Titus 1:15). We must rely on God's self-revelation in his Word to know his character and his commandments, and to recognize both good and evil.

God's holiness carries exceedingly high demands. As a single, unified God, he cannot exercise one attribute in disregard of (let alone in opposition to) another. Therefore the omnipotent God could not save us while leaving his holiness unsatisfied.

If redemption could be purchased at a lower cost, surely God would have chosen it. I think Jesus explored this possibility when he fell to the ground and prayed, "My Father, if it is not possible for this cup to be taken away unless I drink it, may your will be done" (Matthew 26:42). Luke adds, "And being in anguish, he [Jesus] prayed more earnestly, and his sweat was like drops of blood falling to the ground" (22:44).

We may feel tempted to underestimate the horrors of the Cross, because to recognize them is to admit that our monstrous evil demanded a price so horrific. To make light of our sin is to make light of Christ's cross.

Total spiritual inability is a better description of the human condition than *total depravity*.

Scripture insists that all human beings are sinners, that sin touches every part of us, and that we cannot earn God's favor (see Isaiah 64:6; Romans 7:15; 8:8; Hebrews 11:6). God owes us nothing, while we owe him everything. We need God to reach down to us so that we may reach up to him.

Total depravity seems to imply that without Christ, no one can ever do anything *remotely* good. It even appears to suggest that we always do as much evil as possible. If that were true, why would Scripture say of King Jehoshaphat, who had just sinned against God, "There is, however, some good in you" (2 Chronicles 19:3)?

We can successfully complete any number of physical and mental tasks, even some good ones. But we remain helpless sinners with nothing to offer God that could gain us a right standing with him. Therefore I believe Wayne Grudem's term, *total inability*, is more accurate and helpful.[4] I'll add one word, calling it *total* spiritual *inability*. To emphasize that we have no ability to save ourselves may avoid the misinterpretations some have of the term *total depravity*.

THE SIGNIFICANCE OF INHERITED SIN

Inherited sin speaks of our moral condition resulting from the Fall.
People often understand the term *original sin* to refer to Adam and Eve's first sin. This theological term, however, actually speaks of the *effect* of Adam's sin upon *us*, making us sinners from our very conception. Because of this frequent confusion, I will use another term Wayne Grudem prefers, *inherited sin*.[5] Various scriptures speak of or imply the doctrine of inherited sin (see Psalm 51:5; 58:3; Romans 5:12–19; 1 Corinthians 15:22).

These passages tell us we are "sinful at birth" and "from birth...go astray," that "the many died by the trespass of one man," that "through the disobedience of the one man the many were made sinners," and that "in Adam all die."

The evil from inherited sin comes from within; nothing from the outside imposes it on us.
J. C. Ryle wrote, "Dim or indistinct views of sin are the origin of most of the errors, heresies and false doctrines of the present day."[6] Almost as if trying to illustrate Ryle's statement, a hundred years later Robert Schuller wrote,

> To call sin rebellion against God is shallow and insulting to the human being. Where the sixteenth century reformation returned our focus to the sacred Scriptures as the only infallible rule for faith and practice, the new reformation will return our focus to the sacred right of every person to self-esteem. The most serious sin is the one that causes me to say: "I am unworthy."... I don't think anything has been done in the name of Christ and under the banner of Christianity that has proven more destructive to human personality and hence counterproductive to the evangelistic enterprise than the unchristian, uncouth strategy of attempting to make people aware of their lost and sinful condition.[7]

Heresies such as this try to flee biblical truth by appealing to human pride. Though the modern therapeutic movement has done some good, it also can distance us from our sin by blaming it too much on our upbringing, parents, schools, churches, and other influences.

So long as we view evil as coming from sources outside us, we can view ourselves as victims, not perpetrators. When *you* sin, it's *your* fault; but when *I* sin, it's only because *you* "made me" do so. In fact, other sinners don't make me sin.

Certainly their actions may influence me negatively and trigger my heart's sinfulness into revealing itself. As it's sometimes stated, we are not sinners because we sin; we sin because we are sinners.

Jesus taught, "The evil man out of the evil treasure brings forth what is evil; for his mouth speaks from that which fills his heart" (Luke 6:45, NASB). We err when we think we are naturally good and that our environment teaches us to sin. In fact, our evil nature is the catalyst.

"But doesn't that create a moral dilemma," someone asks, "because wouldn't it mean God created us as sinners?" No, it doesn't, and no, he didn't. When we see a flower or a dog, we correctly say that God created them. But centuries of cross-pollination and breeding have also come into play. Likewise, although God truly creates us as individuals, we are also the products of specific historical and hereditary factors linked to our ancestors, including Adam, who functioned as our representative when he sinned against God.

We are accountable to God not only for our disobedience, but for our unbelief in Christ and his redemptive work.

As unbelievers we "were dead in the trespasses and sins" in which we walked (Ephesians 2:1, ESV). God's standard is perfection: "You therefore must be perfect, as your heavenly Father is perfect" (Matthew 5:48, ESV). But how can we, who still sin, be perfect? Paul and John both recognize Christians can and do sin (see Galatians 5:17; 1 John 1:8). On God's moral examination, we don't know whether some would score 1 percent, some 10, some 20, but we know for certain no one scores 100 percent. When perfection is the standard, 99 percent on the final exam is a failing score: "For whoever keeps the whole law and yet stumbles at just one point is guilty of breaking all of it" (James 2:10; see also Galatians 3:10).

So how do we gain the moral perfection God requires of us? Only by trusting Jesus to give us what we cannot attain ourselves. The God who requires moral perfection is the God who supplies it in Jesus.

We need not be sinlessly perfect to please God in this life, but we *must* believe in his work that achieves for us the moral perfection required to live forever with God. Only when God imputes to us the righteous nature of Christ can we be transformed into righteous beings who please God (see 2 Corinthians 5:21).

Whoever believes in him is not condemned, but whoever does not believe stands condemned already because he has not believed in the name of God's one and only Son. (John 3:18)

Abraham believed God, and it was credited to him as righteousness. (Romans 4:3)

Without faith it is impossible to please God. (Hebrews 11:6)

Jesus said that the Holy Spirit would convict the world of its guilt "in regard to sin, because men do not believe in me" (John 16:9). Had Christ not gone to the cross, we would have borne the judgment for all our sins. Since he did go to the cross, the greatest sin is to choose not to trust him for his redemptive work. "Anyone who does not believe God has made him out to be a liar, because he has not believed the testimony God has given about his Son" (1 John 5:10).

Inherited sin provides no basis for self-hatred or devaluing others.

Some think believing in inherited sin is an invitation to view others and ourselves as worthless, thus justifying evil. The theory holds that the more we speak of human virtue, the more we will respect and love one another and ourselves.

In reality, since no aspect of their lives is untouched by their nature, evil people lack the capacity to gauge accurately the extent of their good or evil. We normally commend ourselves and ignore our flaws. But believing in the doctrine of inherited sin provides the ultimate equalizer. Embracing it leads to humility and grace, prompting us to care for the needy—individuals we might otherwise despise.

Ironically, wherever societies recognize the human capacity for evil, evil is restrained and goodness is exalted. Yet whenever people view themselves as basically good, the greatest evils take place. Denying the doctrine of inherited sin leads to elitism and oppression. Why? Partly because people who view themselves as good place no restrictions upon those in power. But apart from checks and balances as well as moral accountability (implemented only when human sin is recognized), leaders inevitably become corrupt. Communism under Stalin, Mao, and Pol Pot provide classic examples.

We all share a strange kinship as desperately needy sinners. We fell together in Adam. And we all benefit from the redemptive work of the second Adam, Christ. While our sins may differ, we all need the same Redeemer.

ISSUES RAISED BY INHERITED SIN

We are sinners in our own right and will be judged for our own lifetime of sins.

Had we been in Adam's place, no doubt we would have made the same evil decision he did; whether months earlier or years later is irrelevant. Remember, it takes only a single sin along the way to become eternally separated from an infinitely holy God.

"The dead were judged according to what they had done as recorded in the books" (Revelation 20:12). Notice the dead are not judged for what *Adam* did, but for what *they* did. God "will render to each person according to his deeds" (Romans 2:6, NASB), not according to Adam's deeds. Yes, we sinned in Adam; but God will judge us for our own sins (which will be plenty). "For he who does wrong will receive the consequences of the wrong which he has done, and that without partiality" (Colossians 3:25, NASB).

Jesus portrays the unredeemed as walking a broad road that leads to destruction (see Matthew 7:13). Coming into the world as a sinner is like beginning your life journey on a downhill slope. You're headed toward a cliff over a fiery pit; gravity, like your sin nature, pulls you downward. But road signs posted along the way (conscience, God's self-revelation in creation and in his Word) warn you of the destruction ahead. Roadside telephones all along the way allow you to summon outside help. If we call upon God in Christ to rescue us and empower us, we can resist the downward pull, moving upward to the narrow road, toward a new center of gravity.

The idea of inherited sin may seem unfair, but God is the proper Judge of fairness.

We have lost the sense of solidarity and connectedness of the human race, once widely assumed. If you feel proud that your ancestor came over on the *Mayflower* or that you're a descendant of a great scientist, but you're embarrassed by your grandfather who was an embezzler, is it really such a stretch to feel shame that your ancestors, Adam and Eve, rebelled against God? Or to feel that in some way the fruit of their sin reaches through all generations to touch your life today?

We see generational connectedness all the time. AIDS gets transferred from generation to generation. Child abusers beget child abusers and alcoholics raise alcoholics. I could not have become an insulin-dependent diabetic without a genetic proclivity. Does the condition of my ancestors affect my life? Of course.

So if we see such obvious physical connections to our ancestors, why not spiritual connections? If drug addicts pass on their addictions, why not sin addicts? Why should we not see sin itself as a communicable disease, one (with the exception of Jesus) universally passed on from parents to children? And since we are who we are, a good God, concerned for our welfare, must no more ignore our sin problem than a good physician would ignore a patient's disease.

The gospel is God's cure for our disease. Jesus paid the ultimate price to heal us—but we will not submit ourselves to the treatment if we deny our disease or bemoan its unfairness. Healing can come only when we recognize we are sinners in need of a Savior. Yes, Adam and Eve's first sin had far-reaching consequences that have extended to each of us. But the Bible teaches us to confess *our* sins and embrace God's forgiveness *for ourselves* (see 1 John 1:9).

The same principle that connects us with Adam allows us to be connected to Christ and his work for us.

Inherited sin demonstrates the connection between a distant representative and us. The good news is that another person's action thousands of years ago can also dramatically influence your life today:

> For just as through the disobedience of the one man the many were made sinners, so also through the obedience of the one man the many will be made righteous. (Romans 5:19)

> For as in Adam all die, so in Christ all will be made alive. (1 Corinthians 15:22)

God sees the human community as an organic whole; the first Adam represents the fallen race. Likewise, "the last Adam" (1 Corinthians 15:45), King Jesus, represents the new community of God's people.

I thank God for the connectedness of humanity that allowed not just the first Adam to introduce evil and suffering to the human race, but the last Adam, Jesus Christ, to take that evil and suffering on himself.

The reality of human sinfulness answers the so-called problem of bad things happening to good people.

It never occurs to most of us that the book title *When Bad Things Happen to Good People* is based on a fundamental falsehood. What if, as the Bible teaches, no people are *truly* good? What if an evil deep within enslaves even the people we consider "good"?

True, in one sense, the book of Job shows that bad things happen to good people, because terrible things happened to Job, who is called "blameless" (Job 1:1).

However, *blameless* is a relative term, since even though he was more righteous than any other man, Job was still a sinner, as he himself recognizes.

Highly educated people who disbelieve in human evil often believe that human government is the root of, and solution to, the world's problems. Alexander Solzhenitsyn, at Harvard's 1978 commencement, spoke of the downward moral direction of American freedom:

> This tilt of freedom toward evil has come about gradually, but it evidently
> stems from a humanistic and benevolent concept according to which
> man—the master of this world—does not bear any evil within himself,
> and all the defects of life are caused by misguided social systems, which
> must therefore be corrected.[8]

Bad things do not happen to good people. Why not? Because in this world truly good people do not exist. Although God created us in his image and we have great worth to him, the fact remains that we are fallen and corrupt, are under the Curse, and deserve Hell.

The arguments against bad things happening to good people often testify to humanity's evil far more than to its goodness.

On the one hand, skeptics argue that bad things shouldn't happen to good people and that the human race consists mainly of good people. On the other hand, their very objections concern the bad things people do to one another: murder, war, rape, child abuse, brutality, kidnapping, bullying, ridiculing, shaming, corporate greed, unwillingness to share wealth or to care for the environment.

I listened to an atheist argue at length against God's existence. Though in passing he mentioned natural disasters, he spent the bulk of his time listing atrocities perpetrated by human beings. He amassed a terrible, cumulative indictment on humanity; a Puritan speaking on human depravity could not have chosen better material. Indeed, were a seminar titled "The Case for Some People Going to Hell," the atheist's illustrations would have fit perfectly.

Yet he went on to state that he believes in human goodness and that he feels offended that good people suffer. He said nothing to recognize the paradoxical nature of his arguments. It almost seemed he believed in two kinds of humans, the hellish ones and the heavenly ones. But this neat distinction finds no evidence to support it. *Human beings* committed all the atrocities he listed. The longer the list of evil things done, the more it demonstrates the truth of what the Bible says: by nature, human beings are evil, not good.

This undercuts the original argument—that humans are good, and therefore it's utterly unjust for bad things to happen to them. Since the same human race that commits these evils also suffers from them—since we are not only victims, but perpetrators, of sin—what would God's critics have him do? Would they insist he strike us all down immediately for our evil? Or would they have him remove human choice in order to protect us from one another?

They might as well say that since we are so good, God shouldn't allow us to be so bad.

Notes

1. Jonathan Aitken, *John Newton: From Disgrace to Amazing Grace* (Wheaton, IL: Crossway Books, 2007), 347.
2. J. I. Packer, quoted in C. J. Mahaney and Robin Boisvert, *How Can I Change?* (Gaithersburg, MD: Sovereign Grace Ministries, 1996), 41.
3. C. S. Lewis, *The Problem of Pain* (New York, Macmillan, 1962), 67.
4. Wayne Grudem, *Systematic Theology* (Grand Rapids, MI: Zondervan, 1994), 497.
5. Grudem, *Systematic Theology*, 494.
6. J. I. Packer, *Faithfulness and Holiness: The Witness of J. C. Ryle* (Wheaton, IL: Good News, 2002), 105.
7. Robert H. Schuller, *Self-Esteem: The New Reformation* (Waco, TX: Word, 1982), 65.
8. Alexander Solzhenitsyn, Harvard commencement address, June 8, 1978, in *The World's Great Speeches,* ed. Lewis Copeland, Lawrence W. Lamm, and Stephen J. McKenna (Mineola, NY: Dover, 1999), 837.

9

A Deeper Consideration of
What Our Sin Nature Does
and Doesn't Mean

We demonstrate our evil not just by what we do, but by what we fail to do and what we stand by and allow others to do.

Fathers abuse their children while mothers look the other way. Nazis rounded up Jews in Germany while most citizens did nothing. Slaves picked cotton while those who wore cotton garments created the demand for slave labor. Men refuse to help raise the children they've fathered, women get abortions, and others look the other way or refuse to help needy women find alternatives.

> Anyone, then, who knows the good he ought to do and doesn't do it, sins.
> (James 4:17)

God commands us to rescue the oppressed, then anticipates our excuses and tells us he knows better:

> Rescue those being led away to death;
> hold back those staggering toward slaughter.
> If you say, "But we knew nothing about this,"
> does not he who weighs the heart perceive it?
> Does not he who guards your life know it?
> Will he not repay each person according to what he has done?
> (Proverbs 24:11–12)

God makes clear it isn't enough to refrain from oppressing or robbing people. The failure to do right is as evil as doing wrong (see Jeremiah 22:2–3). Consider the ship *St. Louis,* dramatized in the 1976 motion picture *Voyage of the Damned.* The *St. Louis,* with its Jewish passengers from Germany seeking asylum, was turned away in Cuba. Then, President Franklin Roosevelt refused permission for it to land in the United States. The ship tried next to enter Canada but was denied again. It returned to Europe, where the United Kingdom, France, Belgium, and the Netherlands accepted some of the passengers. Many later died when Germany invaded three of those countries.

The U.S. and Canada were aware that the Jews on the *St. Louis* already had endured *Kristallnacht,* Germany's state-sponsored pogrom that resulted in hundreds of Jewish shops destroyed, synagogues burned, and thousands put in concentration camps. Yet both nations turned away these Jewish refugees whose ship had already reached their shores. True, U.S. and Canadian immigration regulations restricted the numbers of immigrants of various nationalities, and other German citizens were waiting their turn. But given the violent and escalating aggression against Jews in Germany, couldn't an exception have been made?

We speak of Germany's evil but both the United States and Canada didn't care enough about these defenseless people to open their borders to them, and as a result many of them died. Had Germany not threatened Europe and our own country, but simply executed millions of Jews within its borders, would we ever have come to their defense?

We like to think we're made of better stuff, but we are all part of the same fallen race.

Apart from Christ, we are different from every notorious murderer and ruthless dictator only in degree, not in kind.

Zygmunt Bauman, a Polish sociologist married to an Auschwitz survivor, argues that the Holocaust was not an aberration. The same things that fueled the Holocaust are at work in us today. He says it must not be attributed simply to extraordinary people such as Hitler. It was carried out not by a handful of monsters, but by millions of ordinary people.

Just fifteen miles from our home, Westley Allan Dodd tortured, molested, and murdered three boys. Dodd was scheduled to become the first U.S. criminal hanged in three decades, shortly after midnight on January 4, 1993. At dinner that evening, both our daughters, then eleven and thirteen, prayed earnestly that

Dodd would repent and place his faith in Christ before he died. I agreed with their prayer…but only because I knew I should.

Reporters from all over the country crowded around the prison. Thirty minutes after Dodd died, the twelve media eyewitnesses recounted the experience. I felt stunned as one of them read Dodd's last words: "I had thought there was no hope and no peace. I was wrong. I have found hope and peace in the Lord Jesus Christ."

Gasps and groans erupted from the gallery, fueled by palpable anger. How *dare* someone who had committed such heinous crimes claim that he had found hope and peace in Jesus! Did he really think God would let him into Heaven after what he'd done? Shut up and go to Hell, child killer! You won't get off so easy! The idea of God offering grace to Dodd utterly offended the crowd that had come to see justice done.

That's when it hit me in a deep and personal way—*I* am part of the same human race. I'd imagined the distance between Dodd and me as the difference between the South and North poles. But from God's viewpoint, the distance is negligible. Apart from Christ, I am Dodd. I am Osama bin Laden. I am Hitler. Only by the virtue of Christ can I stand forgiven before a holy God.

This isn't hyperbole; it's biblical truth. Unless we come to grips with the fact that we're of precisely the same stock as Dodd and Stalin and Mao, we'll never get over thinking that we deserve better. Evil done to us will offend us, and having to suffer will outrage us. We'll never appreciate Christ's grace so long as we hold on to the proud illusion that we're better than we are. We flatter ourselves when we look at evil acts and say, "I would *never* do that." Given our evil natures and a similar background, resources, and opportunities, we would.

God says, "My people are fools; *they do not know me*. They are senseless children; they have no understanding. They are skilled in doing evil; they know not how to do good" (Jeremiah 4:22). Look at world history. Look at your own personal history. We skillfully conceive evil and proficiently execute it. The fact that we don't call it "evil" is just further evidence of our evil. The seventeenth-century writer La Rochefoucauld said, "There is hardly a man clever enough to recognize the full extent of the evil he does." The evil within us can stand toe to toe with the evils of human history, for we are all made of the same stuff.

I doubt that those who wanted Dodd to "get what's coming to him" were ready to take what *they* had coming: Hell.

The modern denial of our evil keeps us from the gospel.

G. K. Chesterton claimed that original sin, the most unpopular of all Christian

dogmas, "is the only part of Christian theology which can really be proved....
[Some people] essentially deny human sin, which they can see in the street."[1]

Since humanity's exit from Eden, we've been skilled sinners. Today, however,
many people assume the moral high ground as they defend their immoral choices.
They offer compelling reasons for cheating on their taxes or their spouses, stealing from their workplaces, lying on their résumés, and beating people up physically or verbally. The result of this habitual rationalization? A major obstacle to the
gospel. C. S. Lewis noted,

> When the apostles preached, they could assume even in their Pagan hearers
> a real consciousness of deserving the Divine anger.... It was against this
> background that the Gospel appeared as good news. It brought news of
> possible healing to men who knew that they were mortally ill. But all this
> has changed. Christianity now has to preach the diagnosis—in itself very
> bad news—before it can win a hearing for the cure....
>
> A recovery of the old sense of sin is essential to Christianity. Christ
> takes it for granted that men are bad.... We lack the first condition for
> understanding what He is talking about.[2]

The man swallowing ocean water and going under doesn't need to hear he's
drowning; he needs a life preserver. But countless people today, arms flailing as
they attempt to keep their heads above water, don't believe they are drowning—
and so don't think they need rescue.

Despite our righteous standing in Christ, believers remain prone to sin.

Christians have received the resources in Christ to please him, to turn from sin,
and to live holy and righteous lives (see Titus 2:11–12). God has given to us in
Christ and his indwelling Spirit the ability not to sin. Some, however, take our
righteous standing in Christ to mean we're no longer able to sin. Scripture clearly
contradicts this. "We all stumble in many ways," James lamented (3:2). To stumble is to sin. Since James held a key post of leadership in the early church—and
he affirmed that he sinned—it's hard to imagine a more emphatic rebuttal to the
notion of sinless perfection (see also 1 John 1:8–10).

The apostle Paul said, "Christ Jesus came into the world to save sinners—of
whom I am the worst" (1 Timothy 1:15). Paul said "I am," not "I was." Yes, Paul
had put on Christ's righteousness and lived a Spirit-led life. God had sanctified
him. Those who knew him might view him as the best of men. But Paul knew
himself, his heart, and his tendencies toward evil.

When Paul calls himself the worst of sinners, I don't think he's saying, "There's no one on the planet worse than I am," but rather, "I am more conscious of the depth of my own sin than anyone else's." This is as it should be. Only one who is deeply aware of his evil tendencies will humbly take the necessary steps to guard his heart from sin.

Jesus said, "The truth will set you free" (John 8:32). I've found tremendous freedom in knowing that I am a great sinner. It helps deliver me from pretending I'm better than I am. It makes me more honest before God and others, and hopefully more truly humble (as opposed to merely *appearing* to be humble as a prideful strategy).

A Christ follower is free of sin's lordship, since he has died to sin (see Romans 6:6–9). Sinclair Ferguson writes,

> But this freedom from the dominion of sin is not the end of our struggle against sin. In fact it is the beginning of a new conflict with it. For while we have died to sin, sin has not died in us....
>
> It remains, and it is still sin. What has changed is not its presence within our hearts, but its status (it no longer reigns) and our relationship to it (we are no longer its slaves).[3]

The Christian can persevere in his lifelong struggle against sin with confidence in his core identity as God's child, with the indwelling presence of the Holy Spirit to empower him to obey Christ, rather than sin. But he puts his confidence only in God's grace, for his indwelling sin is still active and deceptive (see Galatians 5:1, 13–24).

The greater our grasp of our sin and alienation from God, the greater our grasp of God's grace.

A woman sang one of my favorite songs, "Amazing Grace," just before I spoke at a gathering. It sounded beautiful, until she got to the tenth word: "Amazing grace! How sweet the sound that saved a *soul* like me!"

My heart sank. The word *wretch* had vanished, replaced by the more positive word *soul.* Can you imagine what John Newton, the composer and former slave trader, might have said? Newton recognized himself as a wretch—and that's what made God's grace so "amazing." The worse we are, the more amazing God's grace.

The Bible says, "Very rarely will anyone die for a righteous man, though for a good man someone might possibly dare to die. But God demonstrates his own love for us in this: While we were still sinners, Christ died for us" (Romans 5:7–8).

If we don't give the word *sinners* its actual meaning, we miss the point. When we cut *wretch* out of "Amazing Grace," we reduce it to something more sensible, less surprising. If we weren't so bad without Christ, then why did he have to endure the cross? Paul said if men were good enough without Jesus, then "Christ died for nothing" (Galatians 2:21).

Charles Spurgeon put it this way: "Too many think lightly of sin, and therefore think lightly of the Saviour."[4] We try to explain away sin in terms of a "bad day" or "that's not what I meant" or "I did what my father always did to me" or "I wouldn't have done this if you hadn't done that." All these statements minimize our evil and thereby *minimize the greatness of God's grace in atoning for our evil.*

Grace isn't about God lowering his standards. It's about God fulfilling those standards through the substitutionary suffering of Jesus Christ. Grace never ignores or violates truth. Grace gave what truth demanded: the ultimate sacrifice for our wickedness.

God's grace is greater than my sin. But my ability to measure the greatness of his grace depends upon my willingness, in brokenness before him, to recognize the greatness of my sin. "God opposes the proud but gives grace to the humble" (1 Peter 5:5). The proud deny their evil; the humble confess it.

A profound awareness of my evil should move my heart to praise God for the wonders of his grace.

Having sin natures doesn't mean we are as evil as we could possibly be or that all people do equal amounts of evil.

"There is not a righteous man on earth who does what is right and never sins" (Ecclesiastes 7:20). This passage affirms that a man can't *always* do right, not that he can *never* do right.

Jesus said that some will bear Judgment Day better than others (see Matthew 11:20–24). Why? Because some have sinned less than others. He said some will be punished more severely than others (see Luke 12:47–48). Do some unsaved humans commit less evil than Hitler, Stalin, Mao, or Pol Pot? Yes. Paul wrote, "Evil men and impostors will go from bad to worse" (2 Timothy 3:13). If evil men can go from bad to worse, then obviously they can be bad without being as bad as possible.

Jesus made clear in the Sermon on the Mount that we can do the right thing with the wrong motives and thereby be evildoers. But clearly an unbeliever can do some things from better or worse motives.

Despite our bondage to sin and our inability to earn God's favor, human beings can make some good choices.

The credit for anyone's good attitude or action ultimately goes to the good God who creates people "made in God's likeness" (James 3:9). We might call the goodness in human beings a residual goodness, a marred form of the goodness of the pre-fallen state. If we retain a likeness to a good God, even as sinners, might that imply the capacity for *some* goodness?

In the case of believers, he graciously empowers us by his Holy Spirit to act in accordance with the righteous nature granted us in Christ (see 1 Corinthians 15:10). This accounts for some of the startling acts of goodness done by Christians throughout the ages, sacrificing their lives not only in martyrdom, but decade after decade cheerfully helping desperately needy people.

But does the Holy Spirit's supernatural empowerment to do good in believers mean that only Christians can do good? I don't think so.

Jesus asked, "Or which one of you, if his son asks him for bread, will give him a stone? Or if he asks for a fish, will give him a serpent? If you then, who are evil, know how to give good gifts to your children, how much more will your Father who is in heaven give good gifts to those who ask him!" (Matthew 7:9–11, ESV). Here Jesus affirms that we are evil *and* that we know how to give good gifts to our children.

People rescue others at great risk. A pedestrian jumps in front of a car to save a child, forfeiting his own life. A soldier falls on a grenade to save his comrades.

On the one hand, I agree with J. I. Packer, who approvingly describes the Puritans as teaching that "our best works are shot through with sin, and contain something that needs to be forgiven."[5]

If that's true of those indwelt by God's Spirit, obviously it's true of unbelievers. Yes, sinners are routinely tarnished by evil motives, stemming from pride and self-congratulation and a desire to please others rather than God. However, it seems doubtful that the man who throws himself on the grenade does it only because he hopes he'll be lauded as a hero. He can die a sinner, yet when he chooses to sacrifice his life to save others, I think God approves his action.

Of course, an unbeliever's good deeds don't win him a place in Heaven. Nonetheless, Paul says unbelievers "who do not have the law, do by nature things required by the law,... since they show that the requirements of the law are written on their hearts, their consciences also bearing witness, and their thoughts now accusing, now even defending them" (Romans 2:14–15). This seems to confirm that sinners can heed a God-given conscience and sometimes do good.

The biblical teaching of common grace helps us understand how God infuses goodness into a fallen world.

Common grace is God's means by which he gives people innumerable blessings that are not a part of salvation. Not every person experiences saving grace, but all people—without exception, even unrepentant sinners—daily experience common grace. Even fallen humanity enjoys a residual goodness in a world that God still oversees and holds together (see Colossians 1:17).

Jesus said God causes his sun to rise on the evil and the good—which must mean some people are good in some sense (see Matthew 5:45). He declared, "Let your light shine before men, that they may see your good deeds and praise your Father in heaven" (verse 16). People *can* do good deeds. The master calls his servant "good and faithful" (Matthew 25:21). Joseph of Arimathea was a "good and upright man" (Luke 23:50).

If humanity lacked all goodness, the human race could not survive.

Drivers would disobey every traffic signal, all police would become utterly corrupt, every pedestrian would be robbed, every house plundered. Murder, rape, and other cruel acts would reign. No driver would nod to let a man cross the street, except to run him down. The poor and disabled would face extinction. Just laws would not exist. All parents would abandon their children to the streets.

In such a world, no "problem of evil" would exist. It would not occur to us to question God's goodness in allowing evil and suffering, unless we had some capacity to understand what goodness really is.

We should be profoundly grateful for God's restraint of evil, his delay of judgment, and his gift of goodness in this fallen world.

TAKING RESPONSIBILITY FOR EVIL AND SUFFERING

Modern culture's habit of denying responsibility and casting blame intensifies evil and suffering.

Ever since Adam blamed Eve for persuading him to eat the forbidden fruit, and Eve blamed the serpent for getting her to eat it, impugning others has become the normal human practice (see Genesis 3:12–13). Accusing another allows us to justify our own sin.

Our culture of blame, exemplified by frivolous lawsuits, goes hand in hand with a sense of entitlement. We think we deserve the best and are offended when we don't get it. We feel outraged at wrongs done to us—whether real or imagined. Most fans of opposing teams watching the same sporting event believe the referees repeatedly made unjust calls against *their* team.

When Hitler was on the verge of losing World War II, his mistress finally wrestled with the problem of evil. Hearing the bombing of Berlin, Eva Braun wrote to a friend from Hitler's besieged bunker, "It's enough to make one lose faith in God."[6]

Eva Braun's lack of perspective may astonish us, but we can suffer from the same twisted mentality. What if we have just as poor a grasp as she did of our true identity and situation, our assumptions of innocence and nobility, and our consequent indictment of God for not treating us fairly?

Blaming ourselves for what happens to us is a lost art we need to recover. G. K. Chesterton wrote perhaps the shortest essay in history. The London *Times* asked various writers for essays on the topic "What's Wrong with the World?" Chesterton replied,

> Dear Sirs:
> I am.
> Sincerely yours,
> G. K. Chesterton

Daniel, a righteous man, came before God confessing the sins of his nation, not saying, "They have sinned," but, "We have sinned" (Daniel 9:5). He took ownership for his own contribution to the problem of national sin. So should we all.

Instead of bemoaning our own predicaments, how often do we look at the world, with all its evil and suffering, and say to God, "Forgive me for my part in the world's sin"?

It's easy to blame God for not doing all he can to stop evil and suffering. But consider that he has graciously allowed the world to continue while postponing final judgment. Consider that he has put us in this world with a mission that includes resisting evil and relieving suffering. Consider that he has entrusted us with vast resources to carry out that mission.

We just might want to ask if we, and not God, are to blame.

Notes

1. G. K. Chesterton, *Orthodoxy* (Vancouver, BC: Regent College Publishing, 2004), 18.
2. C. S. Lewis, *The Problem of Pain* (New York: Macmillan, 1962), 55, 57.

3. Sinclair Ferguson, *Know Your Christian Life* (Downers Grove, IL: InterVarsity, 1981), 125, 138.

4. Charles Haddon Spurgeon, *The Autobiography of Charles H. Spurgeon* (Grand Rapids, MI: Revell, 1899), 76.

5. J.I. Packer, *A Quest for Godliness* (Wheaton, IL: Good News, 1994), 118.

6. Nerin E. Gun, *Eva Braun: Hitler's Mistress* (New York: Meredith, 1968), 252.

10

Natural Disasters: Creation Under the Curse of Human Evil

The December 2004 Asian tsunami killed more than a quarter million people in eleven countries. Huge waves tossed human beings like rag dolls, making Hurricane Katrina's devastation seem small by comparison.

Following the tsunami, a commentator in Scotland's *Herald* (Glasgow) wrote,

> God, if there is a God, should be ashamed of himself. The sheer enormity
> of the Asian tsunami disaster, the death, destruction, and havoc it wreaked,
> the scale of misery it has caused, must surely test the faith of even the
> firmest believer.... I hope I am right that there is no God. For if there
> were, then he'd have to shoulder the blame. In my book, he would be as
> guilty as sin and I'd want nothing to do with him.[1]

In the *Progressive* article titled "God Owes Us an Apology," Barbara Ehrenreich wrote,

> The Christian-style "God of love" should be particularly vulnerable to
> post-tsunami doubts. What kind of "love" inspired Him to wrest babies
> from their parents' arms, the better to drown them in a hurry? If He so
> loves us that He gave his only son, etc., why couldn't he have held those
> tectonic plates in place at least until the kids were off the beach?...
>
> If we are responsible for our actions, as most religions insist, then God
> should be, too, and I would propose, post-tsunami, an immediate with-
> drawal of prayer and other forms of flattery directed at a supposedly moral
> deity—at least until an apology is issued....
>
> If God cares about our puny species, then disasters prove that he is not
> all-powerful; and if he is all-powerful, then clearly he doesn't give a damn.[2]

God's and Humanity's Roles in Natural Disasters

The moral evil of Earth's stewards caused God to curse Earth with natural disasters.

Many people blame God for natural disasters. "How could he allow this?" they ask. But what if the Architect and Builder crafted a beautiful and perfect home for Earth's inhabitants, who despite his warnings carelessly cracked its foundation, punched holes in the walls, and trashed the house? Why blame the builder when the occupants took a sledgehammer to their own home?

Fatalities caused by natural disasters multiply because of morally evil human actions. People frequently cause forest fires and other large-scale disasters. They build houses in areas long proven vulnerable to floods, landslides, fires, tornadoes, and earthquakes. Some perish when they refuse warnings to vacate their homes.

Humans misuse land, resulting in disastrous mud slides. Polluted rivers cause deaths and physical deformities. More people may suffer losses from looting following a hurricane than in the hurricane itself. National leaders may hoard aid sent to help their dying people. People may fail to generously share their God-given resources to rescue the needy.

Natural disasters become most disastrous when they take human life—but they never did so until after humans committed moral evil against God.

God placed a curse on the earth due to Adam's sin (see Genesis 3:17). That curse extends to everything in the natural world and makes it harder for people to live productively. Paul says that "the creation was subjected to frustration" by God's curse, until that day when "the creation itself will be liberated from its bondage to decay" (Romans 8:20–21). The next verse says, "The whole creation has been groaning as in the pains of childbirth." Earthquakes, volcanoes, and tsunamis reflect the frustration, bondage, and decay of an earth groaning under sin's curse.

Natural disasters are not inherently evil, but they can produce secondary evils by thwarting the good of human, animal, and environmental welfare.

Earthquakes and tsunamis are not moral agents and therefore cannot be morally evil. A tidal wave is not malicious—water cannot have malice any more than it can have kindness.

The best answer to the question "Why would God create a world with natural disasters?" is that *he didn't*. Many experts believe the world's atmosphere originally acted like an umbrella, protecting its inhabitants from harm. But now the umbrella has holes in it, sometimes protecting us, sometimes not. While Barbara Ehrenreich blames God for death and disaster, Scripture blames human evil for the cataclysmic Fall and consequent distortion of a once-perfect world (see Romans 8:18–22).

People who have survived disasters often say they understand on a far deeper level the biblical truth that this world *as it now is*—under the Curse—is not our home.

God is sovereign over all nature.

Good weather and bad both come at God's discretion. The meteorologist may explain wind speeds by differences in air pressure, but Scripture says of God, "He makes his wind blow" (Psalm 147:18, ESV). Blowing winds would seem to include hurricanes and tornadoes.

God "brings the clouds to punish men, or to water his earth and show his love" (Job 37:13). Israel's grumbling angered God: "Then fire from the LORD burned among them and consumed some of the outskirts of the camp" (Numbers 11:1; see also Job 37:3, 6; Psalm 29:5, 7; 147:16–18; Jeremiah 14:22).

Jesus said of God, "He causes his sun to rise on the evil and the good, and sends rain on the righteous and the unrighteous" (Matthew 5:45). Note that he did *not* say, "God created natural laws and lets the course of nature go its own way." Those who argue that God has given the operation of the world over to Satan contradict these passages.

The Bible never speaks of nature as an impersonal mechanism. Nature does not govern the universe; God does.

This doesn't mean that Satan, called "ruler of this world" (John 12:31, ESV) and "prince of the power of the air" (Ephesians 2:2, ESV), doesn't have power over weather. Even when Christ calmed the Sea of Galilee, it may speak of his primary power over the secondary powers of pagan demon gods.

The synonym for natural disasters is *an act of God.* Interestingly, beautiful weather isn't widely referred to as "an act of God."

Sometimes God uses natural disasters to punish evil.

God brought the Great Flood upon humanity as a judgment for sin (see Genesis 6–8). He opened the earth to swallow Korah, Dathan, and Abiram, because they had treated him "with contempt" (Numbers 16:30).

God exercised judgment by orchestrating plagues (see Exodus 7–12; Numbers 11:33; 1 Samuel 5:6–9), sending hordes of locusts (Joel 2:25), and releasing swarms of snakes (Numbers 21:4–6).

When the "LORD rained down burning sulfur on Sodom and Gomorrah" (Genesis 19:24), he told Abraham and Lot that he had destroyed the cities because of their sin (see Genesis 18:20, 21; 19:12–13).

Jonah's disobedience prompted God to send a storm to rock the ship that carried Jonah (see Jonah 1:12).

God said, "I gave you empty stomachs in every city and lack of bread in every town.... I also withheld rain from you when the harvest was still three months away.... Many times I struck your gardens and vineyards, I struck them with blight and mildew" (Amos 4:6–7, 9).

Likewise, after saying he would bless them with rain to help grow crops, he warns his people that if they disobey, he would bring down curses, including drought (see Deuteronomy 28:15–68).

Natural disasters ordinarily are general results of the Curse, not specifically linked to the sins of individuals who perish or suffer in them.

Some Christian leaders have embarrassed themselves by pointing to various natural disasters as "God's judgment on sin." How would *they* know? And if it were true for some of those who died, what about the righteous who died alongside them?

Unless God clearly reveals it, we should never assume that a natural disaster or moral atrocity comes upon this earth as his specific judgment on specific people. Jesus made this clear by saying that some people murdered by Pilate and those crushed by a falling tower were no worse sinners than others (see Luke 13:2–5).

Scripture does not distance God from disasters and secondary evils the way his children often do.

God makes an unapologetic statement about himself: "I form the light and create darkness, I bring prosperity and create disaster; I, the LORD, do all these things" (Isaiah 45:7).

As we saw in Jeremiah 11:17 and 32:23, so in Isaiah 45 God brings *ra*, disastrous consequences, to deal with people's *ra*, moral evil. God righteously brings terrible judgment upon human evil.

Amos 3:6 says, "When disaster *[ra]* comes to a city, has not the LORD caused it?" A description of natural disasters follows in Amos 4:6–12, where God says he brought hunger, drought, blight, mildew, locusts, pestilence, and the death of men and horses, "yet you have not returned to me" (verse 11). God intended these disasters not only as punishment, but as discipline designed to draw his people back to himself.

Even when Satan is behind natural disasters and diseases, God hasn't relinquished his world-governing power.

Some authors emphasize that Satan, not God, brings natural disasters, inflicts diseases, orchestrates tragedies, and takes lives. And some passages appear to support that view, including those in the gospels that ascribe demon affliction to certain diseased people.

The book of Job draws back the curtain into the invisible realm, revealing how God and Satan relate in a case of great human adversity that included two natural disasters:

> Then the LORD said to Satan, "Have you considered my servant Job? There is no one on earth like him; he is blameless and upright, a man who fears God and shuns evil."
>
> "Does Job fear God for nothing?" Satan replied. "Have you not put a hedge around him and his household and everything he has? You have blessed the work of his hands, so that his flocks and herds are spread throughout the land. But stretch out your hand and strike everything he has, and he will surely curse you to your face."
>
> The LORD said to Satan, "Very well, then, everything he has is in your hands, but on the man himself do not lay a finger."
>
> Then Satan went out from the presence of the LORD. (Job 1:8–12)

Satan incited the Sabaeans to murder Job's servants and steal his oxen and donkeys. Then one of Job's servants said, "The fire of God fell from the sky and burned up the sheep and the servants" (verse 16). Next, Chaldean raiding parties stole camels and murdered more servants (see verse 17). Finally, while Job's sons and daughters feasted in "the oldest brother's house… suddenly a mighty wind swept in from the desert and struck the four corners of the house. It collapsed on them and they are dead" (verses 18–19).

Were the Sabaeans and Chaldeans responsible for committing the murders and theft? Yes. Was Satan responsible for inciting them? Yes. He brought about two "natural" disasters of severe lightning and gale-force winds.

So, Satan may bring about a natural disaster, but the book of Job makes clear that God continues to reign, even while selectively allowing Satan to do evil things. Satan knew he didn't have the authority to incite humans to do evil, to bring down lightning to cause fires, or to send the wind to blow down a building and take lives *without God's explicit permission.* We should know this too.

Some disasters fall on the blameless.

Since God identified Job as the most righteous of men (see Job 1:1, 8; 2:3), *the book of Job forever refutes the notion that every tragedy that befalls people is a judgment on their sin.* While no one is sinless, and bad things do not happen to morally perfect people (because there are no morally perfect people), they can and sometimes do happen to the best people.

God is free in our lives, as he was in Job's, to permit personal or natural disasters for his own sovereign purposes without ever being an evildoer.

TRANSFORMATION IN TRAGEDY'S AFTERMATH

Disasters can initiate self-examination.

All of us live only by God's mercy. Jesus often reminded his listeners of their mortality. He treated disasters as object lessons to warn people of the far greater eternal disaster of Hell: "Unless you repent, you too will all perish" (Luke 13:5).

Jesus encouraged people to examine their hearts, repent, and turn to God. Why? So they might be ready to face death when it comes and live forever with God in Heaven rather than perish in Hell.

Disasters can bring out the best in people.

Many people remarked that they'd never seen such kindness and sacrificial love as was manifested by tens of thousands of people, many of them Christians, coming in to help the citizens of New Orleans and other areas devastated by Hurricane Katrina.

In 1988, an Armenian earthquake killed forty-five thousand. In the chaos, one man made his way to his son's school, only to find nothing but rubble. Other parents stumbled around dazed and weeping, calling out their children's names. But this father ran to the back corner of the building where his son's classroom once was, and began digging.

To everyone else, it seemed hopeless. How could his son have survived? But this father had promised he would always be there for his boy, so he heaved rocks and dug, calling for his son by name: "Armand!"

Well-meaning parents and bystanders tried to pull him out of the rubble. "It's too late!" "They're dead!" "There's nothing you can do!" The fire chief tried to pull him away saying, "Fires and explosions are happening everywhere. You're in danger. Go home!" Finally, the police came and said, "You're in shock. You're endangering others. Go home. We'll handle it!"

But the man continued to dig, hour after hour—eight hours, then twelve, twenty-four, thirty-six hours. Finally, in the thirty-eighth hour of digging—a day and a half after everyone told him to give up hope—he called his son's name again, pulled back a big rock, and heard his son's voice.

"Armand!" the father screamed.

From under the rocks came the words, "Dad? I told them! I told the other kids that if you were still alive, you'd save me!"

The father helped his son and thirteen other children climb out of the rubble. When the building had collapsed, the children survived in a tentlike pocket. The father lovingly carried his son home to his mother. When the townspeople praised Armand's father for saving the children, he simply explained, "I promised my son, 'No matter what, I'll be there for you!' "[3]

Disasters can lead to spiritual transformation.

I've spoken at many memorial services and am always struck by how hearts are much more responsive to the gospel. Death has the floor. People often listen to God in a way they wouldn't have before tragedy struck. Through suffering and neediness in the aftermath of disasters, many people become receptive to the gospel.

The rate of conversions in Romania significantly increased after the 1977 earthquake. A similar evangelistic outbreak occurred after the 1988 Armenian earthquake. The following year, the massacre of Chinese students in Tiananmen Square became the catalyst for many other Chinese students' conversions.

Time after time throughout history, God has used both man-made and natural disasters to draw people to himself. Philosophy professor Eleonore Stump wrote,

> Natural evil—the pain of disease, the intermittent and unpredictable destruction of natural disasters, the decay of old age, the imminence of death—takes away a person's satisfaction with himself. It tends to humble him, show him his frailty, make him reflect on the transience of temporal goods, and turn his affections towards other-worldly things, away from the things of this world. No amount of moral or natural evil, of course, can *guarantee* that a man will [turn to God].... But evil of this sort is the best hope, I think, and maybe the only effective means, for bringing men to such a state.[4]

When we face a natural disaster, disease, or even a financial hardship, we should ask God, "What are you trying to tell us?"

A world without personal tragedy or natural disasters would produce no heroes.

Life brings more personal disasters than national or global ones—and God can bring good out of any of them. This became clear in the courageous responses not only to Hurricane Katrina but the Asian tsunami. It also becomes apparent in many smaller calamities.

Wesley Autrey, a fifty-year-old construction worker, waited in a Manhattan subway with his two daughters, ages four and six. A twenty-year-old man collapsed nearby. Somehow the convulsing man got up and stumbled to the platform edge, falling to the tracks between the two rails. When Autrey saw a train's headlights coming, he jumped down and placed his body on the fallen man, pressing him down in a space a foot deep. The train cars rolled over them, passing inches from Autrey's head, smudging his cap with grease. Autrey heard onlookers' screams.

When the train came to a stop over him, he yelled, "We're okay down here, but I've got two daughters up there. Let them know their father's okay." When it was all over, he and the other man emerged to the cries and applause of onlookers.[5]

This story probably inspires you. But what if we lived in a world where the man couldn't fall on a train track, or where Autrey wouldn't be risking his life by helping him? If God didn't permit such events, danger and risk wouldn't exist, and therefore neither would heroism.

One day, in Christ's presence, we will be relieved of evil and suffering, yet we'll remember—and our characters will forever benefit from—what we learned in this world. If we did not see life-risking acts of heroism, we would be impoverished. Yet, in order to see such acts, or to be able to make such choices ourselves, we must, for now, live in a world with evil and suffering.

I believe that on the New Earth we will sit around dinner tables and campfires, hearing and telling stories of heroism that happened in that old world, the one that sometimes seemed so confusing to us. And we'll get to meet many of those men, women, and children whom God used to give us little glimmers of his saving grace.

Notes

1. Allan Laing, "Wave That Beggared My Belief," *Herald* (Glasgow, Scotland), January 4, 2005.
2. Barbara Ehrenreich, "God Owes Us an Apology," *Progressive,* March 2005, www.commondreams.org/views05/0216-25.htm.

3. Scott Hahn, *A Father Who Keeps His Promises* (Cincinnati: St. Anthony Messenger Press, 1998), 13-14.

4. Eleonore Stump and Michael J. Murray, *Philosophy of Religion* (Hoboken, NJ: Wiley-Blackwell, 1999), 233.

5. Cara Buckley, "Man Is Rescued by Stranger on Subway Tracks," *New York Times,* January 3, 2007, www.nytimes.com/2007/01/03/nyregion/03life.html.

Problems for Non-Theists: Moral Standards, Goodness, and Extreme Evil

Non-Christians often raise concerns about evil and suffering as if they present a problem exclusively for the Christian worldview. But *every* worldview must attempt to account for them.

Anyone morally outraged about evil and suffering necessarily makes a moral judgment assuming a foundation of objective goodness by which to judge evil as evil. Doing so presents significant problems for world-views that don't recognize God.

11

A Case Study: Bart Ehrman, a "Christian" Who Lost His Faith

WHY THIS CHAPTER?

I'm dedicating an entire chapter to Bart Ehrman and his best-selling book *God's Problem*, because, as a self-described "former evangelical Christian," Ehrman personifies the potential consequences evangelical churches face when they fail to address the problem of evil and suffering. By looking at Ehrman and his book, we can further explore the issue—but with a personal dimension, because we'll see its impact on the life of a real person.

While I will criticize Ehrman, I should clarify that sometimes I find him likable. He can be overconfident, yet occasionally admits his uncertainties. He avoids the bombastic approach that some atheist—and some Christian—authors display.

Unfortunately, Ehrman's Christian-to-non-theist testimony gives apparent credibility to his claims, so he functions as a winsome evangelist for atheism. While he says he doesn't intend to cause believers to lose their faith, it's easy to wonder why else he would write such a book.

One final point before we begin: That Bart Ehrman was a "devout and committed Christian" is his claim, not mine. What isn't debatable is that he once was part of the evangelical subculture.

God's Problem **documents how a "former Christian" denied his faith because he couldn't reconcile evil and suffering with God's goodness.** Ehrman offers a gripping self-introduction to his book:

> The problem of suffering has haunted me for a very long time. It was what made me begin to think about religion when I was young, and it was what

led me to question my faith when I was older. Ultimately, it was the reason I lost my faith.

For most of my life I was a devout and committed Christian.... Early in my high school days I started attending a Youth for Christ club and had a "born-again" experience.... When I became born again it was like ratcheting my religion up a notch. I became very serious about my faith and chose to go off to a fundamentalist Bible college—Moody Bible Institute in Chicago—where I began training for ministry.

I could quote entire books of the New Testament, verse by verse, from memory.... I went off to finish my college work at Wheaton. There I learned Greek.... At Princeton I did both a master of divinity degree—training to be a minister—and, eventually, a Ph.D. in New Testament studies.

I had solid Christian credentials and knew about the Christian faith from the inside out—in the years before I lost my faith.... I served as the youth pastor of an Evangelical Covenant church.... But then...I started to lose my faith. I now have lost it altogether. I no longer go to church, no longer believe, no longer consider myself a Christian. The subject of this book is the reason why.[1]

MAN'S PROBLEM WITH GOD'S PLAN

Ehrman lost faith in Scripture before losing faith in God.

Ehrman refers to his earlier book, *Misquoting Jesus,* to say his belief in the Bible's truthfulness diminished the more he studied it. He decided it was not God's inerrant revelation but "a very human book with all the marks of having come from human hands: Discrepancies, contradictions, errors, and different perspectives." Nonetheless, he writes,

I continued to be a Christian—a completely committed Christian—for many years after I left the evangelical fold. Eventually, though, I felt compelled to leave Christianity altogether. I did not go easily. On the contrary, I left kicking and screaming, wanting desperately to hold on to the faith I had known since childhood.... I could no longer explain how there can be a good and all-powerful God actively involved with this world, given the state of things. For many people who inhabit this planet, life is a cesspool of misery and suffering. I came to a point where I simply could not believe that there is a good and kindly disposed Ruler who is in charge of it.[2]

Ehrman emphasizes that even after coming to believe that parts of the Bible were untrue, he kept his faith. He seems to want the reader to suppose that disbelieving Scripture did not contribute to his loss of faith. But how could it do otherwise? Once we call some parts of the Bible false, on what basis do we judge other parts true?

We all trust *something*. When we abandon trust in God's revelation, we replace it with trust in our own feelings, opinions, and preferences, or those of our friends and teachers—all of which can drift with popular culture, including academic culture.

Ehrman's story should challenge us to come to the problem of evil and suffering with a Christian worldview rooted in a well-informed belief in the reliability and authority of God's Word.[3] If we vacillate on that conviction, we will first reinterpret the Bible, then outright reject it.

Ehrman argues that the answers given in the Bible are not only unsatisfying, but contradictory.

Most of *God's Problem* consists of Ehrman's critical examination of Scripture. He writes, "Given…that God had chosen the people of Israel to be in a special relationship with him—what were ancient Israelite thinkers to suppose when things did not go as planned or expected?… How were they to explain the fact that the people of God suffered from famine, drought, and pestilence?"

Ehrman surveys answers to these questions, including human free will; God's anger at disobedient people; suffering as being redemptive; evil and suffering existing so God can make good out of them; suffering as encouraging humility and undermining pride; suffering as testing faith; evil and suffering as the work of Satan, which Christ will overcome in his return; and suffering and evil as a mystery.

Oddly, he thinks that because the Bible's answers vary, this makes them contradictory. The idea that they supplement one another doesn't seem to occur to him.

While Ehrman finds it troubling that the Bible approaches the issue in different ways, I find it reassuring. No single reason gives a sufficient explanation, but different threads of biblical insight, woven together, form a durable fabric.

I find the book's subtitle ironic: *How the Bible Fails to Answer Our Most Important Question—Why We Suffer.* The problem is *not* that the Bible fails to answer it; Ehrman himself documents that it offers *multiple* answers. He simply doesn't believe them.

Ehrman states unproven premises reflecting his bias, then draws logical conclusions based on his faulty premises.

Ehrman summarizes, often accurately, the biblical teaching. Then he disagrees with it, usually citing no authority beyond his personal opinion. He seems to assume that any rational person would join him in rejecting Scripture's claims. His faith in his own subjective understanding at times seems breathtaking.

Ehrman uses phrases such as "scholars now believe" as if some universally recognized group of experts passes judgment reliably and unanimously, rather than that a large array of authors start with different presuppositions and reach different conclusions. He would write more truthfully, "The scholars *I* agree with believe...."

Ehrman states, "If God tortures, maims and murders people just to see how they will react—to see if they will not blame him, when in fact he is to blame—then this does not seem to me to be a God worthy of worship."[4] But murder is unjustified killing. Where does the Bible speak of God torturing people or killing people without justification? Where does it speak of him doing such things "just to see how they will react"?

If Ehrman began with true premises, he might arrive at valid conclusions. Unfortunately, readers who lack familiarity with the Scriptures will have no way of knowing when his premises are false.

Ehrman identifies with only one biblical book, Ecclesiastes, in determining his worldview; yet he totally ignores that book's God-related teachings.
Ehrman writes,

> I have to admit that at the end of the day, I do have a biblical view of suffering. As it turns out, it is the view put forth in the book of Ecclesiastes.... A lot of bad things happen. But life also brings good things.... And so we should enjoy life to the fullest, as much as we can, as long as we can. That's what the author of Ecclesiastes thinks, and I agree.[5]

Yet, forty times Ecclesiastes directly speaks of the God that Ehrman says doesn't exist. I will summarize what Ecclesiastes says about God, not only for the benefit of its teaching, but to demonstrate the inaccuracy of Ehrman's claims that this book supports his worldview.

According to Ecclesiastes, God is in Heaven (5:2), he is Creator (12:1) and the Maker of all things (11:5), he gave life to human beings (8:15; 9:9), he bestowed our spiritual nature (3:21; 12:7) and set eternity in our hearts (3:11).

God plans the timing of all things, appointing the times for birth, planting, healing, building, joy, searching, keeping, mending, speaking, loving, and enjoying peace (3:1–8). God is sovereign over death, hate, war, and every evil. God providentially controls the sun's rising and setting, the movements of wind, the flowing of rivers, and the evaporation of water (1:5–7). God is the Shepherd (12:11) who seeks people to fear him and tests us to show us we're finite (3:14, 18). He gives us opportunity to enjoy food and work (2:24; 3:13; 5:18–20; 9:7). He gives us wisdom, knowledge, and happiness (2:26), and wealth, possessions, and honor (5:19; 6:2).

God hears and despises (5:2). He can be pleased (2:26; 7:26) and angered (5:2–6). He is good (2:24–26; 3:13; 5:18–19; 6:2) and holy (5:1–2). Though he may delay punishment of the wicked, God will surely bring it (8:13).[6]

Ecclesiastes says, "Be happy, young man, while you are young, and let your heart give you joy in the days of your youth. Follow the ways of your heart and whatever your eyes see." These apparently hedonistic words continue immediately with more sobering ones: "But know that for all these things God will bring you to judgment" (11:9).

Ecclesiastes affirms that despite the apparent emptiness of life as viewed without an eternal perspective, the only answer to the meaning of life is to fear and obey the Creator God, preferably before life's greatest hardships fall (see 12:1–3).

From where does evil come? As The Message words it, Ecclesiastes answers, "God made men and women true and upright; *we're* the ones who've made a mess of things" (7:29).

"Remember your Creator in the days of your youth, before the days of trouble come.… Then man goes to his eternal home…and the dust returns to the ground it came from, and the spirit returns to God who gave it" (12:1, 5, 7).

When we limit our perspective to the horizons of this world, life is indeed meaningless. But that is not how Ecclesiastes ends. It concludes with an emphatic message that cuts through the apparent meaninglessness and uncertainties of life, right to the heart of our existence:

"Now all has been heard; here is the conclusion of the matter: Fear God and keep his commandments, for this is the whole duty of man. For God will bring every deed into judgment, including every hidden thing, whether it is good or evil" (12:13–14).

Does this sound like the godless worldview Ehrman advocates? Or does it make clear that Ehrman has taken passages out of context to support his unbelief?

Ehrman ignores the richness of the biblical teaching about Heaven and the New Earth.

He states, "The Christian notions of heaven and hell reflect a development of this notion of a resurrection, but it is a notion that has been transformed—transformed because of the failed apocalyptic expectations of Jesus and his earliest followers."[7]

In nearly three hundred pages, there are but five sentences comprising the book's one paragraph about Heaven.

As we will see in chapter 28, the biblical teaching of Heaven and the New Earth was not some after-the-fact development by disappointed Christians. Without the teaching of eternal life with God and his people on a resurrected Earth in a redeemed universe, the biblical case for evil being defeated and suffering being redeemed does not stand up.

The climactic teaching of "no more tears, no more crying and no more pain" as well as "no more curse" is the single greatest assurance that God will put an end to evil and suffering while demonstrating that God's redemptive purposes are worth the cost of temporary suffering.

That Ehrman would make this stunning omission reveals a gaping hole in his understanding of the biblical doctrine of eternal life with God in a resurrected universe, reflected in the ancient books of Job and the prophets as well as the teachings of Jesus and the apostles.

Bart Ehrman's case appears persuasive because of what he leaves out.

Bart Ehrman has become an atheist poster boy, presenting himself as a reverse C. S. Lewis, compelled by intellectual honesty to abandon his faith.

Just as Christians elevate the testimonies of former atheists who have come to Christ, so atheists elevate Ehrman. He writes, "I did not go easily. On the contrary, I left kicking and screaming, wanting desperately to hold on to the faith I had known since childhood."[8] He borrows from Lewis, who said, "I came into Christianity kicking and screaming." Lewis wrote,

> You must picture me alone in that room in Magdalen, night after night, feeling, whenever my mind lifted even for a second from my work, the steady, unrelenting approach of Him whom I so earnestly desired not to meet. That which I greatly feared had at last come upon me. In the Trinity Term of 1929 I gave in, and admitted that God was God, and knelt and

prayed: perhaps, that night, the most dejected and reluctant convert in all England.[9]

Note the significant difference between Lewis and Ehrman. Ehrman speaks of his former faith largely in terms of a young person attending churches, schools, and events, and adopting certain religious practices. That his Christianity could withstand neither academic questioning of Scripture nor the realization that this world teems with terrible evil and suffering suggests that he had never embraced a deeply rooted biblical worldview in the first place.

Lewis, by contrast, had come to his atheism as an adult, having seen the horrors of the trenches in World War I, and rejected the trappings of Christianity he'd seen as a child and adolescent. Years later, in his conversion to Christ, he turned away from atheism, even though doing so was particularly difficult in the academic culture of Oxford, where Bible-believing professors could be subjected to condescension and ridicule.

I'm convinced that many Christians, younger and older, have faiths very similar to that which Ehrman abandoned—on the verge of being persuaded to jettison their weak faiths by college professors utilizing Ehrman's kinds of arguments.

In light of the great number of young people who reject their faith as college students or young adults, we need to ask ourselves two questions: What are we doing to help nominally Christian young people come to a true faith in Christ? And what are we doing to help youthful genuine Christians go deeper in exploring Scripture, learning sound theology, and developing a truly Christian worldview, not a superficial one?

Ehrman portrays himself as a courageous figure, when in fact he has moved from an academically unpopular viewpoint to a popular one.
At times Ehrman seems to congratulate himself on his courage. He alludes to strained relationships among family and friends as a result of rejecting Christ. No doubt—but he doesn't address the other side of the story.

On a university campus, how much courage does it take to roll your eyes at and caricature evangelical Christianity? In his professional circles, at least, Ehrman could expect to find far more support for his unbelief than his belief.

One favorable reviewer of Ehrman's book comments, "I much prefer the beneficent gods of my ancestors, who don't cause suffering, who don't pluck people out of existence according to some mysterious plan, who don't send natural disasters to plague us, a world where cause and effect hold sway, where rivers rise because of natural causes, where twisters are the result of meteorological conditions, not because God ordains them."[10]

Notice the word "prefer." This reflects the modern inclination to choose a worldview as you might vote for a candidate on *American Idol.* The beneficent gods of the reader's ancestors—which, if understood better, might not seem so beneficent after all—did not make moral demands as far as he knows. The human heart finds it appealing to reject a God who makes claims on our lives and who promises to judge us.

Ehrman never mentions that while people living in relative comfort reject faith in God due to the problem of evil, those subjected to the worst evil and suffering often turn *to* God.

To his credit, Ehrman acknowledges he's lived "the good life" and has avoided great suffering. But isn't it remarkable that from Sudan to China to Cambodia to El Salvador, faith in God grows deepest in places where evil and suffering have been greatest? The great majority of human beings who have ever lived—nearly all of whom faced evil and suffering worse than Ehrman or I have—still believed in God. Were they all primitive and stupid? Ehrman assumes he knows something that they didn't. But what if *they* knew something *he* doesn't? Just because a belief is modern doesn't make it true.

While Western atheists turn from belief in God because a tsunami in another part of the world caused great suffering, many brokenhearted survivors of that same tsunami found faith in God. This is one of the great paradoxes of suffering. Those who don't suffer much think suffering should keep people from God, while many who suffer a great deal turn *to* God, not *from* him.

Imagine eavesdropping on a conversation between Ehrman and the very people whose suffering he uses as an argument for disbelieving in God. After hearing Ehrman's case, someone says, "You've lost *your* faith because of *my* suffering? But my faith in God has grown deeper than ever. Why would I turn away from the only one who can comfort me, the only one who has planned eternal life for me, the only one who suffered immeasurably, beyond any of us, so that one day I need suffer no longer?"

You won't find the strongest Christian churches in the world in affluent America or Europe, where the problem of evil has the most traction. In Sudan, Christians are severely persecuted, raped, tortured, and sold into slavery. Yet many have a vibrant faith in Christ. People living in Garbage Village in Cairo make up one of the largest churches in Egypt. Hundreds of thousands of India's poor are turning to Christ. Why? Because the caste system and fatalism of Hinduism give them no answers. So they turn to a personal God who loves them and understands suffering. I have interviewed numbers of people who take comfort in knowing that this life is the closest they will ever come to Hell.

As an army of brutal invaders demolished his nation, a man who wrestled with the problem of evil and suffering (on a far deeper level than Bart Ehrman) said this:

> Though the fig tree does not bud
> and there are no grapes on the vines,
> though the olive crop fails
> and the fields produce no food,
> though there are no sheep in the pen
> and no cattle in the stalls,
> yet I will rejoice in the LORD,
> I will be joyful in God my Savior.

> The Sovereign LORD is my strength. (Habakkuk 3:17–19)

Many Christians who have faced evil and suffering embrace their faith with greater conviction.

While reading Ehrman's book, I interviewed Scott and Janet Willis. An unskilled truck driver who obtained his license through bribery allowed a large object to drop onto a Milwaukee freeway in front of the Willises' van. Their gas tank exploded, killing six of their children.

Scott Willis said,

> The depth of our pain is indescribable. However, the Bible expresses our feelings that we sorrow, but not as those without hope. What gives us our firm foundation for hope are the words of God found in Scripture.... Ben, Joe, Sam, Hank, Elizabeth and Peter are all with Jesus Christ. We know where they are. Our strength rests in God's Word.[11]

The Willis family's story is *exactly* the kind that Bart Ehrman features as overwhelming evidence for God's nonexistence. Yet, when I interviewed this couple fourteen years after the tragic event, Janet said, "Today I have a far greater understanding of the goodness of God than I did before the accident." This might have taken my breath away, had I not already heard it from others who've also endured unspeakable suffering.

At the end of our two-hour conversation, Scott Willis said, "I have a stronger view of God's sovereignty than ever before."

Scott and Janet did *not* say that the accident itself strengthened their view of God's sovereignty. Indeed, Scott's overwhelming sense of loss initially prompted suicidal thoughts. Rather, their faith grew as they threw themselves upon God for grace to live each day. "I turned to God for strength," Janet said, "because I had no strength." She went to the Bible with a hunger for God's presence, and he met her. "I learned about Him. He made sense when nothing else made sense. If it weren't for the Lord, I would have lost my sanity."

Is that denial? Is it wishful thinking? Or is it the real power and transforming grace of God that came in suffering?

Bart Ehrman lost what faith he had because of the sort of unspeakable tragedies that have happened not to him, but to people like Scott and Janet Willis. I asked Scott and Janet, "What would you say to those who reject the Christian faith because they say no plan of God—nothing at all—could possibly be worth the suffering of your children, and your suffering over all these years?"

"Eternity is a long time," Janet replied. "It *will* be worth it. Our children's suffering was brief, and they have the eternal joy of being with God. We and their grandparents have suffered since. But our suffering has been small compared to our children's joy. Fourteen years is a short time compared to eternity. We'll be with them there, forever."

La Rochefoucauld may have best captured the difference between Ehrman's lost faith and the Willises' deepened faith: "A great storm puts out a little fire, but it feeds a strong one."

Ehrman would benefit from spending more time talking with people whose faith increased in the midst of horrific suffering.

If he has spoken with people like the Willises, he never mentions it. Ehrman does cite the Holocaust as evidence that God doesn't exist. But why did some who lived through the Holocaust come to a radically different conclusion?

Survivor Stories is a powerful hour of interviews with Jews who survived the concentration camps and came to faith in Christ.[12] It completely defies Ehrman's logic. These people do not deny their suffering; they affirm it. But they simply do not see the reality of evil and suffering as inconsistent with their faith in Christ.

Concentration camp survivor and psychotherapist Viktor Frankl wrote, "The truth is that among those who actually went through the experience of Auschwitz, the number whose religious life was deepened—in spite, not to say because of, this experience—by far exceeds the number of those who gave up their belief."[13]

Ehrman decries God for not doing enough to diminish suffering, then concludes we shouldn't hesitate to spend our money on ourselves.
He argues that a good God would never withhold relief that was in his power to give, then comes to a revealing conclusion:

> I think we should work hard to make the world—the one we live in—the most pleasing place it can be *for ourselves*. ... We should make money and spend money. The more the better. We should enjoy good food and drink. We should eat out and order unhealthy desserts, and we should cook steaks on the grill and drink Bordeaux. ... We should drive nice cars and have nice homes. We should make love, have babies, and raise families. We should do what we can to love life—it's a gift and it will not be with us for long.[14]

Resisting the urge to ask how life can be a gift if it has no Giver, I quote Ehrman's final sentences of *God's Problem:*

> What we have in the here and now is all that there is. We need to live life to its fullest and help others as well to enjoy the fruits of the land. ... But just because we don't have an answer to suffering does not mean that we cannot have a response to it. Our response should be to work to alleviate suffering wherever possible and to live life as well as we can.[15]

Do you see the inconsistency here? If we follow Ehrman's advice to "drive nice cars and have nice homes" and consume expensive meals and drinks and spend as much as we can—in fact, "the more the better"—then we will *not* be working to alleviate suffering whenever possible.

What percentage of the royalties from Ehrman's best-selling book has he earmarked for easing world suffering? If it seems unfair to ask, remember that I am merely applying the standard he expects God to live up to: using all of one's resources to relieve suffering. Does Ehrman place himself under the same condemnation he places God? Based on the lifestyle he seems to advocate, the answer appears to be no.

Bart Ehrman's evangelical heritage serves as a warning to Christian families, churches, and schools: we need to carefully address the problem of evil.

Even Christians who do not outright reject their faith may quietly lose confidence and commitment because of their struggle with this issue. Christian students in every university, including Christian ones, face frequent, impassioned arguments against biblical teachings, whether from professors, fellow students, or textbooks. Most Christian students have seldom personally faced the problem of evil and suffering, and in most cases are inadequately prepared to deal with it. Knowing a few Bible stories proves insufficient when facing an issue of the magnitude of evil and suffering.

Churches and small groups can study and discuss a book such as *If God Is Good* (I recommend others as well).[16] Families can interact with these issues at age-appropriate levels. We should not allow culture or schools to lead the way in shaping our worldview, or our children's.

The book's presumptuous title is off-center; the problem of evil is man's problem with God, not God's problem.

While God suffers with his children, he does not struggle with his attributes and decisions. He knows what will be worth it in the end. He knows how his goodness, omnipotence, and wisdom fit with evil and suffering. It would be more accurate if Bart Ehrman titled his book *My Problem*.

The problem of evil and suffering is not God's problem. It is Bart Ehrman's problem…and yours, and mine.

God asks Job, "Will the one who contends with the Almighty correct him? Let him who accuses God answer him!… Who has a claim against me that I must pay?" (Job 40:2; 41:11). God has not asked us to give him a performance review so that he may do a better job the next time he creates a universe or devises a redemptive plan. Rather, he promises that at the judgment he will give *us* a review.

When we stand before God, we will either thank him for the justifying work of Christ, or we will face the problem of trying to justify ourselves on some other basis.

That will be the real problem.

Notes

1. Bart D. Ehrman, *God's Problem* (New York: HarperCollins, 2008), 1–3.
2. Ehrman, *God's Problem*, 3.

3. See Paul Barnett, *Is the New Testament Reliable?* (Downers Grove, IL: InterVarsity, 1993) and Timothy Paul Jones, *Misquoting Truth* (Downers Grove, IL: InterVarsity, 2007).

4. Ehrman, *God's Problem,* 188.

5. Ehrman, *God's Problem,* 275.

6. In this summary, I am indebted to Roy B. Zuck's excellent article, "God and Man in Ecclesiastes," *Bibliotheca Sacra* 148, no. 589 (January–March 1991): 50–51.

7. Ehrman, *God's Problem,* 258.

8. Ehrman, *God's Problem,* 3.

9. C. S. Lewis, *Surprised by Joy* (New York: Harcourt Brace Jovanovich, 1955), 228–29.

10. Hrafnkell Haraldsson, "Another Ehrman Slam Dunk," Amazon.com Customer Review, June 20, 2008, www.amazon.com/review/R3315JNPKN0ND0/ref=cm_srch_res_rtr_alt_1 (accessed May 4, 2009).

11. ABC7, WLS-TV, Chicago, April 7, 1998, news report; *Through the Flames* book description, www.crossway.org/product/663575724360.

12. Naomi Rothstein, "Seeing and Believing: A Review of Survivor Stories," Jews for Jesus, July 1, 2001, http://jewsforjesus.org/publications/issues/13_8/survivorstoriesreview.

13. Viktor E. Frankl, *The Unconscious God* (New York: Simon & Schuster, 1975), 16.

14. Ehrman, *God's Problem,* 277.

15. Ehrman, *God's Problem,* 277–78.

16. I've compiled an annotated bibliography of many of the books I have most appreciated in my research on evil and suffering; see www.epm.org/sufferingbooks.html.

12

Non-Theistic Worldviews
Lack a Substantial Basis
for Condemning Evil

A MORAL FRAMEWORK WITHOUT A FOUNDATION

Calling evil a problem assumes a standard of goodness; but if God doesn't exist, then by what objective basis can we measure morality?

In a fascinating 1948 debate on BBC Radio, atheist Bertrand Russell discussed with Father Frederick Copleston the naturalistic versus the Christian basis for believing in good and evil. At one point Russell said, "I feel that some things are good and that other things are bad. I love the things that are good, that I think are good, and I hate the things that I think are bad. I don't say that these things are good because they participate in the Divine goodness."

Copleston asked him, "So you distinguish good and bad by what faculty?"

Russell responded, "By my feelings."

Copleston pointed out that Hitler—his atrocities fresh in everyone's mind—did what felt good to him. He pressed Russell on whether he believed in any such thing as moral obligation. Russell answered, "I'm inclined to think that 'ought,' the feeling that one has about 'ought,' is an echo of what has been told one by one's parents or one's nurses.... I think the sense of 'ought' is the effect of somebody's imagined disapproval; it may be God's imagined disapproval, but it's somebody's imagined disapproval. And I think that is what is meant by 'ought.'"

Russell gave his opinion about the *sense* of human moral obligation, but he posed no objective basis for *actual* moral obligation. He ended the debate by saying, "I cannot attribute a Divine origin to this sense of moral obligation, which I think is quite easily accounted for in...other ways."[1]

Our feelings do not constitute a true moral framework for determining good and evil, right and wrong.

It is one thing to account for a *sense* of moral obligation, and quite another to establish that anyone truly *has* a moral obligation. We are left with Russell's three-word answer to how he distinguished good from evil: "by my feelings."

I have read a number of writers who argue, as Russell did, that one does not have to believe in God to have moral categories of good and evil. Some argue from self-defense: we should condemn murder because we don't want to be murdered. Others argue from self-interest: we should do something good to someone else, because he or she will reciprocate (we hope). We should serve others because that will make us feel good about ourselves.

But how do such pragmatic and subjective considerations constitute a true moral framework?

In his article "The Myth of Secular Moral Chaos," Sam Harris writes,

> Clearly, we can think of objective sources of moral order that do not
> require the existence of a law-giving God. In *The End of Faith,* I argued
> that questions of morality are really questions about happiness and suffer-
> ing. If there are objectively better and worse ways to live so as to maximize
> happiness in this world, these would be objective moral truths worth
> knowing. ... Everything about human experience suggests that love is
> better than hate for the purposes of living happily in this world. This is
> an objective claim.[2]

Harris argues that whatever makes people happy, presumably not at the expense of others' happiness, is morally right. Whatever doesn't make people happy is wrong. Does this really qualify as a moral system? Isn't happiness a perception? And as such, is it not subjective rather than objective? I agree that love is indeed better than hate, but is that true simply because love usually creates more happiness? Some people enjoy hating. And sometimes people, out of love, choose great sacrifices leading to personal misery.

Plato and Aristotle argued that we should be moral because that's the best way to live, one that promotes happiness in the sense of human flourishing. That sounds like the "law of love" which Scripture bases on God's loving character and his command to love our neighbors as ourselves. What grounds does atheism have for the law of love beyond it sounding like a good idea?

A Christian can argue that Heaven will replace misery with happiness and that Hell will strip hate of all happiness. But since Harris believes, as Russell did, in no afterlife, the only happiness available—from either love or hate—exists here and now.

Harris's moral framework is not nearly as objective as he claims. I think it necessarily draws on, without realizing it, a theistic worldview that values lasting happiness and sees love as good and hate as evil because of how those attitudes are viewed by God, in whose image we're made.

Non-theistic worldviews may not let God into the family room, but they habitually smuggle him in through the back door. They try to put something in his place to give life meaning, but God remains the primary reference point behind the secondary ones they recognize.

Without borrowing from a worldview that includes God, naturalists cannot successfully argue that either objective good or evil exists.

Let's suppose that humans could exist without a Creator. On what source of goodness could we draw? Why would anyone feel motivated to avoid "evil," whatever that might mean, when there's no Judge to whom they must answer?

The fact that atheists believe in morality, even though their worldview supplies no basis for it, provides evidence for the existence of the very God they deny.

Atheists' argument that goodness and moral standards can exist without God does not hold up.

If there's no God, people don't live after death and aren't held accountable for their actions, good or evil. That's why Dostoevsky said, "Destroy a man's belief in immortality and…everything would be permitted, even cannibalism."[3]

To say that an atheistic worldview provides no basis for the existence of good and evil does *not* mean that atheists have no sense of right and wrong. They do. They live in a culture influenced by a historic belief in God and the morality revealed in Scripture. This provides them a residual basis for believing that moral categories are important, while their own worldview doesn't.

How does an atheistic worldview explain an atheist's morals? Suppose time, chance, and natural forces accounted for us. If we could move from nonlife to life and from irrational to rational—quantum leaps, to say the least—then what more could we do than invent pragmatic social rules to govern group behavior? Since the powerful make the rules and they would survive longer by making the weak serve them, then why would anyone but the weak want life to change?

If the natural world is all there is, would mankind get its morals from animal instincts? A gazelle runs from the cheetah, but gazelles don't sit around the campfire and discuss how unfair it is for cheetahs to kill gazelles. Neither do cheetahs wrestle with the morality of whether they should kill gazelles. Do fish have rights that sharks should recognize and respect? Are sharks evil for eating fish? Would a good shark refrain from taking advantage of vulnerable fish? If so, how long would it survive?

In an evolutionary worldview, why object to stronger human beings stealing from or killing weaker ones? Wouldn't this simply be natural selection and survival of the fittest, not a question of right or wrong?

It doesn't help to define happiness as pleasure, as opposed to pain. Being eaten by cheetahs doesn't make gazelles happy, but eating gazelles makes cheetahs happy. Animals can experience "happiness" or lack of it, but that doesn't provide a moral code. Animal ruthlessness and lack of compassion for the weak is simply how the system works. How could anyone view it as evil?

The naturalist may claim that the survival of the fittest is descriptive, not prescriptive; that it describes the world as it *is,* not as it *should* be. But on what does he base any sense of *should*? Why "should" he operate differently than the way the natural order operates, since he's part of that natural order himself? Any appeal to natural law seems baseless, unless there is a Creator, a Lawgiver, who has built into us a sense of that natural law.

Atheists who have thought through the implications of their worldview occasionally admit its utter moral emptiness. Unbeliever William Provine put it this way in a debate: "Let me summarize my views on what modern evolutionary biology tells us loud and clear.... There are no gods, no purposes.... There is no life after death.... There is no ultimate foundation for ethics, no ultimate meaning in life, and no free will for humans."[4]

Notice his admission that there is no ultimate foundation for ethics. The naturalistic worldview has no basis for declaring some things good and others evil.

But surely something within Dr. Provine can look at good and rejoice, then look at evil and cry out, "This is wrong!" What is it that cries out? The Bible calls it the conscience, God's law written on our hearts (see Romans 2:15). We have a moral code, a natural law built into us. That's what allows us to step outside of what we see around us and call it good or evil.

Belief in evil provides a persuasive argument for God's existence.
Atheists believe that some things are right and others wrong and conclude that their doing so proves they can be good without God. But the logic doesn't hold.

The question isn't whether atheists have morals, but whether atheism is a credible moral framework. The Christian worldview explains why the atheist, God's image-bearer with a divinely created conscience, is a moral being. The atheist worldview, however, does not.

Naturalism teaches that the universe consists of observable phenomena open to scientific investigation; no such thing as an invisible realm exists. Some naturalists remain consistent enough with their worldview to deny the existence of right and wrong, good or evil.

Most naturalists, however, intuitively accept the reality of evil. They then use the existence of evil as evidence for the nonexistence of God. "Since evil exists, there *can't* be a God." But that argument can be turned on its head—if evil exists, there *must* be a God, since evil could not exist without good, and good could not exist without God.

In my novel *Deception,* homicide detective Ollie Chandler denies the existence of God because of the world's injustice, the terrible crimes he's investigated, and his wife's death from cancer. His friend Jake challenges him:

> "Where do you get your sense of justice that makes you believe crime and suffering are so wrong?"
>
> "I guess I was born with it."
>
> "You were born with a sense of justice? Well, then it didn't come from you, did it? It came from the One who made you. You believe evil is wrong because God knows it's wrong and made you know it, too. Ironic, isn't it?"
>
> "What's ironic?"
>
> "You're using standards of justice that could come only from God in order to argue that there is no God."[5]

It's difficult to argue the problem of evil when your worldview provides no basis for believing in evil.

In theory, the atheist could argue that the problem of evil is simply an internal inconsistency within Christianity. Without agreeing that true evils exist in the world, he could still say that the Christian belief in evil is inconsistent with belief in a good God.

I've read many atheists, however, and this is *not* typically what they argue. Instead, they present long lists of things that *they* call evil. But this poses a problem for them. In calling these things evil, the non-theist tries to hold God accountable to moral standards that can exist *only if there is a God.* This puts atheists in a no-win situation. If God does not exist, then there can be no ultimate right or wrong and no objective standards of goodness or evil beyond personal opinion or the majority votes of human cultures. But when he argues against God on the basis of the problem of evil, then he emphatically affirms there *is* such a thing as evil. Two results follow:

If real evil does exist, then the atheist's case collapses.

If real evil does not exist, then the atheist's case also collapses.

Dinesh D'Souza writes,

If we are purely material beings, then we should no more object to mass murder than a river objects to drying up in a drought.... Our ability to distinguish between good and evil, and to recognize these as real, means that there is a moral standard in the universe that provides the basis for this distinction. And what is the source of that moral standard if not God?[6]

The Christian worldview's shaping influence on the Western world, to which most atheists strenuously object, is *exactly* what creates the moral tension needed to reveal evil and suffering as a moral problem.

Atheism's foundation for morality is built on culture's shifting sands.

Many years ago I took a sequence of college philosophy classes from a likable atheist. I found the ethics course most interesting. Every time it came to the question of why the professor believed something to be right or wrong, he could say only that it "seemed" to him to be best, it "seemed" to him to help the most people. In other words, it always boiled down to his personal preference. Thirty of us sat in that ethics class, all with our own personal preferences, many fluxing with the current of popular culture.

I have talked with individuals whose ethics have evolved over time, who now believe that any consensual sex between adults is moral. Adultery is consensual sex. So is it moral? Well, yes, some convince themselves, so long as they commit adultery with a person they genuinely love. But how moral is this same adultery in the eyes of the betrayed spouse? Such hopeless subjectivity is no moral framework at all.

Choosing moral behaviors because they make you *feel* happy can make sense, in a Bertrand Russell/Sam Harris sort of way, but what if it makes you feel happy to torture animals or kill Jews or steal from your employer?

"You misunderstand," someone says. "We atheists do not base our morality on personal preferences, but on the judgments of society as a whole, on what benefits the most people." But how does this help the argument? What if in our class of thirty students, sixteen of us really wanted to kill the professor? Would that be good? Or what if the majority of an entire nation thought it best to liquidate one portion of that population—would that be good? Or what if 51 percent of the world's population decided to obliterate the continent of North America? Would that be good?

Nor does it help to claim the authority of some group of "elites" who supposedly have a finer moral sense. History teaches us that elite groups tend to call good whatever it is they're inclined to do.

If there is no God who created us for an eternal purpose, and no God who will judge us; if there is no God who has revealed his standards and no God who informs our consciences—then surely any morality we forge on our own will ultimately amount to a mirror image of our own subjective opinions that will change with the times.

To say that the Holocaust or child abuse is wrong is a moral judgment. But such a judgment has no meaning without a standard to measure it against. *Why* are the Holocaust and child abuse wrong? Because they involve suffering? Because other people have said they are wrong? Feeling it or saying it doesn't make it so.

William Lane Craig says, "If God does not exist, then life is objectively meaningless; but man cannot live consistently and happily knowing that life is meaningless; so in order to be happy he pretends that life has meaning. ... In a universe without God, good and evil do not exist—there is only the bare valueless fact of existence, and there is no one to say that you are right and I am wrong."[7]

We have only one basis for good moral judgments: the existence of objective standards based on unchanging reference points outside ourselves. Personal opinion falls far short. After all, Nazis and rapists have their opinions too.

A non-theistic worldview logically requires abandoning any moral foundation.

Nietzsche clearly saw the implications of atheism. His story of the madman in the marketplace powerfully captures the moral bankruptcy of rejecting God:

"Whither is God?" he cried. "I shall tell you. *We have killed him*—you and I. All of us are his murderers. But how have we done this? How were we able to drink up the sea? Who gave us the sponge to wipe away the entire

horizon? What did we do when we unchained this earth from its sun?...
Are we not plunging continually? Backward, sideward, forward, in all
directions? Is there any up or down left? Are we not straying as through an
infinite nothing? Do we not feel the breath of empty space? Has it not
become colder? Is not night and more night coming on all the while?...
God is dead.... And we have killed him. How shall we, the murderers of
all murderers, comfort ourselves?"[8]

Atheist Richard Taylor, an ethicist, confesses, "To say that something is wrong
because...it is forbidden by God, is also perfectly understandable to anyone who
believes in a law-giving God. But to say that something is wrong...even though
no God exists to forbid it, is *not* understandable."[9]

Taylor recognizes that "the concept of moral obligation [is] unintelligible
apart from the idea of God. The words remain, but their meaning is gone."[10]

University of Calgary ethicist Kai Nielsen is also an atheist. In a philosophy
journal article, he candidly acknowledges that human reason offers no guidance
in developing a true morality:

We have not been able to show that reason requires the moral point of
view, or that all really rational persons should not be individual egoists or
classical amoralists. Reason doesn't decide here. The picture I have painted
for you is not a pleasant one. Reflection on it depresses me.... Pure practical reason, even with a good knowledge of the facts, will not take you to
morality.[11]

Speaking to the American Academy for the Advancement of Science, Dr. L.
D. Rue argued that people are better off if we deceive ourselves into believing a
"Noble Lie" which will make us *think* (even though it isn't so) that humanity and
the universe have value.[12]

The *New Yorker* called Princeton philosophy teacher Peter Singer "the most
influential philosopher alive." The *New England Journal of Medicine* claims Singer
has had "more success in effecting changes in acceptable behavior" than any
philosopher since Bertrand Russell.

Singer proposed that we shouldn't declare children alive until twenty-eight
days after birth, allowing parents time to decide whether they wish to dispose of
their children without legal consequences.[13]

He wrote, "If we compare a severely defective human infant with a nonhuman animal, a dog or a pig, for example, we will often find the nonhuman to have

superior capacities, both actual and potential, for rationality, self-consciousness, communication and, anything else that can plausibly be considered morally significant."[14]

Singer, like Sam Harris, builds his ethics on the notion of happiness. But notice where it takes him: "When the death of a disabled infant will lead to the birth of another infant with better prospects of a happy life, the total amount of happiness will be greater if the disabled infant is killed. The loss of happy life for the first infant is outweighed by the gain of a happier life for the second. Therefore, if killing the hemophiliac infant has no adverse effect on others, it would… be right to kill him."[15]

When Singer was appointed a Princeton professor, a disabilities rights group named Not Dead Yet protested his arrival. They objected to Singer's books, which promote the legalization of killing disabled infants as well as children and adults with severe cognitive disabilities. (Parents paying for their children to attend Singer's classes might be interested in knowing that he also provides a "moral justification" for killing the elderly.)

Each of us should reflect seriously on this question: If everyone acted as if Singer's worldview were true, then what would our culture look like? Would there be more good and less evil?

And more to the point: if you have a physical disability, cognitive impairment, or senior citizen's discount, would you want to live in Singer's world? (Even if the answer is yes, you wouldn't be allowed to live there very long.)

When God is removed from the equation, no basis remains for the recognition of human rights.

It's no surprise that atheism was the centerpiece of Soviet and Chinese communism's worldview that allowed its leaders to murder more than a hundred million people. Richard Wurmbrand, tortured in communist prisons, wrote, "The cruelty of atheism is hard to believe. When man has no faith in the reward of good or the punishment of evil, there is no reason to be human. There is no restraint from the depths of evil which is in man. The communist torturers often said, 'There is no God, no hereafter, no punishment for evil. We can do what we wish.'"[16]

We know murderers and rapists violate human rights. But *how* do we know this? We have a consensus about objective moral standards, and we even agree on many of them. But if God does not exist, then on what objective basis could human rights exist?

Rights must come from *somewhere*. The Declaration of Independence claims "all men are created equal, that they are endowed by their Creator with certain unalienable Rights." But what if no Creator exists? Imagine a declaration saying, "Human beings, even those dumber than toast and too weak to survive on their own, are equal and have the same rights as the smart and strong." Leave out the Creator and you leave out human rights.

In contrast to non-theistic worldviews, the biblical worldview offers a foundation for determining both good and evil.
Poll a culture of cannibals about the ethics of eating human flesh (you might have difficulty conducting such a poll) and you'll find consensus: it's not evil.

If a subjective sense of happiness or well-being constitutes a moral system, then Charles Manson, terrorists, and genocidal dictators have an equally authoritative moral ground when they appeal to their own personal preferences. Of course we all know they are wrong—but *how* do we know?

The Christian worldview affirms that God's character provides the objective standard that determines good and evil: "Be holy because I, the LORD your God, am holy" (Leviticus 19:2). But how can we know what God is like? Because he has revealed in Scripture moral laws that reflect his character qualities. For instance, the Bible offers an objective moral stance against adultery. Marital unfaithfulness violates God's character and is specifically forbidden in his Word. Therefore we can know—without depending on our feelings—that it is evil. A Christian's subjective feelings, in light of his current temptations, may tell him adultery is right. But he can still hold to the view that it is wrong, because a credible authoritative source outside himself says so.

That God has planted in all his image-bearers an ability to recognize good and evil in their consciences (see Romans 2:15) accounts for why people who do not believe Scripture can nonetheless feel guilty when they do wrong and feel good when they do right.

Even those who reject the claims of the Christian worldview should acknowledge that it does in fact offer a moral foundation upon which to discern good and evil. And they should ask themselves whether, without realizing it, they sometimes borrow from the Christian worldview because their own worldview cannot provide a foundation on which to judge good and evil.

Notes
1. Bertrand Russell, *Bertrand Russell on God and Religion*, ed. Al Seckel (New York: Prometheus Books, 1986), www.bringyou.to/apologetics/p20.htm.

2. Sam Harris, "The Myth of Secular Moral Chaos," Council for Secular Humanism, www.secularhumanism.org/index.php?section=library&page=sharris_26_3.

3. Fyodor Dostoevsky, *The Brothers Karamazov* (New York: Random House, 1970), 88.

4. William Provine (transcript of a debate with Phillip E. Johnson, Stanford University, Palo Alto, CA, April 30, 1994).

5. Randy Alcorn, *Deception* (Colorado Springs: Multnomah, 2007), 60.

6. Dinesh D'Souza, *What's So Great About Christianity* (Washington, D.C.: Regnery, 2007), 276.

7. William Lane Craig, *Reasonable Faith* (Wheaton, IL: Good News, 1994), 61.

8. Friedrich Nietzsche, "The Gay Science," in *The Portable Nietzsche,* ed. and trans. W. Kaufmann (New York: Viking, 1954), 95.

9. Richard Taylor, *Ethics, Faith, and Reason* (Englewood Cliffs, NJ: Prentice Hall, 1985), 90. This quote and several others from this chapter are cited by William Lane Craig in *Reasonable Faith.*

10. Taylor, *Ethics, Faith, and Reason,* 84.

11. Kai Nielsen, "Why Should I Be Moral?" *American Philosophical Quarterly* 21 (1984): 90.

12. Loyal D. Rue, "The Saving Grace of Noble Lies" (address to the American Academy for the Advancement of Science, February 1991), cited by Craig, *Reasonable Faith,* 85.

13. Peter Singer, *Rethinking Life and Death* (New York: St. Martin's Griffin, 1996), 217.

14. Peter Singer, "Sanctity of Life or Quality of Life," *Pediatrics* 72, no. 1 (July 1983): 129.

15. Peter Singer, "Taking Life: Humans," www.petersingerlinks.com/taking.htm, excerpted from Peter Singer, *Practical Ethics* (New York: Cambridge University Press, 1993), 186.

16. Richard Wurmbrand, *Tortured for Christ* (Bartlesville, OK: Living Sacrifice Book, 1990), 38.

13

The Unbeliever's Problem
of Goodness

WHY DOES GOOD EXIST?

Those who argue that the Christian worldview doesn't adequately account for evil need to explain how theirs can account for goodness.

Beginning with Sam Harris's *Letter to a Christian Nation* in 2006, a string of books promoting atheism hit top spots on the *New York Times* bestsellers' list, including Richard Dawkins's *The God Delusion* and Christopher Hitchens's *God Is Not Great.* Harris writes,

> If God exists, either He can do nothing to stop the most egregious calamities, or He does not care to. God, therefore, is either impotent or evil.... There is another possibility, of course, and it is both the most reasonable and least odious: the biblical god is a fiction, like Zeus and the thousands of other dead gods whom most sane human beings now ignore.[1]

While atheists routinely speak of the problem of evil, they usually don't raise the problem of goodness. But if evil provides evidence against God, then shouldn't goodness count as evidence for him? And wouldn't that be evidence against atheism?

From a non-theistic viewpoint, what is evil? Isn't it just nature at work? In a strictly natural, physical world, shouldn't everything be neither good nor evil? Good and evil imply an "ought" and an "ought not" that nature is incapable of producing.

Augustine summarized the argument in two great questions: "If there is no God, why is there so much good? If there is a God, why is there so much evil?"[2]

To many, only the second question occurs. But the first is just as important. If a good God doesn't exist, what is goodness's source?

We have no logical reason to take good for granted; its existence demands an explanation.

Much of the good of this world, such as the beauty of a flower or the grandeur of a waterfall or the joy of an otter at play, serves no more practical purpose than great art. It does, however, serve a high purpose of filling us with delight, wonder, and gratitude.

Why does anyone feel gratitude? And why do people, even irreligious survivors of a plane crash, so often thank God? Do people thank time, chance, and natural selection for the good they experience? No, because innately we see life as a gift from God.

People speak of gratuitous evil. But what about gratuitous *good*—purely impractical, over-the-top good that seems to have no explanation?

That we don't question good's existence affirms we consider good the norm and evil the exception.

Don't evil and suffering grab our attention precisely because they are *not* the norm in our lives? We "get the flu" because we normally don't have it. We break an arm that normally remains unbroken. Our shock at evil testifies to the predominance of good. Headlines we consider terrible wouldn't be headlines if they described usual events. At any given time, fewer people are at war than at peace. Even in the bloody twentieth century, a person had less than a 2 percent chance of dying from war or violent civil strife.[3]

The atheist who points out the horrors of evil unwittingly testifies to good as the norm. When we speak of children dying, we acknowledge they usually don't. When a natural disaster hits, 99 percent of the world remains untouched. Most people in the world go through a lifetime without personally experiencing a devastating natural disaster. Fatal car accidents and murder are rare, relatively speaking. Though fallen, nature still contains more beauty than ugliness.

The average person sees considerable good in the world. This may be why the great majority of societies believe that, despite evil and suffering, God is good. (Polytheists believe in some demon gods, but no monotheistic religion views God as anything but good.)

In *The Problem of Pain*, C. S. Lewis said, "If the universe is so bad, or even half so bad, how on earth did human beings ever come to attribute it to the activity of a wise and good Creator? Men are fools, perhaps; but hardly so foolish as that."[4]

Granted, in certain lives and times, suffering becomes the norm. Yet even then sufferers often retain a remarkable capacity for laughter and can find pleasure in flowers, a movie, a pet, or a friend.

How Can Good Exist?

Some of the world's goodness can be described only as supernatural, since from a naturalistic viewpoint we should all ruthlessly step on one another to survive.

The worldview of naturalism holds that physical matter is all that exists and all phenomena can be explained by natural causes. Popular astronomer Carl Sagan embraced naturalism when he said, "The cosmos is all there is, all there ever was, and all there ever will be."[5]

In contrast, the Bible affirms, "In the beginning God created the heavens and the earth" (Genesis 1:1). The Creator called the cosmos "very good" (verse 31). Even in a fallen world, God's common grace infuses goodness, implants a measure of it in the consciences of his image-bearers, and restrains much evil.

So how does naturalism explain the world's goodness? Setting aside the issues of how something can come from nothing and how life can come from nonlife, great goodness and nobility pose a serious problem: why would we expect to find such goodness in a world that came about through blind force, time, and chance?

Bumper stickers encourage us to practice random acts of kindness. A company named *Life is good* started stores called Celebrate Life; four thousand retailers carry its products. Their festivals, eighteen of them in 2008, raise millions of dollars for needy children. People wear *Life is good* T-shirts—over twenty million of them. Of course, not all of life is good; but, as a whole, enough people believe it's good, and want to celebrate it, to buy and wear such products. This level of optimism seems implausible for a world of disease, struggle, war, and conflict, in which death awaits everyone. Yes, there are truckloads of evil, but there are also boatloads of good.

The Christian worldview explains goodness as rooted in God, revealed by God and rewarded by him. It gives reason for optimism to those who embrace it. What explanation for goodness and what basis for optimism does naturalism offer?

In the post-Enlightenment era Voltaire asked, "How can God be so cruel?" In the pre-Enlightenment Reformation era Luther asked, "How can God be so merciful?"

Without God, the world would be amoral, with no objective goodness or evil.

I heard Christopher Hitchens say in a debate, "The world looks as it would if there were no God." But if there were no God, would you really expect this world to look just as it does? I don't think so.

Where does goodness come from? How could it come from nothing? Why would people have such a strong sense of right and wrong? Why would the powerful sometimes sacrifice their lives to save the weak, handicapped, and dying?

Evolution can explain greed, selfishness, insensitivity, survival-preoccupation, and even a certain amount of ruthlessness; but does anything in the blind evolutionary process explain demonstrating kindness, putting other people first, and even risking your life to help a stranger? If so, what? How much good should we expect to see in an impersonal, self-generated world of mere molecules, chemicals, and natural forces?

A system that operates on brute strength, genetic superiority, and the survival of the fittest can explain and justify racism, sexism, and oppression. But it cannot explain goodness, humility, kindness, compassion, and mercy, especially when exercised on behalf of the weak and dying. What should surprise atheists is not that powerful people crush those weaker than themselves—that would be entirely natural. The surprise is that powerful people would sacrifice their welfare to aid the weak. And yet, that very thing often happens. Why?

The ruthlessness seen in abortion should characterize our society at every level. The existence of children's hospitals that spend vast resources to help the terminally ill, the provision of special parking for handicapped people, Special Olympics for disabled children—they all reveal shocking aberrations from natural selection. If naturalism were an accurate worldview, the human race should welcome the death of the weak, diseased, and disabled, for its genetic betterment and its own survival.

Jeffrey Dahmer, the notorious sexual predator and cannibal, stated in an interview, "If it all happens naturalistically, what's the need for a God? Can't I set my own rules? Who owns me? I own myself."[6]

We read of parents prosecuted for abusing their children. But think of how many sleep-deprived parents have restrained themselves from hurting a crying child whom they could easily kill or gravely injure in a moment of frustration.

Think of sacks of money found and turned in to the authorities. Ponder why people stop to help a stranded motorist or dive into frigid water to save a stranger from drowning. Would you expect to see *any* of this in a world without a good Creator?

The world looks remarkably different than a world without God should look.

Richard Dawkins wrote, "The universe we observe has precisely the properties we should expect if there is, at bottom, no design, no purpose, no evil and no good, nothing but blind pitiless, indifference."[7]

"Pitiless indifference" did not motivate Christians to care for those dying of the Black Death, at great risk to their own lives. "Pitiless indifference" did not take Father Damien to the lepers of Molokai, whom he served for sixteen years before dying of leprosy at age forty-nine. Nor, on the other extreme, did "pitiless indifference" fuel the Holocaust. Rather, Nazis slaughtered millions of Jews because their hatred was so deep that it defied all natural explanation.

Suppose we believe in a Creator who made people in his image, fashioning them to make effectual choices. Suppose those people chose sin, condemning themselves to live under death and curse, but that God still blessed them with his providence and common grace. In that case, wouldn't we expect the world to look as it does, with much goodness and evil coexisting? I think the answer is yes.

The sacrificial good done by many Christians in the face of evil testifies to God's existence.

Dawkins, Hitchens, and other atheists emphasize the evils done in religion's name. But they say virtually nothing about how modern education, science, and health care all emerged out of Christianity. Consider the Red Cross, an organization that has done incalculable good to millions across the world. Compare this to the much publicized witch hunts of old New England, in which a total of nineteen people died, or even the Inquisition, responsible for an average of five deaths a year in its four-hundred-fifty-year history.[8]

While some professing Christians have certainly perpetrated injustice in the name of Christ, the numbers pale in comparison to the multimillions slaughtered by the eager disciples of atheists such as Nietzsche and Lenin—including Hitler, Stalin, and Mao.

While hatred of religion motivated Stalin and Mao, Hitler was a utilitarian who used everything at his disposal, including the nominal churches of Germany, to advance his evil agenda. (Many have mistakenly called Hitler a Christian; in fact, he wrote, "I shall never come to terms with the Christian lie… Our epoch will certainly see the end of the disease of Christianity.")[9]

Look around the world at the goodness you see, particularly at the groups and individuals dedicated to helping those who suffer. And then consider: Where are the hospitals and famine-relief organizations founded by atheists? Where are the groups of atheists reaching out to drug addicts, troubled youth, and prisoners?

Matthew Parris wrote in the London *Times* a remarkable 2009 article titled "As an Atheist, I Truly Believe Africa Needs God." He grew up in Africa and noted the profound difference in the goodness and resistance to evil he saw among Christians in contrast to unbelievers. He concluded, "Removing Christian evangelism from the African equation may leave the continent at the mercy of a malign fusion of Nike, the witch doctor, the mobile phone and the machete."[10]

We see goodness even in unexpected places, including in persecution and suffering.

Countless persecuted Christians and prisoners of war testify that goodness flourishes even where it seems it could not. Alexander Solzhenitsyn wrote in *The Gulag Archipelago*,

> It was only when I lay there on rotting prison straw that I sensed within myself the first stirrings of good. Gradually, it was disclosed to me that the line separating good and evil passes not through states, nor between classes, nor between political parties either—but right through every human heart—and through all human hearts. …
>
> I nourished my soul there, and I say without hesitation: "Bless you, prison, for having been in my life!"[11]

Thomas Schmidt tells of an old woman he met in a nursing home. Blind and almost deaf, Mabel was eighty-nine. She'd lived there for twenty-five years and now sat strapped in a wheelchair. The cancer eating her face had pushed her nose to the side, dropped one eye, and distorted her jaw, so she drooled constantly.

Schmidt handed Mabel a flower and said, "Happy Mother's Day."

She tried to smell it. "Thank you," she said, her words garbled. "It's lovely. But since I'm blind, can I give it to someone else?" When he wheeled her to another resident, she held out the flower and said, "Here, this is from Jesus."

Schmidt asked, "Mabel, what do you think about when you lie in your room?"

"I think about my Jesus."

"What do you think about Jesus?"

As she spoke slowly and deliberately, he wrote down her words: "I think how good he's been to me. He's been awfully good.... I'm one of those kind who's mostly satisfied.... I'd rather have Jesus. He's all the world to me."

Then Mabel started singing, "Jesus is all the world to me, my life, my joy, my all. He is my strength from day to day."

Thinking of this woman bedridden, blind, nearly deaf, cancer eating her for twenty-five years, Schmidt said, "Seconds ticked and minutes crawled, and so did days and weeks and months and years of pain without human company and without an explanation of why it was all happening—and she lay there and sang hymns. *How could she do it?*"[12]

The only good answer to that question, I think, is supernatural. The Jesus Mabel loves is the Jesus who sustains her.

Our desire to live proves that good is greater than evil and that most suffering can be tolerated.

For five days Aron Ralston's right arm was pinned under an eight-hundred-pound boulder. Alone, with long odds against his rescue, he didn't give up.

On the morning of April 29, 2003, Aron began using a dull pocketknife to saw off his pinned arm. It took two days, but once he was freed, he wrapped his arm stump in a plastic bag and covered it with a small canvas backpack. After he rappelled down a sixty-foot rock face with one arm and hiked six miles, a search helicopter finally found him.

Hundreds of people have contacted Aron, telling him how his story has inspired them to take a fresh look at their own personal tragedies. Aron said he was at peace with the idea of dying. On the other hand, his will to live was very strong because there were so many things he wanted to do with his life.[13]

Cicero said, "After the supreme happiness of not being born, and of avoiding the shoals of life, the most happy lot for every one who has come into the world would be to die on the spot, and escape from life as one escapes from a conflagration."[14] Authorities put Cicero to death at age sixty-three. He could have ended his life anytime sooner, but didn't.

Why not?

David Hume, famous for his formulation of the problem of evil, wrote, "The first entrance into life gives anguish to the newborn infant and to its wretched parent: Weakness, impotence, distress, attend each stage of that life: and 'tis at last finished in agony and horror."[15] Such dismal words! Yet Hume, too, chose to keep living, dying of cancer at age sixty-five.

A major study of those suffering from three or more chronically painful conditions reported that 14 percent have suicidal thoughts and 8 percent have attempted suicide.[16] I find it remarkable that 86 percent of those living with extreme pain do not even *consider* suicide and 92 percent have never attempted it. We hear of a rising suicide rate, but that rate in the United States stands at eleven per one hundred thousand people, or about 0.01 percent.[17]

If the quantity and intensity of evil and suffering in the world is so intolerable, why don't more people commit suicide, or at least seriously consider it? Could it be that the good they see in this world gives them hope for a better future?

Philosopher William Hasker points out that most of us don't regret our existence and that of our loved ones. Yet, he says, that existence depends on a long line of ancestors, all of whom sinned and suffered and endured life in a world of evil and suffering:

> Only if we argue that we and our loved ones should not exist do we have a grounds for saying God shouldn't have made the world that produced us and our loved ones, even as we are. On the whole, we prefer the world, even with its evil and sufferings, to a possible world with fewer evils and sufferings that would have resulted in the nonexistence of ourselves and our loved ones.[18]

Despite its current flaws, the world's beauty and goodness testify to a Creator who designed it with order and purpose.

Theist David Wood asks in his debates with atheists whether it is rational to look at the Venus de Milo statue, note its condition, and conclude that no intelligent artist would be incompetent or perverse enough to sculpt it without arms.

Surely it makes more sense to view the delicate greatness of what *remains* of Venus de Milo and conclude instead that a great artist's work has suffered serious damage.

I have visited museums throughout the world where many great statues are disfigured. Nonetheless, people see past the flaws to the magnificent, intrinsic beauty of the art, giving high praise to the artists who fashioned them.

Not once have I heard a guide or visitor suggest that because the art is marred, it must have come into existence *ex nihilo*.

Many have come to faith by contrasting the depths of evil and suffering with the goodness of Christians who responded to it.

Philip Hallie's marvelous book *Lest Innocent Blood Be Shed* tells the true story of Le Chambon, a French town where Pastor André Trocmé's church, under the Nazi occupation, provided Jews with food, shelter, protection, and means of escape. Despite the disapproval of many, Trocmé and his church persevered in doing what they believed was right. As a result, "Le Chambon became the safest place for Jews in Europe."[19] Over a period of about four years, the church rescued nearly twenty-five hundred Jews.

The Holocaust's cruelty obsessed Hallie. He said he'd become "bitterly angry" and "over the years [of studying the Holocaust] I had dug myself into Hell." Hallie speaks of a life-changing day when he discovered the stories of Christians in Le Chambon rescuing Jews, at peril of their own imprisonment and death. As he read, it surprised him to break into tears in what he called "an expression of moral praise." Hallie later described the love of the church at Le Chambon:

> It was this strenuous, this extraordinary obligation that…Trocmé expressed to the people in the big gray church. The love they preached was not simply adoration; nor was it simply a love of moral purity, of keeping one's hands clean of evil. It was not a love of private ecstasy or a private retreat from evil. It was an active, dangerous love that brought help to those who needed it most.[20]

The day Hallie read of those flawed but loving Christians, he caught a view of God in the goodness they had done. He went home and spent a busy evening with family, then found himself in bed, weeping again over what happened in Le Chambon. Hallie wrote,

> When I lay on my back in bed with my eyes closed, I saw more clearly than ever the images that had made me weep. I saw the two clumsy khaki-colored buses of the Vichy French police pull into the village square. I saw the police captain facing the pastor of the village and warning him that if he did not give up the names of the Jews they had been sheltering in the village, he and his fellow pastor, as well as the families who had been caring for the Jews, would be arrested. I saw the pastor refuse to give up these people who had been strangers in his village, even at the risk of his own destruction.

Then I saw the only Jew the police could find, sitting in an otherwise empty bus. I saw a thirteen-year-old boy, the son of the pastor, pass a piece of his precious chocolate through the window to the prisoner, while twenty gendarmes who were guarding the lone prisoner watched. And then I saw the villagers passing their little gifts through the window until there were gifts all around him—most of them food in those hungry days during the German occupation of France.

Lying there in bed, I began to weep again. I thought, Why run away from what is excellent simply because it goes through you like a spear? Lying there, I knew...a certain region of my mind contained an awareness of men and women in bloody white coats [committing unspeakable atrocities to] six- or seven- or eight-year-old Jewish children.... All of this I knew. But why not know joy?... Why must life be for me that vision of...children [hideously brutalized]? Something had happened, had happened for years in that mountain village. Why should I be afraid of it?

To the dismay of my wife, I left the bed unable to say a word, dressed, crossed the dark campus on a starless night, and read again those few pages on the village of Le Chambon-sur-Lignon. And to my surprise, again the spear, again the tears, again the frantic, painful pleasure that spills into the mind when a deep, deep need is being satisfied, or when a deep wound is starting to heal.[21]

Philosophy professor Eleonore Stump tells of coming to know Jesus through studying the problem of evil and suffering. Reflecting on her own experience (and Hallie's), Stump writes,

So, in an odd sort of way, the mirror of evil can also lead us to God. A loathing focus on the evils of our world and ourselves prepares us to be the more startled by the taste of true goodness when we find it and the more determined to follow that taste until we see where it leads. And where it leads is to the truest goodness...to the sort of goodness of which the Chambonnais's goodness is only a tepid after-taste. The mirror of evil becomes translucent, and we can see through it to the goodness of God.... So you can come to Christ contemplating evil in a world of goodness, or contemplating goodness in a world of evil.[22]

One mother—her three children saved by the people of Le Chambon—said, "The Holocaust was storm, lightning, thunder, wind, rain, yes. And Le Chambon was the rainbow."[23]

The history of the human race cannot be reduced to the Holocaust. There was and is considerable goodness in the world outside the Holocaust. Yet even inside it, in places like Le Chambon, a costly and beautiful goodness lives.

Notes

1. Sam Harris, *Letter to a Christian Nation* (New York: Knopf, 2006), 55–56.
2. Augustine as quoted by Peter Kreeft in Lee Strobel, *The Case for Faith* (Grand Rapids, MI: Zondervan, 2000), 45.
3. John Mueller, *Overblown* (New York: Simon & Schuster, 2006), 153.
4. C. S. Lewis, *The Problem of Pain* (New York: Macmillan, 1962), 15.
5. Carl Sagan, *Cosmos* (New York: Ballantine Books, 1980), 4.
6. "Jeffrey Dahmer: The Monster Within," *Biography*, A&E, 1996.
7. Richard Dawkins, *River Out of Eden* (New York: Basic Books, 1995), 133.
8. My thanks to Dinesh D'Souza for making this point while speaking at our church in October 2008.
9. Jonathan Glover, *Humanity* (New Haven, CT: Yale University Press, 2000), 355.
10. Matthew Parris, "As an Atheist, I Truly Believe Africa Needs God," *Times* (London), December 27, 2008, www.timesonline.co.uk/tol/comment/columnists/matthew_parris/article5400568.ece.
11. Alexander Solzhenitsyn, *The Gulag Archipelago* (New York: Harper and Row, 1985), 312–13.
12. Thomas E. Schmidt, *Trying to Be Good* (Grand Rapids, MI: Zondervan, 1990), 180–83, quoted in William Lane Craig, *Hard Questions, Real Answers* (Wheaton, IL: Crossway Books, 2003), 109–10.
13. See Aron Ralston, *Between a Rock and a Hard Place* (New York: Simon & Schuster, 2004).
14. Cicero, quoted in Ernest Naville, *The Problem of Evil*, trans. John P. Lacroix (New York: Carlton and Lanahan, 1871), 136.
15. David Hume, *Dialogues Concerning Natural Religion* (London: William Blackwood, 1907), 126.
16. Mark A. Ilgen, Kara Zivin, Ryan J. McCammon, and Marcia Valenstein, "Pain and Suicidal Thoughts, Plans, and Attempts in the United States," *General Hospital Psychiatry* 30, no. 6 (November–December 2008): 521–27.
17. *American Journal of Preventive Medicine*. www.cnn.com/2008/HEALTH/10/21/Healthmag.suicide.increase/.

18. William Hasker, "On Regretting the Evils of This World," *Southern Journal of Philosophy* 19 (1981): 425–37, quoted in *The Problem of Evil: Selected Readings,* ed. Michael L. Peterson (Notre Dame, IN: University of Notre Dame Press, 1992), 153–67.

19. Philip Paul Hallie, *Lest Innocent Blood Be Shed* (New York: HarperCollins, 1994), 4.

20. Hallie, *Lest Innocent Blood Be Shed,* 129.

21. Hallie, *Lest Innocent Blood Be Shed,* 110–11.

22. Eleonore Stump, "The Mirror of Evil," in *God and the Philosophers,* ed. Thomas V. Morris (New York: Oxford University Press, 1994), 235.

23. Os Guinness, *Unspeakable* (San Francisco: HarperCollins, 2005), 227.

14

The Unbeliever's Problem of Extreme Evil

Throughout this book I use illustrations of what I would call superhuman goodness, acts of loving sacrifice and courage that go beyond anything we might expect of human beings. These serve as evidence for the Christian worldview that includes the supernatural prescence of a good God and righteous angels.

The problem of extreme evil, however, usually takes center stage. It's the most frequently cited argument against God, and many consider it the most devastating.

Surprisingly, however, upon closer examination, extreme evil may actually be seen as evidence *for* God's existence, not against it. (This chapter contains graphic examples of evil, necessary, I think, to address this crucial issue.)

WHY EXTREME EVIL POSES A PROBLEM FOR UNBELIEVERS

The Christian worldview explains the existence of extreme evil far better than atheism does.

If you have toured medieval castles and learned of the tortures inflicted there, have you marveled at how it all defied reason? In most cases, the torturers had little interest in extracting information. It cost much time and material resources to keep prisoners alive rather than simply killing them. Why commit evil just for evil's sake, or why take pleasure in inflicting suffering? All pragmatic, naturalistic, and evolutionary explanations of such evil prove inadequate.

The Bible, on the other hand, speaks of an unseen realm full of powerful spirit beings that project their cruel and malignant thoughts and wills on humans. These beings, far more powerful than humans, also exceed them in their evil. These malevolent beings push us to expand our evil beyond the boundaries of what could be expected even of fallen humans.

Since non-theists believe in nothing outside of the visible realm, they must explain such evils on the basis of human perversity alone.

As Americans reeled from the events of September 11, 2001, no one explained the terrorists' actions from a naturalistic worldview. No one argued that the deliberate flying of commercial airliners into the World Trade Center and the Pentagon was merely natural selection at work. People knew in their guts that such evil transcended human explanation. A naturalistic worldview just couldn't account for such wickedness.

Acts of extreme evil, though routinely used as arguments against God, are arguments for supernaturalism.

I spent hours walking through Cambodia's Killing Fields. Vek and Samoeun Taing, a gentle Cambodian couple who had survived there with a young child for two years, escorted our small group. Feeling numb, I saw the skulls piled up and stood by the mud pits where killers threw hundreds of bodies. A human jawbone lay at my feet. I picked it up, held it in my hand, and wept.

The darkness felt overwhelming. Pol Pot and the Khmer Rouge murdered nearly *one-third* of the country's population. Yet the three million slaughtered in Cambodia amount to less than *one-fiftieth* of the murders by twentieth century tyrants, who killed mostly their own people. Hitler, Stalin, and Mao accounted for most of the carnage, but the ongoing state-sponsored killing in Sudan, including the Darfur region, follows the same script. (And this figure ignores the staggering number of preborn children aborted throughout the world.)

Samoeun's parents both starved to death. One of her brothers was murdered; they never again heard from another brother. Vek's brother and sister-in-law and six of their children all perished. We stood together at a tree where Khmer Rouge soldiers held children by their little feet, swinging them into the tree to smash their heads. Unthinkable evil! Who could imagine such horrible crimes?

I just looked again at a photograph of one sign written in Cambodian, referring to the "sea of blood and tears." The sign reads as follows, its awkward English translation powerfully capturing the sentiment:

We are hearing the grievous voice of the victims who were beaten by Pol
Pot men with canes, bamboo stumps or heads of hoes. Who were stabbed
with knives or swords. We seem to be looking at the horrifying scenes and
the panic-stricken faces of the people who were dying of starvation, forced
labour or torture without mercy upon the skinny body.... How bitter they

were when seeing their beloved children, wives, husbands, brothers or sisters were seized and tightly bound before being taken to mass grave! While they were waiting for their turn to come and share the same tragic lot.

The method of massacre which the clique of Pol Pot criminals was carried upon the innocent people of Kampuchea cannot be described fully and clearly in words because the invention of this killing method was strangely cruel. So it is difficult for us to determine who they are for they have the human form but their hearts are demon's hearts.

After all the horrors I'd learned of on that unforgettable day, human skulls at my feet, that one sentence rocked me: "They have the human form but their hearts are demon's hearts."

Yes! That was it. Nothing on a merely human level could explain the gratuitous torture, the tireless cruelty inflicted even on helpless children. This was *super*human evil.

Nanci and I felt overwhelmed as we walked through the Holocaust Memorial in Washington, D.C. Years before we'd had an even more unforgettable experience at Yad Vashem, Jerusalem's Holocaust museum. The burning candles and the reading of the names of children killed in the Holocaust remain among the most haunting and unforgettable experiences of my life. We watched sobbing men and women poring through books to find the names of their murdered relatives. What surrounded us cried out for an explanation even bigger than human depravity.

I think often of that young man I mentioned a few chapters ago, the one on the plane who told me he didn't believe in evil. When I asked him whether the Holocaust was evil, he replied, "I guess it was a mistake." But his body language betrayed him. It was *evil*...and he knew it.

One test of a worldview is whether you sometimes have to borrow from another because yours doesn't work. That's what this young man had to do. I believe he recognized what he refused to verbalize. To admit the Holocaust was evil, he would have to abandon his worldview and borrow the concepts of both human and demonic evil from a worldview he didn't *want* to believe.

Extreme evil committed by "regular" people demands a superhuman explanation.

Emmanuel Ndikumana is a Hutu married to a Tutsi. This is remarkable, since in the 1994 Rwandan slaughters, Hutu militia massacred a million Tutsis, many of them hacked to death with machetes. Tutsis then took revenge on Hutus. Teenage classmates at Emmanuel's school targeted him for murder.

Do you know what struck me most when Emmanuel told me of his survival? It was that the Tutsi students who tried to murder him were, in every respect, very normal young people. So were most of those Hutus who butchered innocent Tutsis. Yet the gruesome murders perpetrated by both sides transcend natural explanation—so what explanation remains but a supernatural one?

And once we affirm there is supernatural evil, can we fail to recognize supernatural good? God and Satan are not equal opposites, but if there is a Satan and demons who do evil, then doesn't it make sense that there is a God and righteous angels who do good?

Robert Lifton's *The Nazi Doctors: Medical Killing and the Psychology of Genocide* documents how intelligent medical professionals participated in cruel and deadly experimental surgeries on Jewish children, with appalling ease. Among the best-trained medical personnel in Europe, they enjoyed normal family lives and loved their children and pets; but day after day, they committed shockingly cruel evils.

Susan Smith went to prison after drowning her two small sons because a man she was dating hinted that he didn't like children. When Chuck Colson visited that prison, he heard that Smith had signed up to hear him speak. Colson looked for her in the audience but never saw her. Afterward he found out she'd been sitting right in front of him. His point? "The face of evil is frighteningly ordinary."[1]

I've watched interviews with family, friends, and classmates of serial killers who all say the same chilling words: "He was such a nice boy."

In *People of the Lie,* psychologist Scott Peck tells the story of Bobby, a young man suffering from depression. Bobby struggled with the recent suicide of his older brother, Stuart. His condition plummeted after Christmas.

Dr. Peck asked him what presents he'd received for Christmas. Bobby told him, "A gun." This alarmed Peck because of Bobby's depression, and especially since the boy's brother had shot himself. Then came the horrifying truth: his parents gave Bobby the *same* gun Stuart had used to commit suicide. Bobby's post-Christmas depression suddenly made sense. His seemingly normal parents, with their Christmas gift, had invited him to take his life like his brother had.

Satan and demons provide the most rational explanation for unnatural evil.

In *The Brothers Karamazov,* Ivan cites terrible evil after evil to his Christian brother,

Alyosha. He speaks of Turks nailing their prisoners by the ears to fences, only to let them suffer all night and then hang them in the morning. He says,

> People talk sometimes of bestial cruelty, but that's a great injustice and insult to the beasts; a beast can never be so cruel as a man, so artistically cruel. The tiger only tears and gnaws, that's all he can do. He would never think of nailing people by the ears, even if he were able to do it. These Turks took a pleasure in torturing children, too; cutting the unborn child from the mother's womb, and tossing babies up in the air and catching them on the points of their bayonets before their mothers' eyes.[2]

While Ivan considered this an argument against God, it actually provides a compelling argument against naturalism. Ivan is right. Mere animals would never do such a thing.

Ivan speaks of apparently normal people, responsible and civil to fellow adults, who delight in torturing children:

> It is a peculiar characteristic of many people, this love of torturing children, and children only. To all other types of humanity these torturers behave mildly and benevolently, like cultivated and humane Europeans; but they are very fond of tormenting children.... It's just their defenselessness that tempts the tormentor, just the angelic confidence of the child who has no refuge and no appeal, that sets his vile blood on fire. In every man, of course, a demon lies hidden—the demon of rage, the demon of lustful heat at the screams of the tortured victim, the demon of lawlessness let off the chain.[3]

Where did the ideas for such malignant evil come from? Read the Bible and C. S. Lewis's *The Screwtape Letters* and you'll discover the answer.

Demons prompt the killing of children. The false god Molech, a demon, demanded the sacrifice of children. In the first of a dozen passages warning against this bloodthirsty demon, God says, "Do not give any of your children to be sacrificed to Molech, for you must not profane the name of your God" (Leviticus 18:21). God loves children, his tiniest image-bearers. Demons hate them. In killing them, demons lash out at God.

The atheistic worldview simply cannot account for superhuman evil. Death, yes; suffering, yes. But calculated, relentless, exhausting brutality toward the weak and innocent? The death camps? The Nazi doctors? The Killing Fields? The despicable acts of apparently "normal" people such as Bobby and Stuart's parents? Jesus gave us the answer when he said of Satan, "He was a murderer from the beginning" (John 8:44).

Three times in my life, each unexpected, I have faced the palpable presence of supernatural evil. In each case it was *distinctly* not of this world. Given the world's atrocities, should it surprise us that supernatural powers can influence human beings?

After witnessing the members of Sudan's so-called Lord's Resistance Army force children to hack their parents to death with machetes (or be killed along with them), my friend heard one man respond, "I now believe in God, for I have met the devil."

Extreme evil can wake us up to the reality of both good and evil, testifying to the invisible realities of God and Satan.
Unbelievers and believers both call certain things utterly evil, including child abuse. Some will cite such evil as evidence against God. But others will see things for what they are and come face to face with the supernatural. When evil grows awful enough, the unbeliever may abandon the sinking ship of moral relativism and its conviction that absolute evil doesn't exist.

Because the Christian worldview offers a well-grounded explanation for both human and superhuman evil, and a solid basis for moral outrage, those who find themselves morally outraged owe themselves a careful look at it.

THE INADEQUACY OF THE ATHEISTIC VIEW

In arguing against God's existence, atheists often display anger at God, but why be angry with Someone who doesn't exist?
Many atheistic books and blogs seethe with anger. Remarkably, the authors do not limit their anger to Christians. They seem most livid with God.

I don't believe in leprechauns, but I haven't dedicated my life to battling them. I suppose if I believed that people's faith in leprechauns poisoned civilization, I might get angry with members of leprechaun churches. But there's one thing I'm quite sure I wouldn't do: I would *not* get angry with leprechauns. Why not? Because I can't get angry with someone I know doesn't exist.

Though I see why atheists get irate at Christians, I don't understand why they seem so furious with God—unless, deep inside, their atheism isn't a rational denial of God as much as an attempt to retaliate against him.

Andrea Weisberger, an atheist philosopher, argues that the problem of evil makes it irrational to believe God exists. She wrote an article evaluating an online debate, explaining she refused to call God "he," and would only say "it." Then she says she will not even capitalize God, but render him (it) as "god." [4]

I find this extraordinary. Dr. Weisberger believes that God does not exist. He (it) is a mere fiction. But surely she doesn't refuse to capitalize Ebenezer Scrooge or Sherlock Holmes, both fictional characters. Or Zeus, Poseidon, or Hera, all fictional gods. I am left with the eerie feeling that demoting God to the lower case might be her way of taking grammatical revenge against a deity who has profoundly disappointed her. The fact that she doesn't bother exacting such revenge against Thor or Odin suggests that she believes he's different from those fictional gods.

How might he be different? Well, perhaps he actually exists.

Non-theists don't consistently live by the moral relativism of their naturalistic worldview; they object to many evils, particularly when done to them.

The "it all depends" morality, controversial fifty years ago when called *situational ethics,* denies the existence of any objective standards of right and wrong. What's wrong for one person, so it insists, may be right for another. One uses internal, not external, standards to judge morality.

People who say they believe in such a shifting ethic, however, constantly make moral judgments. They may not oppose abortion or euthanasia, but they decry rape, environmental exploitation, genocide, and child abuse. Why?

How ironic that the September 11, 2001, attacks came when American moral relativism had reached a peak. Some people, who on one day emphatically denied the existence of moral absolutes, on the next spoke against these absolutely hideous evils.

Fifteen years ago, while teaching a college ethics course, I read an account of a university professor who'd discovered that half of his students had received photocopies of the final exam and cheated on the test. Ironically, the professor was an outspoken advocate of moral relativism. The professor felt outraged at his students' behavior. Instead, shouldn't have he congratulated them for living out the very moral framework he had taught them?

This man, like all of us, innately recognized moral absolutes. The fact that his worldview couldn't account for them should have prompted him to seek an alternative.

Notes

1. Charles Colson, *How Now Shall We Live?* (Carol Stream, IL: Tyndale, 1999), 185.
2. Fyodor Dostoevsky, *The Brothers Karamazov* (New York: Modern Library, 1995), 265.
3. Dostoevsky, *The Brothers Karamazov*, 268.
4. David Wood, "A Reply to Andrea Weisberger, Part 5," The Problem of Evil, March 24, 2007, www.problemofevil.org/2007_03_01_archive.html.

Proposed Solutions to the Problem of Evil and Suffering: Limiting God's Attributes

15

Is God's *Limited Power* a Solution?

The book *When Bad Things Happen to Good People* and "process theology" promote the notion that God's weakness leaves him understandable and likable.

Rabbi Harold Kushner's only son, Aaron, suffered from a rare disease; aging rapidly, he died in his teens, looking like an old man.

In *When Bad Things Happen to Good People,* Kushner wrote that some things are "too difficult even for God." He said, "I can worship a God who hates suffering but cannot eliminate it, more easily than I can worship a God who chooses to make children suffer and die, for whatever exalted reason."[1] The book, published in 1981, sold over four million copies and continues to influence many today.

Our culture's eroded view of God prepared the way for the book's staggering success. People welcomed a kindhearted God who would stop anything bad from happening to us...*if only he could.* Kushner's explanation that some things lie outside God's control resembles polytheism, in which competing gods, like superheroes, have more power than mortals but lack omnipotence.

Born largely in the writings of Alfred North Whitehead (1861–1947), "process theology" provides an alternative to viewing God in the classical framework of an unchangeable, all-knowing, all-powerful, and everywhere-present deity. Instead, process theologians see God as constantly changing, learning, and evolving, right along with humanity—just at a higher level. God affects history indirectly through gentle persuasion, never by coercion. He doesn't intrude directly into human history and never violates nature's laws by performing miracles.

Process theologian David Ray Griffin writes, "Most of the problems of Christian theology, I contend, have been created by the traditional doctrine of divine omnipotence.... We must fully surrender this doctrine if we, while recognizing that genuine evil occurs, are to hold without any inconsistency or equivocation that our creator is unambiguously loving."[2]

Prior to process theology, nearly all monotheists believed in an all-powerful God. Although men and women in Scripture express confusion about why God doesn't remove their suffering, they never suggest he *cannot* remove it.

Stephen Davis summarizes process theology: "Faced with evil, God has his powerlessness as his excuse. He aims, intends, seeks, works and 'tries his best' to overcome evil: rather than blame, he deserves sympathy, even pity."[3]

It has become theologically trendy to speak of God's weakness, powerlessness, and vulnerability. Writers argue that Jesus didn't restrain himself from exercising power to liberate himself from his captors and the Cross—they believe he had no power to do so.[4]

Scripture emphatically reveals God as all-powerful.

If process theology is correct, then the writers of Scripture completely missed the boat. And if Scripture is inspired, even God doesn't know his own nature: "I am God, and there is no other; I am God, and there is none like me. I make known the end from the beginning, from ancient times, what is still to come. I say: My purpose will stand, and I will do all that I please.... What I have said, that will I bring about; what I have planned, that will I do" (Isaiah 46:9–11).

God is "the LORD strong and mighty, the LORD mighty in battle!" (Psalm 24:8). The rhetorical question "Is anything too hard for the LORD?" implies a "no" answer (see Genesis 18:14; Jeremiah 32:27).

Gabriel says to Mary, "Nothing is impossible with God" (Luke 1:37). Jesus says, "With God all things are possible" (Matthew 19:26).

God is the "Almighty" (2 Corinthians 6:18; Revelation 1:8). He is "able to do far more abundantly than all that we ask or think" (Ephesians 3:20, ESV). John the Baptist says, "God is able from these stones to raise up children for Abraham" (Matthew 3:9, ESV).

A God of limited power would raise other problems; a God who can't deliver us *from* suffering cannot deliver us *through* suffering.

When asked what allowed her to endure the concentration camp where her beloved sister died, Corrie ten Boom responded, "Not what, but *Who.*" Then she added, "The devil is strong, but his power is limited; Jesus' power is unlimited."[5]

Jesus sustained Corrie in Ravensbrück. She believed his words: "All authority in heaven and on earth has been given to me" (Matthew 28:18). Suppose instead Jesus had said to his disciples, "I have a lot of authority, but I'm only in process; human and demonic choices can thwart my limited power. But I sincerely hope things work out for you." How many of his disciples do you think would have willingly died for him?

Scripture speaks of Christ's "incomparably great power" and "mighty strength" that made possible his resurrection. Today he sits at God's right hand, "far above all rule and authority, power and dominion, and every title that can be given, not only in the present age but also in the one to come. And God placed all things under his feet and appointed him to be head over everything" (Ephesians 1:19–21).

What in these passages hints at his "limited" power?

If God lacks power, his good intentions are inadequate.

A God who has high aspirations but limited power to bring them about resembles our mothers. We love them for loving us and wanting our best, but those nice intentions go only so far in a world they can't control.

Probably you already have friends who can't control the universe. Do you really need another one, named "God"?

Those who believe in a God of limited power might respond, "It isn't that God can't do anything, just that he can't do everything." But what *can* he do? If God is doing the best he can, then he doesn't *permit* evil and suffering, rather he is *overtaken* by them, since he can't stop them. Why frustrate God with prayers he can't answer, since if he could, he already would have?

Many men might be willing to *try* to rescue my loved ones from a burning building, but I want someone who actually *can*. If God can't prevent our suffering even if he wanted to, then why should we believe he can successfully save us in the end?

Limiting God may appear to get him off the hook for life's difficulties. It might make us feel warmer toward him. But this is a god of man's invention, not the God revealed in Scripture.

An omnipotent God cannot do what is intrinsically impossible.

God can do what is humanly impossible. He can perform miracles. But he can't do anything that contradicts himself. God can't make a square circle or a round rectangle. He cannot make a rock so big that he can't lift it. That's not a limitation; it's an absurdity.

Since this omnipotent God is also omniscient and rational, he cannot contradict his own rational nature that governs the universe. The law of gravity cannot hold him down, but he cannot move a solid, unchanging object upward and downward at the same time. Such a thing would not require omnipotence, but nonsense.

Scripture tells us God cannot deny himself (2 Timothy 2:13) and he cannot lie (Hebrews 6:18). It's not lack of power that accounts for this inability, it's his nature. That's why the universe, though full of paradoxes, is not full of contradictions.

God could easily *make* anyone obey him. But he cannot compel beings, against their will, to *freely* obey him. God can invite, draw, and woo. But he cannot force us to love him, for love, by nature, cannot be forced.

Peter Kreeft wrote, "To be wholly trustable, a God must be both all-good and all-powerful. For if he is not all-good, he might deliberately do you harm, and if he is not all-powerful, he might accidentally do you harm."[6]

The misguided notion of humans "forgiving God" puts us in God's place and God in ours.

Rabbi Kushner wrote,

> Are you capable of forgiving and loving God even when you have found out that He is not perfect, even when He has let you down and disappointed you by permitting bad luck and sickness and cruelty in His world, and permitting some of those things to happen to you? Can you learn to love and forgive Him despite His limitations?[7]

In recent years I have heard even Bible-believing Christians talk about "forgiving God." But what can be forgiven, except moral evil? The one who forgives assumes the moral high ground. Telling God we forgive him accuses him of wrongdoing and implies we are qualified to judge him. This is both blasphemy and silliness.

God is the source of all good and the standard by which good is measured. We may not like what God does, but we are in no position to accuse him of wrongdoing. Every breath he gives us—we who deserve immediate and eternal death—is a gift.

We should ask for God's pardon, not his confession. He owes us no apology; we owe him many. If you're waiting for God to say he's sorry for what he's done to you, don't hold your breath.

But if, on the other hand, you want to hear him say he cares about you, and sympathizes with you for the pain you've had to endure, if you are downtrodden and brokenhearted, listen to what he says to his people:

As a father has compassion on his children,
> so the LORD has compassion on those who fear him. (Psalm 103:13)

Can a mother forget the baby at her breast
> and have no compassion on the child she has borne?
Though she may forget,
> I will not forget you!
See, I have engraved you on the palms of my hands. (Isaiah 49:15–16)

God compares himself to both father and mother, and if you are his child, he says his care for you is greater than anyone's. He loves you beyond measure and freely offers forgiveness. God is surely loving, but we dare not attempt to purchase his love at the expense of his power. His attributes are not a menu for us to choose from but are each an essential part of his eternal being.

God's omnipotence and love are not in conflict. Jeremiah 32:17–19 affirms God's love in the midst of a passage not minimizing his power but exalting it: "Ah, Sovereign LORD, you have made the heavens and the earth by your great power and outstretched arm. *Nothing is too hard for you. You show love to thousands....* O great and powerful God, whose name is the LORD Almighty, great are your purposes and mighty are your deeds."

Notes

1. Harold S. Kushner, *When Bad Things Happen to Good People* (New York: Schocken Books, 1981), 134.
2. David Ray Griffin, "Creation out of Nothing, Creation out of Chaos, and the Problem of Evil," in *Encountering Evil,* ed. Stephen T. Davis, (Louisville, KY: Westminster John Knox, 2001), 96.
3. Stephen T. Davis, "God the Mad Scientist: Process Theology on God and Evil," *Themelios* 5, no. 1 (1979): http://s3.amazonaws.com/tgc-documents/journal-issues/5.1_Davis.pdf.
4. See, for example, John D. Caputo, *The Weakness of God* (Bloomington: Indiana University Press, 2006), 44.
5. Corrie ten Boom interview with Pat Robertson on 700 Club, 1974. (www.youtube.com/watch?v=6VZYFDCS3Gw&NR=1).
6. Peter Kreeft, *Making Sense Out of Suffering* (Ann Arbor, MI: Servant Books, 1986), 39.
7. Kushner, *When Bad Things Happen to Good People,* 148.

16

Is God's *Limited Knowledge* a Solution?

Most proposed solutions to the problem of evil and suffering have been around for a long time; "open theism" is recent.

Open theists believe that God does not and cannot know in advance the future choices that his free creatures will make. A leading proponent of open theism, Gregory Boyd, writes, "The open view, I submit, allows us to say consistently, in unequivocal terms, that the ultimate source of all evil is found in the will of free agents rather than in God."[1] Since Boyd includes suffering in the category of "all evil," he believes God never sends us suffering.

A loving God took a calculated risk, open theists suggest, but had he known the horrible things that would occur—the rapes and killings and tortures and abuse—he might never have created this world as he did. Hence, proponents of open theism argue, God cannot be held responsible for his creatures' evil, since he could not foresee it.

Years ago when I first read an open theist's article, it surprised me, but it didn't deeply concern me, because I thought this view would never gain traction among evangelical Christians. How wrong I was! Both in research and in conversations with suffering people, I've discovered that open theism has become surprisingly influential—and its popularity continues to rise.

It is difficult to oppose a doctrine that suffering brothers and sisters, including some of my friends, find comforting. I do not question the integrity of those who embrace this viewpoint. Still, I must try to explain why I reject it and why this question is so important.

Open theists argue that our free choices preclude God's knowledge of future circumstances.
Boyd writes,

In one correspondence my father asked me why God would allow Adolf Hitler to be born if he foreknew that this man would massacre millions of Jews. It was a very good question. The only response I could offer then, and the only response I continue to offer now, is that this was not foreknown as a certainty at the time God created Hitler.[2]

While God can know in advance what *he* has planned to do, open theists claim he cannot know what his free *creatures* will choose to do. They believe this distances God from evil human choices and the consequent suffering they bring. Clark Pinnock said, "The future is really open and *not available to exhaustive foreknowledge even on the part of God.* It is plain that the biblical doctrine of creaturely freedom requires us to reconsider the conventional view of the omniscience of God"[3] (italics added).

Process theology has long taught that God grows in knowledge, learning more, becoming more knowledgeable as events unfold. Events can surprise him. While Pinnock denies he is advocating it, he admits, "I am sympathetic with a number of motifs in process theism." He claims his view harmonizes with Scripture's portrayal of God.[4]

Open theism stands in contrast to the biblical and historical teaching that God knows absolutely everything.

God is *"perfect in knowledge"* (Job 37:16). He *"knows everything"* (1 John 3:20). "He determines the number of the stars and calls them each by name" (Psalm 147:4). That's countless trillions of stars, each named by God.

Jesus says, "Your Father knows what you need before you ask him," and, "Even the very hairs of your head are all numbered" (Matthew 6:8; 10:30). Even of plentiful sparrows, he says, "Not one of them is forgotten by God" (Luke 12:6).

"Yes," an open theist will say, "I believe the passages that teach God's vast knowledge. But while he knows everything that *can* be known, future choices of his free creatures *can't* be known."

What does Scripture tell us?

David says, "O LORD, you have searched me and known me! You know when I sit down and when I rise up; you discern my thoughts from afar.... *Even before a word is on my tongue,* lo, O LORD, you know it altogether" (Psalm 139:1–2, 4, ESV). From eternity past, God knew everything that will happen on every day of our lives: "Your eyes saw my unformed substance; in your book were written, every one of them, the days that were formed for me, when as yet there was none of them" (Psalm 139:16, ESV). God knows all the choices, free or not, we will ever make and all the consequences they will ever produce.

When David asked God questions about the future, God gave him detailed answers about what Saul would do, revealing that the men of Keilah would surrender to him (see 1 Samuel 23:11–13). Saul and these men would make specific choices, and God knew them in advance.

God doesn't only know what choices his creatures will make, but what would have happened (what philosophers call *middle knowledge*) if his creatures made different choices. God reveals to Elisha *what would have happened* if King Joash had struck the ground five or six times with arrows (see 2 Kings 13:19). To Korazin and Bethsaida Jesus states, "If the miracles that were performed in you had been performed in Tyre and Sidon, they *would have* repented long ago" (Matthew 11:21).

The charge that they don't really believe in God's omniscience offends open theists. Nevertheless, Christians throughout church history have believed that God's omniscience encompasses *all* knowledge—past, present, *and* future. Both Arminian and Calvinist theologians have consistently taught this. A. H. Strong's definition of omniscience is typical: "God's perfect and eternal knowledge of all things which are objects of knowledge, whether they be actual or possible, past, present, or future."[5] A. W. Tozer wrote that God "knows instantly and with a fullness of perfection that includes every possible item of knowledge concerning everything that exists or could have existed anywhere in the universe at any time in the past or that may exist in the centuries or ages yet unborn."[6]

Bruce Ware points out, "The open view has not been advocated by any portion or branch of the Orthodox, Roman Catholic, or Protestant church throughout history."[7]

For open theists to insist on using the term *omniscience* while departing from its historical, not to mention logical, meaning is unfortunate and misleading.

Open theists claim God knows all possible future events, but not the actual ones that will result from human and demonic choices.

If that's true, given the number of free beings and the quantity of daily choices they make, this leaves countless *billions* of choices, and events coming from those choices, that God cannot know with certainty since they haven't yet happened. If people make meaningful choices to turn to Christ, as open theists believe, and God doesn't know such choices in advance, then how could their names be "written in the book of life from the creation of the world"? (Revelation

17:8). (Open theism contradicts both the Calvinist perspective of God's elective or causative foreknowledge *and* the Arminian perspective of his simple or non-causative foreknowledge.)

How much does it help God to know future possibilities, but not future actualities? "By analogy, if one is working on a mathematics problem, how will it help to know all the *possible* answers that might be given—*all* of which are wrong, *save one*—yet not know which answer, of that infinite list of possible answers, is the correct answer?"[8]

Open theists believe that a partially unaware God brings greater comfort than a God who knows everything that's coming.

In *Is God to Blame?* Boyd calls the traditional definition of God's omniscience both misguided and harmful.[9] He tells the heartbreaking story of a woman who came to him for pastoral counsel, wondering why God had taken her only child, who at birth strangled on her umbilical cord.

> I asked, "Does that seem like something a loving God would do? Can you
> picture Jesus doing that to someone?" Melanie was completely stunned by
> my reply.... I felt such grief for the tormented state her theology had put
> her in.[10]

Boyd told Melanie that God didn't know in advance that her baby would die. He writes,

> We have no reason to assume God put Melanie and her husband through
> this tragic ordeal. Rather, we have every reason to assume God was and is
> at work to deliver Melanie and her husband from their ordeal.... Does
> Melanie see the hand of God at work in the death of her child, or does she
> interpret it in some other fashion? It all depends on her picture of God. It
> is most biblical and most helpful not to see God involved in the evils in
> this world but to interpret it in some other fashion.[11]

The key to Melanie's spiritual health, Boyd believes, lay in accepting that her child's death remained beyond God's knowledge and therefore was not part of his plan.

If Boyd is right and God has knowledge only of the past and present, not contingent future choices and events, then God wouldn't know the baby was going to suffocate until it was actually happening. But how does that solve the problem? Once God knew, *why didn't he intervene?*

Open theists believe that God's limited knowledge showcases his unlimited power.

In another book Boyd tells of a different woman, Suzanne, who asked God to provide a husband with whom she could serve on the mission field. She met a man at college and sensed God's leading to marry him. Tragically, he turned out to be an unrepentant adulterer. After she became pregnant, he left her to raise the child herself. Boyd recounts Suzanne's bitterness toward God and says,

> I suggested to her that God felt as much regret over the confirmation he had given Suzanne as he did about his decision to make Saul king of Israel.... Not that it was a bad decision—at the time her ex-husband was a good man with a godly character. The prospects that he and Suzanne would have a happy marriage and fruitful ministry were, at the time, very good. Indeed, I strongly suspect that he had influenced Suzanne and her ex-husband toward this college with their marriage in mind.

The woman found comfort in Boyd's viewpoint. He concludes, "By framing the ordeal within the context of an open future, Suzanne was able to understand the tragedy of her life in a new way. She didn't have to abandon all confidence in her ability to hear God and didn't have to accept that somehow God intended this ordeal 'for her own good.' Her faith in God's character and her love toward God were eventually restored and she was finally able to move on with her life."[12]

But why should it help Suzanne to believe she could still hear God and sense his leading? God might have a well-meaning prediction of a happy future, only to be proven wrong *again*. Shouldn't she think, *Since God directed my paths toward the wrong man the last time, how can I now lean on his understanding, instead of mine, in view of his limited knowledge? He already led me into a terrible marriage; who's to say he won't lead me somewhere worse the next time?*

Scripture calls upon Suzanne to trust God. Isn't part of God's trustworthiness based on his *total,* not partial, knowledge of the future?

Boyd dismisses as naive the notion "that somehow God intended this ordeal 'for her own good.'" But is it really cruel of God to permit evil and intend it for our good, as he did with Joseph? Romans 8:28 suggests that God *does* intend life's ordeals for our good—but there's a difference between *immediate* good and *ultimate* good. Seeing that difference requires faith.

The God of historic orthodox Christianity is a God who cares deeply about us, but also has a purpose and plan even for the bad things we encounter. Open theism interprets this viewpoint as cruel and tries to persuade us we can love God more because he doesn't have a purpose and a plan in our suffering. God may seem more approachable and lovable, but at what expense? His greatness.

Believing in God's limited future knowledge does *not* solve the problem of God withholding justice or allowing evil in the present.

Open theism sacrifices God's future knowledge, but what does it gain in exchange? Whether God has known a child would die from eternity past, or has figured it out only in the last two minutes, either way, he still allows the child's death when he could have prevented it.

Boyd's claim that God brought Hitler into the world only because he didn't know Hitler would commit great evils does not solve the problem. Why not? Because God did not intervene when he *knew* Hitler was doing evil things. Discerning human beings predicted the harm Hitler would do if left unhindered, so why couldn't God see it coming?

Just by eavesdropping on Hitler's private conversations with his henchmen, God could have known of the coming Holocaust. So if God could have stopped Hitler from murdering the Jews, why didn't he? A car accident, a heart attack, or a successful assassination attempt all could have fixed the problem and saved millions of lives. Wouldn't a God with limited knowledge of the future bear the same responsibility for failing to restrain the adult Hitler, as a God with complete foreknowledge would have for bringing the infant Hitler into the world?

Open theists suppose we should find comfort in believing God has not ordained our suffering from eternity past. But open theism's answer to the problem of evil is an illusion. The only way to fully defend God's goodness would be to believe that God not only lacks knowledge of the future, but also of the present. I find it easier to trust a God who has known all along and planned how he will use the tragedy for his glory and our good, than one who just found out about it but chose not to stop it anyway.

Open theism is not only biblically wrong; it's a shallow answer to the problem of evil.

Open theism portrays God as making mistakes.

While open theists try to avoid stating that God can make mistakes, John Sanders candidly asserts that Scripture "does leave open the possibility that God might be 'mistaken' about some points." He acknowledges, "The notion that God could be dismayed or wrong about anything may not sit well with some people."

I agree; I am one of them. (The question is whether it sits well with God.)

Sanders then offers some qualifications about the meaning of the word *mistake* and says, "Even if we affirm that God is sometimes 'mistaken' in the sense that God believes that something would happen when, in fact, it does not come about, there is a question as to how often this happens. The biblical record gives a few occasions, but we are in no position to judge just how many times this occurs with God."[13]

Apparently, while God sometimes make mistakes, we can't know how often. I don't find that the least bit comforting. Do you?

While people have found comfort in open theism, I see no logical basis for their comfort.

Compare Melanie's and Suzanne's situations from two perspectives. In the traditional view, God knew from eternity past what would happen, and allowed it or ordained it (either theological perspective works), and did so with a good purpose informed by his foreknowledge of all its consequences. In the open view, God knew not in advance, but only *at the time* as it was unfolding, yet he still permitted it. He had the power to stop it but chose not to. He had no purpose and plan in it, and still cannot know all that will come from it.

What is there to feel better about in the open view? That God has known of the evil and suffering a shorter time? It seems to me that in addition to contradicting Scripture, this viewpoint gives us much to feel *worse* about.

We might compare the God of the Bible to a gifted surgeon who has studied a patient's case in advance and has planned a specific procedure to accomplish a particular purpose. He operates with a detailed foreknowledge of his patient's condition.

The God of open theism is more like an emergency room physician, also highly knowledgeable and skilled, but because he doesn't know his patient's condition when that patient gets wheeled in the door, the doctor must improvise—sometimes successfully, sometimes not.

Any surgeon will testify that surgeries planned and prepared for in advance have a higher success rate than emergency surgeries done on the fly. Which physician would give you greater comfort?

Some open theists claim that when God created the world, he didn't know evil would follow. But this shrinks the gospel by reducing it to God's Plan B. The unfolding drama of redemption is seen not as God's best plan, just the best he could do once creatures derailed his original plan.

To suggest that if God had known in advance the evils and suffering of this world he might not have created it is to say that an uncreated world would have been better than the world in which Christ did his redemptive work. Such a viewpoint is utterly foreign to Scripture. The gospel of redemption was not an afterthought; it was an all-knowing God's plan from the beginning.

Because God knows the whole future, he can be good while allowing pain that a good human being would try to stop.

John Stuart Mill argued that God should live under the same moral expectations he places on us; if it is wrong for us not to save the innocent, then it is also wrong for God. Mill's statement sounds rational until we think through its implications.

God knows everything, including every contingency, and he knows what is ultimately best in ways we cannot. God can see ultimate purposes and plans that we can't. He can know it is better for someone to die now rather than later: "The righteous perish, and no one ponders it in his heart; devout men are taken away, and no one understands that the righteous are taken away to be spared from evil" (Isaiah 57:1).

We have no way of knowing, for instance, whether a disability might be used to cultivate personal qualities that would more profoundly honor God and bring the person greater eternal reward in Heaven.

Because God knows all things in the past, present, *and* future, God is uniquely qualified to know when to ordain or permit evil and suffering and when not to.

God's foreknowledge of future events does not necessarily *cause* those events.

Clark Pinnock states, "If God now knows that tomorrow you will select A and not B, then your belief that you will be making a genuine choice is mistaken.... God can surmise what you will do next Friday, but cannot know it for certain because you have not done it yet."[14]

Open theists claim that human freedom and divine omniscience are mutually exclusive. If God knows you will drink a white chocolate mocha at 3:00 p.m. tomorrow, then you are not free to abstain from drinking that mocha. You can't make any other choice, because if you did, then God would be wrong. This argument may sound plausible—but is it? (Though foreknowledge sometimes has a deeper theological meaning involving God ordaining or predestining doctrines Scripture also affirms, I am here referring to God's foreknowledge only in the sense of prescience, his simple knowledge of an event before it occurs.)

Of course, God causes many things he knows about, but he can also know about something without causing it. He knew in advance of Satan's fall and Adam and Eve's sin, but he did not cause it, for God neither tempts people to evil nor causes them to commit evil (see James 1:13). Yes, he could have kept them from sinning, and yes, he is accomplishing an ultimate plan of redemption that will glorify him through his conquest of sin and death. But knowledge is not the same as causation.

Suppose I travel to the future and see a certain quarterback throw the winning touchdown pass with two seconds left on the clock. Would my knowledge mean that this quarterback will not freely choose to throw that pass? No. What I know is that he will choose to throw that pass. My knowledge doesn't *cause* anything—it is a simple awareness of the quarterback's future choice. He would make the same choice whether I knew about it or not. Freedom to choose is not incompatible with God knowing our choices in advance.

God sees the future with the same fixed certainty that we see the past. (That's why Jesus is called the Lamb slain from before the foundation of the world, not merely the Lamb God *knew* would be slain.)[15]

Some theologians believe God knows future events because he has ordained that they will happen, through the willing choices of his creatures. Others affirm that God knows the future even though his creatures' willing choices are not all part of his plan. In either case, what God knows will happen "must" happen because God is never wrong, *not* because people cannot make meaningful choices.

Open theism credits Satan with too much power and God with too little.
In *Satan and the Problem of Evil,* Boyd says, "Where free agents are involved, some outcomes cannot be guaranteed.... The God of the Bible is not a God who has or needs 'inside information' on what is going to transpire."[16]

But if human and demonic free agents can choose differently than what God supposes they will, couldn't they derail God's promise to work "all things" together for the good of those who love him (see Romans 8:28)? How can he make such a promise if he did not know what "all things" would entail?

Open theists offer many examples of bad things God supposedly did not anticipate. How can God keep all his promises if so much remains uncertain in his mind? What promises of Scripture would God now want to edit or retract? If he could rewrite Romans 8:28 now that he's seen the Holocaust, how would it read?

God could still promise, "I will *try* to make everything work together for your good." He might even have a high success rate. But Romans 8:28 isn't about God *trying*, it's about God actually working together *all* things for our good.

The warfare against demonic powers depicted in Scripture is very real but does not put God's power or knowledge in doubt.

Boyd believes that spiritual warfare implies that a battle's outcome must remain in doubt. And Scripture's use of warfare terminology does indeed indicate that rebels can resist and violate God's will. But though angels can fight God, they cannot overpower him:

> And there was war in heaven. Michael and his angels fought against the dragon, and the dragon and his angels fought back. But he was not strong enough, and they lost their place in heaven. The great dragon was hurled down—that ancient serpent called the devil, or Satan, who leads the whole world astray. He was hurled to the earth, and his angels with him. (Revelation 12:7–9)

This passage should keep us from three errors. First, we shouldn't believe that everything that happens pleases God. What ruler is gratified by his beloved subjects turning against him?

Second, we should never believe that the conflict between good and evil is only figurative, not real. This passage vividly shows its reality—Michael and his angels fight in a great battle, with much at stake.

Third, the passage should keep us from believing that anyone can thwart God's *ultimate* plan. The rebellion is real, the warfare is real—but Satan "was not strong enough" to stay in Heaven. God accomplished his will by casting out the devil.

We, too, war against these evil beings: "For our struggle is not against flesh and blood, but against the rulers, against the authorities, against the powers of this dark world and against the spiritual forces of evil in the heavenly realms" (Ephesians 6:12). We should take up our armor yet not fear the future, for the outcome is certain: "The reason the Son of God appeared was to destroy the devil's work" (1 John 3:8).

Job recognized that regardless of Satan's role, God remained in charge.
When everything Job had, including his children, was taken from him, he said, "The LORD gave and the LORD has taken away; blessed be the name of the LORD'" (Job 1:21). Under divine inspiration, the writer comments, "In all this Job did not sin or charge God with wrong" (verse 22, ESV).

Satan did appalling things, but *Job saw them as coming from God's hand.* Job did not say, "The LORD gave and Satan has taken away."

Open theists argue, as in Boyd's example of Melanie whose child died at birth, that we shouldn't view God as taking away our loved ones in death. Yet after he'd lost ten children, Job said God *had* taken them away—and still he blessed God's name. So the psalmist can say, "Precious in the sight of the LORD is the death of his saints" (Psalm 116:15).

Contrary to the claims of open theism, God does not change his mind or learn and grow in understanding.
Open theists cite 1 Samuel 15:11 to prove that God changes his mind. God says, "I regret that I have made Saul king, for he has turned back from following me" (ESV). The word translated "I regret" is also rendered "I am grieved" (NIV) and "I am sorry" (NLT). Similarly, verse 35 tells us again, "And the LORD regretted that he had made Saul king over Israel" (ESV).

Open theists argue that when God says he "regrets" something, he implies that he didn't know what would happen. After gaining further knowledge, God changes his mind. God acted on the best knowledge he had at the time, but the bottom line is, regardless of the terminology used, God made a mistake.

Throughout history Christians have understood that in 1 Samuel 15 (and similar passages), God accommodates his language so that we can better understand him. To say he "regrets" making Saul king is to communicate powerfully that he grieves over sin. God is *not* saying, "If only I had known then what I've learned since…" (Even among finite beings, a mother can feel sorrow about disciplining her child, still knowing she'd repeat her actions in a similar situation.)

Remarkably, between the two verses about God "regretting" making Saul king, another verse warns us against wrong conclusions about God: "The Glory of Israel will not lie or have regret, for *he is not a man, that he should have regret*" (verse 29, ESV).

Here we find an emphatic statement that God does *not* regret as humans do. We couldn't ask for a clearer interpretive guideline. Knowing in advance our tendency to misunderstand, God sovereignly places this clarification in the immediate context, using the same Hebrew word from verses 11 and 35, warning us *not* to conclude *exactly* what open theists do conclude: that God regrets in the same way humans do.

On the contrary, he directly tells his people, "I the LORD do not change" (Malachi 3:6). He is a God "who does not change like shifting shadows" (James 1:17). Jesus Christ, the very "image of God" (1 Corinthians 4:4), "is the same yesterday and today and tomorrow" (Hebrews 13:8)—and doesn't that seem to rule out constant change, whether in knowledge or anything else?

I agree with Bruce Ware, who argues that the proper interpretation of 1 Samuel 15 about God "regretting" is this: God never regrets in the strong and ultimate sense, but he does regret in a weaker and more immediate sense.[17] He is not uncaring (he does regret), but he remains unchanging (he does not regret).

How do we explain passages such as God promising judgment on Nineveh (see Jonah 3:4), then deciding to withhold judgment when the Ninevites repent (see verse 10)? Wayne Grudem says, "These instances should all be understood as true expressions of God's *present* attitude or intention *with respect to the situation as it exists at that moment.* If the situation changes, then of course God's attitude or expression of intention will also change."[18]

Such change does not indicate an inconsistency in God's being; he remains true to his unchanging nature by responding to repentance differently than he responds to evil.

God knows the end from the beginning; if he didn't, he wouldn't be God.

Fulfilled biblical prophecies are not good guesses on God's part but proof that God knows the future in detail. Isaiah 40–45 demonstrates that false gods make faulty predictions. Why? Because false gods are either human projections or demons, and therefore finite. Demons and false prophets may be able to guess certain aspects of the future, but they err on some points because finite beings can't know everything about the future.

In contrast, the Creator says, "I am God, and there is none like me. I make known the end from the beginning, from ancient times, what is still to come. I say: My purpose will stand, and I will do all that I please" (Isaiah 46:9–10). God can make known the end from the beginning only because he *knows* the end from the beginning.

When God said through the prophets that Messiah would be born in a certain place and be crucified between two evildoers, he was not speculating but stating what he has always known. When he prophesied that Judas would betray Jesus for thirty pieces of silver and throw the money back to the priests, he knew exactly what choices people would make (see Zechariah 11:13; compare Matthew 27:3–7).

That's why God can say, "If what a prophet proclaims in the name of the LORD does not take place or come true, that is a message the LORD has not spoken" (Deuteronomy 18:22). God absolutely *knows* the future. In contrast to the god of open theism, God doesn't merely predict the future with a high degree of accuracy; he sees it all in advance and cannot make a mistake.

Jesus told Peter that before the rooster crowed, he would deny Jesus three times (see John 13:38). A specific rooster at a specific place will crow at a specific time, after Peter (at that same place and time) will deny Christ not just twice, not four times, but *three* times.

Earlier, Jesus had said to Peter, "Simon, Simon, behold, Satan demanded to have you, that he might sift you like wheat, but I have prayed for you that your faith may not fail. And *when* you have turned again, strengthen your brothers" (Luke 22:31–32, ESV).

Notice that Jesus knew Peter's future choices, both that he would turn away from him *and* turn back to him. If he knew those details about Peter's future choices—not only denials and repenting, but the number of denials and the place and time down to when a particular rooster would crow—why wouldn't he know the details about all our future choices?

Some argue that Jesus knew Peter well enough to accurately predict what he would do. But if prophecies about human free choices can never be certain even to God, was Christ merely making lucky guesses about the details? Might Peter have chosen differently and Christ have been proven wrong? If so, what else might Christ have been wrong about?

Those who believe that God doesn't know about billions of future choices and the events that flow out of those choices must simply hope for the best. Those who believe in a God who knows "the end from the beginning" (Isaiah 46:10), however, can relax because even though *they* don't know what lies ahead, their sovereign God does.

We can find great assurance in believing God knows the future and that he works even evil and suffering together for our good.
Twenty years ago, on nine occasions I participated in peaceful, nonviolent civil disobedience in what was (particularly in my home state of Oregon) an extremely unpopular cause—speaking up for the civil rights of unborn children. I briefly

went to jail, and abortion clinics brought lawsuits against me and others. It seemed possible that if the lawsuits succeeded, the abortion clinics might take away our house and a good part of our monthly income.

In the several years we found ourselves in the middle of this stressful situation, Nanci and I would talk with our daughters—eight and ten when the legal problems began, and ten and twelve when they culminated—assuring them that God remained in control, that he knew everything that would happen, and that we could trust him to use it for good. True, I was no longer able to serve as a pastor or make more than minimum wage, but God would take care of us.

Our daughters believed this and prayed with a kind of trust in God that still brings tears to my eyes. One night when an abortion clinic tried to drop us from a lawsuit (they required our permission to do so, but our agreement would have appeared to help their case), we asked our daughters, "What do you think God wants us to do?" Though they understood their answer might mean losing our house and leaving the private school they loved, my twelve-year-old daughter said, as her sister and my wife nodded agreement, "Daddy, if the abortion clinic doesn't want you there, I think God does."

We prayed together again; I called our attorney and spent the next month in court in one of the most difficult experiences of our lives. While there were no actual damages to the clinics except the money lost for abortions prevented, the jury found our group liable for $8.2 million in punitive damages.

My family faced this situation with the firm belief that God is all-knowing, all-powerful, and all-loving, and that no matter what happened, he would work things out for our ultimate good. That is exactly what he did. The fact that we lost the case was irrelevant. We're fortunate not to have to wait for eternity to see how God worked it for good. We've already seen it in countless ways, though no doubt we'll learn more when we're with him.

Now suppose we had believed in open theism. Our conversations with our children would have gone in a remarkably different way: "Girls, we don't know how this lawsuit is going to turn out. We don't know if we'll lose our house. We don't know if you'll be able to continue in school. *And God doesn't know either.* God wishes the best for us and he'll do what he can to help, but he doesn't have a definite purpose or plan in this and there's no assurance that this will work out for our good. So don't blame him if the choices of demons, abortion clinic owners, a judge, or a jury ruin our lives. God must respect their free will."

I cannot express how radically different our children's prayers, lives, and peace of mind—as well as our own—would have been, had we believed that. Instead, we believed what Scripture teaches, and God helped us trust him and his purpose to work for our ultimate good, despite the evil intentions of demons and people. I am eternally grateful for that.

God, because of his comprehensive knowledge of the future, can bring eternal value out of evil and suffering.

God saw what would happen in a world of human beings, all able to choose. He saw the horrors that would come with the Fall and millennia of evil and suffering. But he also saw, from the very beginning, exactly how the ultimate good of manifesting his love and revealing the wonders of his grace would bring an eternal richness to the universe. He does not *hope* this to be the case. He *knows* this to be the case.

We may imagine that, on balance, it's not a fair trade. We feel less happy than we'd like to. But God looked ahead at the benefits and saw they outweighed the costs, even the incalculable cost to his Son on the cross.

If God had to do it all over again—knowing what he knows and has always known—he would create the same world and permit the same evils. And if the world's suffering (and his own) is worth it to God, then in the end without end, surely it will be worth it to us too.

Attempts at limiting God's omniscience or other attributes have far-reaching consequences.

I don't believe in picking fights about secondary doctrinal issues. But I'm convinced there's a great deal at stake in the issue of open theism. God does not need us to rescue him from the problem of evil, and particularly not at such great cost.

Justin Taylor wrote, "Open theism is not just another intramural squabble among evangelicals. It is not a debate about second-order doctrines, minutiae, or peripheral matters. Rather, it is a debate about God and the central features of the Christian faith."[19]

I have noticed a domino effect in books that promote open theism. When someone diminishes or topples one of God's attributes, other attributes inevitably start to fall. Deny God's omniscience, and you deny his immutability. In the cases of Melanie and Suzanne, God's *lack of knowledge* produced a *lack of power* to lovingly protect them. Once we begin to dismantle God's attributes, the God we wish to relate to ceases to be the only true God, revealed in Scripture. This cannot please him.

"You thought I was altogether like you," God says in Psalm 50:21. "But I will rebuke you and accuse you to your face."

D. A. Carson says open theism "so redefines the God of the Bible and of theology that we wind up with a quite different God." Wayne Grudem warns that open theism "ultimately portrays a different God than the God of the Bible."[20]

If we feel free, no matter how well intentioned, to abandon the doctrine of God's omniscience as presented in Scripture and reaffirmed by councils and creeds, then what other divine attributes will we redefine next? Is God *really* everywhere present, or are some places beyond his reach? Is he absolutely holy and just, or only 98 percent of the time? Whatever meager gains we suppose our revisions bring us, the losses pile up to Heaven.

Fortunately, God will always remain who he is. The question is, as we try to modify him, what will become of us?

Notes

1. Gregory A. Boyd, *God of the Possible* (Grand Rapids, MI: Baker Book House, 2000), 98.
2. Boyd, *God of the Possible*, 98.
3. Clark Pinnock, "God Limits His Knowledge," in *Predestination and Free Will*, eds. David Basinger and Randall Basinger (Downers Grove, IL: InterVarsity, 1986), 150.
4. Pinnock, "God Limits His Knowledge," 147.
5. Augustus Hopkins Strong, *Outlines of Systematic Theology*, (American Baptist Publication Society, 1908), 77.
6. A. W. Tozer, *The Knowledge of the Holy* (San Francisco: HarperOne, 1992), 87.
7. Bruce Ware, *Their God Is Too Small* (Wheaton, IL: Good News, 2003), 16.
8. Bruce Ware, "The Gospel of Christ," in *Beyond the Bounds*, ed. John Piper, Justin Taylor, and Paul Kjoss Helseth (Wheaton, IL: Good News, 2003), 312–13.
9. Gregory A. Boyd, *Is God to Blame?* (Downers Grove, IL: InterVarsity, 2003), 11.
10. Boyd, *Is God to Blame?* 13.
11. Boyd, *Is God to Blame?* 16, 21.
12. Boyd, *God of the Possible*, 105–6.
13. John Sanders, *The God Who Risks* (Downers Grove, IL: InterVarsity 1998), 132–33.
14. Pinnock, "God Limits His Knowledge," 156–57.
15. Revelation 13:8 may be speaking instead of names written in the book of life before the world's foundation; if so, the notion of the absolute certainty of Christ's eventual redemptive work is still apparent in passages such as Acts 2:23; 4:27–28; 1 Peter 1:20.

16. Gregory A. Boyd, *Satan and the Problem of Evil* (Downers Grove, IL: InterVarsity, 2001), 112, 115.

17. Ware, *Their God Is Too Small,* 32–34.

18. Wayne Grudem, *Systematic Theology* (Grand Rapids, MI: Zondervan, 1994), 164.

19. Justin Taylor, introduction to *Beyond the Bounds,* 13.

20. Grudem, quoted in *Beyond the Bounds,* 13.

17

Is God's *Limited* Goodness a Solution?

John K. Roth writes what he calls a "theodicy of protest" against God. In his own words he "puts God on trial, and in that process the issue of God's wasteful complicity in evil takes center stage.... Human repentance will have to be matched by God's." He argues, "Such a wasteful God cannot be totally benevolent. History itself is God's indictment."[1]

Roth continues, "I affirm that God is good, but not perfectly good, and that both God and humanity could be better.... The amount, degree, intensity of evil are too great to justify fully God's creation of the world we inhabit.... If God has a 'plan,' it is wanting."[2]

If evil lurked within God—if he were not entirely good—then this could explain why God would not only permit evil, but actually commit it. If he were partly good and partly evil, like a flawed human, his mixture of goodness and evil could explain the world's partial goodness and evil. God would then be guilty of Roth's charges.

Satan attacks us by bringing us to doubt God's goodness. The statement "God is not perfectly good" comes from the pit of Hell. It is an accusation the Bible firmly rejects.

Larry Crabb writes, "Doubt of God's *goodness* creates the terror of aloneness in an unreliable world, which leads to rage against God for doing so little to protect us from suffering." He states, "When I am not convinced that God is good, I will quietly—but with tight-lipped resolve—take over responsibility for my own well-being."[3]

God is good.
God is the Greatest Good and is the source of all lesser goods: "Every good and perfect gift is from above, coming down from the Father" (James 1:17). Wayne Grudem says, "The goodness of God means that God is the final standard of good, and that all that God is and does is worthy of approval."[4]

Scripture contains many direct affirmations of God's goodness, such as:

Good and upright is the LORD;
.   therefore he instructs sinners in his ways. (Psalm 25:8)

You are good, and what you do is good;
teach me your decrees. (Psalm 119:68)

Give thanks to the LORD Almighty,
for the LORD is good;
his love endures forever. (Jeremiah 33:11)

The LORD is good,
a refuge in times of trouble.
He cares for those who trust in him. (Nahum 1:7)

God extends his goodness to his people.

God's goodness entails a number of his other attributes. Grudem says, "God's mercy is his goodness toward those in distress, his grace is his goodness toward those who deserve only punishment, and his patience is his goodness toward those who continue to sin over a period of time."[5]

God's goodness is linked to his love: "Surely goodness and love will follow me all the days of my life, and I will dwell in the house of the LORD forever" (Psalm 23:6). His goodness also connects with his holiness: "We are filled with the good things of your house, of your holy temple" (Psalm 65:4). "How great is your goodness, which you have stored up for those who fear you, which you bestow in the sight of men on those who take refuge in you" (Psalm 31:19). God has stored up his goodness for those who fear him. That means in the future he plans to bestow upon us a storehouse full of goodness.

God manifests his goodness to all people.

God does not restrict his goodness to believers only. He is good to all his creatures: "The LORD is good to all; he has compassion on all he has made" (Psalm 145:9); "He has shown kindness by giving you rain from heaven and crops in their seasons; he provides you with plenty of food and fills your hearts with joy" (Acts 14:17; see also Matthew 5:45).

God grants his goodness to humanity at large, manifested in both nature and culture, in such good things as animals, forests, rivers, music, art, and sports.

God's goodness is absolute; there is no evil in him.

Henri Blocher writes, "Evil is defined by its opposition to God and its utter dissimilarity to him; God shows no compliance whatsoever with evil."[6]

"Holy, holy, holy is the Lord God Almighty" (Revelation 4:8). God's holiness speaks of his transcendent otherness, which includes his absolute moral purity.[7]

The prophet says to God, "Your eyes are too pure to look on evil; you cannot tolerate wrong" (Habakkuk 1:13).

"Why do you ask me about what is good?" Jesus asked a rich young man. "There is only One [God] who is good" (Matthew 19:17).

God has no evil within him and will never change to accommodate evil: "When tempted, no one should say, 'God is tempting me.' For God cannot be tempted by evil, nor does he tempt anyone.... The Father of the heavenly lights...does not change like shifting shadows" (James 1:13, 17).

We define goodness from our finite and fallen perspective, then criticize God for failing to be good in our eyes.

A good man does not knowingly allow his neighbor to beat his child. He intervenes. If he had all power, he would not only stop the man from beating the child, he would not allow him to begin beating the child in the first place. Such an appraisal is completely apt regarding humans.

Then we say, "If God allows it, then he must not be good; I'm better than God, or there is no God at all." But we err in judging God by our standards.

Imagine your dog saying, "If *I* were my master, I would never discipline me or give me a shot or a big pill; I would let myself run free in the neighborhood and take steaks from any barbecue I find. Since he does not do this, my master must not be good." The master, who claims to be a good dog owner, *never bases his claim on the dog's standards,* but on his own. We can envision a dog recognizing his master as good when he feeds and walks him, but questioning his goodness when he doesn't let him have a Hershey bar. He might even write a book *(Dog's Problem?)* or go on the lecture circuit telling everyone why his master isn't good.

Applying human standards to God is like dogs applying canine standards to us. Our conclusions will invariably come up short.

The existence of evil does not contradict God's goodness, since God can ultimately use evil to bring about a greater good.

Many college philosophy classes have discussed the problem of evil as framed by J. L. Mackie. He maintained that belief in a good and all-powerful God is logically contradictory and therefore untrue. Mackie wrote,

God is omnipotent; God is wholly good; yet evil exists. There seems to be some contradiction between these three propositions so that if any two of them were true the third would be false. But at the same time all three are essential parts of most theological positions; the theologian, it seems at once, must adhere and cannot consistently adhere to all three.[8]

In response to Mackie's argument, Alvin Plantinga affirmed not just three, but *six* tenets of biblical Christianity: God exists; he is omnipotent; he is omniscient; he is omnibenevolent; he created the world; and the world now contains evil. He then laid out the challenge: "What exactly is the explicit contradiction between these proposals?" After all, couldn't God create human beings with a free will that allowed them to do evil?

Mackie suggested two more premises that he thought would at least make theism implausible: "Good is opposed to evil in such a way that a being who is wholly good eliminates evil as far as he can" and "There are no limits to what an omnipotent being can do."[9] Now Mackie thought the contradiction was clear.

But this logic has serious problems. First, even an omnipotent God cannot grant free choice while keeping people from doing evil, because this is a logical contradiction. Second, God could eliminate some evil, but the result might be a greater evil or the failure to produce a greater good.

The assumption that a good being must always eliminate evil as much as possible doesn't work as well as it sounds. If it were true, for instance, God would not have been good to allow Adam and Eve to keep living after doing evil. To eliminate them because of their evil would mean they wouldn't bear children and there would be no human race. The following statement gets closer to the truth: "A good God will eliminate evil as far as he can without either losing a greater good or bringing about a greater evil."[10] Notice this presents no logical contradiction between God being good and yet allowing evil.

To say that God is good is *not* to say God will always *appear* to be good, or that when he is good we will always like him for it.

Consider the anguished cry of Jeremiah: "He has driven me away and made me walk in darkness rather than light; indeed, he has turned his hand against me again and again, all day long. He has made my skin and my flesh grow old and has broken my bones. He has besieged me and surrounded me with bitterness and hardship" (Lamentations 3:2–5).

This outcry doesn't appear to affirm God's goodness, does it? Jeremiah sounds like Epicurus or David Hume. It seems remarkable that God would include in his inspired Word such human displays of confusion and frustration.

In *The Lion, the Witch and the Wardrobe,* Susan asks Mr. Beaver if Aslan the Lion is safe. "Who said anything about safe?" Mr. Beaver answers. "'Course he isn't safe. But he's good. He's the King, I tell you."[11]

This is sound theology—God can be good without being safe; he can be loving without bowing to our every wish or desire.

God's acts of goodness may appear harsh or even cruel.

Mary, who did not know Christ at the time, was dying of cancer. One day she seemed perfectly healthy, the next she found herself in unending chemotherapy. She asked my wife why, if a loving God existed, he had let her life fall apart.

Nanci shared with Mary an analogy of a three-year-old boy who swallows poison. The father calls poison control, and they say, "You have to get him to the hospital. And whatever you do, don't let him fall asleep. If he falls asleep, he'll die."

It's a cold winter night. His father rushes the boy to the car, sits beside him in the front seat, and rolls all the windows down. The boy's head starts to drop. His father slaps him in the face. The boy cries. His head starts to nod again. The father slaps him again and again, all the way to the hospital.

Can the child understand why his father is slapping his face? Of course not. He's only three years old. His father, through tears, says, "I love you, son." But if this is love, the boy doesn't want any more of it.

Even though the child cannot understand, the father is acting in his son's best interests. The father is doing good. What the child considers cruelty is actually kindness. Is it possible that God shows his love for us in the midst of human suffering and, like that three-year-old, we sometimes don't understand?

Nanci's story touched Mary. During her illness, she came to faith in Christ. A short time later she died. We look forward to seeing her in Heaven and hearing her tell of God's bountiful love, including how he used her illness to draw her to him.

Kindness is not the same as love and goodness.

C. S. Lewis points out that kindness as such "cares not whether its object becomes good or bad, provided only that it escapes suffering."[12] But love cares for the welfare, not the momentary preferences, of the one loved. This explains why a kind stranger might buy children ice cream, while their parents—who love them far more—might not.

Hardship often cultivates Christlikeness in us and prepares us for greatness. Sheer kindness might keep us from the hardship that true love doesn't—especially all-knowing love that clearly sees the final result.

Some parents force their children to stay home most nights, do chores, study, and practice the piano, while other parents let their children hang out at the mall and play video games every night. Which parents, down the line, will prove to have been good? To the child, the answer may seem obvious.

But that answer is wrong.

Sinners don't need help *feeling* good; they need help *being* good.

Sinners need more than pleasantness. In fact, if they received only life's delights, they would never come to terms with the sin that separates them from God. Though there's no lasting happiness without God, sinners could at best live their short time on Earth relatively content, only to die and go to Hell for eternity.

Envision a canoe heading down a river. Smiling campers wave from the shore, sending the message, "Everything's fine." Oblivious to what's coming, the canoeists feel good—right up to the moment of panic when they realize they are about to plunge over a waterfall. The helpful person—the one who truly does them good—yells at them from the shore and warns them of the danger ahead.

We are not merely travelers who need to be guided. We are rebels who need to surrender. But no one surrenders until he suffers his adversary's strength.

We argue against God's goodness in allowing suffering, not because our goodness exceeds God's, but because it falls so far short of it.

God's goodness entails more than whatever makes us feel warm and happy. We argue that if God were as good as we are, then evil and suffering wouldn't exist. On the contrary, evil and suffering wouldn't exist if we were as good as God is.

The fact that our standards are so much lower than God's makes us prone to view this world's sufferings as disproportionate. So we ask, "How could a horrible place like Hell exist?" We pose the question because we understand neither the vileness nor the extent of our sin. We conclude that God is not good because, ironically, we are so far from good that we do not understand what severe justice that true goodness must exact against sin.

"Or do you show contempt for the riches of his kindness, tolerance and patience," Paul asks, "not realizing that God's kindness leads you toward repentance?" (Romans 2:4). We show contempt for God's kindness, tolerance, and patience because those very attributes lead him to refrain from immediately bringing judgment upon us. Yet his goodness gives us time and opportunity to repent—which requires that we have time and opportunity to sin, get hurt, get sick, grow old, and face death. Ironically, then, it is God's very goodness that leads men to question his goodness.

Sometimes we conclude God is not good, because he's far better than we'd like him to be.

In God's presence are eternal pleasures, but God's goodness doesn't make him an endless dispenser of pleasures to sinners. Goodness involves holiness and justice. Rather than indulge us with what we think we want, God considers the long-term effects that may keep us from what we actually need and *really* want.

We do not like to suffer, but that preference does *not* establish as fact that our suffering cannot work for our ultimate good. Most of us understand that the pain felt by soldiers, athletes, farmers, and even children dragged away from video games is not inherently evil. Once we acknowledge this, the debate concerns only acceptable degrees of pain—and only our presumption makes us think we can judge what's acceptable better than God can.

In 1967 a diving accident left Joni Eareckson a quadriplegic at age seventeen. Years later Joni wrote about this time:

> I desperately wanted to kill myself....
>
> Why on earth should a person be forced to live out such a dreary existence? How I prayed for some accident or miracle to kill me. The mental and spiritual anguish was as unbearable as the physical torture.
>
> But...there was no way for me to commit suicide. This frustration was also unbearable. I was despondent, but I was also angry because of my helplessness. How I wished for strength and control enough in my fingers to do something, anything, to end my life.[13]

Who at that time would have said, "God is clearly working out his gracious purpose in this young woman's life"? Yet thirty-five years later, Joni, still a quadriplegic, wrote what may seem counterintuitive, but one day we will see through different eyes:

> God cares most—not about making us comfortable—but about teaching us to hate our sins, grow up spiritually, and love him. To do this, he *gives us salvation's benefits only gradually, sometimes painfully gradually.* In other

words, he lets us continue to feel much of sin's sting while we're headed for heaven...where at last, every sorrow we taste will one day prove to be the *best possible thing* that could have happened.[14]

God's superior goodness is the source of all lesser goodness, beauty, and pleasure in the universe.

Jonathan Edwards said in a 1733 sermon,

> God is the highest good of the reasonable creature, and the enjoyment of him is the only happiness with which our souls can be satisfied. To go to heaven fully to enjoy God, is infinitely better than the most pleasant accommodations here. Fathers and mothers, husbands, wives, children, or the company of earthly friends, are but shadows. But the enjoyment of God is the substance. These are but scattered beams, but God is the sun. These are but streams, but God is the fountain. These are but drops, but God is the ocean.[15]

We should see God as the source of all good and our sustainer through everything bad. While he wants us to express our heartbreaks and ask our questions, I think it must hurt God when we look at evil and suffering and conclude he isn't completely good. Consider the perspective of one accustomed to suffering, who can still say, "They feast on the abundance of your house; you give them drink from your river of delights. For with you is the fountain of life" (Psalm 36:8–9).

God alone is the fountain of life. Without him there could be neither life nor joy, neither abundance nor delights.

When I take pleasure in a good meal or a good book, I take pleasure in God. The meal and book do not substitute for God, nor do they distract me from him. According to the Westminster Shorter Catechism, "Man's chief end is to glorify God, and to enjoy him forever."

Thomas Aquinas wrote, "If the goodness, beauty and wonder of creatures are so delightful to the human mind, the fountainhead of God's own goodness (compared with the trickles of goodness found in creatures) will draw excited human minds entirely to itself."[16]

King David wrote, "In Your presence is fullness of joy; at Your right hand are pleasures forevermore" (Psalm 16:11, NKJV). Nothing but joy surrounds the presence of God. The world where he dwells—where one day we will dwell—has nothing but goodness. At the other end of the spectrum, the world from which he will completely withdraw, Hell, will utterly lack his goodness, and therefore will have nothing except what unredeemed humans take into it: insatiable lust, greed, hatred, fear, anxiety, jealousy, envy, pride, resentment, and pain.

Everything good, enjoyable, refreshing, fascinating, and interesting derives from God. People who reject God now can maintain the illusion that life is good without him, only because in his kindness he has not withdrawn all his good gifts.

God can accomplish good through our affliction.

Psalm 119 says, "In faithfulness you have afflicted me" (verse 75). It also says, "It was good for me to be afflicted, so that I might learn your decrees" (verse 71). If it was good for the psalmist to be afflicted, then for God to send that affliction would be to send good, wouldn't it? To withhold that affliction would be to withhold good.

My friend David O'Brien told me that God used his cerebral palsy to draw him to depend on Christ. Is he better off? He's convinced he is. His seventy-five years of suffering are no cosmic accident or satanic victory, but a severe mercy from the good hand of God. I haven't met many people more convinced of God's goodness than David O'Brien. He's experienced a lifetime of serious afflictions that many consider senseless evil, but David sees them as tools in the hands of a good God.

God's goodness seen on this fallen Earth is merely a sampling of God's goodness in Heaven.

God promises to ultimately remove all evil so that we will live in a world of utter goodness. Consider this picture of the world where we will live forever:

> Now the dwelling of God is with men, and he will live with them. They
> will be his people, and God himself will be with them and be their God.
> He will wipe every tear from their eyes. There will be no more death or
> mourning or crying or pain, for the old order of things has passed away.
>
> He who was seated on the throne said, "I am making everything
> new!" (Revelation 21:3–5)

The goodness we see around us now amounts to a whiff of Mama's stew while it simmers on the stove—just a foretaste of the full meal awaiting us.

You and I have never seen men and women as God intended them to be. We've never seen animals as they existed before the Fall. We see only marred remnants of what once was. So if the "wrong side" of Heaven can look so beautiful, what will the "right side" look like? If the smoking ruins appear so stunning, what will Earth look like when God resurrects it and makes it new?

C. S. Lewis and J. R. R. Tolkien saw core truth in the old mythologies. In their books they give us a glimpse of people and beasts and trees all vibrantly alive. Lewis and Tolkien realized, "Pagan fables of paradise were dim and distorted recollections of Eden."[17]

We won't lose the earthly beauty we now see. We won't trade Earth's beauty for Heaven's, but will retain Earth's beauty while gaining even deeper beauty. As we live with the redeemed people of this world, we will enjoy forever the redeemed beauties of this world.

Lewis said, "We want something else which can hardly be put into words— to be united with the beauty we see, to pass into it, to receive it into ourselves, to bathe in it, to become part of it. And so we shall."[18]

Through eternal perspective and faith we can see God's goodness in our weaknesses and rejoice that our weakness provides a platform for showing his strength.

"To keep me from becoming conceited because of these surpassingly great revelations," Paul wrote, "there was given me a thorn in my flesh, a messenger of Satan, to torment me. Three times I pleaded with the Lord to take it away from me. But he said to me, 'My grace is sufficient for you, for my power is made perfect in weakness.' Therefore I will boast all the more gladly about my weaknesses, so that Christ's power may rest on me. That is why, for Christ's sake, I delight in weaknesses, in insults, in hardships, in persecutions, in difficulties. For when I am weak, then I am strong" (2 Corinthians 12:7–10).

As a teenager who had just come to faith in Christ, I read this passage with perplexed interest. I believed it because it was God's Word—but it made little sense to me. Now, forty years later, it makes a great deal of sense. As an insulin-dependent diabetic I have lain helpless, stiff as a board, not in my right mind, needing my wife to get sugar in my mouth. My once-strong body grows weak. Low blood sugar clouds my judgment and leaves me with a memory of having said stupid things, like a drunken man. Several times a year I have severe reactions in which I don't know what's happening to me.

This humbles me, but I can honestly say I am grateful for it; yes, I even delight in it, because I recognize the value of being humbled, for "when I am weak, then I am strong." My weakness drives me to greater dependence upon Christ. I wouldn't begin to trade the spiritual benefits I've received.

As a young pastor I loved God sincerely; but like my tavern-owner father, I was independent, self-sufficient, and prone to do things on my own. Christ's words, "Apart from me you can do nothing" (John 15:5), rang true—but I did a lot of things without drawing on his strength. So from eternity's viewpoint, those things amounted to nothing.

Seventeen years ago I sat in a courtroom and heard abortion-clinic employees tell lie after lie, all under oath. When I heard a judge tell the jury they *must* (it was a directed verdict) find us guilty and impose severe financial punishments on us—all for peaceful, nonviolent civil disobedience—I knew I had no power to get what I wanted. None. Yet despite the difficulty and injustice, what God did in that situation was wonderful. I delighted in my weakness, for I found joy in depending on Christ.

During that thirty-day court trial, I often recited to myself God's Word, including the assurance that the Judge of all the earth will do right (see Genesis 18:25). Like Jesus, I needed to entrust myself to a faithful Creator who will work all things together for good. (And I have subsequently seen amazing ways he has done just that, none of which I could see at the time.)

God uses my weakness and inadequacy not only to build my character, but also to manifest his strength and grace to me and through me. That's why I see his goodness in giving this weakness to me to accomplish his good purposes. Not only will I celebrate those purposes in eternity, I am celebrating them now.

Through eternal perspective and faith we can know God's goodness even when our hearts break.

When George Müller's wife of thirty-nine years died, he preached her funeral sermon from the text "Thou art good, and doest good" (Psalm 119:68, KJV).

Müller recounts how he prayed when he discovered she had rheumatic fever: "Yes, my Father, the times of my darling wife are in Thy hands. Thou wilt do the very best thing for her, and for me, whether life or death. If it may be, raise up yet again my precious wife—Thou art able to do it, though she is so ill; but howsoever Thou dealest with me, only help me to continue to be perfectly satisfied with Thy holy will."

When she died, Müller said, "I bow, I am satisfied with the will of my Heavenly Father, I seek by perfect submission to his holy will to glorify him, I kiss continually the hand that has afflicted me... Without an effort my inmost soul habitually joys in the joy of that loved departed one. Her happiness gives joy to me. My dear daughter and I would not have her back, were it possible to produce it by the turn of a hand. God himself has done it; we are satisfied with him."[19]

Through eternal perspective and faith we can help one another affirm his goodness, even though he seems silent and we feel deserted.

As a young Christian who didn't come from a church background, it seemed strange for me to sing Sunday school songs with words such as "Now I am happy all the day." While Jesus was very real to me, I did *not* feel happy all the day. Moses, David, the prophets, Paul, and Jesus didn't feel happy all the day either. In fact, there's a superficial happiness some experience by shutting out the world's misery.

Saint John of the Cross wrote of "the dark night of the soul." In *Deserted by God?* Sinclair Ferguson discusses what our forefathers in the Christian church called "spiritual desertion," the sense that God has forgotten us, leaving us feeling isolated and directionless.[20] Rather than reject his goodness, God invites us to come to him and see that he is good. "Come near to God and he will come near to you" (James 4:8). He makes this promise, and he will not break it.

Ken Gire writes, "Unanswered questions can form an impasse in our relationship with God that is Himalayan in its expanse. Stopped there, we look to the highest mountain in that range, to the God we once knew—or thought we knew—and the God whose paternal arms we once felt wrapped so protectively around us now seems an Everest of indifference."[21]

Martin Luther's wife, Katherine, saw him discouraged and unresponsive for some time. Nothing she did encouraged him. One day she dressed in black mourning clothes. Luther asked her why.

"Someone has died," she said.

"Who?" Luther wondered.

"It seems," Katherine said, "that God must have died!"

Luther got her point. Since God hadn't died, he needed to stop acting as if he had.[22]

Many of us, without realizing it, have walked the Emmaus road (see Luke 24:13–32). Sorrow overwhelms us. Questions plague us. We wonder where God is…when all along he walks beside us.

All arguments to the contrary, God is utterly good and worthy to receive our worship.

Sinclair Ferguson tells the story of English missionary Allen Gardiner. In January 1852, a search party found Gardiner's lifeless body. He and his companions had shipwrecked on Tierra del Fuego. Their provisions had run out. They starved to death.

Gardiner, at one point, felt desperate for water; his pangs of thirst, he wrote, were "almost intolerable." Far from home and loved ones, he died alone, isolated, weakened, and physically broken.

Isn't this one of those stories told to raise the problem of evil and suffering? Indeed, if the story ended like this, we would find it tragic beyond description.

Despite the wretched conditions of his death, Gardiner wrote out Scripture passages, including Psalm 34:10: "The young lions do lack, and suffer hunger: but they that seek the LORD shall not want any good thing" (KJV). Near death, his handwriting feeble, Gardiner managed to write one final entry into his journal: "I am overwhelmed with a sense of the goodness of God."[23]

Notes

1. John K. Roth, "A Theodicy of Protest," in *Encountering Evil*, ed. Stephen T. Davis (Louisville, KY: Westminster John Knox, 2001), 6–7.
2. Roth, "A Theodicy of Protest," 31–32.
3. Larry Crabb, *Finding God* (Grand Rapids, MI: Zondervan, 1995), 37, 86.
4. Wayne Grudem, *Systematic Theology* (Grand Rapids, MI: Zondervan, 1994), 197.
5. Grudem, *Systematic Theology*, 197.
6. Henri Blocher, *Evil and the Cross* (Grand Rapids, MI: Kregel, 1994), 59.
7. Bruce Waltke and Charles Yu, *An Old Testament Theology* (Grand Rapids, MI: Zondervan, 2007), 507.
8. J. L. Mackie, "Evil and Omnipotence," in *The Philosophy of Religion*, ed. Basil Mitchell (Oxford: Oxford University Press, 1971), 92–93.
9. J. L. Mackie, *The Miracle of Theism* (Oxford: Oxford University Press, 1983), 150.
10. Ronald H. Nash, *Faith and Reason* (Grand Rapids, MI: Zondervan, 1988), 186.
11. C. S. Lewis, *The Lion, the Witch and the Wardrobe* (New York: HarperCollins, 1978), 80.
12. C. S. Lewis, *The Problem of Pain* (New York: Macmillan, 1962), 40–41.
13. Joni Eareckson Tada, *Joni* (Grand Rapids, MI: Zondervan, 1976), 74–75.
14. Joni Eareckson Tada and Steven Estes, *When God Weeps* (Grand Rapids, MI: Zondervan, 1997), 56.
15. Jonathan Edwards, quoted in Randy Alcorn, *Heaven* (Wheaton, IL: Tyndale House, 2004), 179.
16. Thomas Aquinas, quoted in Alistair E. McGrath, *Christian Spirituality* (Hoboken, NJ: Wiley-Blackwell, 1999), 30.
17. Alistair E. McGrath, *A Brief History of Heaven* (Malden, MA: Blackwell, 2003), 70.

18. C. S. Lewis, "The Weight of Glory," in *A Chorus of Witnesses,* ed. Thomas G. Long and Cornelius Plantinga Jr. (Grand Rapids, MI: Eerdmans, 1994), 89.

19. John Piper, "A Very Precious and Practical Doctrine," September 29, 1981, www.desiringgod.org/ResourceLibrary/TasteAndSee/ByDate/1981/2888_A_Very_Precious_and_Practical_Doctrine.

20. Sinclair B. Ferguson, *Deserted by God?* (Grand Rapids, MI: Baker Books, 1993), 11.

21. Ken Gire, *The North Face of God* (Wheaton, IL: Tyndale House, 2005), 14.

22. Ferguson, *Deserted by God?* 18.

23. Ferguson, *Deserted by God?* 19.

18

Is God's *Limited* Love a Solution?

While few critics make a philosophical argument that God lacks love, many, when personally facing evil and suffering, interpret the terrible things happening to them to mean that God doesn't love them after all. Doubt about their salvation may grip them, causing them despair.

Others view God's love in a way that eclipses all his other attributes. God's love doesn't surprise them. ("Why *shouldn't* God love us? We're lovable, aren't we?") But his holiness and hatred of sin *does* surprise and trouble them. And they feel terribly disappointed that his love for them does not exempt them from suffering. Some feel hurt and confusion; others anger and resentment.

The Old Testament repeatedly affirms God's love for his people.
After God revealed his name to Moses, "He passed in front of Moses, proclaiming, 'The LORD, the LORD, the compassionate and gracious God, slow to anger, abounding in love and faithfulness, maintaining love to thousands, and forgiving wickedness, rebellion and sin'" (Exodus 34:6–7).

God's people call upon him to keep his promises of love: "Remember the great love promised to David your servant" (2 Chronicles 6:42).

Nehemiah appeals to God's love and asks him to intervene in a time of great hardship:

> But you are a forgiving God, gracious and compassionate, slow to anger
> and abounding in love. Therefore you did not desert them....
>
>   Now therefore, O our God, the great, mighty and awesome God, who
> keeps his covenant of love, do not let all this hardship seem trifling in your
> eyes. (Nehemiah 9:17, 32)

God's love *abounds*. It proliferates. It's overflowing, even excessive—something all sufferers need to hear.

The New Testament repeatedly affirms God's love, through Christ, to his people.

With amazement, John writes, "How great is the love the Father has *lavished* on us, that we should be called children of God! And that is what we are!" (1 John 3:1; see also 4:16). If ever exclamation marks were justified in a translation, surely they are here.

"God has poured out his love into our hearts by the Holy Spirit, whom he has given us" (Romans 5:5; see also 8:39; Galatians 2:20; Ephesians 3:17–19; Titus 3:4–7).

We are God's "dearly loved children" (Ephesians 5:1) and "brothers loved by God" (1 Thessalonians 1:4).

Christ's incarnation and atonement provide the ultimate demonstration of love and the basis for our loving others. "This is love: not that we loved God, but that he loved us and sent his Son as an atoning sacrifice for our sins. Dear friends, since God so loved us, we also ought to love one another" (1 John 4:10–11).

God's constant love for us will never let us down, no matter how things appear.

We often define love in superficial and trivial ways, setting us up to question God's love in hard times. Yet notice how our spiritual forebears saw his love:

> The LORD's unfailing love
> surrounds the man who trusts in him. (Psalm 32:10)

> Have mercy on me, O God,
> according to your unfailing love. (Psalm 51:1)

> Though he brings grief, he will show compassion,
> so great is his unfailing love. (Lamentations 3:32)

We cannot see the end God has in mind. If we could, we would likely see that the hardships God allows prevent even more debilitating hardships—the by-products of the diminished character that results from a life of ease.

Our problem is not that we make too much of divine love, but too little. God does not love us on our preferred terms, but on his own. His infinite wisdom ensures us that he gives to us a higher love, not a lower one. C. S. Lewis writes,

We want, in fact, not so much a Father in Heaven as a grandfather in heaven—a senile benevolence who, as they say, "liked to see young people enjoying themselves," and whose plan for the universe was simply that it might be truly said at the end of each day, "a good time was had by all.".... I should very much like to live in a universe which was governed on such lines. But since it is abundantly clear that I don't, and since I have reason to believe, nevertheless, that God is Love, I conclude that my conception of love needs correction."[1]

God is as just and holy as he is loving.

In order to understand God's love in our current culture, it's necessary to distinguish what love doesn't mean and to see it in relationship to God's other attributes. That's why in a chapter on love I need to explore God's holiness. (We will come back to God's love in subsequent chapters about Christ's redemptive work.)

Yes, God is love, but it is not his only attribute, nor is it always his defining attribute. More and more we hear that God's love overshadows all his other attributes, as if the rest have only secondary importance.

Gregory Boyd writes, "God is unsurpassable love. The foundational difference between the true image of God and every version of the serpent's lie is that Jesus Christ first and foremost reveals God as unsurpassable love: 'God *is* love.'... The most fundamental distinguishing characteristic of every false picture of God is that it qualifies and compromises the truth about God's love."[2]

Unfortunately, this viewpoint guarantees that affirmations of God's holiness or justice, which *also* should never be qualified or compromised, will appear to qualify and compromise God's love.

God is loving, but he is not *only* loving. Isaiah says, "I saw the Lord seated on a throne, high and exalted.... Above him were seraphs, each with six wings.... And they were calling to one another: 'Holy, holy, holy is the LORD Almighty'" (6:1–3). Notice that the angels before his face day and night do not cry, "Love, Love, Love is the LORD Almighty."

Lest we believe that God's love in the New Testament eclipses his holiness in the Old Testament, the final book of the Bible reveals the present and future in a picture similar to Isaiah's vision: "Each of the four living creatures had six wings and was covered with eyes all around, even under his wings. Day and night they never stop saying: 'Holy, holy, holy is the Lord God Almighty, who was, and is, and is to come'" (Revelation 4:8).

God did not cease to be uncompromisingly holy when Jesus came into the world. God's eternal character does not change (see Malachi 3:6; James 1:17). That means the following Old Testament declarations remain just as true now as when they first appeared in Scripture:

> Who is like you—
> majestic in holiness,
> awesome in glory,
> working wonders? (Exodus 15:11)

> Who can stand in the presence of the LORD, this holy God? (1 Samuel 6:20)

> Your ways, O God, are holy. (Psalm 77:13)

> Exalt the LORD our God
> and worship at his footstool;
> he is holy....

> You were to Israel a forgiving God,
> though you punished their misdeeds.
> Exalt the LORD our God
> and worship at his holy mountain,
> for the LORD our God is holy. (Psalm 99:5, 8–9)

Of course, holiness is not God's only other attribute, which makes it all the more important that we refuse to reduce him only to love. But we can distinguish holiness from love, so it serves as a good example. Notice how Joshua appealed to God's holiness, not his love:

> You are not able to serve the LORD. He is a holy God; he is a jealous God.
> He will not forgive your rebellion and your sins. If you forsake the LORD
> and serve foreign gods, he will turn and bring disaster on you and make an
> end of you, after he has been good to you. (Joshua 24:19–20)

To demons, God's defining characteristic is his holiness. A demon said to Jesus, "What do you want with us, Jesus of Nazareth? Have you come to destroy us? I know who you are—the Holy One of God!" (Mark 1:24).

Only one attribute of God forms part of the name of a member of God's triune person—not the *Loving* Spirit, but the *Holy* Spirit. The angel announcing Messiah's incarnation referred to all three members of the Trinity. Note the prominence of God's holiness and power: "The Holy Spirit will come upon you, and the power of the Most High will overshadow you. So the holy one to be born will be called the Son of God" (Luke 1:35).

When Paul alludes to two godlike qualities, the Lord's righteousness and holiness come to his mind: "Put on the new self, created to be like God in true righteousness and holiness" (Ephesians 4:24).

God cares as much that we share in his holiness as in his love: "God disciplines us for our good, that we may share in his holiness.... Make every effort to live in peace with all men and to be holy; without holiness no one will see the Lord" (Hebrews 12:10, 14).

It's a mistake to think God's love overshadows his holiness, or to think his holiness limits his love.
In *The Difficult Doctrine of the Love of God*, D. A. Carson writes,

> The love of God in our culture has been purged of anything the culture finds uncomfortable. The love of God has been sanitized, democratized, and above all sentimentalized....
>
> It has not always been so. In generations when almost everyone believed in the justice of God, people sometimes found it difficult to believe in the love of God. The preaching of the love of God came as wonderful good news. Nowadays if you tell people that God loves them, they are unlikely to be surprised.[3]

If we asked people to vote on a divine character quality they most appreciate, God's love would surely receive far more votes than his holiness. Christians tend to reflect our culture, and because our culture values love and devalues holiness, we do the same. We have taken one precious divine attribute, love, defined it as we please, then used our redefinition to neutralize others of God's attributes that don't appeal to us.

Arguing that we should view all God's attributes in terms of his love, Gregory Boyd says, "The essence of God's holiness is his eternal triune love.... God's righteousness is simply the justice of his unsurpassable love.... God's power is simply the power of his love."[4]

But on what grounds should we subordinate God's other attributes to his love? Would we say, "The essence of God's love is his eternal holiness"? By defining other attributes as if they are all subordinate to love, we end up with a one-attribute God. Peter Hicks writes,

> God is one, and all the elements of his nature, however disparate they may seem to us, make up one integrated whole. For this reason we should resist the suggestion that some elements of his nature are to be set over against others, that they exist "in tension." There is no tension in God; none of his attributes sits uneasily with any other. We may feel there is a tension between justice and mercy, or between the God who loves and the God who punishes. But that is because our understanding of these things is warped and inadequate. In God they fit perfectly together.[5]

God states a reason for his pleasure in his Son: "You have loved righteousness and hated wickedness" (Hebrews 1:9). If we imagine God only loves and doesn't hate, we will think he calls upon us to only love. Yet he commands us, "Hate evil, love good" (Amos 5:15).

God's attributes of holiness, purity, and righteousness prompt him to hate evil, including some human attitudes and actions; and yes, even some people (see Deuteronomy 12:31; Proverbs 6:16–19; Jeremiah 44:4; Malachi 1:2–3). David writes, "He [God] is angry with the wicked every day" (Psalm 7:11, NLT). David also says, "You are not a God who takes pleasure in evil; with you the wicked cannot dwell. The arrogant cannot stand in your presence; you hate all who do wrong. You destroy those who tell lies; bloodthirsty and deceitful men the LORD abhors" (Psalm 5:4–6).

These statements make clear that our loving God won't allow the wicked to dwell in his presence. Certainly, he hates sin; but passages such as this go further by saying, "You hate all who do wrong." If we place God's love above his holiness, such statements will seem appalling. And they will seem especially jarring when we hear John, the "apostle of love," say something like, "Whoever rejects the Son will not see life, for God's wrath remains [present tense] on him" (John 3:36).

God calls upon us to love our enemies, yet to be Christlike means to love good and hate evil. "To fear the LORD is to hate evil" (Proverbs 8:13). We cannot separate the two, nor should we try to separate God's love from his holiness. Whenever we set one above the other, we fail to honor God as God and fail to accurately represent his character to our families, churches, and culture.

The God of love is also a God of wrath (see Romans 1:18). Evil angers God. He hates evil, despises it, and will punish it. Yet the God who punishes is the same loving God who chose to bear our punishment in Christ and offer us pardon. If we don't accept his atoning work, however, we remain subject to eternal punishment. Any affirmation of God's love that fails to acknowledge the demands of his holiness distorts God's character and truth, undermines the gospel.

If in our eyes his holiness contradicts his love and his justice conflicts with his mercy, then that is our problem, not his. The almighty God who created us is the same holy God who condemned us as sinners and the same loving God who went to extraordinary lengths that we might go to Heaven. God's self-consistency demands the simultaneous and full expression of his holiness, his love, and all his other attributes.

God reveals his multifaceted character in Jesus, who is eminently loving, but not only loving.

Boyd says, "The anchor God gives us is Jesus Christ. This alone is what we can trust: God is decisively revealed in Jesus Christ."[6]

I agree that Jesus is our anchor. But Christ reveals God's love *and* his holiness. John cites Isaiah 6:10, then adds, "Isaiah said this because he saw Jesus' glory and spoke about him" (John 12:41). When had he seen God's glory? Seven verses earlier, when he beheld God and heard the seraphim cry, "Holy, holy, holy is the LORD Almighty" (Isaiah 6:3). Jesus came not only full of grace, but full of truth (see John 1:14). We should never choose grace over truth or truth over grace, love over holiness or holiness over love.

Jesus shows us exactly what God looks like. Problems arise when we trust our own subjective picture of Jesus over what the Bible says and shows. The same Jesus who spoke words of tender love and forgiveness also spoke some of the harshest words of condemnation in Scripture. Jesus spoke more about Hell, and in more terrible terms, than anyone else in the Bible. When we speak only of love, inevitably we will diminish or reject the biblical teaching of Hell. If we imagine it unloving to speak of Hell, we imagine Jesus to be unloving.

If God's love outstripped his holiness, then why send Jesus to the cross? If love trumps holiness, then why not dispense with the Crucifixion altogether—especially since Jesus asked for this very thing (see Matthew 26:39)? The truth is, God's holiness and love combined at Calvary constitute the only way possible to save sinners and still satisfy God's perfect nature.

God's love divorced from the full picture of his infinite glory reduces him to a false god, made in our own likeness. God's love defined in light of the totality of his all-encompassing majesty, depicts him as he truly is and invites our heart-felt praise.

God could have created or governed us without loving us, but he would not have gone to the Cross without loving us.

The most compelling proof of God's love is giving his Son to die for us. "This is how God showed his love among us: He sent his one and only Son into the world that we might live through him. This is love: not that we loved God, but that he loved us and sent his Son as an atoning sacrifice for our sins" (1 John 4:9–10).

We were all God's enemies: "Once you were alienated from God and were enemies in your minds because of your evil behavior" (Colossians 1:21). Even so, "God demonstrates his own love for us in this: While we were still sinners, Christ died for us" (Romans 5:8).

As our *Abba,* God knows our hurts intimately and remains lovingly attentive to our cries.

When God's children suffer, Paul says they cry out, "*Abba,* Father" (Romans 8:15). *Abba* is an Aramaic word for the babbling of a child who says, "Papa," because he can't pronounce the word for "father." Crying indicates the need of a wounded or frightened child.

This striking picture of intimacy comes in the context of the elevated role of fathers in the ancient world. Jews would pray, "Our Father *who is in Heaven,*" because "Father" alone sounded too intimate. But *Abba* goes further still, like "Papa" or "Daddy." We step into God's intimate love when we call God *Abba* with the affection of a child.

Children who know their Father as good and loving find great security. And the Bible assures us that the God who spun galaxies into being "gathers the lambs in his arms and carries them close to his heart" (Isaiah 40:11).

I heard a story of a kindhearted king who finds a blind, destitute orphan boy while hunting in a forest. The king takes the boy to his palace, adopts him as his son, and provides for his care. He sees that the boy receives the finest education. The boy is extremely grateful, and he loves the king, his new father, with all his heart.

When the boy turns twenty, a surgeon performs an operation on his eyes, and for the first time he is able to see.

This boy, once a starving orphan, has for some years been a royal prince, at home in the king's palace. But something wonderful has happened, something far greater than the magnificent food, gardens, libraries, music, and wonders of the palace. The boy is finally able to *see* the face of the father he adores.

He loves his father because his father loved him. The love in the son's heart is thunder produced by the lightning of his father's love.

The father's rescue of the starving child is like our conversion. We come to know God's love and enjoy his indwelling presence, but still we cannot fully see. The day is coming when we will live in a glorious world where all will be beautiful beyond our imagination, with feasts, gardens, fruit trees, rivers and mountains, music and art, and perhaps libraries, games, and dramas.

But all these magnificent wonders will be secondary, mere tributes to the King. For by far our greatest thrill will be when, with resurrected eyes, we see for the first time the face of the God who loved us so much as to pour out his life for us.

John Donne put it beautifully:

> I shall rise from the dead.... I shall see the Son of God, the Sun of Glory, and shine myself as that sun shines. I shall be united to the Ancient of Days, to God Himself, who had no morning, never began.... No man ever saw God and lived. And yet, I shall not live till I see God; and when I have seen him, I shall never die.[7]

Notes

1. C. S. Lewis, *The Problem of Pain* (New York: Macmillan, 1962), 40.
2. Gregory A. Boyd, *Is God to Blame?* (Downers Grove, IL: InterVarsity, 2003), 36.
3. D. A. Carson, *The Difficult Doctrine of the Love of God* (Wheaton, IL: Crossway Books, 2000), 11.
4. Boyd, *Is God to Blame?* 36.
5. Peter Hicks, *The Message of Evil and Suffering* (Downers Grove, IL: InterVarsity 2007), 31–32.
6. Boyd, *Is God to Blame?* 39.
7. John Donne, Sermons 3:751 quoted in Randy C. Alcorn, *Heaven* (Carol Stream, IL: Tyndale, 2004), 165.

Evil and Suffering in the Great Drama of Christ's Redemptive Work

19

Evil and Suffering as Seen in Scripture's Redemptive Story

The story of redemption began before God created the world.

God speaks of "all whose names have not been written in the book of life belonging to the Lamb that was slain from the creation of the world" (Revelation 13:8). Before creation itself, God had written myriad names in the book of life. That book belongs to "the Lamb that was slain." Before God took his first step in forming this universe, already he had determined to sacrifice his Son for our sins, like a lamb on the sacrificial altar.

From the perspective of a timeless God, Christ's sufferings and death did not confine themselves to a few years or hours. Before the world fell—even before he created it—God knew *exactly* what he would do to redeem the world. He knew the horrors of evil before Adam and Eve knew them. When you consider that the distant future is as real to God as the present is to us, then this passage takes on paradigm-shifting meaning.

God's redemptive plan was not an ad-lib response to unanticipated events. From before the very beginning, God knew the very worst. And the very best it would one day bring.

Paul writes, "This grace was given us in Christ Jesus before the beginning of time" (2 Timothy 1:9). How could God give us grace before our lives began, even before the universe itself existed? Only because God knew and determined in advance the work of Christ for us on the Cross.

God wrote the script of the unfolding drama of redemption long before Satan, demons, Adam and Eve—and you and I—took the stage. And from the beginning, he knew that the utterly spectacular ending would make the dark middle worth it.

The earliest scriptures document evil's pervasiveness in the human heart.

We find the first four biblical references to evil in Genesis 2:9; 2:17; 3:5; and 3:22. The first two refer to the tree of the knowledge of good and evil, the second pair to man becoming like God in knowing good and evil.

The next reference provides a frightening commentary on the extent of human evil: "The LORD saw how great man's wickedness on the earth had become, and that *every* inclination of the thoughts of his heart was only *evil all the time*" (Genesis 6:5). After tolerating generations of increasing evil, God sent the Flood as a catastrophic judgment to sweep away evil and start civilization over.

God's present postponement of worldwide judgment gives the human race time to repent and turn to God, thereby avoiding eternal condemnation.

After the Flood, God again affirms man's evil nature but announces his decision to mercifully withhold sweeping judgment: "The LORD smelled the pleasing aroma [of Noah's sacrifice] and said in his heart: 'Never again will I curse the ground because of man, even though every inclination of his heart is evil from childhood. And never again will I destroy all living creatures, as I have done'" (Genesis 8:21).

Noah's sacrifice represented the coming sacrifice of Christ, which gave God cause to postpone judgment. Elsewhere he expresses his gracious purpose: "God isn't late with his promise as some measure lateness. He is restraining himself on account of you, holding back the End because he doesn't want anyone lost. He's giving everyone space and time to change" (2 Peter 3:9, MSG).

When we call upon God to end all evil, we should consider what we're really asking. He *did* once judge evil *almost* completely, but doing so required that he sweep away nearly every human being on the planet. Is this what we want him to do today?

We should be careful what we wish for.

God's judgment at Babel kept evil in check, allowing sufficient time for his redemptive story to reach the nations.

God originally commanded humankind to spread across the earth and occupy it (see Genesis 1:28). But fallen humanity had another idea. Rebellious people said, "Come, let us build ourselves a city, with a tower that reaches to the heavens, so that we may make a name for ourselves and not be scattered over the face of the whole earth" (Genesis 11:4).

Despite their blatant disobedience, God kept his promise not to judge the earth as in the Flood. But he did confuse their language so they couldn't understand one another. God then "scattered them from there over all the earth" (verse 8).

God used both the Flood and Babel to restrain sin, allowing the earth to continue on its course before final judgment. Babel, however, served another ultimate redemptive purpose. God later promised Abraham, "Through your offspring all nations on earth will be blessed" (Genesis 22:18). The Messiah would redeem not only Israel, but representatives of every nation, nations that would not exist apart from God's judgment on Babel.

At any time God could eliminate evil, suffering, death, and curse. He does not, because he wants more of the human race to participate in his redemptive plan. He wants people to worship him "from every nation, tribe, people and language" (Revelation 7:9). Heaven praises the Redeemer, Jesus, the Lamb of God: "With your blood you purchased men for God from every tribe and language and people and nation. You have made them to be a kingdom and priests to serve our God, and they will reign on the earth" (Revelation 5:9–10).

God never gave up on his original plan for sinless humans to rule the earth. But the development of nations served his purpose to enrich and expand humanity into cultures and societies that ultimately would bring more glory to God and Christ our Redeemer.

Meanwhile, God wants more people to have time to come into the world, then come to repentance and into a right relationship with him. He wants more of us to reign and live with him on the glorious New Earth.

God lets the story unfold by restraining evil until his final verdict.

Paul speaks of "the man of lawlessness" (2 Thessalonians 2:3) who sets himself up as God. He says, "You know what is holding him back, so that he may be revealed at the proper time. For the secret power of lawlessness is already at work; but the one who now holds it back will continue to do so till he is taken out of the way" (verses 6–7).

Clearly it is God who restrains both the man of lawlessness and lawlessness itself. He holds back the tide of human and demonic evil. God infuses this fallen world with his goodness, restraining evil until the moment he brings final judgment.

Like Job, we live in a cosmic drama, in full view of Heaven's audience.

In the first chapter of Job, the drama's Director tells us what the characters don't know—what's *really* going on. Job knew nothing about God commending

Job to Satan and calling him blameless. God let Job face terrible trials with no explanation.

We share this in common with Job—*God doesn't specifically explain why he permits evil and suffering to fall upon us.* He wants us to trust him. In one sense, Job is everyman.

Right now, you and I may be subjects of discussion between God and Satan, or between God and righteous angels, or angels and redeemed people in Heaven. You may lie in a rest home or a hospital, or sit alone at home. But you're *not* alone—an unseen universe is watching.

Perhaps a wager has been placed involving the testing of your faith. A cosmos of invisible beings, good and evil, may be observing you with intense interest. Powerful warriors battle one another, some for us, some against us (see Daniel 9:20–10:21).

You may feel your choices have been reduced to whether you want Jell-O, or a window opened, or an extra blanket. On the contrary, your choice of whether you will trust God and worship him today reverberates throughout the universe, honoring or dishonoring your God. It also has enormous implications for eternal rewards God promises us in the next life.

Human suffering genuinely moves the heart of God, the Storyteller.
The Lord said to Moses,

> I have indeed seen the misery of my people in Egypt. I have heard them
> crying out because of their slave drivers, and I am concerned about their
> suffering. So I have come down to rescue them from the hand of the
> Egyptians and to bring them up out of that land into a good and spacious
> land, a land flowing with milk and honey.... And now the cry of the
> Israelites has reached me, and I have seen the way the Egyptians are
> oppressing them. So now, go. I am sending you to Pharaoh to bring my
> people the Israelites out of Egypt. (Exodus 3:7–10)

Just a few years after Jesus wept over his beloved city (see Matthew 23:37–38), God brought terrible judgment on Jerusalem. Our suffering affects God just as any child's suffering concerns his parent. David says to God, "You keep track of all my sorrows. You have collected all my tears in your bottle. You have recorded each one in your book" (Psalm 56:8, NLT).

God's rich variety of feelings, including compassion, are vital to the story.
Some time ago theologians formulated the doctrine of God's *impassibility.* They

argued that God was "without passions." Their motive was to distinguish God from the mood swings and more erratic and unstable aspects of human emotions. Unfortunately, many Christians came to believe that God doesn't have emotions.

It's critical that we know the heart of God. He genuinely loves and cares about us. If we believe he has no emotions, then we will never feel his love for us, nor will we experience deep love for him.

An abundance of biblical passages show that God experiences a broad range of emotions. God commands us not to "grieve" the Holy Spirit (Ephesians 4:30). God is said to be "angry" (Deuteronomy 1:37), "moved by pity" (Judges 2:18, ESV), "pleased" (1 Kings 3:10), and "to rejoice over you with singing" (Zephaniah 3:17). Genesis 6:6 says, "So the LORD was sorry he had ever made them and put them on the earth. It broke his heart" (NLT).

Some explain these verses as ascribing human emotions to God so that we can relate to him better. But surely God wants us to relate to him *as he really is,* and passages that don't describe him as he is would mislead us. God wants us to understand that he can genuinely grieve, his heart full of pain. Surely he didn't choose these powerful words so we would respond, "Of course, God didn't *really* feel moved—he has no emotions."

Since God made us in his image, we should assume our emotions are reflective of his, even though ours are subject to sin while his are not. Consider a small sampling of verses illustrating God's emotions:

Now leave me alone so that my anger may burn against them and that I
may destroy them. (Exodus 32:10)

As a father has compassion on his children,
    so the LORD has compassion on those who fear him.
        (Psalm 103:13)

"In a surge of anger
    I hid my face from you for a moment,
but with everlasting kindness
    I will have compassion on you,"
    says the LORD your Redeemer. (Isaiah 54:8)

As a bridegroom rejoices over his bride,
    so will your God rejoice over you. (Isaiah 62:5)

Nor does God limit his compassion to his children. He says, "I wail over Moab, for all Moab I cry out" (Jeremiah 48:31).

A passage about God's goodness and compassion contains a remarkable statement: "In all their distress he too was distressed" (Isaiah 63:9). A form of the same word is used to describe God's people's distress as to depict God's own. Yes, our distress can involve feelings God's doesn't, such as helplessness and uncertainty. But clearly God intends us to see a similarity between our emotional distress and his.

The fact that the second member of the triune God suffered unimaginable torture on the cross should explode any notion that God lacks feelings. In the suffering of Jesus, God himself suffered. No one who grasps this truth can say, "God doesn't understand my suffering." Dietrich Bonhoeffer wrote in a Nazi prison camp, "Only the suffering God can help."[1]

While in the larger story this is not the best possible world, it may be the best possible means of achieving the best possible world.
A world that had never been touched by evil *would* be a good place. But would it be the best place possible? If we acknowledge that evil and suffering facilitate the development of significant human virtues, then we must answer no.

If you tell God he should not have allowed evil and suffering, then you are saying he should not have allowed us to experience compassion, mercy, and sacrificial love. In order for those characteristics to develop and become part of us, God had to permit evil and suffering. Can we fault God for ordaining the kind of world in which we could experience such great good?

And suppose that once developed, the attributes of patience, mercy, love, and strength of character could last forever, even long after evil had disappeared. Could this justify God's allowance of evil? I believe the answer is yes.

If God merely wanted to develop men and women who would behave correctly, he could have bypassed freedom, evil, and suffering. But if he intended that his image-bearers see their genuine need for him and be brought to loving obedience, then how would we propose that he improve the processes he uses in our lives?

The story culminates in a new world made breathtaking because God has overcome evil and suffering.
God prepared me to hear the gospel when, as a junior higher, I read fantasy and science fiction stories and gazed at the night sky through my telescope. I'd read of

other worlds, of great battles and causes, and I knew that the universe was huge beyond comprehension. I remember the profound loneliness I felt, being on the outside of something so great. Some of the alien worlds I read of captivated me. I believed there *had* to be something better than this world. Without knowing the story of this universe, I sensed that evil and suffering didn't fit into the story's beginning.

In high school I first read the Bible and saw how the world had gone wrong. Three-fourths of the way through the story I met Jesus and realized he was the One my heart had always longed for. When I got to the end of the story, I saw that God will never give up on this world. The new world I longed for will be this world reborn.

Christ is the main character of God's story. His redemptive work brings goodness to this world beyond all cost and value.

John Piper writes,

> The suffering of the utterly innocent and infinitely holy Son of God in the place of the utterly undeserving sinners to bring us to everlasting joy is the greatest display of the glory of God's grace that ever was, or ever could be. Everything leading to it and everything flowing from it is explained by it, including all the suffering in the world.[2]

When we live peacefully on the New Earth, where joy will permeate the very air we breathe, we will look back at this present world and affirm not by faith but by sight that all the evil and suffering was worth it—and that Christ's incarnation and redemption have made the universe eternally better.

Notes

1. Dietrich Bonhoeffer, *Letters and Papers from Prison,* ed. Eberhard Bethge (New York: Simon & Schuster, 1997), 361.
2. John Piper, "The Suffering of Christ and the Sovereignty of God," in *Suffering and the Sovereignty of God,* ed. John Piper and Justin Taylor (Wheaton, IL: Crossway Books, 2006), 82.

20

If You Were the Author, How Would You Have Written the Story?

We value in story the conflict we avoid in life.

Though I write mostly nonfiction, I've written nine works of fiction, seven of them full-length novels. Like many fiction writers, I've spent considerable time developing the craft of storytelling.

What makes a good story? Interesting characters, significant conflict, the thwarting of desires, and a satisfying (if not triumphant) resolution. It must avoid predictability and its characters have to continuously develop—and the higher the stakes, the better the story.

If I were to write a book about lives without conflict, where the characters get everything they want, where life marches on predictably and no one ever loses anything, no one would read it. Who likes a boring story?

Now, consider God as the great Storyteller. With grand artistry, he writes into the story the characters, both angels and people, with different names, personas, and circumstances. He tells us of Michael and Lucifer, brother archangels. Lucifer rebels and becomes Satan. He takes a third of the angels down with him. When Satan first appears in the garden, we know none of this; God doesn't tell us this backstory until much later.

As the culmination of his new universe, God creates Adam and Eve. He could have kept them from temptation and so prevented evil, suffering, and the Curse. But no rebellion, no drama, no story. Without the great problem, there can be no wondrous solution. Without the high stakes of humanity's alienation from God, there can be no redemption.

Evil enters the world. And right then and there God promises a Redeemer, the woman's offspring. His people, century after century, expect the Redeemer to come soon, overthrow his enemies, and set up his kingdom—end of story.

But that's not how it happens.

Instead, thousands of years pass as humanity continues its struggle with evil and suffering. Finally, in a fantastic plot twist, God becomes a humble carpenter, heals the sick, raises the dead, and allows others to kill him. He does it all to redeem the people he loves. He rises from the dead, commands and empowers his followers to serve him, then leaves but promises to return. With compelling resurrection evidence to back it up, he reiterates the promise—one day he'll make all things right and will live forever with his people.

The first three chapters of God's story, as told in the Bible, set up the unfolding drama of redemption. The last three chapters show how God will judge evil, reward good, and come down to the New Earth to live with his children forever. He will wipe away every tear from their eyes, and there will be no more suffering and evil.

But this greater eternal happiness could not happen without evil and suffering, those foreign invaders, attacking God's original good creation, with its great but lesser happiness that will be eclipsed by the One to come.

This is the greatest story ever told. Secular reviewers often say of a book, "This is a powerful redemptive story." The very concept of a redemptive story flows from the Bible's story of redemption. It's the prototype of all great stories.

Suppose you could remove from the story Lucifer's fall and Adam and Eve's sin. Take away Cain and Abel's conflict, the Flood, Babel, and the battles Joseph, Job, Moses, David, and Elijah had with evil and suffering. Remove all wars and heartbreaks and yearnings for something better. Take them all away and *you would also take away Jesus,* who would not become one of us in order to reveal God's character and save us from our sins.

The second person of the triune God would still exist, of course, but no God-man, no incarnation, no *need* for incarnation. No first coming, no second coming. No New Heaven and New Earth, only the same one continuing forever. The result? Less appreciation for peace because war had never broken out; less appreciation for food because famine had never occurred; less appreciation for righteousness because sin never appeared. Less love for life because death never happened. Less glory to God and heartfelt worship because we'd never have seen his attributes of grace and mercy and patience.

As a member of the real-life story's cast, you might wish for a world untouched by evil and suffering. That's understandable, because life is hard as the story unfolds; and it *will* be hard until it culminates or you leave the stage, having played your part.

But if you sat in the audience, which story would you prefer to watch? And if you wrote the story, which version would you prefer to write? And even as a cast member, having endured such difficulty, ten thousand years from now at the ongoing cast party in honor of the Writer and Director, when grand tales make the rounds at dinner tables on the New Earth—which story do you think you would cast your vote for?

The greatest character virtues we know would never appear in a story without evil and suffering.

Don't most, if not all, of the greatest virtues surface in response to evil and suffering? Think of your favorite books and movies. Take *Braveheart, Saving Private Ryan, Schindler's List, Amistad, Star Wars,* or *The Lord of the Rings.* The virtues and camaraderie, the courage and sacrifice central to these stories simply would not exist without a context of evil and suffering.

Do you agree that some great goods such as courage and sacrifice and compassion materialize only in the presence of evil and suffering? If you do, then you recognize that if God allowed less evil in the world, there would also be less good.

If you could snap your fingers and remove all evil and suffering that has ever happened, would you? If you did, then Frederick Douglass, Sojourner Truth, Abraham Lincoln, Harriet Tubman, Susan B. Anthony, and William Wilberforce would just be names. Without his deafness, we don't know whether Beethoven would have written his symphonies. Had John Bunyan not been unjustly imprisoned, he almost certainly would not have written *The Pilgrim's Progress.*

On January 13, 1982, Air Florida Flight 90 faced icy weather upon departing Washington, D.C. The Boeing 737 skidded off the runway, slammed into the Fourteenth Street Bridge, and careened into the deathly cold Potomac River. Five passengers clung to the broken-off tailpiece, floating in icy water.

A rescue helicopter dropped a lifeline, pulling up one person. When the second lifeline fell to Arland Williams, forty-six, he quickly passed it on to save another. The third and fourth lifelines came, and again he passed them to others. By the time the fifth and last lifeline dropped, Williams had drowned in the frigid water. Rescuer Gene Windsor wept as he described what Williams had done: "He could have gone on the first trip, but he put everyone else ahead of himself. Everyone."[1]

My heart aches for the many families whose loved ones perished in that crash. Yet this act of heroism, as have countless others, enriches us and challenges us to strengthen our own characters so in a similar circumstance we might do the same.

Remember the story of Armand and his classmates buried for days beneath the rubble of the Armenian earthquake, while his father relentlessly moved rocks by himself and finally saved them all? Terrible events, such as earthquakes costing untold lives, make up part of this world under the Curse. But without them we'd miss heart-gripping stories, New Earth campfire-type stories, like one man's relentless love that saved his son's life and thirteen others', some of whom, I hope, we'll hear tell the story.

I don't ask my characters for permission to let them suffer and face evil because, as the author, I know the best ending for the story.

Let's, for a moment, grant life to fictional characters. If, in an interview with a character from one of my novels, you were to ask whether he'd like to be written out of the story, he would answer no. Nonexistence appeals to no one. Now, ask him if he would like to suffer less, and he'll answer yes.

Ah, but I'm the author, and I know I have something greater in store for my characters. So I do not let them walk out of my novels in protest. I know that in the end, it will all be worth it.

I sympathize with my characters, since I too am a character in God's story. At times I'd like to take a break from the drama. Three months off without stress would feel nice. But I honestly wouldn't want a permanent break, because the story gives meaning to my life. I'm part of something great, far bigger than myself. And I trust God not only to bring the whole story together, but to do with my part of it what he knows to be best.

How many of us would have chosen to leave the warmth and security of our mother's womb for a world of noise, bright lights, cold, hunger, and thirst? Think how much we gave up when we left the womb. Yet, knowing what you know now, would you want to go back?

In my novels, the main characters face great conflict, turmoil, uncertainty, and suffering. Some die. So who am I to say God shouldn't write such things into his story, including my part?

God created *all* the characters in his story. He loves a great story, and he has made us to love it. Before we fault him for the plot twists we don't like, we should remember that Jesus has written this story in his own blood.

Wise authors don't let their characters dictate their circumstances, as wise parents don't let their children dictate theirs.

Of course, we're not merely God's characters, we're also his children. But like any good parent, God doesn't give us happiness at any cost.

Parents who try to make their children happy in the short term unwisely allow their children to set the agenda. Children question even the best parent's goodness and love. "Why can't I have ice cream? I don't want to go to bed. I want to watch this movie. Why can't I?" Notice the keyword in the questioning of parental authority, wisdom, and goodness: *Why?*

Why also dominates our thinking in the problem of evil and suffering. If God is good, *why* does he let us suffer? *Why* doesn't he stop the things that make us unhappy? Or as the child puts it, *why* doesn't he let us eat what we want, *why* doesn't he let us go where we want? *Why* does he discipline us?

God was a parent before the first humans became parents. Our experience as parents should teach us much about the gap between what we know to be best for the child and what the child *thinks* she knows to be best for herself.

What if forever attaining the highest good in the universe means *not* getting what we think we want now? What if the highest good means learning to trust God and becoming more Christlike? What if the Author chose the right setting and plot twists after all, and in the end we'll be eternally grateful for our God-given part in the story?

Given the option, surely Joseph would have walked off the stage of God's story. After betrayal and abuse and the false accusation by Potiphar's wife, Joseph had surely had enough for one life.

Talk to Job in the middle of his story—with ten children dead and excruciating boils covering his body, his friends haranguing him and his feeling abandoned by God. Ask him if he wants out. I know what he'll say: "Why did I not perish at birth, and die as I came from the womb?" (Job 3:11).

But that's all over now. On the New Earth, sit by Job and Joseph at a banquet. Ask them, "Be honest, Job. You too, Joseph. *Was it really worth it?*"

"Absolutely," Job says. Joseph smiles, nodding emphatically.

"But Job, had God given you the choice back then, wouldn't you have walked out of the story?"

"In a heartbeat. I'm just glad he didn't let me."

We would not want God's story to be about a choiceless utopia.

In hundreds of science-fiction and fantasy books and dozens of movies, life in the future looks safe and orderly. No crime. No conflict. People have limited choices…and life is deadly boring. In some stories the characters travel back in time to see what the good old days looked like, when choices had consequences and people took risks.

Peter Kreeft points to this popular anti-utopian theme: A futuristic society uses science to abolish suffering, cure disease, and end poverty. Accidents don't happen, and sometimes there's even artificial immortality.[2] But all such societies are colossal fakes. People are supposed to act happy, but dissatisfaction drips from every pore. A wall of protective technology strips them of the freedom that defines humanity. Attempting to abolish all suffering essentially abolishes freedom and eradicates what makes living worthwhile.

Brave New World, where supposedly "everybody's happy now," is actually "a streamlined, soulless Eden." As Kreeft puts it, "No Beethoven, no Shakespeare, no da Vinci, and no suffering."

What if you could have both complete freedom and complete happiness? Scripture promises exactly that, in the New Heaven and New Earth—not an artificial utopia, but a genuine one. All will serve Jesus because they want to *with all their hearts.* We'll rejoice as we fall down before him who sits on the throne, laying our crowns before him, crying "You are worthy, our Lord and God, to receive glory and honor and power" (Revelation 4:11). What could be greater than not only worshiping him, but watching in wonder as he places his nail-scarred hands upon our shoulders and says, "Well done, my good and faithful servant," as we participate in our Master's joy?

It literally *doesn't* get any better than that.

One paragraph into chapter 1 on the New Earth will make up for eighty hard "chapters" on Earth; but even if it took another eighty to compensate, the joys would have only just begun.

How long will we need to be in Heaven before our new home will make up for all the suffering we've faced in this life? Two months? Two weeks? Two days? Two hours? Two minutes?

The bleakest pessimist might answer, "More like a hundred years." But even if you say ten *thousand* years, that will be but the beginning of an eternal life of joy and pleasures at God's right hand (see Psalm 16:11). When we realize God has promised us a redeemed universe and time without end, we'll finally "get it." We'll have opportunity to develop and fulfill dreams bigger than anything we ever had on this fallen Earth. Heaven will be anything but boring!

At the end of Peter Jackson's production of *The Return of the King,* Bilbo Baggins—by then aged and decrepit—gets invited to board an Elven ship bound for Valinor (Heaven). He smiles, and a youthful energy returns to his eyes. "I think I'm quite ready for another adventure," he says.

For the Christian, death is not the end of adventure but a doorway to a world where dreams and adventures forever expand. No matter how bad the present, an eternity with Christ in Heaven will be incomparably better. So if *God* thinks the whole thing is worth it—and we know it will be worth it to *us* once we reach Heaven—then why not affirm by faith, even in the midst of suffering, that it's worth it now?

We live between *Paradise Lost* and *Paradise Regained;* recalling the story's beginning and ending gives perspective to our lives between the two.

Though the Lord exiled us from Eden because of our evil, that place remains forever embedded in our hearts. We feel homesick for Eden. We long for what the first man and woman once enjoyed, a perfect and beautiful Earth with free and untainted relationships with God and each other. Every effort at human progress has tried to regain what we lost in the Fall.

Our heartsick nostalgia for the earth we've never known leaves us longing. But the Hero of the story has come to rescue us from evil and suffering, and from ourselves. And he's coming back, with a new world in tow.

Our friends John and Ann watched helplessly as their eighteen-month-old son, Gary, died. Ann says, "In that one moment our life was shattered. My big question was, how could God love me and allow this? If he could have stopped it, why didn't he?" Nothing could take away the pain, but John and Ann faced a choice concerning their perspective. Ann says, "Even though we still have questions, we've decided to dwell on what we know to be true. I see Heaven in a whole new light. After all, my treasure is there. I look forward to joining him. I can't wait to see him, hug him, hold him, and spend eternity with him."[3]

Instead of dreading the short-term future and further losses it will bring, we can daily look forward to the eternal future, to the joys—including the joys of reunion—that God has promised await us.

One day we will view our present pain with very different eyes.

I'll never forget my first thirty seconds of high school. I walked in the front door, tripped, and fell on my face...right in front of three junior cheerleaders. They laughed hysterically. Not a good start for a freshman desperately wanting to be cool!

That incident *hurt,* worse than my serious ankle injury while playing football. But today, as I look back at both of those incidents, neither of them brings me the slightest pain, even though I distinctly *remember* feeling pain. I have gained the benefit of perspective.

Of course, my teenage troubles do *not* compare to fighting cancer, being tortured, or seeing a child die. I only mean that although my experiences brought me genuine pain, with the passing of time and gaining of perspective, they no longer do. The same is true of several years of lawsuits, job loss, and uncertainty my family experienced two decades ago. Oh, I remember that we experienced pain, I remember some of the feelings, but what I am left with now is the joy of what God did for us in those days. Similarly, many women remember the pain of giving birth, yet today can recall those times without the suffering recurring. (They can tell the story without reaching for a pain reliever.)

Shouldn't we suppose that many of our most painful ordeals will look quite different a million years from now, as we recall them on the New Earth? What if one day we discover that God has wasted *nothing* in our life on Earth? What if we see that every agony was part of giving birth to an eternal joy?

Some consider the strongest case against God ever made was Ivan's argument cited earlier from Dostoevsky's *Brothers Karamazov:*

> Imagine that you are creating a fabric of human destiny with the object of making men happy in the end, giving them peace and rest at last, but that it was essential and inevitable to torture to death only one tiny creature— that baby beating its breast with its fist, for instance—and to found that edifice on its unavenged tears, would you consent to be the architect on those conditions?[4]

Some consider the answer self-evident. But suppose that one day you were to meet that baby, now grown into a woman. What if you found she had been gloriously rewarded and enjoyed an unending depth of happiness beyond anything she could have known on the old Earth? What if, after the resurrection, you came to her, now gloriously and joyfully serving her king on the New Earth and asked her, "Was your suffering worth it for you?" And what if, without a moment's hesitation or doubt, she replied from her heart, "Oh *yes,* it was absolutely worth it!"

What would you say *then*? Would you still claim that God committed a great wrong to permit her horrific (but fleeting) suffering, even though it contributed to her eternal joy? Even though her eternal delight had completely eclipsed her momentary pain? Would you *still* insist that nothing could make up for what happened to her on this fallen Earth?

Is it possible that not only God, but the girl herself, would be better qualified than you to answer that question?

When the drama culminates in a happy ending, our suffering will have raised the stakes and increased our eternal happiness.
"All's well that ends well" is a cliché, but there's truth in it. There's no substitute for a happy ending.

If you've read the book or seen the movie, you feel good about *The Count of Monte Cristo,* a story about Edmond Dantes, who endured years of terrible, unjust suffering in a vile and dank prison. An inscription on his cell wall read, "God will bring justice." At first it comforted him, but as the years went on it mocked him.

Finally, with the help of a friend, he escapes from prison, finds vast wealth, and carries out terrible vengeance—which ultimately he finds unsatisfying. At the movie's end, Edmond Dantes, his wife, son, and best friend look over the rocks from the hellhole where he'd been imprisoned, a place he's now redeemed.

Now imagine as you look at Edmond that none of his long years of suffering had ever taken place. How do you feel? Relieved? No. Happy? No. You feel that something great has disappeared. The *story* has been lost. No more triumph! You've been robbed. So has Edmond.

The Count of Monte Cristo would leave us terribly depressed, *if not for its ending.* But the happy ending turns everything on its head. The same is true of *Les Misérables* and nearly every great story. It's also true of the Bible, the archetypal redemptive story.

I watched an interview with two families whose daughters, students at Taylor University, suffered a terrible car accident in 2006. A truck hit a van head on, killing five people.

At the accident scene, someone found Laura Van Ryn's purse next to Whitney Cerak. Workers at the scene mistook the students, both blondes, for each other. Laura, misidentified as Whitney, was pronounced dead at the scene, while Whitney, misidentified as Laura, fought for her life on the way to the hospital. Some fourteen hundred people attended "Whitney's" funeral, and her father spoke at the service. No one suspected that the body they buried that day belonged to Laura Van Ryn.

Meanwhile, physicians told Don and Susie Van Ryn that their daughter had severe head injuries and would not look like herself, and brain damage could leave her confused. Whenever "Laura" (in fact, Whitney) didn't look or respond like their daughter, they assumed her trauma had caused the problem.

For five weeks the Ceraks believed their daughter had died, while the Van Ryns thought their daughter lived.

When this monumental error finally came to light, both families expressed faith in God. In one conversation, the Ceraks told the Van Ryns, "We are so sorry that we have the happy ending." Don Van Ryn responded, "We do, too...we just haven't seen it yet."

The Van Ryns await their reunion with Laura in a better world.

God promises that the eternal ending will break forth in such glorious happiness that all present suffering will pale in comparison. *All* who know Jesus will have a happy ending.

We just haven't seen it yet.

Notes

1. Juan Williams, "A Hero—Passenger Aids Others, Then Dies," *Washington Post,* January 14, 1982.
2. Peter Kreeft, *Making Sense Out of Suffering* (Ann Arbor, MI: Servant Books, 1986), 98.
3. Ann Stump, video, November 22, 1997. www.epm.org/annstump.html.
4. Fyodor Dostoevsky, *The Brothers Karamazov,* (New York: Modern Library, 1995), 272.

21

Jesus: The Only Answer Bigger Than the Questions

THE CROSS: WHERE GOD'S SUFFERING CONQUERED EVIL

The Cross is God's answer to the question "Why don't you do something about evil?"

Bart Ehrman writes, "I came to think that there is not a God who is actively involved with this world of pain and misery—if he is, why doesn't he do something about it?"[1]

But what if God *did* do something about it? What if what he did was so great and unprecedented that it shook the angelic realm's foundation, and ripped in half, from the top down, not only the temple curtain but the fabric of the universe itself?

A powerful moment in the movie *The Passion of the Christ* occurs when Jesus, overwhelmed with pain and exhaustion, lies on the ground as guards kick, mock, and spit on him. A horrified woman, her hand outstretched, pleads, "Someone, stop this!"

The great irony is that "Someone," God's Son, was doing something unspeakably great that required it *not* be stopped.

Had someone delivered Jesus from his suffering that day, he could not deliver us from ours.

God allowed Jesus' temporary suffering so he could prevent our eternal suffering.

Consider God's history of reaching down to men. He sent angels and prophets. "The LORD, the God of their fathers, sent word to them through his messengers again and again, because he had pity on his people and on his dwelling place. But they mocked God's messengers, despised his words and scoffed at his prophets" (2 Chronicles 36:15–16).

When men would not listen to angels or prophets, God sent his Son (see Hebrews 1:1–4). He came in humiliation; many imagined him conceived out of wedlock, a shameful thing in that era. He grew up in a town of ill repute: "Nazareth! Can anything good come from there?" (John 1:46).

"He had no beauty or majesty to attract us to him, nothing in his appearance that we should desire him" (Isaiah 53:2). He worked as a humble carpenter, which made many people rule him out as the Messiah (see Mark 6:2–3). He lived in relative poverty: "Foxes have holes and birds of the air have nests, but the Son of Man has no place to lay his head" (Matthew 8:20).

They called him a liar: "No, he deceives the people" (John 7:12). Long before his crucifixion, he endured these indignities and much more.

Christ's atonement guarantees the final end of evil and suffering.

As an unbeliever raised with no knowledge of God, part of what drew me to Christ is how the gospel accounts seem so contrary to typical human reasoning. Yet I found them completely credible. No human would make up such a story! It had (and still has) the ring of truth.

Sometimes our familiarity with the gospel story prevents us from understanding its breathtaking nature. That's one benefit of reading other redemptive stories that give us glimpses of the greatest one. To me, *The Lion, the Witch and the Wardrobe* offers particular help in understanding Christ's atoning sacrifice.

Aslan, the all-powerful lion, created Narnia and all worlds. After Lucy hears that her brother has to die for his treachery, she asks Aslan, "Can anything be done to save Edmund?"

"All shall be done," Aslan responds. "But it may be harder than you think." Knowing the terrible suffering and death that await him, Aslan becomes very sad. But he can save Edmund only through his self-sacrifice.

Those serving Aslan's foe, the White Witch, roll Aslan onto his back and tie his paws together. "Had the Lion chosen, one of those paws could have been the death of them all," Lewis writes. Finally, the witch orders that Aslan, their rightful king, be shaved. They cut off his beautiful mane and ridicule him. Aslan surrenders to his enemies, trading his life for Edmund's.[2]

Likewise, Jesus felt overwhelming sadness in the Garden of Gethsemane. He told his disciples, "My soul is crushed with grief to the point of death. Stay here and keep watch with me" (Matthew 26:38, NLT). The soldiers who guarded Jesus mocked him and hit him (see Luke 22:63). And in actual history, Jesus went to the cross to die for us. That's how much he loves us.

The drama of evil and suffering in Christ's sacrifice addresses the very heart of the problem of evil and suffering. One day it will prove to have been the final answer.

THE CROSS: GOD'S PLAN FROM THE BEGINNING

Jesus is the perfect and permanent intermediary between God and man.
In the midst of his suffering, Job cried out for someone who could understand, someone who could bridge the apparently infinite gap between God and man. He lamented, "He is not a man like me.... If only there were someone to arbitrate between us, to lay his hand upon us both, someone to remove God's rod from me, so that his terror would frighten me no more" (Job 9:32–34).

But who could lay his hand upon both God and man, to connect them in loving relationship? Only the God-man, the One who would take God's rod upon himself to pay for the sins of mankind: "For there is one God and one mediator between God and men, the man Christ Jesus" (1 Timothy 2:5).

Every reference to "Good Friday" should remind us that the greatest good in human history came out of the greatest evil.
On the cross Jesus suffered the worst pain in history. Yet that event will forever remain at the center of our worship and wonder.

In his book *The Cross Centered Life,* C. J. Mahaney sees the Cross as the heart of the gospel, and the gospel as the heart of everything else: "If there's anything in life we should be passionate about, it's the gospel. And I don't mean passionate only about sharing it with others; I mean passionate in thinking about the gospel, reflecting upon it, rejoicing in it, allowing it to color the way we look at the world and all of life."[3]

The Cross exposes us for what we are. The punishment our evil warrants answers the question "How evil are we?" The Cross is a mirror showing us the heart-stopping magnitude of our depravity and offers a terrible glimpse of Hell's misery.

The Cross is also a lens showing us God's uncompromising holiness and wrath that demand such a price for sin. It's also a magnifying glass showing us the sweeping vastness of God's grace and love, that he would be willing to pay a price he knew would be so horrific.

Everything before the Cross points forward to it. Everything since the Cross points back to it. Everything that will last was purchased on it. Everything that matters hinges on it.

Children learn a great deal about Jesus by watching Aslan on the stone table, knowing he could kill his mocking enemies with a single word, but instead allowing himself to be bound, laying down his life for Edmund. Jesus said, "Do you think I cannot call on my Father, and he will at once put at my disposal more than twelve legions of angels? But how then would the Scriptures be fulfilled that say it must happen in this way?" (Matthew 26:53).

The temptation to end it all must have been overwhelming. With no more than a thought, just the unspoken word *Come,* Christ could have called upon waiting armies to strike down his torturers and bring him instant relief. Perhaps the greatest wonder is not that Jesus *went* to the cross but that he *stayed* on it.

Why did Jesus suffer the relentless beatings before the Cross? Why did he hang on it for six hours rather than six seconds or six minutes? Perhaps as a reminder that suffering is a process. God does not end our suffering as soon as we would like. He did not end his Son's suffering as soon as he would have liked. We stand in good company.

Spurgeon said, "One short glimpse, one transitory vision of his glory, one brief glance at his marred, but now exalted and beaming countenance, would repay almost a world of trouble."[4] It's one thing to suffer terribly, another to *choose* to suffer terribly. Evil and suffering formed the crucible in which God demonstrated his love to mankind.

What is good about "Good Friday"? Why isn't it called "Bad Friday"? Because out of the appallingly bad came what was inexpressibly good. And the good trumps the bad, because though the bad was temporary, the good is eternal.

God's love comes to us soaked in divine blood. One look at Jesus—at his incarnation and the redemption he provided us—should silence the argument that God has withdrawn to some far corner of the universe where he keeps his hands clean and maintains his distance from human suffering.

God does not merely empathize with our sufferings. He actually suffers. Jesus is God. What Jesus suffered, God suffered.

THE CROSS: GOD'S LOVE PROVEN

Christ's prophesied suffering disproves the accusations against Jesus.

The messianic text found in Isaiah 52:13–53:12 depicts the worst suffering any one person has ever endured. Remarkably, his suffering wasn't because of his own sin; it was for "our" infirmities, "our" sorrows, "our" transgressions, "our" iniquities. Before you read it, ask God to let the weight of this passage fall upon you:

Many who were appalled at him...his appearance...disfigured beyond that of any man...his form marred beyond human likeness.... He was despised and rejected by men, a man of sorrows, and familiar with suffering.... He took up our infirmities and carried our sorrows,...stricken by God, smitten by him, and afflicted...pierced for our transgressions...crushed for our iniquities...the punishment that brought us peace was upon him, and by his wounds we are healed.... The LORD has laid on him the iniquity of us all. He was oppressed...he was led like a lamb to the slaughter...it was the LORD's will to crush him and cause him to suffer.

Rose Price says, "My mother and the rest of the family were murdered in Treblinka. I was in three camps in Poland and three camps in Germany. And the beatings were constant. 'It's all Jesus' fault!' Every time we were hit, the guards would tell us, 'Jesus told us to hit you. Jesus hates you.'" This was Rose's view of Jesus for many years. Then, she says,

I picked up my daughter's Bible. And I started reading it, and reading it, and reading it.... And after I just couldn't find any more excuses, I noticed that he was the lamb.... And he didn't kill me, he didn't put me in a camp, he didn't kill my family. He died for me, did you know that? He died for me! He loved me this much. That he gave himself for me.[5]

Marion Parkhurst, another Holocaust survivor, studied Isaiah 53 and the Messiah's suffering on her behalf. She quotes Isaiah, "He was pierced for *our* transgressions, he was crushed for *our* iniquities; the punishment that brought us peace was upon him, and by his wounds we are healed." Marion finally realized what she could no longer deny: the prophet spoke of Y'shua, Jesus. Marion says, "After I started believing in Y'shua, all the hate left me.... And that was very important because hate is really destructive, it destroys you eventually."[6]

As a girl, Dr. Vera Schlamm and her family suffered in the Bergen-Belsen concentration camp. She said,

Being drawn to Jesus and yet feeling I couldn't believe in Jesus as a Jewish person, you know, having gone through the Holocaust and all that. How could I go into enemy territory, you know, that's the thinking. And yet when I read that "we turned our faces from him," I couldn't deny that that whole chapter [Isaiah 53] was talking about Jesus.... They had the Scriptures out in the temple where I went and the next Friday night I got the Scriptures out and I looked for Isaiah 53 and there it was, same thing. And then I thought, how come I never heard that before?[7]

Ruth Horack says, "I spent three and a half years in the worst concentration camps. Teresienstadt, Auschwitz, Hamburg and Bergen-Belsen." Later she considered the Scriptures, speaking of Messiah and his sacrifice for us. She says, "And I thought about it and thought about it. And then I said to myself, how could we have blamed Jesus for what happened to our people?"[8]

Those who have suffered most are most deeply touched when they grasp Christ's suffering for them.

Christ's suffering does not mean God is weak and vulnerable.

Though many recent writers have spoken of God's vulnerability and weakness demonstrated on the Cross, we must see this truth in the context of God's sovereignty. Christ chose this "weakness."

Christ humbled himself. His obedient death on the cross reflects a deliberate weakness. "The reason my Father loves me," Jesus said, "is that I lay down my life—only to take it up again. No one takes it from me, but I lay it down of my own accord" (John 10:17–18). He willingly chose to suffer as a victim. Scripture portrays a God so strong he can take on weakness to overpower all opposition and accomplish his eternal purposes:

God made him who had no sin to be sin for us, so that in him we might become the righteousness of God. (2 Corinthians 5:21)

[Jesus] made himself nothing,
   taking the very nature of a servant,
   being made in human likeness.
And being found in appearance as a man,
   he humbled himself
   and became obedient to death—even death on a cross. (Philippians
      2:7–8)

Christ also suffered once for sins, the righteous for the unrighteous, that he might bring us to God. (1 Peter 3:18, ESV)

The proven character of Christ, demonstrated in his sacrifice on our behalf, makes him trustworthy even when evil and suffering overwhelm us.
If I had to believe that what we now see represents God's best for this world, I would not be a Christian. If not for the redemptive work of Christ, I would not believe in God's goodness. The fault would lie with me, for God would remain good even if he hadn't gone to the cross for us. But no matter how persuasive the argument that we sinners deserve judgment, I couldn't overcome the obstacles of suffering children, or slaughters like the Holocaust and Killing Fields.

That Jesus Christ, the eternal Son of God, would choose to endure the holocaust of the Cross to pay for sin, that he would take on the sufferings of *all* people in Golgotha's Killing Field, changed the way I look at suffering and evil, and how they reflect upon God's character.

For me, Jesus changes everything.

Earlier I wrote of eighteen-year-old Kevin Butler, who died a few months before I met his father, Randy, in a class I taught on Heaven. For weeks after Kevin's death, his dad, a pastor, cried out to God each morning:

> I asked God, "What were you thinking?" God answered, "I was thinking of what I experienced with my son."
>
> Every time God spoke to me He took me back to the cross. I didn't want to go to the cross. I wanted my son back. There is a silence and a darkness of the soul. There is likewise, a silence beyond the silence, and darkness beyond the darkness of the soul. This is where my journey took me. All roads lead to the cross. While I was gaining peace, I still did not see what God was doing in me. We rarely do.

Randy Butler's healing came from going to the cross. You cannot *truly* go to the cross without realizing God went there before you. And there he purchased the means to wipe away every tear from your eyes.

When you feel God's silence, or think him absent, look at Christ, the "lamb...silent before the shearers" (Acts 8:32, NLT). He shouts to us without opening his mouth: "I *do* care. Don't you see the blood, bruises, and scars? Whatever you may think, never doubt that I care for you."

THE CROSS: GOD'S EMPATHY DEMONSTRATED

God paid the highest price on our behalf; we have no grounds for believing he doesn't "get it."

In all human history, who has paid the highest price for evil and suffering? Poll a hundred people on this question and only a few would come up with the right answer: *God.*

"This is love: not that we loved God, but that he loved us and sent his Son as an atoning sacrifice for our sins" (1 John 4:10). Many complaints against the Creator boil down to this: "God, you don't 'get it.'" Christ's suffering says back to us, "No, actually, I *do* get it. It's *you* who don't get it."

Jesus suffered the same trials and temptations we do. God understands our worst losses and heartbreaks, even our temptations: "Because he himself suffered when he was tempted, he is able to help those who are being tempted" (Hebrews 2:18).

He knows suffering and temptation from firsthand experience. God calls us to hold firmly to our faith precisely because "we do not have a high priest who is unable to sympathize with our weaknesses, but we have one who has been tempted [tested] in every way, just as we are" (Hebrews 4:15).

God might say to us, "I have intimate understanding of what it is to be in your place. You have no clue what it is to be in *my* place. If you'd experienced Gethsemane and the march to Golgotha and the horrors of the Cross, you'd not question for a moment either my understanding or my love."

And he might add, "After you've created a world, and seen your creatures betray you, and you've chosen to die for all their sins and offer them forgiveness...*then* come back and let's talk about it."

Whenever you feel tempted to ask God, "Why did you do this *to* me?" look at the Cross and ask, "Why did you do that *for* me?"
The Bible describes Christ in the garden before he went to the cross: "Being in anguish, he prayed more earnestly, and his sweat was like drops of blood falling to the ground" (Luke 22:44). The enormous stress upon him broke his blood vessels. He chose to die for our evils, to be alienated from his Father, to bear an emotional pain that exceeded even his physical misery.

Bloody, realistic imagery disturbed many who watched the movie *The Passion of the Christ.* But Christ's very worst suffering on the cross—his bearing of sins that separated him from the loving presence of his Father—no one could capture that on screen.

History's worst event happened to history's best person.

God knows what it's like to watch his Son die. Handing over your child to executioners to save others is a far greater sacrifice than losing your child to death when you have no choice.

John Stott, in *The Cross of Christ,* tells a story about billions of people seated on a great plain before God's throne. Most shrank back, while some crowded to the front, raising angry voices.

"Can God judge us? How can He know about suffering?" snapped one woman, ripping a sleeve to reveal a tattooed number from a Nazi concentration camp. "We endured terror...beatings...torture...death!"

Other sufferers expressed their complaints against God for the evil and suffering he had permitted. What did God know of weeping, hunger, and hatred? God leads a sheltered life in Heaven, they said.

Someone from Hiroshima, people born deformed, others murdered, each sent forward a leader. They concluded that before God could judge them, he should be sentenced to live on Earth as a man to endure the suffering they had endured. Then they pronounced a sentence:

Let him be born a Jew. Let the legitimacy of his birth be doubted. Let his close friends betray him. Let him face false charges. Let a prejudiced jury try him and a cowardly judge convict him. Let him be tortured. Let him be utterly alone. Then, bloody and forsaken, let him die.

The room grew silent after the sentence against God had been pronounced. No one moved, and a weight fell on each face.

For suddenly, all knew that God already had served his sentence.[9]

God's Son bore no guilt of his own; he bore ours. In his love for us, God self-imposed the sentence of death on our behalf. One thing we must never say about God—that he doesn't understand what it means to be abandoned utterly, suffer terribly, and die miserably.

Dorothy Sayers wrote,

For whatever reason God chose to make man as he is—limited and suffering and subject to sorrows and death—God had the honesty and the courage to take his own medicine. Whatever game he is playing with his creation, he has kept his own rules and played fair. He can exact nothing from man that he has not exacted from himself. He has himself gone through the whole of human experience, from the trivial irritations of family life and the cramping restrictions of hard work and lack of money to the worst horrors of pain and humiliation, defeat, despair, and death. When he was a man, he played the man. He was born in poverty and died in disgrace and thought it well worthwhile.[10]

That God did this willingly, with ancient premeditation, is all the more remarkable. Jesus said, "I lay down my life for the sheep.... No one takes it from me, but I lay it down of my own accord" (John 10:15, 18).

Some people can't believe God would create a world in which people would suffer so much. Isn't it more remarkable that God would create a world in which no one would suffer more than he?

In his haunting cry, "Why have you forsaken me?" Christ identifies with our despair.

On the cross—echoing David in Psalm 22—Jesus, the messianic Son of David, cried out, "My God, my God, why have you forsaken me?"

The beloved Son who had "well pleased" his Father (see Matthew 3:17) *became* our sin (see 2 Corinthians 5:21). So the Father turned away. For the first time in all eternity, the oneness within the Godhead knew separation. In ways we cannot comprehend—ways that would amount to blasphemy had not God revealed it to us—the Atonement somehow tore God apart.

Some believe Jesus' cry showed he didn't know why his Father had poured out his wrath on him. But Scripture says otherwise. Speaking of his death, Jesus said, "Now my heart is troubled, and what shall I say? 'Father, save me from this hour'? No, it was for this very reason I came to this hour. Father, glorify your name!" (John 12:27–28). Jesus knew why he had to die. He cried out because any separation from his Father constituted an infinite horror.

Tim Keller explains,

> The physical pain was nothing compared to the spiritual experience of cosmic abandonment. Christianity alone among the world religions claims that God became uniquely and fully human in Jesus Christ and therefore knows firsthand despair, rejection, loneliness, poverty, bereavement, torture, and imprisonment. On the Cross he went beyond even the worst human suffering and experienced cosmic rejection and pain that exceeds ours as infinitely as his knowledge and power exceeds ours.[11]

The unrighteous have no grounds for asking God why he has forsaken them—all who understand his holiness and our sin know the reasons. But God's beloved Son had the right to ask, even knowing the answer. In some qualitative, not quantitative, way, Jesus endured the punishment of Hell. When he said, "It is finished," signaling he had paid the redemptive price, Jesus ceased to bear the penalty for our sin. Then "Jesus called out with a loud voice, 'Father, into your hands I commit my spirit.' When he had said this, he breathed his last" (Luke 23:46). The triune God had been restored to utter and complete oneness.

When Jesus cried, "My God, my God, why have you forsaken me?" he bridged the gap between God and us not only theologically, in the Atonement, but emotionally, between our suffering and God's, between our agonizing cries and God's.

How could he endure such suffering for us? And why, since he has done so, would I ever accuse or reject him?

If God can use the horror of Christ's crucifixion for good, then surely he can use our suffering for good.
Christ foresaw the good even as he faced the bad, and that helped him to endure the bad: "[Jesus] who for the joy set before him endured the cross, scorning its shame, and sat down at the right hand of the throne of God" (Hebrews 12:2).

If God brought eternal joy through the suffering of Jesus, can he bring eternal joy through my present suffering, and yours? If Jesus endured his suffering through anticipating the reward of unending joy, can he empower you and me to do the same?

Malcolm Muggeridge, a high-profile British journalist, satirist, and agnostic, sent major ripples across British culture through his conversion to Christ at age sixty-four. Eleven years later he wrote,

> Were it possible to eliminate affliction from our earthly existence by means
> of some drug or other medical mumbo jumbo, as Aldous Huxley envis-
> aged in *Brave New World*, the result would not be to make life delectable,
> but to make it too banal and trivial to be endurable. This, of course, is
> what the Cross signifies. And it is the Cross, more than anything else, that
> has called me inexorably to Christ.[12]

The Christ of the Cross: Our Best Answer

The answer to the problem of evil and suffering is not a philosophy, but a Person; not words, but the Word.
A grieving father asked, "Where was God when my son died?"

A friend answered, "The same place he was when his Son died."

Despite the statement's power, it's not entirely accurate. For God turned away from his Son when he died. Why? So he would not have to turn away when the grieving man's son died. The man and his son can enjoy eternity together in a world without suffering and death because God's Son died for them.

I agree with John Stott:

> I could never myself believe in God, if it were not for the cross.... In the real world of pain, how could one worship a God who was immune to it? I have entered many Buddhist temples in different Asian countries and stood respectfully before the statue of Buddha, his legs crossed, arms folded, eyes closed, the ghost of a smile playing round his mouth, a remote look on his face, detached from the agonies of the world. But each time after a while I have to turn away. And in imagination I have turned instead to that lonely, twisted, tortured figure on the cross, nails through hands and feet, back lacerated, limbs wrenched, brow bleeding from thorn-pricks, mouth dry and intolerably thirsty, plunged in God-forsaken darkness. That is the God for me! He laid aside his immunity to pain. He entered our world of flesh and blood, tears and death. He suffered for us. Our sufferings become more manageable in light of his.[13]

The Cross perpetually establishes God's close relationship to his children.

Many people imagine that though God once suffered on the cross, he's now remote and distant from suffering. Not so! After his ascension, Jesus says to the Pharisee on the Damascus road, "Saul, Saul why do you persecute *me*?" (Acts 9:4). Persecution, of course, entails suffering. One verse later Christ says to Saul, "I am Jesus, whom you are persecuting." Note the present tense—although Christ's atoning sacrifice occurred in the past, he continues to identify with and participate in his people's suffering until he returns to end all suffering.

Christ made it clear that to persecute his people is to persecute him. Whatever others do to his people, positively or negatively, he regards as being done to him (see Matthew 25:40, 45). Christ no longer suffers on the cross, but he suffers with his suffering people.

Edward Shillito, after seeing the horrors of the First World War, wrote this prayer to Christ:

> The other gods were strong, but Thou wast weak;
> They rode, but Thou didst stumble to a throne;

But to our wounds only God's wounds can speak,
And not a god has wounds, but Thou alone.[14]

When we feel upset with God and tempted to blame him, we should look at the outstretched arms of Jesus and focus on his wounds, not ours.
When we lock our eyes on our cancer, arthritis, fibromyalgia, diabetes, or disability, self-pity and bitterness can creep in. When we spend our days rehearsing the tragic death of a loved one, we will interpret all life through the darkness of our suffering. How much better when we focus upon Jesus!

"Let us fix our eyes on Jesus…who for the joy set before him endured the cross." The following verse commands us, "Consider him who endured such opposition from sinful men, so that you will not grow weary and lose heart" (Hebrews 12:2–3).

However great our suffering, his was far greater. If you feel angry at God, what price would you have him pay for his failure to do more for people facing suffering and evil? Would you inflict capital punishment on him? You're too late. No matter how bitter we feel toward God, could any of us come up with a punishment worse than what God chose to inflict upon himself?

Tim Keller writes,

> If we again ask the question: "Why does God allow evil and suffering to continue?" and we look at the cross of Jesus, we still do not know what the answer is. However, we know what the answer isn't. It can't be that he doesn't love us. It can't be that he is indifferent or detached from our condition. God takes our misery and suffering *so* seriously that he was willing to take it on himself. … So, if we embrace the Christian teaching that Jesus is God and that he went to the Cross, then we have deep consolation and strength to face the brutal realities of life on earth.[15]

If you know Jesus, then the hand holding yours bears the calluses of a carpenter who worked with wood and carried a cross for you. When he opens his hand, you see the gnarled flesh of the nail scars on his wrists. And when you think he doesn't understand your pain, realize that you don't understand the extent of his pain. Love him or not, he has proven he loves you.

If you hate suffering, does it make sense to choose eternal suffering when God has already suffered so much to deliver you from it?

In your most troubled moments, when you cry out to God, "Why have you let this happen?" picture the outstretched hands of Christ, forever scarred…for you.

Do those look like the hands of a God who does not care?

Readers should not rely on others' judgments but see for themselves who Jesus is.

Jesus became a man and went to the cross for us, paying for our sins and offering us the gift of eternal life. Jesus asked his Father for another way to the same end. There was none. We cannot be saved another way. And believing in him, trusting in him, is the only way to experience his redemptive work (see John 1:12).

Jesus said, "I am the way and the truth and the life. No one comes to the Father except through me" (John 14:6). The early church believed this and the apostles preached it: "Salvation is found in no one else, for there is no other name under heaven given to men by which we must be saved" (Acts 4:12).

Yet twenty centuries later, a 2008 poll of thirty-five thousand Americans showed that "57 percent of evangelical church attenders said they believe many religions can lead to eternal life."[16]

Jesus asked his disciples the most important question: "Who do you say I am?" (Matthew 16:16). If we get it right about Jesus, we can afford to get some minor things wrong. But if we get it wrong about Jesus, it won't matter in the end what else we get right.

"Come and see what God has done," the psalmist says, "how awesome his works in man's behalf!" (Psalm 66:5).

"Taste and see that the LORD is good" (Psalm 34:8).

Scripture gives us many such invitations to come to God and personally experience him. The best way to do this is to open the Bible and learn about Jesus. Ask yourself who he is and whether you could believe in him. If you hold him at a distance, you will never see him for who he is. Philip simply invited his friend Nathanael to "come and see" Jesus (John 1:45–46).

Have you come? Have you seen him? If not, brace yourself. Because once you see Jesus as he really is, your worldview, your goals, your affections, *everything*— including your view of evil and suffering—will change.

Do you remember the story I told in the introduction about the physician, a young Christian who contracted AIDS while conducting research in Africa? At the end of his life, he could scrawl out only one letter, J, meaning Jesus. Jesus filled his thoughts. "Jesus" was all he needed to say. Jesus was enough for that man.

And, whether or not you know it yet, he is enough for you.

Notes

1. Bart D. Ehrman, *God's Problem* (New York: HarperOne, 2009), 128.

2. C.S. Lewis, *The Lion, the Witch, and the Wardrobe* (New York: HarperCollins, 1978), 151-155.

3. C. J. Mahaney, *The Cross Centered Life* (Colorado Springs: Multnomah, 2002), 15.

4. Charles Haddon Spurgeon, "The Beatific Vision" (sermon 61, New Park Street Pulpit, January 20, 1856), www.spurgeon.org/sermons/0061.htm.

5. Rose Price, *Survivor Stories: Finding Hope from an Unlikely Source,* Purple Pomegranate Productions, Jews for Jesus video, http://store.jewsforjesus.org/ppp/product/210.

6. Marion Parkhurst, *Survivor Stories.*

7. Vera Schlamm, *Survivor Stories.*

8. Ruth Horack, *Survivor Stories.*

9. John R. W. Stott, *The Cross of Christ* (Downers Grove, IL: InterVarsity, 1986), 327.

10. Dorothy L. Sayers, "The Greatest Drama Ever Staged," in *The Whimsical Christian* (New York: Collier Macmillan, 1987), 12.

11. Timothy Keller, *The Reason for God* (New York: Dutton, 2008), 30.

12. Malcolm Muggeridge, *A Twentieth Century Testimony* (Nashville: Thomas Nelson, 1978), quoted in Charles R. Swindoll, *Living on the Ragged Edge* (Nashville: Word, 1985), 71.

13. Stott, *The Cross of Christ,* 335–36, the last sentence quoting P. T. Forsyth, *Justification of God* (London: Duckworth, 1916), 32.

14. Edward Shillito, "Jesus of the Scars," quoted in Mark Dever and John MacArthur, *The Message of the New Testament* (Wheaton, IL: Good News, 2005), 199.

15. Keller, *The Reason for God,* 31.

16. "Americans: My Faith Isn't the Only Way to Heaven," Foxnews.com, June 24, 2008, www.foxnews.com/story/0,2933,370588,00.html.

SECTION 6

Divine Sovereignty and

Meaningful Human Choice:

Accounting for Evil and Suffering

The six chapters of this section take us into deep waters. Some readers may find it fascinating, others difficult, some both. I encourage you to persevere, because this is a vital aspect of the problem of evil and suffering. How we view God's choices and those made by ourselves, other people, and demons isn't merely academic; it's immensely practical. It will shape how we see life's events and how we respond to them.

Our theological position on sovereignty and free will depends on which scriptures we include and which we ignore, or which we see through the lens of the others.

I once spoke to a group of eighty college students on a sensitive theological topic: "Can true Christians lose their salvation?" I asked them to raise their hands and commit themselves to one position or the other. I divided the students on opposite sides of the room according to their answers.

Next I gave everyone a handout consisting of twenty passages of Scripture. After they looked up and read the passages, they were to decide, "If these were the only Scripture passages you had, would you answer yes or no?" In the thirty minutes that followed, tension rose. On both sides of the room, many were confused, some angry. Why? Because to follow the instructions, they had to write down an answer opposite to the one they believed.

After the discussion finished, I explained that I'd given each group different handouts. Those who'd answered, "Yes, Christians can lose their salvation," had Scripture passages appearing to say they couldn't. The no's had passages appearing to say they could.[1] We then pooled the passages and discussed the need to understand others' positions and inform our own positions in light of *all* Scripture. Yes, I had a definite conviction on the issue, but my point was that neither John Calvin nor John Wesley were idiots. They both loved God; they both believed God's Word, but they emphasized different aspects of it.

The Bible says a great deal about human choice and responsibility. It also says a great deal about God's sovereignty. If you look only at hundreds of biblical passages that teach or assume human choice and responsibility, then you will have a small view of God's sovereignty. If you look only at hundreds of biblical passages that teach or assume God's sovereignty, then you will likely assume humans have no meaningful capacity for choice. But we must compare scripture with scripture and discern "the whole counsel of God" (Acts 20:27, ESV).

I believe we should affirm both divine sovereignty and meaningful human choice, and I will do so in this section in ways that may frustrate readers accustomed to affirming one but not the other.

I do have a bias, and it is this: when one must be viewed in light of the other, I think it wiser to view passages addressing human choice through the lens of God's sovereignty, rather than the other way around. Why? Because the universe begins and ends with God, not humankind. The universe is first and foremost not about us but about the purposes, plan, and glory of God. Because he is infinite and we are finite, his choices naturally hold more sway. If we see humanity through the lens of God's nature, as revealed in his Word, we see ourselves accurately. But if, as we read Scripture, we see God through the lens of human nature we are bound to distort him.

These chapters should be viewed as a whole to see them in proper biblical balance. No single chapter in this section is balanced, especially the first three, where I deliberately separate the biblical teachings related to God's sovereignty and human choice, treating them one at a time. These chapters, if read on their own, could be misleading and to some readers irritating, just as being shown only one set of passages was to in that college group.

Only in the last three chapters of these six do I look at passages that affirm both divine sovereignty and human choice in the same context, providing a healthy balance.

My request then is this: before drawing firm conclusions about any portion of the next six chapters, please read them all.

Some who have suffered great evil feel skeptical of the teaching of God's sovereignty, because they understand it to mean that God has personally inflicted evil on them and perhaps even takes pleasure in their suffering. Given the horrors that they and others have faced, they think that believing in God's sovereignty would make him a sadist. How could they turn for comfort to a God who has tortured them?

Others doubt that creatures have the ability to make choices that inflict genuine harm on others, especially on God's children. They believe God couldn't grant such power to creatures while remaining sovereign. If choices of humans and demons have significant negative impact on our lives, they think, then we are out of God's hands, subject to others' evil whims, and God must not really be in control of the universe.

Both of these perspectives lead to something undesirable—a diminished trust in God and his purposes—and both reactions need correction by the whole teaching of Scripture.

Please ask God to speak to you through the scriptures presented in each chapter. And try to reserve judgment on the whole until you see the entire picture.

Notes

1. Randy Alcorn, "Scriptures on Whether True Christians Can Lose Their Salvation (Cited by Arminians and Calvinists)," www.epm.org/articles/security.html.

22

God's Sovereignty and Its Reach

God's sovereignty gives him ownership and authority over the universe.

G od's sovereignty is the biblical teaching that all things remain under God's rule and nothing happens without either his direction or permission. God works in all things for the good of his children (see Romans 8:28). These "all things" include evil and suffering. God doesn't commit moral evil, but he can use any evil for good purposes.

"Dominion belongs to the LORD, and he rules over the nations" (Psalm 22:28). Because he has absolute power, no one, including demons and humans who choose to violate his moral will, can thwart his ultimate purpose.

Christ "upholds the universe by the word of his power" (Hebrews 1:3, ESV). The Greek word translated "upholds" is *phero*, "to carry," the same word used in Luke 5:18 of the friends of the paralyzed man who carried him on his bed to Jesus for healing. God carries the entire universe as men may carry a bed.

"In him we were also chosen, having been predestined according to the plan of him who works out everything in conformity with the purpose of his will," wrote Paul (Ephesians 1:11).

"Everything" is comprehensive, allowing for no exceptions. God works even in those things done against his moral will, to bring them into conformity with his purpose and according to his plan. God can and will redeem the worst thing that ever happens to his child.

When Jesus said certain things "must" happen, he assumes an inevitability related to God's predetermined purpose.
Jesus often declared that certain events "must" happen in line with Scripture and God's sovereign will. Among them:

From that time on Jesus began to explain to his disciples that he *must* go to Jerusalem and suffer many things at the hands of the elders, chief priests and teachers of the law, and that he *must* be killed and on the third day be raised to life. (Matthew 16:21)

When you hear of wars and rumors of wars, do not be alarmed. Such things *must* happen, but the end is still to come. (Mark 13:7)

And the gospel *must* first be preached to all nations. (Mark 13:10)

But first he [the Son of Man] *must* suffer many things and be rejected by this generation. (Luke 17:25)

Did not the Christ *have to* suffer these things and then enter his glory? (Luke 24:26)

Similar wording describes various prophecies that *must* be fulfilled. Why "must" these things happen? Because God *knows* they will happen, some say. Though they involve evil human and demonic choices, God fully anticipates them, even though he doesn't desire them to happen.

Others argue that God knows exactly what he will and will not *permit,* and has a specific redemptive purpose in doing so. Still others say God knows these things will happen because he will *cause* them to happen.

In any case, because of what the triune God knew and decided in eternity past, Jesus not only *might* or *could* go to the cross, but certainly *would* do so. His redemptive work *must* happen.

Though evil had no part in God's original creation, it was part of his original plan.

Christ is "the Lamb that was slain from the creation of the world" (Revelation 13:8). God "chose us in him [Christ] before the creation of the world" and "predestined us to be adopted as his sons through Jesus Christ" (Ephesians 1:4–5).

This means God didn't devise his redemptive plan on the fly. Evil didn't take him by surprise. God isn't the author of evil, but he is the author of a story that includes evil. He intended from the beginning to permit evil, then to turn evil on its head, to take what evil angels and evil people intended for evil and use it for good. In the face of the lowest evil, God intended to show his highest good.

It is possible to plan for something you know is coming without forcing that thing to happen. God didn't *force* Adam and Eve to do evil, but he did create them with freedom and permitted Satan's presence in the garden, fully knowing they would choose evil and knowing that what he would do in his redemptive plan would serve a greater good.

Christ's crucifixion was God's set purpose, known from eternity past.

Peter, speaking to a Jerusalem crowd, said of Christ, "This man was handed over to you by God's set purpose and foreknowledge; and you, with the help of wicked men, put him to death by nailing him to the cross" (Acts 2:23).

If God planned Christ's death, do others die according to his plan? Does the God who had purpose in the death of his Son also have purpose, even though a different one, in the deaths of his other children? Does the same God who intended evil for good in the life of Joseph intend evil for good in the life of other believers? Romans 8:28 suggests the answer is yes.

Countless passages affirm God's control over human lives and circumstances.

Our Creator is "God, the blessed and only Ruler, the King of kings and Lord of lords" (1 Timothy 6:15). The Bible says of him:

> You are the ruler of all things.
> In your hands are strength and power
>   to exalt and give strength to all. (1 Chronicles 29:12)

> But He stands alone, and who can oppose him?
>   He does whatever he pleases. (Job 23:13)

> The Most High rules the kingdom of men and gives it to whom he will
> and sets over it the lowliest of men. (Daniel 4:17, ESV)

Even what appears random is not: "The lot is cast into the lap, but its every decision is from the LORD" (Proverbs 16:33). Jesus said, "Are not two sparrows sold for a penny? Yet not one of them will fall to the ground apart from the will of your Father. And even the very hairs of your head are all numbered" (Matthew 10:29–30). If we believe these things, our reactions to many of the difficulties we face will change. Problems will seem smaller; though we can't control them, we know God can.

A distraught man frantically rode his horse up to John Wesley, shouting, "Mr. Wesley, Mr. Wesley, something terrible has happened. Your house has burned to the ground!" Weighing the news for a moment, Wesley replied, "No. The Lord's house burned to the ground. That means one less responsibility for me."

Wesley did not give a sanctimonious or clever response; I think he recognized not only God's ownership but his sovereign control. We might say, "Get real," but his reaction didn't deny reality. Rather, it affirmed the reality that God owns everything and reigns over all. (Of course, his response to the death of a loved one would have reflected far greater trauma, despite his belief in God's sovereignty.)

God intended for good the evil actions of Joseph's brothers, as well as Joseph's subsequent life in Egypt.

Joseph recognized God's sovereignty when he said to his brothers, who betrayed and sold him into slavery, "It was to save lives that God sent me ahead of you.... God sent me ahead of you to preserve for you a remnant on earth and to save your lives by a great deliverance. So then, it was not you who sent me here, but God" (Genesis 45:5–8). God didn't only *permit* Joseph's journey to Egypt, he *sent* him there through his brothers' evil deeds.

Later Joseph told his brothers, "As for you, you meant evil against me, but God meant it for good, to bring it about that many people should be kept alive, as they are today" (Genesis 50:20, ESV). "God meant it for good" communicates something far stronger than God being handed lemons and making lemonade. God did not merely make the best of a bad situation; on the contrary, fully aware of what Joseph's brothers would do, and fully permitting their sin, God *intended* that the bad situation—which he could have prevented, but didn't—be used for good. He did so in accordance with his plan from eternity past.

We see two wills at work in Genesis 50:20. The brothers successfully did evil, and God successfully brought about good from their evil—but his good dramatically eclipsed their evil. While God did not *force* them to do evil, he sovereignly worked so that the moral evil they committed, and the consequential evils that came from it, accomplished his ultimately good purposes. These purposes extended not only to Israel, but to Joseph and even to Joseph's brothers, the evildoers. (Similarly, some of those who crucified Jesus later embraced the redemption accomplished in his crucifixion. Hence, in a sense inexplicable except by God's sovereign grace, they became beneficiaries of their own evil deed.)

An earlier passage dramatically sets up Genesis 50. God said to Abraham, "Know for certain that your offspring will be sojourners in a land that is not theirs and will be servants there, and they will be afflicted for four hundred years" (Genesis 15:13, ESV). God knew the exact time frame, even though the national enslavement involved the choices of countless people. God then explained that the sin of the Amorites, the inhabitants of the Promised Land, had yet to reach its full measure (see verse 16). God would bring Israel into the Promised Land to drive out the land's inhabitants, exactly when Israel, sick of slavery, would be ready for deliverance and the Amorites, entrenched in sin, would be ready for judgment.

Nothing about God's sovereign work in Joseph's life suggests that God works differently in the lives of his other children. Though events in our lives may have less drama or historical prominence, God didn't act out of character with Joseph. Rather, he revealed for our benefit how he sovereignly works in *our* lives as well.

To understand that short-term evil and suffering sometimes accomplishes long-term good, we must recognize God's sovereignty. John Feinberg, who had written extensively about the problem of evil, tells the story of his wife's diagnosis with Huntington's disease and their deep concern not only for her, but also for their children. They requested a copy of his mother-in-law's medical chart. They discovered that twenty years earlier she had been diagnosed with Huntington's disease, but no one had told the family. Feinberg felt angry, realizing this diagnosis came five years before he met his wife. He writes,

> For twenty years that information had been there, and at any time we
> could have found it out. Why, then, did God not give it to us until 1987?
>
> As I wrestled with that question, I began to see his love and concern
> for us. God kept it hidden because he wanted me to marry Pat, who is a
> great woman and a wonderful wife. My life would be impoverished with-
> out her, and I would have missed the blessing of being married to her had
> I known earlier. God wanted our three sons to be born. Each is a blessing
> and a treasure, but we would have missed that had we known earlier. And
> God knew that we needed to be in a community of brothers and sisters in
> Christ at church and at the seminary who would love us and care for us at
> this darkest hour. And so he withheld that information, not because he
> accidentally overlooked giving it to us, and not because he is an uncaring
> God who delights in seeing his children suffer. He withheld it as a sign of
> his great care for us. There is never a good time to receive such news, but
> God knew that this was exactly the right time.[1]

Now, it could be argued that if Feinberg had known of his wife's condition and the potential for his children inheriting it (what doctors called a 50/50 chance), he should have married her anyway. But that, I think, is part of his point. Perhaps God knew that at the time Feinberg lacked the maturity to do the right thing.

How many options has God withheld from me by not giving me clear knowledge at the time? On two occasions I doubt I would have written a book if I'd known in advance how extremely difficult and time-consuming—over a period of years—it would prove to be. Yet God graciously didn't make this clear, and he has used both of these books in powerful ways that far exceeded my expectations.

God clearly and repeatedly affirms and assumes his sovereignty over all. Many verses make clear that though God's creatures can oppose him, they cannot ultimately prevail. For example:

> I make known the end from the beginning,
> from ancient times, what is still to come.
> I say: My purpose will stand,
> and I will do all that I please. (Isaiah 46:10)

> All the peoples of the earth
> are regarded as nothing.
> He does as he pleases
> with the powers of heaven
> and the peoples of the earth.
> No one can hold back his hand
> or say to him: "What have you done?" (Daniel 4:35)

That he does what pleases him does not mean that all that happens pleases him. Yet the following passages emphasize God's sovereignty in this broken world.

God gives and withholds children. Many couples struggle with infertility, but the Bible consistently ascribes this problem to God. It's said of Hannah "the LORD had closed her womb" (1 Samuel 1:5). God opened Leah's womb (see Genesis 29:31). Sarah said, "The LORD has kept me from having children" (Genesis 16:2). Samson's mother and John the Baptist's mother both had children by God's intervention (see Judges 13:3; Luke 1:13). God oversees the conception of children and works directly to shape the child: "[God] knit me together in my mother's womb" (Psalm 139:13).

God sends poverty and wealth. First Samuel 2:7–8 says, "The LORD sends poverty and wealth; he humbles and he exalts. He raises the poor from the dust and lifts the needy from the ash heap."

God grants limited and conditional power to people, but he, the power-dispenser, still maintains control. Pilate arrogantly said, "Don't you realize I have power either to free you or to crucify you?" Jesus answered, "You would have no power over me if it were not given to you from above" (John 19:10–11).

God determines the times and places people will live. Acts 17:25–26 says God "gives all men life and breath and everything else" and that "from one man he made every nation of men, that they should inhabit the whole earth; and he determined the times set for them and the exact places where they should live."

GOD IS SOVEREIGN OVER DISABILITIES AND DISEASES

Scripture sometimes regards physical afflictions as consequences of the Fall, sometimes as the work of demons, but ultimately sees them from God.

God said to Moses, "Who gave man his mouth? Who makes him deaf or mute? Who gives him sight or makes him blind? Is it not I, the LORD?" (Exodus 4:11). Remarkably, God takes full credit for giving these disabilities. God does not say the Fall makes people deaf or Satan makes them blind, but that *he* does. God doesn't attempt to give a full list. But doesn't he intend us to understand that he also gives people Down syndrome, deformities, cancer, and insulin-dependent diabetes? The fact that we don't like the idea that deformities, diseases, and suffering come from God's own hand does not alter Scripture. Our discomfort will not change God's mind.

Many Christians distance God from disabilities, sometimes arguing that people won't trust a God who would deliberately dispense handicaps. Yet I have spoken with many disabled people who didn't find comfort until they came to believe God had made them as they are.

Right-thinking believers find great comfort in knowing that such life-altering abnormalities don't happen randomly or because of bad luck, but are granted to us with divine purpose. God doesn't helplessly watch us suffer because of bad genes or an accident that Satan or people caused. He offers us help dealing with any disability he has given us.

I've seen clearly how God has used my insulin-dependent diabetes to humble me. It's no accident that it appeared the same month my first book came out in 1985. God wanted me to depend on him. Every day since, I've recognized that need.

If we see God's involvement in people's deformity or disease, we will view them differently than if we think they suffer because of Satan or sin. Whether we believe *God* makes the Down syndrome, trisomy 18, or anencephalic child as they are, profoundly affects our hearts toward them. A large percentage of children diagnosed with diseases before birth are aborted. If we believe Satan alone deforms the child or gives the adult a disease, then we might view taking their lives as battling evil instead of committing it. If we believe God has made these individuals as they are, then we can love them as he intends.

God knows what good may arise from a disease or disability and what evil could come if that disease or disability were withheld or healed.

Vicki Anderson was born with hypertelorism, a facial abnormality. Vicki says,

> I don't really like the phrase "birth defect"—it contradicts my theology. A "defect" implies a mistake and I believe that God is sovereign. If he had the power to create the entire universe according to his exact specifications, then my face was certainly no challenge for him! If God is loving, why did he deform my face? I don't know—maybe because with a normal face I would have been robbed of the thousands and thousands of blessings that I have received because of my deformities. It seems odd, but usually our greatest trial is what most molds and shapes us. It gives us character, backbone, courage, wisdom, discernment, and friendships that are not shallow.[2]

Vicki's mother dealt with this condition from the time of her daughter's birth. She writes,

> I believe that God chose this sorrow for our family. And surprisingly, what I at first felt was a sorrow, I see now as a joy. In all sincerity, if given such a chance, I would not change the journey our family has traveled. We have all learned, we have all grown, and we love the Lord and His sovereign direction in our lives.[3]

God uses disabilities to accomplish his unique purpose.

David O'Brien has had a severe form of cerebral palsy since birth. David demonstrates a joy that transcends his body's bondage. David once asked me to join him at a conference for disabled people. I spoke at three sessions, David at one. Despite David's brilliance, he's not always easy to understand. So he asked me to serve as his interpreter. He laboriously spoke what he'd written, then I read it so everyone could understand.

David's message began, "Is it possible that God has his hand in shaping the events that could lead to a handicap or suffering?" Following David's notes, I read from Genesis 32:24–28, the story of Jacob wrestling with a man identified as God in human flesh, most likely the preincarnate Christ. David observed, "We see Jacob's thigh touched by the Hand of God. Thereafter, his hip was out of joint. This handicap was caused directly by God's Hand." He went on to say, "I believe that the result of God's blessings [David called Jacob's handicap a blessing] were preservation of Jacob's life and a lifelong dependency upon God's ability to carry out his plan."

As a room full of disabled people listened intently, David went on to speak of God's affirmation in Exodus 4:11 that he makes people deaf, mute, and blind. David pointed out that God didn't merely say he *permitted* deafness and blindness, but that he *created* people with those conditions. Then David said, "God knows the spirit and will in each person and he shapes the body to mold that will to his purpose. A gardener uses gradual tension to shape a tree into a beautiful arch. A special body is the gradual tension that shapes spirit and will to glorify God."

I still remember the faces in that roomful of twisted and atrophied bodies, all confined to wheelchairs and beds on wheels. I can still hear the groans of affirmation of David O'Brien's words that rose up to God that day. Those groans reminded me of Romans 8, the Holy Spirit's groanings too deep for words.

David then turned to John 9:1–3. The disciples wanted to attribute a man's blindness to human sin, either his or his parents'. Jesus corrected them: "Neither this man nor his parents sinned." Then Jesus stated the disability's purpose: "This happened *so that* the work of God might be displayed in his life." The "so that" is critical. David said it rules out haphazardness, demonic control, or bad luck. Rather, Jesus declares a deliberate, divine purpose in that blindness. While God would receive great glory in the man's healing, surely he had a purpose for the man's life long before his healing.

David also highlighted Hebrews 2:10 and 5:8, passages that speak of Christ learning obedience and being perfected through his sufferings. David marveled, calling this "a complete surprise" and said, "If it were not in the Scriptures, we would say it's impossible." I could see how this point deeply encouraged people in that room. Christ didn't suffer for us on the cross only. As a human being, he suffered throughout his life, and God used it to accomplish a staggering purpose. I realized that nearly everyone in that room appreciated this truth more than I ever had.

David commented, "If Christ had to suffer to be made complete, how can we expect not to have some form of suffering?" Then he said something unforgettable: "God tailors a package of suffering best suited for each of his own. We all have the opportunity to grow through these." David spoke the following, in words difficult to understand, yet prophetically clear: "Dare I question God's wisdom in making me the way I am?"

As I repeated his words, I realized I could never have said such a thing to these people, not only because I had no right, but because at that time I lacked David O'Brien's perspective.

He added, "If God knew that Christ had to suffer to make him complete, certainly he knows what I need."

David ended his presentation with these words: "I'm sure that if I were not handicapped I would not be here with you. Actually, I would probably be out on a racetrack driving the fastest car I could find."

Laughter erupted. But David had made his point: his disability kept him from doing many things. And while there's nothing wrong with racing a car—perhaps he'll do that on the New Earth—such a distraction might have become his life's focus and kept him from Christ. Deprived of lesser objects of affection, my friend David turned to the greatest, Jesus Christ.

Skeptics may say of these disabled people, "They're denying reality and finding false comfort. They'd do better to admit they were dealt a bad hand and get on with it. If there's a God who loves them, he wouldn't treat them like this."

The people at the conference that night—living as they had for many years, understanding what skeptics don't—found better reasons to believe and worship the God who purchased their resurrection with his blood and offers them comfort and perspective, than to believe the skeptics who've purchased them nothing and offer only hopelessness.

God Is Sovereign in Our Own Suffering

Your state of mind determines whether the doctrine of God's sovereignty comforts you or threatens you.

In his nineteenth-century poem *Invictus*, William Ernest Henley captures the proud human spirit. He speaks of his "unconquerable soul" and brags, "My head is bloody, but unbowed." Charging forward, he claims, "The menace of the years finds, and shall find, me unafraid." He finishes, declaring,

It matters not how strait the gate,
How charged with punishments the scroll,
I am the master of my fate:
I am the captain of my soul.

Spurgeon wrote, "There is no attribute of God more comforting to His children than the doctrine of divine sovereignty. On the other hand, there is no doctrine more hated by worldlings."[4]

Why? Because the proud human heart doesn't want to submit to almighty God. We want to make our own plans, do our own thing, and have it our way. We don't want anyone, including God, to impose his way on us. James identifies the arrogance and evil boasting underlying our presumption that we can do whatever we wish without submitting to God's plan:

Now listen, you who say, "Today or tomorrow we will go to this or that city, spend a year there, carry on business and make money." Why, you do not even know what will happen tomorrow. What is your life? You are a mist that appears for a little while and then vanishes. Instead, you ought to say, "If it is the Lord's will, we will live and do this or that." As it is, you boast and brag. All such boasting is evil. (4:13–16)

We delude ourselves when we think we have ultimate control over our lives. We imagine that God should let us have our way. And when he doesn't, we resent him.

We can trust God's loving sovereignty throughout a lifetime of hardship.

Benjamin B. Warfield, world-renowned theologian, taught at Princeton Seminary for thirty-four years until his death in 1921. Students still read his books today. Few people know his story, that in 1876, at age twenty-five, he married Annie Kinkead. They traveled to Germany for their honeymoon. In an intense storm, lightning struck Annie and permanently paralyzed her. After Warfield cared for her for thirty-nine years, she died in 1915. Because of her extreme needs, Warfield seldom left his home for more than two hours at a time during all those years of marriage.[5]

Imagine your marriage beginning like this on your honeymoon. Imagine how it might affect your worldview. So what did this theologian with shattered dreams have to say about Romans 8:28: "And we know that in all things God works for the good of those who love him, who have been called according to his purpose"?

> The fundamental thought is the universal government of God. All that comes to you is under His controlling hand. The secondary thought is the favour of God to those that love Him. If He governs all, then nothing but good can befall those to whom He would do good.... Though we are too weak to help ourselves and too blind to ask for what we need, and can only groan in unformed longings, He is the author in us of these very longings...and He will so govern all things that we shall reap only good from all that befalls us.[6]

Really, Dr. Warfield? *Only* good from *all* that befalls us? Even from a personal tragedy that deeply hurts your beloved wife and dramatically restricts her personal liberties and your daily schedule, for the rest of her life and for most of yours? Warfield spoke not from the sidelines but from the playing field of suffering, answering an emphatic "Yes!" to the loving sovereignty of God.

Paul wrote Romans 8:28 from a long track record of hardship, beatings, shipwrecks, cold, hunger, and sorrow. He had just spoken of the sufferings of this present time and the groanings of all creation, from God's children and the Holy Spirit himself. Paul brought solid credentials of adversity to writing Romans 8:28. Countless people such as B. B. Warfield have affirmed the same truth, earning the right to do so in the school of suffering.

When we consider the best and the worst things that have happened to us, we often see a startling overlap.
Nancy Guthrie writes of a speaker asking people to fold a paper in half. She then instructed them to write on the top half the worst things that had happened to them, and on the bottom half the best things.[7]

Invariably, people find things at the top of the page that they also include at the bottom. Experiences they'd labeled as the worst things that ever happened to them had, *over time,* become some of the best things that ever happened. That's because God uses the painful, difficult experiences of life for our ultimate good.

In making my own list, I find exactly the same thing—a number of the worst things have turned out to be the best. Try making your own list. If you've lived long enough, if enough time has passed since some of those "worst things" happened to you, then you will almost certainly find an overlap.

How is this possible? Because God is both loving and sovereign. Our lists provide persuasive proof that while evil and suffering are not good, God can use them to accomplish immeasurable good. Knowing this should give us great confidence that even when we don't see any redemptive meaning in our suffering, *God* can see it—and one day we will too. Therefore, we need not run from suffering or lose hope if God doesn't remove it. We can trust that God has a purpose for whatever he permits.

Perhaps the greatest test of whether we believe Romans 8:28 is to identify the very worst things that have happened to us, and then ask if we believe that, in the end, God will somehow use them for our good.

Reflecting on his long life, Malcolm Muggeridge wrote,

Contrary to what might be expected, I look back on experiences that at the time seemed especially desolating and painful with particular satisfaction. Indeed, I can say with complete truthfulness that everything I have learned in my seventy-five years in this world, everything that has truly enhanced and enlightened my existence, has been through affliction and not through happiness, whether pursued or attained.[8]

Notes

1. John S. Feinberg, *The Many Faces of Evil* (Wheaton, IL: Crossway Books, 2004), 464–65.
2. Vicki Anderson, http://aboutfacenow.blogspot.com/2005/01/hypertelorism_23.htmlhttp://aboutfacenow.blogspot.com.
3. http://aboutfacenow.blogspot.com/2005/07/moms-story-final-chapter.html.
4. Charles Haddon Spurgeon, sermon titled "Divine Sovereignty," quoted in Warren W. Wiersbe, *The Bible Exposition Commentary* (Colorado Springs: David C. Cook, 2004), 51.
5. John D. Woodbridge, *Great Leaders of the Christian Church* (Chicago: Moody, 1989), 344.
6. Benjamin Breckinridge Warfield, *Faith and Life* (Edinburgh, Scotland: Banner of Truth, 1991), 20.
7. Nancy Guthrie, *Holding On to Hope* (Carol Stream, IL: Tyndale, 2002), 39.
8. Malcolm Muggeridge, *A Twentieth Century Testimony* (Nashville: Thomas Nelson, 1978).

23

"Free Will" and Meaningful Choice

L iviu Librescu was a seventy-six-year-old professor of aerospace engineering at Virginia Tech. On April 16, 2007, when a murderous gunman tried to enter his classroom, Liviu managed to barricade the door, blocking the shooter's entrance. He held his ground long enough to give all but one of his twenty students time to escape out the window. The killer shot Librescu five times. The final shot to the head killed him.

A Holocaust survivor, Librescu made his choice to stand between a mass murderer and his students, and give his life for them, doing so on, of all days, Holocaust Remembrance Day.

God gave free will to the original humans—perhaps as part of their being made in his likeness.
Scholars debate the meaning of "God's image." But what might creating men and women in his own image and in his own likeness mean? (see Genesis 1:27; 5:1).

God is intelligent, creative, communicative, and free to choose. To be made in his likeness likely includes having these attributes, though on a finite level. We think because he thinks, we speak because he speaks, we create because he creates, and we choose because he chooses. These things all come from God and comprise part of what it means to be human.

God sovereignly created angels and human beings and gave them freedom to choose. He knew what choices angels and humans would make under what circumstances. While he could have intervened to stop them from sinning, he wanted them to choose freely, not under constraint. Furthermore, he planned to use the evil and suffering he foresaw to reveal himself in Christ and his redemptive plan.

Adam and Eve freely chose to sin.
Genesis 2:16–17 tells us, "And the LORD God commanded the man, 'You are free

to eat from any tree in the garden; but you must not eat from the tree of the knowledge of good and evil, for when you eat of it you will surely die.'"

We should take God's words at face value: "*You are free* to eat from any tree." Perhaps hundreds of trees filled Eden, but God forbade eating from only one of them. If Adam could not help but eat from the forbidden tree, then would God tell him he "must not" do so?

Nothing in the biblical account suggests that outside influences or God-given internal desires required Adam and Eve to make a sinful choice. Satan influenced them but did not control them. They weighed God's words and could have obeyed them, but chose evil instead.

God permitted Satan's influence and knew exactly the choice humanity would make under those circumstances. But God did not force Adam and Eve to choose evil. Not only does God not sin, Scripture says God does not tempt anyone (see James 1:13). We should not think of angels and human beings as pawns on a chessboard. God is not the author of evil. He was, however, the author of his creatures' *capacity to choose between good and evil.*

God said to Eve, "What is this you have done?" (Genesis 3:13), not, "What is this that Satan has made you do?" or "What is this I have caused you to do?" Likewise, God declared that Adam had chosen to disobey him, and so God held him fully responsible for his choice. Adam, Eve, and Satan all made real choices— and God judged them accordingly.

The Free-Will Debate

The term "free will" misleads when applied to slaves of sin.

Our free will is limited first because we are finite. Even when morally perfect, Adam and Eve were not free to choose to do whatever came into their mind. Even if they wanted to, they couldn't fly, visit the moon, swim underwater for two hours, run as fast as a cheetah, or make themselves taller or shorter. There are a lot of things they weren't smart enough or strong enough to do. God alone is infinite, and therefore *God alone has completely free will* that permits him to do whatever he wants (and which will always be in keeping with his flawless character).

What may be less obvious to us is that *our* free will is far more limited still due to our sin natures. *We are not just finite, we are fallen.*

Jesus said, "Everyone who sins is a slave to sin" (John 8:34). Romans 6 and 7 repeatedly state that human beings, without the transforming power of God's indwelling Holy Spirit, are "slaves to sin" (6:16, 17, 18; 7:14, 25). Slaves, by definition, have seriously restricted freedom. A slave to sin cannot be righteous: "When you were slaves to sin, you were free from the control of righteousness" (6:20).

True, God can change this condition within us. Paul says, "But now that you have been set free from sin and have become slaves to God, the benefit you reap leads to holiness, and the result is eternal life" (verse 22).

Sinners do not have the freedom to choose in exactly the same way as Adam and Eve did. Freedom still exists, but our fallenness greatly limits our capacity to obey God. Scripture tells us, and experience confirms, that sin holds us in bondage.

Only three human beings have enjoyed moral innocence: Adam, Eve, and Jesus. Adam and Eve lost theirs in the Fall, making slavery to sin the natural human condition. Liberation from that slavery requires supernatural intervention.

Paul wrestles with the reality that even the regenerate person feels inclined toward evil: "When I want to do good, evil is right there with me.... What a wretched man I am! Who will rescue me from this body of death? Thanks be to God—through Jesus Christ our Lord! So then, I myself in my mind am a slave to God's law, but in the sinful nature a slave to the law of sin" (Romans 7:21, 24–25).

Luther and Erasmus engaged in a timeless debate about free will that still frames our modern discussions.

Let's step back five centuries to understand the issue of free will. In 1524 Desiderius Erasmus wrote *On Free Will* to refute Martin Luther's teachings. In response, Martin Luther penned *On the Bondage of the Will*—one of his most important books.

The exchange between Luther and Erasmus remains lively and current because although culture has changed, the issues have not. Erasmus claimed that fallen people have a genuine ability to choose to obey God. Luther argued that sin incapacitates us and that we are, on our own, incapable of choosing obedience. Luther believed that the sin nature, sometimes exploited by demons, dominates unredeemed human beings. Only when God brings new birth to an individual does man receive power to love God and serve him instead of sin.

Luther clarified that he did believe in free will in matters that didn't accompany salvation. "Free choice is allowed to man only with respect to what is beneath him and not what is above him," he said. "In relation to God, or in matters pertaining to salvation or damnation, a man has no free choice, but is a captive."[1]

Erasmus believed God wouldn't command us to do anything unless we could obey; Luther viewed God's commands as a measuring standard to show us our inability to choose righteously.

Grace alone saves us, Luther maintained, and God's empowerment to choose righteously comes to us only with his saving grace. While affirming God's grace, Erasmus believed that repenting and turning from sin to God was within the power of human wisdom and free choice. Luther said to Erasmus, "When you are finished with all your commands and exhortations…I'll write Romans 3:20 over the top of it all." Romans 3:20 states, "Therefore no one will be declared righteous in his [God's] sight by observing the law; rather, through the law we become conscious of sin."

Why did Luther believe this single verse ended the argument? Because it says observing the law will not impart righteousness *since no one will observe the law.* We cannot do so. We are slaves to sin.

Because God repeatedly commands us to obey him, Erasmus argued, we *must* have the capacity or "free will" to do so. Erasmus's argument appears to make sense. After all, I would not command my dog to read a book. I wouldn't even command him not to eat a plate of raw meat set in front of him. (Perhaps a dog somewhere could obey this command, but that dog is not mine.) We never commanded our children to fly around the room, but we did tell them to stay away from drugs, because they could make that choice.

Luther replied that God had a higher purpose in giving us his law. The second half of Romans 3:20 says we are not righteous enough to obey the law, "rather, through the law we become conscious of sin." Luther wrote, "The commandments are not given inappropriately or pointlessly; but in order that through them the proud, blind man may learn the plague of his impotence, should he try to do as he is commanded." Luther argued that even schoolboys know that commands indicate "what *ought* to be done, and ought, for sinners, does not mean *able.*"[2]

Erasmus believed God gives the unbeliever free choice that does not require further divine empowerment; Luther emphasized the human need for God's grace and empowerment to obey.

Believing that Erasmus's view of "free will" made much of man's power and little of God's, Luther wrote, "All the passages in the Holy Scriptures that mention assistance are they that do away with 'free-will,' and these are countless.… For grace is needed, and the help of grace is given, because 'free-will' can do nothing."[3]

Thanks to God's commandments that repeatedly call us to a life we cannot live without him, we can realize our bondage to sin. In desperation we should call on God's grace to do for us what we cannot do for ourselves.

This calling upon God requires God's work in us, since in our own bondage to sin, we cannot escape from our self-made prison. According to Luther, whenever a sinner repents, free will didn't make it possible. Sinners are not only slaves, they're also dead in sin (see Ephesians 2:1). How responsive are dead people? How capable are they of getting up out of the coffin and making right choices? Salvation is *God's* free will at work, to draw, convict, and rescue sinners, miraculously liberating them. Jesus said, "No one can come to me unless the Father who sent me draws him" (John 6:44).

When the sinner comes to Christ, he takes on Christ's righteousness, and the indwelling Holy Spirit empowers him. He's now free and capable of choosing to obey God. Without being redeemed, we have no freedom to do anything that makes us holy and acceptable to God.

On the other hand, by God's common grace, unsaved people, whether secular or religious, remain free to do acts of kindness. However, they may do them without consciousness of God or gratitude to God, and are inclined to do good things with poor motivations (see Matthew 6:1–5).

Given the biblical teaching about bondage to sin, *free will* may be a less-helpful term than *reasonable self-determination* or *meaningful choice.*

Augustine wrote that God has given us "reasonable self-determination." Wayne Grudem explains this: "We think about what to do, consciously decide what we will do, and then we follow the course of action that we have chosen.... Our choices really do determine what will happen. It is not as if events occur *regardless* of what we decide or do, but rather that they occur *because of* what we decide and do."[4]

In light of the debate between Luther and Erasmus, we should consider what different people mean by *free will.* Usually it refers to the capacity of rational beings to choose a course of action from among various alternatives. It can be defined as the "freedom of humans to make choices that are not determined by prior causes or by divine intervention."[5] It can also be seen as "the deliberative choosing on the basis of desires and values."[6]

Jonathan Edwards defined free will as "the ability to choose as one pleases." He explained, "A man never, in any instance, wills anything contrary to his desires, or desires anything contrary to his will."[7]

In that sense, a sinner has free will, but given his sinful nature, he is not free to desire righteousness or live righteously without God's empowerment.

I believe in free will if it means the ability to make voluntary choices that have real effects. I do not believe in free will if it means what evangelist Charles Finney said: "Free-will implies the power of originating and deciding our own choices, and of exercising our own sovereignty, in every instance of choice upon moral questions of deciding or choosing in conformity with duty or otherwise in all cases of moral obligation."[8] This gives more credit to the human condition than Scripture does.

Since I've engaged in discussions and read books where these and other definitions of *free will* are assumed without being stated, I've seen how confusing it can get. Before the argument starts, be sure to define terms.

MEANINGFUL AND CONSEQUENTIAL HUMAN CHOICE

Scripture calls human beings to choose and continuously describes them as making choices.

Having addressed the limits of human free will, we should recognize that the Bible certainly assumes human beings have the ability to make meaningful choices.

Look up all the Bible verses containing the word *choose,* and you'll find that a remarkable number of them speak of God's choices. *His* free will dominates Scripture. But God's Word also speaks of humans making meaningful choices, often with the stated or implied option of choosing otherwise.

After God set forth his laws to Israel and laid out the consequences of obedience and disobedience, Moses assured his fellow Israelites, "Now what I am commanding you today is *not too difficult for you or beyond your reach.* It is not up in heaven.... Nor is it beyond the sea.... No, the word is very near you; it is in your mouth and in your heart so you may obey it" (Deuteronomy 30:11–14). Moses goes on to implore them, *"Choose life,* so that you and your children may live and that you may love the LORD your God, listen to his voice, and hold fast to him. For the LORD is your life" (verses 19–20).

"As surely as I live, declares the Sovereign LORD, I take no pleasure in the death of the wicked, but rather that they turn from their ways and live. Turn! Turn from your evil ways! Why will you die, O house of Israel?" (Ezekiel 33:11). God's heartfelt plea surely implies that he offers his people sufficient resources to make the right choice and turn to him. Would he make such an emotional plea with those who had no choice except to refuse him?

Consider Proverbs 4:13–15: "Hold on to instruction, do not let it go; guard it well, for it is your life. Do not set foot on the path of the wicked or walk in the way of evil men. Avoid it, do not travel on it; turn from it and go on your way." Some will choose to obey these nine commands; some will not. Are those choices real and meaningful so that all will be held accountable for them? Yes.

Through his servants God laid out choices for his people: "Choose for yourselves this day whom you will serve, whether the gods your forefathers served beyond the River, or the gods of the Amorites, in whose land you are living. But as for me and my household, we will serve the LORD" (Joshua 24:15).

God sent the prophet Gad to give David three options. David deliberated and made his choice, which God honored and acted upon (see 2 Samuel 24:12–14).

If a slave seeks refuge, God commands, "Let him live among you wherever he likes and in whatever town he chooses" (Deuteronomy 23:16). Significantly, God regards slaves, who lived with restricted freedom, as having the right and capacity to exercise their wills.

Sinners also make real choices to sin:

Anyone who chooses to be a friend of the world becomes an enemy of God. (James 4:4)

For you have spent enough time in the past doing what pagans choose to do—living in debauchery, lust, drunkenness, orgies, carousing and detestable idolatry. (1 Peter 4:3)

Hebrews 11 commends person after person for their godly choices. Paul calls upon individuals to do what lies within the general power of human choice: "Do your best to come to me quickly.... Bring the cloak that I left with Carpus at Troas, and my scrolls, especially the parchments" (2 Timothy 4:9, 13). No doubt Timothy prayed for God's guidance and mercy on this journey, but the God-given power of choice granted to all men enabled him to gather Paul's books and bring them to Rome. An atheist could choose to do the same.

While Scripture reveals truths such as sovereignty, election, and predestination, it doesn't reveal the reality of human choice as much as it simply *assumes* it, but it does so repeatedly. It's as if something so self-evident as our ability to make choices doesn't require special revelation or commentary. *Of course* we can choose. We do so constantly.

Pastors whose theology might not appear to leave much room for human choice nevertheless continuously call upon their people to make choices to follow Christ, repent, be pure, be honest, share their faith, give, lead, serve, reject false doctrine, and embrace truth, including the truth about God's sovereignty, which people may choose to either accept or reject. All these depend on exercising the human will. They don't only ask God to change the hearts of unbelievers; they challenge unbelievers to weigh Scripture's testimony, consider the evidence for Christ's resurrection, repent of their sins, and place their faith in Christ. Surely we all must believe in *some* degree of meaningful human choice, both for believers and unbelievers.

God gives us choices to test us.

After Abraham showed his willingness to obey God even if it meant sacrificing his son, the Lord said to Abraham, "Now I know that you fear God, because you have not withheld from me your son, your only son" (Genesis 22:12).

God said to Moses, "I will rain down bread from heaven for you. The people are to go out each day and gather enough for that day. In this way I will test them and see whether they will follow my instructions" (Exodus 16:4).

If loving God really means something, then the choice to follow him must be real and meaningful. Consider God's words to his people:

Wash and make yourselves clean.
Take your evil deeds
    out of my sight!
Stop doing wrong,
    learn to do right!
Seek justice,
    encourage the oppressed.
Defend the cause of the fatherless,
    plead the case of the widow.

"Come now, let us reason together,"
    says the LORD.
"Though your sins are like scarlet,
    they shall be as white as snow;
though they are red as crimson,
    they shall be like wool.

> If you are willing and obedient,
>> you will eat the best from the land;
> but if you resist and rebel,
>> you will be devoured by the sword." (Isaiah 1:16–20)

Ask yourself, in this passage doesn't God call upon people, appealing to their reason, to make meaningful, consequential choices for which he will hold them accountable?

Even if we lack strength to do some things, we can do others.

A rebellious child selectively disobeys. He may open the forbidden drawer, yet not play on the road or climb on the roof. Likewise, we may choose to obey God in some areas and not others.

Is it possible to stay away from Internet pornography? Can an unbelieving alcoholic stay sober? Absolutely. As recovery groups all over the world demonstrate, not only believers but millions of unbelievers have learned to make choices contrary to their temptations. This requires that their desire to change, often fueled by remembering the disastrous consequences of their past behaviors, must outweigh their desire to repeat those behaviors.

To believe that God preordains *everything* I do creates problems. If God causes me to make *all* choices, then he causes me to do evil. And if I have no choice, then how do I bear his image? God sovereignly appoints governing authorities (see Romans 13:1), yet judges rulers for their evil choices (see Psalm 110:6).

If meaningful choice does not exist, then life isn't real. Do you have the choice to read this book? Did I have the choice to write it? Right now I'm tired of sitting here thinking and pounding keys day after day, month after month for the last year. I feel like quitting. But I'm still working, because God has given me the power of choice. He's given it to atheists too, but he graciously grants me, as he does all believers, a supernatural enablement that sometimes amazes me.

Our own freedom to choose, though restricted, remains meaningful and consequential.

Some affirm a far too expansive "free will." The human sin nature and consequent moral condition, addictions, choice-making history, and other dominant influences can greatly diminish our volitional freedom.

In his book *The Next 100 Years,* George Friedman states what makes forecasting human behavior possible: "If human beings can simply decide on what they want to do and then do it, then forecasting is impossible. Free will is beyond forecasting. But what is most interesting about humans is how unfree they are."[9]

Treatments on free will sometimes emphasize that no one can predict future choices. But apart from radical steps of intervention, those with addictions know otherwise. A pornography addict, given the opportunity, will look at pornography (unless he has a compelling reason not to, which is also predictable based on past behavior). A football fanatic will always watch the game. A doughnut addict won't turn down a doughnut.

Even at the level of preferences, not addictions, we can rightly say we're free to do what we desire. Our addictions, desires, need for approval, and vulnerability to peer pressure may turn what appears to be a free choice into a "forced choice." To know such dynamics about a person makes it possible to predict their choices—not always, but usually—as many spouses and parents commonly do. (When Nanci offers me a choice of two dinners, she knows which I will choose.) We may make free choices uncoerced by any external force, but powerful *internal* coercions may compel certain choices over others.

Sinners by nature desire what's sinful. In the absence of an external constraint, normally they will choose to sin. They don't *have* to do so—under threat of instant death they would refrain.

Jeremiah 13:23 captures our dilemma: "Can the Ethiopian change his skin or the leopard its spots? Neither can you do good who are accustomed to doing evil." We are evildoers by nature; while we may modify certain behaviors, and even some attitudes, we cannot alter our fundamental nature.

Our real but limited freedom is instinctively misdirected and dangerous.

Four chapters after God says through Jeremiah that we lack the power to transform ourselves from evildoers into doers of good, he speaks of our fallen condition: "The heart is deceitful above all things, and desperately sick; who can understand it?" (Jeremiah 17:9, ESV).

We may freely follow our desires, but this is not entirely good news. Why not? Because *we lack freedom to dictate our desires.* We are not innocent beings inclined to choose whatever's best. We are not even morally neutral beings, objectively weighing and measuring our options. We are congenitally selfish.

Jesus said of the human heart, "From within, out of men's hearts, come evil thoughts, sexual immorality, theft, murder, adultery, greed, malice, deceit, lewdness, envy, slander, arrogance and folly. All these evils come from inside and make a man 'unclean'" (Mark 7:21–23).

How free are we? Free enough to be human, free enough to be morally responsible and accountable, free enough to make consequential choices that matter. Free enough to make choices, some better and some worse—yet not free enough to transform our own hearts or make ourselves righteous before God.

Even prisoners exercise limited freedom with meaningful and consequential choices.

A prisoner may choose to read, watch television, lift weights, shoot baskets, write letters, pray, think about his family, or plot an escape. He can eat or not eat what's on his plate, or trade pancakes for sausage with another prisoner. But he cannot leave his cell and visit a coffee shop downtown or catch a plane to London. The man in bondage makes meaningful choices, free within limits. But those limits are very real.

People who live in the "free world" also live under restraints. To love children requires imposing restrictions on their freedom. Nanci and I put up a fence to keep our grandsons away from the road. We constantly place things out of their reach. They freely make many choices. But knowing them, we realize it isn't enough to say, "Don't do that." Their choices are real, but limited.

We cannot make right or wrong choices unless we can make *real* choices. Yet we are not autonomous, always able to make any choice independently of our natures or external limitations.

Salvation in Christ not only changes our destiny in the afterlife, it radically affects our capacity to resist evil in this life.

Believers' justification by faith in Christ changes our legal status before God, satisfying the just demands of the law, by imputing our sins to Christ and Christ's righteousness to us (see Romans 3:21–26). In regeneration, God grants to the believer a new nature that, as he draws upon God's power, can overcome evil, giving him a greater freedom of choice than he had when he was in bondage to sin.

Regeneration changes our hearts, thereby changing the inclination of our wills. Once regenerated, we choose a better way because, as new people in Christ, we *want* a better way (see 2 Corinthians 5:17). "You, however, are controlled not by the sinful nature but by the Spirit, if the Spirit of God lives in you" (Romans 8:9).

Regeneration empowers the formerly blind to see and comprehend the things of God (see 1 Corinthians 2:12–16; 2 Corinthians 4:4, 6; Colossians 3:10). It renews the will, enabling us to make godly choices (see Philippians 2:13; 2 Thessalonians 3:5). God speaks of the "washing of regeneration and renewal of the Holy Spirit" (Titus 3:5, ESV). Once born again, believers cannot continue to sin as a lifestyle because of our new nature (see 1 John 3:9). Sin is still present in our lives (see Romans 6:11–14; 1 John 1:8–2:2). But we have supernatural power to overcome sin, for we've died to sin and are free from slavery to it (see Romans 6:6–9). God's Holy Spirit indwells us and helps us to obey him (see 2 Timothy 1:14).

Being slaves to sin does not mean unregenerate people can't ever make good choices.
Those without Christ are tied to their sin. While they can modify many sinful behaviors, they can't escape the sin built into their nature. However, Romans 7 says that sinners can't stop doing evil, *not* that they can never do good.

Adulterers, thieves, the greedy, and gossipers can all risk their lives to save a child. Without Christ, we remain spiritually separated from God and cannot earn our way to Heaven, but this doesn't mean we are as evil as we could be or that we lack any capacity to do good.

Does God grant power to his creatures? Yes, the power to choose to get up in the morning, go to work, raise a family, make meals and consume them, paint and sing and laugh and play. He gives us the power to tell the truth or to lie, to cheat on an exam or to be honest.

Does a man have a choice of whom to marry, whether to be faithful to his wife, and whether to protect his child or abuse him? Call it free will, meaningful choice, or anything else, it is God-given and real. If it isn't, our decisions and our lives are merely illusions.

I began this chapter with the heroic choice Professor Liviu Librescu made, saving the lives of his students on a day when an evildoer killed thirty-two people at Virginia Tech. I don't know whether the professor was a Christ-follower, but I do know on that day, in the face of death, Librescu made a meaningful and consequential choice. What made it powerful and significant is that *he didn't have to do it.* He was free to have chosen differently. He made the right choice, and for that his students and their families will always be grateful.

Notes
1. Martin Luther, *On the Bondage of the Will,* 143.
2. Luther, *On the Bondage of the Will,* 159.

3. Luther, *On the Bondage of the Will,* 270.

4. Wayne Grudem, *Systematic Theology* (Grand Rapids, MI: Zondervan, 1994), 192–93.

5. *Merriam-Webster Online Dictionary,* s.v. "free will," www.merriam-webster.com/dictionary/free%20will.

6. Timothy O'Connor, "Free Will," in *Stanford Encyclopedia of Philosophy,* April 14, 2005, http://plato.stanford.edu/entries/freewill/.

7. Jonathan Edwards, *A Careful and Strict Inquiry,* Books for the Ages, AGES Software (Rio, WI: Master Christian Library Series, 2000), 10.

8. Charles G. Finney, *Systematic Theology,* Lecture 2, *"Conditions for Moral Obligation"* from Books for the Ages, AGES Software (Rio, WI: Master Christian Library Series, 2000), 25.

9. George Friedman, *The Next 100 Years* (New York: Doubleday, 2009), 252.

24

This World's Structure Is Necessary for Meaningful Choice

CAUSE AND EFFECT

In a universe where God is Creator and Judge, doing good is always smart while doing evil is always stupid.

Deuteronomy 28 pronounces God's blessing on good choices and his curse on bad ones. In Proverbs a father exhorts his son to distinguish between wise choices and foolish ones; generally, wise choices bring positive consequences while foolish choices bring negative consequences.

While wrongdoing appears to offer benefits, doing right may seem to bring serious disadvantages. Moses "chose to be mistreated along with the people of God rather than to enjoy the pleasures of sin for a short time" (Hebrews 11:25). The right choice brought him short-term pain, while the wrong choice would have brought him short-term pleasure. But in the long run, often in this life and always in the afterlife, God rewards right choices and confers consequences for wrong ones (for believers, this may be loss of reward; see 1 Corinthians 3:12–15; 2 John 8).

"Do not be deceived: God cannot be mocked. A man reaps what he sows" (Galatians 6:7). Justice may seem delayed, but it always comes: "The sins of some men are obvious, reaching the place of judgment ahead of them; the sins of others trail behind them" (1 Timothy 5:24).

Meaningful choice requires a cause-and-effect system in which choices generate consequences.

I've heard people argue that a good and all-powerful God should miraculously intervene every time someone intends to do harm.

But a world of freedom requires cause and effect. For choice to be real it must be effectual, and for it to be effectual it must have structure and predictability. Miracles must be the exception, not the rule. Otherwise, our choices would have no real consequences. I could step off the top of a tall building or hit someone with a baseball bat without fear of the cost, since God would prevent the consequences from my bad choices. (And therefore I would not see them as bad.)

The nature of wood, which allows us to use it as a baseball bat, also allows us to use it as a murder weapon. C. S. Lewis invited us to imagine a world structured so that wooden beams would become soft as grass when used as a weapon and sound waves would not carry lies or insults:

> But such a world would be one in which wrong actions were impossible,
> and in which, therefore, freedom of the will would be void; nay, if the
> principle were carried out to its logical conclusion, evil thoughts would be
> impossible, for the cerebral matter which we use in thinking would refuse
> its task when we attempted to frame them.... Try to exclude the possibili-
> ty of suffering which the order of nature and the existence of free-wills
> involve, and you find that you have excluded life itself.[1]

If God disarmed every shooter and prevented every drunk driver from crashing, this would not be a real world in which people make consequential choices. It would not be a world of character development and faith building. It would not be a world where families put their arms around one another to face life's difficulties. It would be a world where people went blithely along with their lives, content to do evil and put up with it, feeling no need to turn to God, no incentive to consider the gospel and prepare for eternity. In such a world, people would die without a sense of need, only to find themselves in Hell.

Peter van Inwagen writes, "If God simply 'canceled' all the horrors of this world by an endless series of miracles, he would thereby frustrate his own plan of reconciliation. If he did that, we should be content with our lot and should see no reason to cooperate with him."[2]

The evil and suffering of this world fit a God who despises evil but values freedom. God desires meaningful relationships with his creatures, and that requires a degree of freedom on our part.

Ironically, those who most value the freedom to choose are quickest to condemn God for allowing evil and suffering.

Critics of a God who allows evil and suffering may feel deeply that they should have the freedom to smoke, or drive at the speed they wish, or not to wear seat belts or bicycle helmets. Then when they get injured or inflict injury on others, they question God's goodness, unwilling to take responsibility for the consequences of the choices they so value.

Freedom to do good, which brings good consequences, cannot exist without the corresponding freedom to do evil, which brings suffering.

God said, "It is not good for the man to be alone" (Genesis 2:18). Interdependence lies at the core of the human community. The fact that I wrote this book and you are reading it testifies to our need for each other. But in this world as it is, we can't influence each other for good unless we can also influence each other for evil. If I could not hurt you, I could not help you. If you could not kill me, you could not die for me.

God made the world as he did so that we could live in relationships where our choices have consequences in the lives of others. If we value freedom, we value a world that allows both good and evil choices. If we say we wish God made humans without the freedom to do evil, we are saying we don't think humans should have freedom. Which is to say that humans shouldn't be human.

God could not make human beings while eliminating the process by which humans mature; he could create us innocent, but we must *become* righteous.

We come into the world as infants, gradually growing physically and mentally. We learn by experience. Human beings don't enter the world as twenty-year-olds. For God to fast-forward our lives to an eternity in Heaven would be to bypass the life experiences that define us. Christ could not just snap his fingers and declare us redeemed. He had to actually come into this world, in space-time history, to redeem us. Even Adam and Eve, though created innocent, weren't created wise. They needed to grow in understanding.

Scripture teaches a continuity of our identity from this life to the next.[3] For us to become the best people we can be for eternity, something needs to happen in us while we live here. As we move through a world of choice and consequences, we need to come to see God for who he is and his goodness for what it is. We need to see his power, love, grace, mercy, and patience. As finite humans we can learn those virtues only by observation and experience.

God has allowed moral evil in this world to show its ugliness, that we might forever know the difference between good and evil and cherish the goodness he purchased for us at Calvary. To skip the process of life under the Curse and get ushered into eternity already declared righteous, without facing suffering, might sound good. But it would not accomplish God's highest purpose for us. He intends to bring about an eternal world where righteousness reigns because he has marvelously overcome evil.

This world under the Curse will be remade into a new world. Meanwhile, God is not only preparing a place for us; he is, through our suffering and character growth, preparing us for that place (see 2 Peter 3:11–14).

If God protected us from poor choices, he wouldn't be protecting us, because there would be no "us."

In a question-and-answer session with teenagers at my church, one student asked, "Why doesn't God just overrule our choices whenever we're about to hurt ourselves or someone else?"

My eyes fell on two students I'd coached that week at the district tennis tournament. "Suppose," I said, "I had the power to keep Ryan and Stefan from making any choices that would hurt them. And suppose I had the power to keep anyone else from making choices that would hurt Ryan and Stefan. Should I do it? At first the obvious answer seems yes.

"But it's not so simple. I value Stefan and Ryan because they are human beings, distinct individuals, with their own personalities, qualities, and abilities. A fundamental part of their identity is their ability to make choices that have consequences. They're part of a human community, including their families and neighbors and society, who have the same capacity to choose.

"If I intervened to stop Stefan and Ryan from making hurtful decisions and keep others from hurting them, in the end I wouldn't be protecting Stefan and Ryan, because they would no longer *be* Stefan and Ryan. I would save them from evil and suffering, but they would lose their freedom, and become incapable of learning and maturing. They would no longer be the people I value."

Eliminating choice or its consequences would mean eliminating people, marriage, family, and culture, and signal the end of meaningful life. Isn't that too high a price to pay?

The Need for Effectual Choice

Meaningful choice must exist for love to exist.

Human freedom is a good that justifies the reality of a temporary evil; to argue that God should not permit evil or suffering is to argue against not only human choice, but love. In other words, a world without the choice to hate would be a world without the choice to love.

C. S. Lewis said, "Why, then, did God give them free will? Because free will, though it makes evil possible, is also the only thing that makes possible any love or goodness or joy worth having. A world of automata—of creatures that worked like machines—would hardly be worth creating."[4]

Can real love exist without freedom? Suppose that through threats, drugs, or hypnotism I could coerce my wife to love me. First, it would be a contradiction in terms. Her "loving" words and actions would be an illusion, meaning nothing if they originated in me, not in her. I don't want to force her to love me; I want her to love me simply because she does, because she wants to. I may inspire or "win" her love through my devotion to her, but I cannot dictate it, nor would I if I could. Forced love is no love at all. Love requires the freedom not to love.

In the movie *The Stepford Wives,* husbands program "perfect" wives. Of course, these robotic wives are perfect only in the sense that they will do whatever their husbands want. But what men really desire, despite the difficulties and conflicts it brings, is to have a relationship with a real person who responds as she chooses. When she says, "Thank you," or, "I love you," or laughs at his jokes or kisses him, she really means it. Fake or programmed love is cheap and empty.

God is our Father, Christ is our Bridegroom. The Father wants real children, not Stepford children. The Bridegroom wants a real wife, not a Stepford wife. The kind of people you would fashion to make a utopia might satisfy a museum curator or an engineer, but they would never satisfy a father or a husband.

The Free Will Defense offers what may be a *partial* and *limited* answer to the problem of evil.

Alvin Plantinga's Free Will Defense[5] has had a powerful influence on modern philosophers, most of whom concede it to be a valid response to the logical problem of evil as classically stated. Plantinga says,

> A world containing creatures who are significantly free (and freely perform
> more good than evil actions) is more valuable, all else being equal, than a
> world containing no free creatures at all. Now God can create free crea-
> tures, but He can't cause or determine them to do only what is right. For
> if He does so, then they aren't significantly free after all; they do not do
> what is right freely. To create creatures capable of moral good, therefore,
> He must create creatures capable of moral evil; and He can't give these
> creatures the freedom to perform evil and at the same time prevent them

from doing so. As it turned out, sadly enough, some of the free creatures
God created went wrong in the exercise of their freedom; this is the source
of moral evil.[6]

Even many who don't believe in God have acknowledged that his argument
seems reasonable.

Still, some theologians offer arguments against the Free Will Defense.[7] For
instance, it doesn't account for natural evil such as suffering caused by earthquakes, birth defects, and disease, which do not occur as a direct consequence of
human choice.

A counter-argument is that natural disasters do indeed occur as a consequence
of humanity's free choice to sin, which brought ruin to the earth (see Genesis
3:17; Romans 8:19–22). Another proposed solution claims that natural evil
results from Satan's free choices.

Peter van Inwagen says, "The simple form of the free-will defense can deal
with at best the existence of *some* evil—as opposed to the vast amount of evil we
actually observe—and the evil with which it can deal is only that evil that is
caused by the acts of human beings."[8]

Though many people think the free-will argument gives the best response to
the problem of evil, it doesn't seem to me that the value of human autonomy,
even if necessary for love, could alone outweigh all the world's suffering and evil.
The greater-good argument seems more compelling and springs directly from
the Bible (see, for example, Romans 8:18; 2 Corinthians 4:17). In fact, the building of Christlike character alone might be enough to outweigh evil and suffering, as might be the eternally celebrated unveiling of God's grace in his drama of
redemption.

But could the greater-good argument itself work without meaningful choice?
Without such choice, could we have a meaningful relationship with God? The
greatest commandment is that we love God with our whole beings (see Matthew
22:37). Could we do that without being capable of meaningful choice? Could we
even be "we" without it?

If families and churches could never choose to turn against each other and
break each other's hearts, would we have fallen to our knees to beg God's miracle
of reconciliation? Would we as much appreciate in the coming ages the everlasting loyalty and oneness of God's family? Choice is a bittersweet gift, is it not?

Yet all this talk of human free will must be balanced with the reminder of
God's sovereignty. Paul anticipates our natural response to his argument for God's

sovereignty and election: "One of you will say to me: 'Then why does God still blame us? For who resists his will?' But who are you, O man, to talk back to God? 'Shall what is formed say to him who formed it, "Why did you make me like this?"' Does not the potter have the right to make out of the same lump of clay some pottery for noble purposes and some for common use?" (Romans 9:19–21).

Scripture appeals here to God's free will, not man's, to Creator's rights, not creatures' rights. And lest we think that calling himself the potter and us the clay is playing God, we should remember that God does not play God. He *is* God.

Notes

1. C. S. Lewis, *The Problem of Pain* (New York: Macmillan, 1962), 33–34.
2. Peter van Inwagen, ed., *Christian Faith and the Problem of Evil* (Grand Rapids, MI: Eerdmans, 2004), 71.
3. Randy Alcorn, *Heaven* (Wheaton, IL: Tyndale House, 2004), 65, 273–74, 278.
4. C. S. Lewis, *Mere Christianity* (New York: Macmillan, 1952), 52.
5. See Alvin Plantinga, *God, Freedom, and Evil* (Grand Rapids, MI: Eerdmans, 1974).
6. Plantinga, *God, Freedom, and Evil*, 30.
7. John Frame, *Apologetics to the Glory of God* (Phillipsburg, NJ: Presbyterian and Reformed, 1994).
8. Van Inwagen, *Christian Faith and the Problem of Evil*, 65.

25

Meaningful Human Choice and Divine Sovereignty Working Together

Any discussion of sovereignty and free will is challenging. I don't want to get too technical, but trying to make things too easy results in oversimplification and misstatement. So if you want to stretch your brain a little more on this issue, this chapter is for you. If not, skip to the next chapter.

God being sovereign does not mean the world as it is now is the best possible world.

German philosopher and mathematician Gottfried Leibniz believed God is sovereign and wise. Since God had his choice of what kind of world to create, this world must be "the best of all possible worlds." Leibniz's logic worked better when applied to the original world God created. God called it "very good" (Genesis 1:31). Even the ability for his image-bearers to choose freely was good, despite the evil and suffering that might arise.

Yet couldn't that original world have been even better? Couldn't he have added on one more spectacular waterfall or fantastic animal? Or could he have made it better by delaying Satan's access and postponing the Fall a little longer?

That God considered the original Earth "very good" is not to say it couldn't have been better.[1] No one, including Adam and Eve, has yet experienced the best possible world. Certainly the New Earth will be a better world, in light of Christ's redemptive work that purchased it and the glimpses we're given of it in Scripture (see, for example, Isaiah 60–65; Revelation 21–22). Assuming that God will continue to create in the coming world, might not the new universe continue to get better and better? Our infinitely creative God may always on each new day bring a greater good to the universe, so that with all its magnificence, even the New

Earth as we first experience it will not be the best possible world, though every day it will be the best world there has ever been.

Clearly, however, the world as it exists *now* does not qualify as the best possible world. For it is neither as God created it nor as it one day will be. It was once better and it will eventually be better. It is at most the best possible world *under the circumstances,* those circumstances being that it is fallen. But even then it would seem that a single evil removed from this world or a single good added to it could make it a better world.

A few years after a major earthquake devastated Lisbon in 1755—taking an estimated ninety thousand lives—Voltaire wrote *Candide.* He mockingly repeated Leibniz's position: "All is for the best in the best of all possible worlds." That worldview appeared silly in the wake of such a horrific tragedy.

The Lisbon earthquake had an interesting feature that prevented Christians from arguing that God had brought judgment on a corrupt society. The earthquake occurred on All Saints' Day, when churches had filled up with worshiping saints. Nearly all those church buildings collapsed, killing the worshipers inside.

Voltaire wrote in *Candide,* "If this is the best of all possible worlds, then what are the others like?"

We become Voltaire-like cynics if we judge the Creator by the way the world is now. But if we look back to what it once was and fast-forward to what it will one day be, everything changes. And if we view the present world as an essential part of the preparation for that future world, then we may see the present world, even with all its evil and suffering, as *the best possible way for God to get us to that best possible world* that awaits us.

Years ago, in Milan, Nanci and I saw da Vinci's painting *The Last Supper.* Faded and marred, the disappointing work didn't seem beautiful unless you reminded yourself of how it once appeared. A restoration process had begun, according to a sign, but we couldn't see any progress. Had someone said, "This is the best of all possible paintings," we would have laughed. But today, post-restoration, its beauty sparkles once more.

The Sistine Chapel, with Michelangelo's ceiling paintings badly faded, underwent a similar restoration. It took our breath away when we saw it in 2008. No thinking person would call the deteriorated works of da Vinci or Michelangelo "the best of all possible paintings." But the original and now the restored versions were and are magnificent.

God has hung a sign on this Earth that says, "Condemned: Plans in place for radical restoration, to begin soon. Come back and see. You'll love it."

God's Influence on Our Wills

God invites us and sovereignly empowers us to choose to come to him.
God's invitation to come to him assumes the possibility of a real and meaningful choice to accept it.

> Come to me, all you who are weary and burdened, and I will give you rest. (Matthew 11:28)

> "The Spirit and the bride say, 'Come!' And let him who hears say, 'Come!' Whoever is thirsty, let him come; and whoever wishes, let him take the free gift of the water of life" (Revelation 22:17).

As a young Christian I recited memory verses printed on small cards. One of them said, "Him who comes to me I will not cast out" (John 6:37, RSV). But the first part of the same verse apparently didn't fit someone's theology, since it was left out: "All that the Father gives me will come to me, and..."

Similarly, Jesus goes on to say, "No one can come to me unless the Father who sent me draws him" (verse 44). And in case we still don't get the message, he adds, "No one can come to me unless the Father has enabled him" (verse 65).

Apparently we freely choose Christ because he empowers us to do so. That may not make sense to us, but when we compare all scriptures, discarding none, that seems to be the truth.

People genuinely respond to God, yet God first opens their hearts: "One of those listening was a woman named Lydia, a dealer in purple cloth from the city of Thyatira, who was a worshiper of God. *The Lord opened her heart to respond* to Paul's message" (Acts 16:14).

God calls us spiritually dead without Christ (see Ephesians 2:1). We did not, by acts of our will, make ourselves alive. Rather, "when you were dead in your sins and in the uncircumcision of your sinful nature, *God made you alive with Christ. He forgave us all our sins*" (Colossians 2:13). Lazarus serves as an illustration of what it means to be dead, then made alive. When Jesus said, "Lazarus, come out!" (John 11:43), the dead man lacked the capacity to obey until Jesus made him alive. Who's more helpless than a dead man?

Still...God extends a *genuine*, not a *pretend* invitation to choice-making people to come to him. They can do so as he sovereignly empowers them.

Jesus said, "And I, when I am lifted up from the earth, will draw all people to myself" (John 12:32, ESV). "All people" is broad and inclusive. The book's larger context shows not all will be saved, yet when Jesus speaks of dying for the world and drawing all men to himself, he seems to deliberately cast his net wide.

Sometimes Christians assume we have a full capacity to respond to God. But this doesn't square with any number of scriptures, including this one: "For just as the Father raises the dead and gives them life, even so the Son gives life to whom he is pleased to give it" (John 5:21). It appears that a person doesn't simply choose life; Jesus gives it to him.

Notice carefully what Paul wrote about repentance: "Those who oppose him [the Lord's servant] he must gently instruct, in the hope that God will grant them repentance leading them to a knowledge of the truth, and that they will come to their senses and escape from the trap of the devil, who has taken them captive to do his will" (2 Timothy 2:25–26).

Sinners should choose to repent, yet only God grants saving repentance. God calls upon us not only to surrender and lay down our arms, but to switch sides. We need his empowerment to do this.

Without Christ, we have freedom to act upon our desires, but by nature we do not desire to please God and cannot fully obey him.

Romans 8:7 tells us the sinful mind "does not submit to God's law, nor *can* it do so." In our sinful state, we have no innate ability to follow God. People who lack the Spirit cannot begin to understand spiritual things (see 1 Corinthians 2:14).

Our problem is both our unwillingness to understand *and* our incapacity to turn our wills toward God. Once we grasp the depths of this problem, we will fully appreciate the wonders of his grace. Without that insight, we might imagine ourselves in Heaven congratulating one another that we had the savvy and strength of will to turn to Christ. But God leaves no room for such boasting (see Ephesians 2:8–9; Titus 3:5).

God's amazing grace doesn't end at our conversion. Even the regenerated human will depends upon the divine will to live as it should. Philippians 2:12–13 corrects both those who understate and those who overstate the role of the human will: "Continue to work out your salvation with fear and trembling, for it is God who works in you to will and to act according to his good purpose." We must will and work, *and* God must will and work.

SOVEREIGNTY AND HUMAN CHOICE-MAKING

Because God wills things in two different senses, God's will does not always get done, yet his will is never frustrated.

I've heard people say, "God's will cannot be thwarted." If by "God's will" we mean his ultimate, decreed purpose, then yes, that is true, since Ephesians 1:11 says that God "works out everything in conformity with the purpose of his will."

But if we mean that God's moral laws and stated desires cannot be violated, that is clearly wrong. Wherever evil exists, we see a violation of God's moral will. The prayer "Thy will be done in earth, as it is in heaven" (Matthew 6:10, KJV) assumes that God's will often is *not* presently done on Earth.

If everything on Earth takes place as God wills it, then why would he have agonized over the human evil that moved him to judge the earth with the Flood? Why did Jesus weep over the death of Lazarus? Is it God's will that sexual predators rape women and enslave children? No.

Jeremiah says of God, "He does not willingly bring affliction or grief to the children of men" (Lamentations 3:33)—and yet the prophet writes in the context of the God-ordained destruction of Jerusalem by Babylon. Other passages show that God does indeed bring affliction, but with reluctance. No father enjoys seeing his child in pain.

Scripture says the omnipotent God desires many things that don't happen; for instance, he "desires all people to be saved and to come to the knowledge of the truth" (1 Timothy 2:4, ESV). Taking these words at face value, since not all people will be saved, then God's desire will go unfulfilled. He wants people to repent of sin, to love him and love their neighbor, but often they don't.

Jesus wept over Jerusalem when he wanted one thing and Jerusalem wanted another: "O Jerusalem, Jerusalem, the city that kills the prophets and stones those who are sent to it! How often *would* I have gathered your children together as a hen gathers her brood under her wings, and you *would* not!" (Matthew 23:37, ESV). Remarkably, the same Greek word for "wishing, wanting, or willing" *(thelo)* is used for what Jesus wanted and what the people of Jerusalem wanted. Yet Jesus didn't get what he said *he* wanted, while Jerusalem did, successfully resisting *his* will (to its own ruin).

Of course, as God's Son, Jesus could have overpowered the will of Jerusalem's people and forced them to accept him. But he sovereignly chose not to do so. One day Jesus will reign over the New Jerusalem, filled with people who love him and willingly and eagerly bow to his lordship. So Christ's will shall *ultimately* prevail, even though he permitted it to be *immediately* resisted. Ironically, Jerusalem's immediate *rejection* of his will was necessary to accomplish the ultimate *fulfillment* of his will through his redemptive work.

If you were asked, "Can humans reject God's purposes for us?" how would you answer? My instinct is to answer no. Yet the Bible, without qualification, claims the Pharisees "rejected the purpose of God for themselves" (Luke 7:30, ESV). I stand corrected.

How do these passages fit with God's sovereignty? After all, if an omnipotent God really wants something, then won't he simply make it so? Well, not necessarily—and even if he does, he won't necessarily make it so *now*.

Although humans lack sovereignty, we often choose not to exercise the power we do have. Parents can overpower their children to force them to do their will, but often they choose not to. A teacher may give students opportunities to try something their way, before forcing her will upon them.

Since humans can disobey God, they can violate God's stated will. So in that sense, God's will can be both opposed and thwarted, though no one can thwart the ultimate purposes of God. This distinction is vital for women who think that God desired and willed their fathers to rape them for years. How can they turn to God for redemption and ultimate deliverance from horrors they believe God himself has inflicted upon them? One does not turn to the torturer for deliverance.

Those who believe and teach, without clarification, that no one can ever violate God's will need to take a closer look at Scripture and their message. They should balance their stress on God's sovereignty—a *vital* emphasis—with the full biblical teaching, including passages such as those we're examining.

Scripture does not teach that God wills everything, in the sense that he forces everything or is pleased with everything that happens in this fallen world.

Fatalism holds that everything, including evil and suffering, happens in a predetermined and inevitable way, with human beings powerless to effect change. It results in an attitude of acquiescence. Fatalism predominates among many, though not all, Hindus and Muslims. The term *Insha'Allah* implies that whatever happens is God's will. Unfortunately, some Christians also think like fatalists.

Where does such logic take us? If God permits racism, slavery, and child sex trafficking, then why should we battle them? Here's why: the Bible speaks much about God's sovereignty, yet constantly calls upon people to take action, and to speak up for and help the poor and needy (see, for example, Proverbs 31:8–9)— this is the polar opposite of fatalism.

Albert Einstein said, "The world is too dangerous to live in—not because of the people who do evil but because of the people who sit and let it happen."[2] Some of that problem stems from indifference, some from fatalism.

Since God can use evil for his glory, if I abstain from a sin or try to stop a sin, am I in danger of trying to thwart God's will? No, because God commands us to intervene to stop injustice, so that his moral will is done. Why? Because his moral will is *not* currently being done.

Humans can resist God and do reject him: "Yet they rebelled and grieved his Holy Spirit. So he turned and became their enemy and he himself fought against them" (Isaiah 63:10). "You stiff-necked people, with uncircumcised hearts and ears! You are just like your fathers: You always resist the Holy Spirit!" (Acts 7:51).

Scripture teaches that humans make real choices and that we must resist evil, yet God remains sovereign in a nonfatalistic way, offering us choices and encouraging us to pray for him to bring changes, and to do what we can to change our lives and the world itself. This may confuse us, but the Bible plainly teaches both truths.

Determinism, libertarianism, and compatibilism offer differing views on the relationship between God's sovereignty and human choice.

Disclaimer: My point here is not to bog you down with terminology, but rather to help you understand these different positions. Whether you use these terms doesn't matter, but whether you understand the concepts they refer to does. I hope you'll gain insight by comparing and contrasting these positions and deciding which you think Scripture most supports. (I recommend you consult further sources taking various positions on these views.)[3]

Determinism affirms that "acts of the will, occurrences in nature, or social or psychological phenomena are causally determined by preceding events or natural laws."[4] Simply put, everything happens because it must.

Some who follow astrology and horoscopes believe in determinism. Some Christian determinists believe God orchestrates in advance each reality, including every demonic and human choice.

Libertarianism claims humans have free will and that free will and determinism cannot coexist. In philosophy (not politics), the term refers to the idea that human free will, undetermined, is necessary for moral responsibility.

Compatibilism holds that free will—understood as people able to make meaningful choices for which they are morally responsible—can coexist with determinism—understood as God remaining completely sovereign, his decrees not being thwarted by his creatures' choices.

Despite the paradoxical nature of sovereignty and free will, Christian compatibilists believe God reveals both ideas to be true and understands how they fit together, even if we do not.[5]

Hard determinism is incompatible with meaningful human choice.

The terms *hard determinism* and *soft determinism* aren't as commonly used anymore but offer a helpful distinction.

There are non-theistic hard determinists. They may believe that heredity, environment, unconscious impulses, defense mechanisms, and other influences absolutely determine how people will act. There are also theistic hard determinists, who believe God determines how people will act. Essentially, the hard determinist believes that freedom is an illusion.

Among Christians, a hard determinist would be what Spurgeon, a Calvinist and compatibilist, called a "hyper-Calvinist." The hard determinist believes that God orchestrates every single choice, good or evil. If a woman is raped, God sends the rapist. If a child is beaten, God moves the hand of the abuser against the child. This seems to deny meaningful choice, and our genuine capacity to love, hate, learn, rebel, or follow. It violates countless scriptures that assume we can and do make meaningful decisions daily.

A famous example of hyper-Calvinism occurred at a British ministers' gathering in 1787, when William Carey affirmed his desire to go to India as a missionary. One of the pastors responded, "Sit down, young man. When God decides to save the heathen, He will do it without your help."[6]

Hard determinism appears to put a holy and good God in the role of devising and carrying out moral evil through demonic and human henchmen. Creatures serve as his instruments of evil. This makes God the author of sin, which Calvin affirmed he is not.[7] It trivializes the nature of God's image-bearers, and undercuts the persuasive power and beauty of God's wondrous redemptive plan. It presents an impersonal engine of cause and effect quite different than the dynamic, loving, and sometimes tragic relationships between God and humans portrayed in Scripture.

The hard determinist must answer these questions: If God makes moral evil happen, why would he be outraged and grieved at the human evil he orchestrates, and why would he punish people in Hell for doing precisely what he made them do in the first place? And if he causes moral evil, how can the Bible declare him to be holy and separate from moral evil, and to despise it?

Soft determinism allows room for meaningful human choice.

Many Christian compatibilists think of themselves as "soft determinists." They are determinists in the sense that they believe God is absolutely sovereign and that nothing occurs that he cannot use to fulfill his plan and further his glory. They don't accept the notion that life is random or that one's destiny can be in the hands of demons and other people.

Their determinism is *soft* as opposed to hard, because compatibilists fully affirm the reality and consequences of voluntary evil choices demons and humans make. They do not ascribe these choices to God. These creatures do wrong, acting in accordance with their desires which stem from their fallen natures.

I do not embrace hard determinism and believe it contradicts much we see in God's Word. But if there is not *some* degree of divine determinism, at least in its softer form, how can God predestine his people according to his plan and work out everything in conformity with the purpose of his will per Ephesians 1:11? And what is the meaning of Romans 9:16, "So then it does not depend on the man who wills or the man who runs, but on God who has mercy"(NASB)?

Libertarianism is not consistent with biblical teaching about God's sovereignty.

We should take a closer look at libertarianism, a view that many people hold, even if unknowingly.

The philosophical position of libertarianism teaches that human beings possess free will, that free will is incompatible with determinism, and that determinism is false. No definition can go much further than this, because libertarians embrace a variety of beliefs. (I discovered this when they disagreed with each other's input on this manuscript; and though I consider myself a compatibilist, other compatibilists will also disagree with some of what I am saying.)

Some libertarians speak of "the power of contrary choice." While recognizing that various influences may affect it, they claim that the will sometimes (or normally, according to others), remains free to choose apart from any causation.

According to libertarianism, free actions are ones which could have been different. Despite other influences, people's choices remain their own, without outside causes forcing them to choose a certain way. Some libertarians believe our wills exist independently from our natures and can act out of keeping with desires. Only if this is true, they argue, can we be held responsible for our actions.

While Scripture teaches we make meaningful choices, I believe it also teaches that fallen people have greater limits on their freedom than libertarians suggest. As Luther pointed out to Erasmus, we cannot have extensive freedom if our wicked hearts make us slaves to sin. True, those who come to faith in Christ have been "set free from sin and have become slaves to righteousness" (Romans 6:18).

We now have a capacity to choose what's right and honoring to God, yet even then, we must rely on the Holy Spirit's empowerment to resist sin.

We remain responsible before God and accountable to him because he is the Creator and we are his creatures. He is our judge. So our human freedom, though real, is less radical than the freedom of libertarianism. Our real but lesser freedom fits with verses such as the following, which appear incompatible with libertarianism:

> The LORD foils the plans of the nations;
>> he thwarts the purposes of the peoples.
> But the plans of the LORD stand firm forever,
>> the purposes of his heart through all generations. (Psalm 33:10–11)

> Our God is in heaven;
>> he does whatever pleases him. (Psalm 115:3)

> The LORD works out everything for his own ends—
>> even the wicked for a day of disaster. (Proverbs 16:4)

Those of us who believe that humans have real choices may feel tempted to minimize these verses. But their cumulative weight, with similar passages throughout Scripture, leaves no doubt that God controls the events of human history as well as our daily lives.

We want to reconcile what seems irreconcilable—human choice and divine sovereignty. We want to remove God from any hint of blame for injustice or suffering. But biblically, it just doesn't work. We shouldn't take on the mantle of God's public relations team. We do not need to put a spin on Scripture, airbrushing the Almighty so he can win the popular vote. He doesn't ask us to get him off the hook of public opinion, but to believe what he has told us about both our meaningful choice and his complete sovereignty.

FREE WILL IN HEAVEN

Free will in Heaven will not require that we be capable of sinning or that humanity may fall again.

People often argue that if true human freedom in Eden required the ability to choose evil, then either we will not be free in Heaven or we will have to be able to sin again.

A sinless, perfect environment doesn't rule out the possibility of sin; Adam and Eve proved that. While Satan tempted them, he too was originally a perfect being living in a perfect environment. Yet Satan sinned. Hence, Heaven's perfection, it seems, does not in itself guarantee the absence of future sin.

Yet I believe the Bible is clear: though we will have freedom to choose in Heaven, we will have no ability to sin. Christ promises of the New Earth, "There will be no more death or mourning or crying or pain" (Revelation 21:4). Since "the wages of sin is death" (Romans 3:23), the promise of no more death in fact requires that there be *no more sin*. Sin causes mourning, crying, and pain; and if those will never occur again, then sin can never occur again.

Consider the last part of Revelation 21:4: "For the old order of things has passed away." What follows the word *for* explains why the evil that caused death, mourning, crying, and pain will no longer exist. When the old order has passed away, we need not fear another Fall.

Scripture emphasizes that Christ died *once* to deal with sin and will never again need to die (see Hebrews 9:26–28; 10:10; 1 Peter 3:18). We'll have the full experience of our new nature so we will in Christ "become the righteousness of God" (2 Corinthians 5:21). Possessing God's own righteousness, we won't sin in Heaven for the same reason God doesn't: he *cannot*. Christ purchased with his blood our eternal inability to sin: "For by a single offering [himself] he has perfected *for all time* those who are being sanctified" (Hebrews 10:14, ESV).

"Nothing impure will ever enter it [the New Jerusalem], nor will anyone who does what is shameful or deceitful, but only those whose names are written in the Lamb's book of life" (Revelation 21:27). The passage doesn't say: "If someone becomes impure or shameful or deceitful, that person will be evicted." That's unthinkable. The text presents an absolute contrast between eternal sinners and the eternal righteous.

That Satan and evildoers are cast forever into the lake of fire (see Revelation 20:10; 21:8) shows an absolute separation of evil from the New Earth. Jesus indicates that evil will have no footing in Heaven and no leverage to affect us: "The Son of Man will send out his angels, and they will weed out of his kingdom *everything* that causes sin and all who do evil. They will throw them into the fiery furnace.... *Then* the righteous will shine like the sun in the kingdom of their Father" (Matthew 13:41–43).

With an air of finality, Hebrews 9:26 says that Christ sacrificed himself "to put away sin" (NASB) or "to do away with sin" (NIV). Sin will be a thing of the past.

Even in the present Heaven, prior to the resurrection, people cannot sin, for they are "the spirits of the righteous made perfect" (Hebrews 12:23). Ultimately, we'll be raised "incorruptible" (1 Corinthians 15:52, NKJV). *Incorruptible* is a stronger word than *uncorrupted.* Our risen bodies, and by implication all that we are, will be immune to corruption.

We will have true freedom in Heaven, but a righteous freedom that never sins.

Christ will not allow us to become vulnerable to the very thing he died to deliver us from (see Romans 4:25). Since our righteousness comes from Christ, who is eternally righteous, we will never lose it (see Romans 5:19).

Heaven will harbor no evil desires and no corruption, and we will fully participate in the sinless perfection of Christ. What does this mean in terms of human freedom? It's hard to believe our worship would please God if we had no choice but to offer it. Christ woos his bride; he doesn't program her so she has no choice but to love him.

Once we become what the sovereign God has made us to be in Christ and once we see him as he is, then we'll see all things—including sin—for what they are. God won't need to restrain us from evil. It will have absolutely no appeal. It will be, literally, unthinkable. The memory of evil and suffering in this life will serve as an eternal reminder of sin's horrors and emptiness. "Sin? Been there, done that. Seen how ugly and disastrous it was."

My inability to be God, an angel, a rabbit, or a flower does not violate my free will. It's the simple reality of my nature. The new nature that will be fully ours in Heaven—the righteousness of Christ—cannot sin. Remember, though God can't sin, no being has greater free choice than he does. That we won't be able to sin does not mean we won't have free will.

Paul Helm said, "The freedom of heaven, then, is the freedom from sin; not that the believer just happens to be free from sin, but that he is so constituted or reconstituted that he cannot sin. He doesn't want to sin, and he does not want to want to sin."[8]

Notes

1. John Frame, interview by Andy Naselli, August 20, 2008, www.theologica.blogspot .com/2008/08/interview-with-john-frame-on-problem-of.html.
2. Steven Best and Anthony J. Nocella, eds., *Terrorists or Freedom Fighters?* (New York: Lantern Books, 2004), 157.

3. See David Basinger and Randall Basinger, eds., *Predestination and Free Will* (Downers Grover, IL: InterVarsity, 1986); Jack Cottrell, *What the Bible Says About God the Ruler* (Eugene, OR: Wipf and Stock, 2000); R. K. McGregor Wright, *No Place for Sovereignty* (Downers Grove, IL: InterVarsity, 1996).

4. *Merriam-Webster Online Dictionary,* s.v. "determinism," www.merriam-webster.com/dictionary/determinism.

5. A good presentation of compatibilism is D. A. Carson's *Divine Sovereignty and Human Responsibility* (Eugene, OR: Wipf and Stock, 2002).

6. *The Reformed Reader,* www.reformedreader.org/history/ivey/ch06.htm.

7. John Calvin, *Institutes of the Christian Religion,* I.18.4; see www.reformed.org/master/index.html?mainframe=/books/institutes/entire.html.

8. Paul Helm, *The Last Things* (Carlisle, PA: Banner of Truth, 1989), 92.

26

Further Thoughts on God's Sovereignty and Human Will

FATE, FREEDOM, AND TRUST

Human will under God's sovereignty has been compared to passengers crossing the ocean on a ship.

Some think of human beings as automatons with no true freedom to choose—mechanical men, some destined to clean decks, some stuck in the engine rooms, some to enjoy the luxury rooms, others to steal purses. Meaningful human choice is illusory. All is fate or hard determinism.

Others envision themselves as fully free to govern the course of their lives, to be captain of their own ship, capable of doing whatever they wish, taking the ship to any harbor and destiny.

The ship illustration as it is sometimes presented is misleading, but it can be helpful provided we make some important qualifications. Passengers have true freedom to walk the ship, to choose when and where and what to eat, and whether or not to befriend others. We can act kindly or with malice, though our hearts lean toward evil; and left to ourselves we will live in bondage. We cannot change the course of the ship—the owner (who is also the captain) makes that decision, and furthermore, unlike any human being, God controls the weather and foresees the icebergs and will bring the ship into harbor where he wants, when he wants.

We are passengers, living under God's rules. We can rebel, even attempt mutiny, and may appear for the moment to have our way. But we will not succeed. We cannot take over the ship and change its course. When the ship reaches its predetermined destination, we will be held accountable for our actions.

A. W. Tozer used the ship analogy and concluded:

Both freedom and sovereignty are present here and they do not contradict each other. So it is, I believe, with man's freedom and the sovereignty of God. The mighty liner of God's sovereign design keeps its steady course over the sea of history. God moves undisturbed and unhindered toward the fulfillment of those eternal purposes which He purposed in Christ Jesus before the world began.[1]

God's purpose and glory are the life-breath of the universe. Everything—including the real choices that Satan, angels, and every person makes—is subordinate to God's redemptive plan, which he carries out with deliberate purpose.

If anything in the universe can happen outside of God's control, then ultimately we can't trust his promises.
I wince when a movie character goes off to battle and promises a child or a spouse, "I'll be back," or, "You'll be safe." The person means well, but he or she lacks the power to keep that promise. God, however, does not.

Some views depict God as so limited by his creatures' free choice that they, not he, assume control of their lives. This would mean I pray to a God who loves me and hurts with me, but who doesn't supervise the events of my life. He cannot keep the ship on course, because crew and passengers can revolt and overthrow the captain.

The Bible overflows with promises. But if things happen outside the sovereign control of God, how can he guarantee those promises will be kept?

Paul said, "I know whom I have believed, and *am convinced that he is able to guard what I have entrusted to him* for that day" (2 Timothy 1:12). Margaret Clarkson wrote,

> The sovereignty of God is the one impregnable rock to which the suffering human heart must cling. The circumstances surrounding our lives are no accident: they may be the work of evil, but that evil is held firmly within the mighty hand of our sovereign God.... All evil is subject to Him, and evil cannot touch His children unless He permits it. God is the Lord of human history and of the personal history of every member of His redeemed family.[2]

We should use our memories of God's past acts of providence to increase our trust in his present and future providence.

At ten years of age, our daughter Karina sat behind me, next to her friend Andrea, in a small plane that went down in Alaska. Bleeding off altitude after the loss of our single engine, Barry Arnold, the missionary pilot, made an emergency landing by a river at the base of two mountains. Eight hours later, around midnight, a search and rescue helicopter flew us out.

After our rescue Karina told me, "God must have a purpose for my life." Six years later a van full of high schoolers, bringing her home from a summer mission trip, lost control going full speed on a highway, rolling over yet causing only bumps and bruises. She told me, "This is the second time God spared my life. He must have a purpose."

When our daughter Angela was a teenager, doctors removed a large tumor from her body. As we awaited the test results in her hospital room, I received a call saying one of her high school classmates, the son of Pat and Rakel Thurman, a missionary couple in our church, had been in a terrible accident. A few hours later we learned he'd died in another hospital five miles away. Angie's tumor was benign. God spared her life. Why didn't he spare Jonathan's?

We don't know.

But I wonder how many times God has spared us from such tragedies without our knowing it? If God saved us from death five times a day, how would we know? How many close calls do we have that we don't recognize, and how many never happen because God intervenes?

God hates sin and judges it, yet predetermines a plan in which he uses human evil to accomplish his purposes.

Speaking of the indefensible evil actions of Herod, Pilate, Gentiles, and Jews in conspiring against Jesus in Jerusalem, Peter and John prayed, "They did what your power and will had decided beforehand should happen" (Acts 4:28).

Herod, Pilate, and the others acted according to their sinful nature. Likewise, God acted according to his sovereign nature, using their sinful choices to accomplish what he had already *decided* should happen. God holds men accountable for the sin they choose to do. But it is not inconsistent or unjust of him to utilize their low-purposed, finite evil for his high-purposed, infinite good.

This reality should prompt us to worship him for his greatness and his ability to use even what displeases him to accomplish what will ultimately please both him and us. Our fates do not rest with people who file lawsuits against us, or with unjust politicians, lawyers, teachers, coaches, military officers, or employers. They can do their worst against us—and God is fully capable of turning it around and using it for our best (no matter how much it hurts in the meantime).

A criminal raped a precious friend of ours. I would never minimize her pain or downplay the terrible evil committed against her. But she believes, and I agree, that God has a purpose in this. The child conceived in her rape has an appointed future. The man who raped her will not get away with it: "It is a fearful thing to fall into the hands of the living God" (Hebrews 10:31, ESV).

Our friend does not live in the hands of the evil man who raped her, but in the hands of almighty God, who created her and went to the cross to die for her. And though the words do not come easily and could be misunderstood, I say this with conviction: God did not let her out of his sight the day the rapist attacked her.

Some imagine that God's use of evil means that he commits it, approves of it, or fails to hate, judge, and be angered by it.
This is categorically wrong. God remained sovereign when our friend was raped, but I believe his fierce anger erupted at the evil done to this precious woman, his beloved daughter.

> Who knows the power of your anger?
>> For your wrath is as great as the fear that is due you. (Psalm 90:11)

> I myself [God] will fight against you with an outstretched hand and a
> mighty arm in anger and fury and great wrath. (Jeremiah 21:5)

Some claim that affirming God's sovereign grace in the context of human evil justifies evildoing. Paul refutes this erroneous thinking:

> Someone might argue, "If my falsehood enhances God's truthfulness and
> so increases his glory, why am I still condemned as a sinner?" Why not
> say—as we are being slanderously reported as saying and as some claim
> that we say—"Let us do evil that good may result"? Their condemnation
> is deserved. (Romans 3:7–8)

God's sovereign grace and ability to use evil doesn't justify or minimize evil-doing, it simply shows that he is infinitely superior to any evildoer and that his plan to do good to his people will not be derailed by *any* creature.

It's true that God hated the crime done against our friend. It angered him and stirred his great wrath. It's also true that he could have stopped the rape and in so doing prevented much heartache; yet, if Romans 8:28 applies to the great groan-causing suffering of its immediate context, it surely applies to hers also. If God permits evils not randomly, but with deliberate purpose so that he will reverse the Curse and bring eternal blessing, then even though we don't understand how, he deserves not our attacks, but our trust.

We are puzzled sometimes because God could have shown his power by preventing tragedies and healing diseases, but chose not to. We would prefer that God crush and remove evil, not allow it to hurt us. But power isn't his sole attribute. He is also glorified in showing his wisdom. While his power gains immediate praise, his wisdom is seen over time. Sometimes in this life, but one day in his presence, we will marvel at his wisdom in not preventing certain evils that he used, in ways we could never have imagined, for our ultimate good.

Jerry Bridges writes,

> If God is truly sovereign, if He truly loves you, and the teaching of Scripture is correct, then God will never allow any action against you that is not in accord with His ultimate purpose to work for your good. If the evil done against you is fresh and haunting, then I know my words may seem terribly calloused. But I say them because I believe they are true. Scripture teaches them, and one day we will all believe them, when we are with Him.[3]

A CLOSER LOOK AT COMPATIBILISM

Scripture teaches both God's sovereignty and meaningful human choice. Many verses clearly declare God's absolute sovereignty. God "works out everything in conformity with the purpose of his will" (Ephesians 1:11). He not only assigns us our times and places (see Acts 17:26), but takes credit for natural processes, feeding birds and caring for the grass (see Matthew 6:26, 30).

Here's a passage that seems to deny libertarian freedom: "I know, O LORD, that a man's life is not his own; it is not for man to direct his steps" (Jeremiah 10:23).

While God used the Assyrians to accomplish a divine purpose, he held them accountable for the evil of their hearts as they served that purpose (see Isaiah 10:5–7). He said that when he finished using them against Israel, "I will punish the king of Assyria for the willful pride of his heart and the haughty look in his eyes" (verse 12).

Arrogant Assyria viewed itself as controlling its own destiny, but God said, "Does the ax raise itself above the one who swings it, or the saw boast against him who uses it?" (verse 15). Hard determinists cite this passage to prove that humans are but instruments in God's hands. While there are other passages that speak of meaningful choice, those who reject all forms of determinism should remember that such texts as Isaiah 10 are God-breathed. We dare not ignore them. Assyria acted from an evil heart, doing what it desired, yet God, from a heart of goodness and justice, remained free to use Assyria as a tool to accomplish his purposes in Israel.

God commands people to consecrate themselves and make themselves holy, to keep his decrees and follow them (see Leviticus 20:7–8). But immediately God says, "I am the LORD, who makes you holy" (verse 8). God makes us what he commands us to be. This is one of countless passages that has led me to favor compatibilism as a worldview. God is no puppeteer and we are not puppets, yet he remains in charge. We choose, and we are responsible and accountable for our choices. Yet God reigns.

Wayne Grudem states, "However we understand God's relationship to evil, we must *never* come to the point where we think that we are not responsible for the evil that we do, or that God takes pleasure in evil or is to be blamed for it. Such a conclusion is clearly contrary to Scripture."[4]

God's sovereignty and meaningful human choice sometimes appear in the same verses, with no sense of contradiction.

God promises he will harden Pharaoh's heart (see Exodus 4:21; 7:3; 14:4). Pharaoh's heart did harden (see 7:13–14, 22; 9:7, 35; 14:8) "as the LORD had said" (7:13, 22; 8:15, 19). But Pharaoh also hardened his own heart (see 8:15, 32; 9:34), just as God hardened Pharaoh's heart (see 9:12; 10:1, 20, 27; 11:10; 14:8, 17).[5]

Scripture refers seven times to Pharaoh's heart being hardened before the first time it says Pharaoh hardened his own heart. God's sovereignty and Pharaoh's meaningful choice both came into play.

Rehoboam refused to listen to wise counsel. He sinned and remained fully responsible for that sin. And yet we're told, "The king did not listen to the people, *for it was a turn of affairs brought about by God*" (2 Chronicles 10:15, ESV).

People come to Christ because God elects and draws them: "All who were appointed for eternal life believed" (Acts 13:48). But in the immediate context we're given another reason, involving Paul and Barnabas: "They spoke so effectively that a great number of Jews and Gentiles believed" (14:1). So did the people come to saving faith as a result of God choosing them or as a result of effective preaching? The answer is both.

In Romans 9, Paul refers to Israel's unbelief as God's sovereign work, but in chapter 10 he says Israel refused to respond to the preaching of the gospel. Which is it? Both. God saves people, but Paul asks, "How can they hear without someone preaching to them?" (10:14).

Paul claims it's his responsibility to "win as many as possible" (1 Corinthians 9:19). In fact, he says, "I have become all things to all men so that by all possible means I might save some" (verse 22). He reveals not the slightest hint of the attitude, "It's up to God to save people, so I'm content to sit passively by."

We should seek to be consistent with the Bible, not with a particular theological persuasion.

Any position that denies either God's complete sovereignty or our meaningful choice does not stand up to Scripture. While arguments exist against every position and not all compatibilists agree on all issues, I consider the compatibilist position to be most in keeping with Scripture.

Non-Calvinists opposed Charles Spurgeon because of his understanding of God's sovereignty. Hyper-Calvinists opposed him because his public invitations to respond to the gospel affirmed meaningful human choice and responsibility. Spurgeon reminded us that no theological system is authoritative, but Scripture alone:

> My love of consistency with my own doctrinal views is not great enough
> to allow me knowingly to alter a single text of Scripture. I have great
> respect for orthodoxy, but my reverence for inspiration is far greater. I
> would sooner a hundred times over appear to be inconsistent with myself
> than be inconsistent with the word of God.[6]

The Bible is God-breathed, theological systems aren't. They are valid *not* to the extent that they are self-consistent, but to the degree they are consistent with Scripture. Spurgeon didn't try to reconcile the paradoxical doctrines we've looked at for five chapters. He said,

> That God predestines, and that man is responsible, are two things that few
> can see. They are believed to be inconsistent and contradictory; but they
> are not. It is just the fault of our weak judgment. Two truths cannot be
> contradictory to each other. If, then, I find taught in one place that every-

thing is fore-ordained, *that is true;* and if I find in another place that man is responsible for all his actions, *that is true;* and it is my folly that leads me to imagine that two truths can ever contradict each other. These two truths, I do not believe, can ever be welded into one upon any human anvil, but one they shall be in eternity: they are two lines that are so nearly parallel, that the mind that shall pursue them farthest, will never discover that they converge; but they do converge, and they will meet somewhere in eternity, close to the throne of God, whence all truth doth spring.[7]

Spurgeon warned against theologies that attempt to reconcile, by means of shortsighted human logic, every apparent biblical inconsistency: "Men who are morbidly anxious to possess a self-consistent creed—a creed which they can put together, and form into a square, like a Chinese puzzle—are very apt to narrow their souls.... Those who will only believe what they can reconcile will necessarily disbelieve much of Divine revelation."[8]

The Bereans "examined the Scriptures every day to see if what Paul said was true" (Acts 17:11). Paul's friend Luke, the author of Acts, portrays this as a commendable practice, and if it applies to the words of a man who eventually wrote thirteen inspired biblical books, it surely applies to my words and everyone else's, be they theologian, professor, pastor, or writer! We can benefit from their work, but we should not search the writings of John Wesley or John Calvin to examine whether a teaching is true. We should search the Scriptures.

Over the years, as I've studied Scripture, I have come to conclusions different from those I had as a young Christian. At one time I was reluctant to accept biblical teachings that seemed to contradict the theological positions I inherited from the church where I came to Christ and the Bible college and seminary I attended. I have found it freeing to remind myself that Scripture is my authority and we should never let a theological system ignore or tinker with Scripture to make it fit the system. If we do, we place our faith in the system's authority, not Scripture's, and consequently avoid and reinterpret portions of the Bible.

When Scripture teaches apparently contradictory ideas, we should embrace both. Spurgeon said, "The system of truth is not one straight line, but two. No man will ever get a right view of the gospel until he knows how to look at the two lines at once."[9]

Many years ago my Greek professor repeatedly urged us not to get too comfortable with our theology, but to let Scripture say what it says and revise our theology accordingly. More than ever, I believe he was right. May we read Scripture and believe it, not explaining away what doesn't fit our theology, but stretching our theology to embrace the full breadth of God's revealed truth.

God's sovereignty is consistent with human responsibility.

We can believe in God's sovereignty and still lock the door. "If a man is lazy," says Ecclesiastes, "the rafters sag; if his hands are idle, the house leaks" (10:18). Proverbs 20:4 says, "A sluggard does not plow in season; so at harvest time he looks but finds nothing."

These verses don't simply attribute sagging rafters and leaking houses to God's sovereignty. They lay responsibility on people to take action. Students who don't study and set the alarm to get up for class aren't trusting God; they're just being irresponsible.

The book of Nehemiah reflects God's sovereign plan to rebuild Jerusalem. Yet it repeatedly shows Nehemiah preparing, strategically positioning, and arming the people: "But we prayed to our God and posted a guard day and night to meet this threat" (4:9). They prayed, recognizing God's sovereignty and posted a guard, recognizing their responsibility to choose wisely.

No contradiction exists between praying, "Lord, please protect us and the children on this drive," and then putting on seat belts. Prayers for healing do not conflict with the common grace of medical treatment. Carl Sagan wrote, "We can pray over the cholera victim, or we can give her 500 milligrams of tetracycline every 12 hours."[10] But why should we choose between the two? Believers understand that giving tetracycline before, after, and while we pray for the sick helps them in two vital ways, rather than just one.

We find the greatest example of divine sovereignty and meaningful human choice in the Crucifixion: "Jesus of Nazareth…was handed over to you by God's set purpose and foreknowledge; and you, with the help of wicked men, put him to death by nailing him to the cross" (Acts 2:22–23).

God's set purpose brought about Christ's atoning death. Yet, wicked men nailed him to the cross. While they committed the ultimate evil, God used their evil to accomplish the ultimate good.

Two chapters later Peter says, "In this city there were gathered together against your holy servant Jesus, whom you anointed, both Herod and Pontius Pilate, along with the Gentiles and the peoples of Israel, *to do whatever your hand and your plan had predestined to take place*" (Acts 4:27–28, ESV).

Here again in the same verse, two causes are identified for the same event—wicked people and a righteous, sovereign God.

How can Christ's crucifixion, the worst event in history, also be—in concert with his resurrection—the best event? If we can begin to wrap our minds around this, we start to see that if the greatest evil in the universe could serve the greatest good, then the same God—our God—can surely bring good out of even the darkest evils.

Holocaust survivor Bob Kertesz described in an interview his conversion to Christ:

> Most of my father's family died in the concentration camp, and I don't understand why. I'm sure God had a reason, but I don't know why. Maybe one of these days, I'll ask Him. (Crying).... God must have had a reason to get me through all these times, all these bad times that I have had and all these good times, and I have had some good times in my life.
>
> It took me a long time to realize that I'm not losing being a Jew. I'm just adding Jesus as my Savior. I'm still a Jew inside, I always will be, I will never change that.
>
> There's too many clues in the OT that there is a Messiah coming and there is a Messiah here already. I just think it's faith that you have that this is the right thing. I can't really describe how come I all of a sudden accepted Jesus. I just know it is true.[11]

Notes

1. A. W. Tozer, *The Knowledge of the Holy* (San Francisco: HarperOne, 1992), 174.
2. Margaret Clarkson, *Grace Grows Best in Winter* (Grand Rapids, MI: Eerdmans, 1984), 40–41.
3. Jerry Bridges, *Is God Really in Control?* (Colorado Springs: NavPress, 2006), 50.
4. Wayne Grudem, *Systematic Theology* (Grand Rapids, MI: Zondervan, 1994), 323.
5. English Standard Version Study Bible, notes on Exodus 7, (Wheaton, IL: Crossway Bibles, 2008), 151.
6. Charles Haddon Spurgeon, "Salvation by Knowing the Truth" (sermon 1516), *Metropolitan Tabernacle Pulpit* 26 (1880): 49–52, www.spurgeon.org/sermons/1516.htm.
7. Charles Haddon Spurgeon, "Sovereign Grace and Man's Responsibility" (sermon 207), *New Park Street Pulpit* 4 (August 1, 1858): 337, www.spurgeon.org/sermons/0207.htm.
8. Spurgeon, "Faith," *An All-Round Ministry,* 1872, www.spurgeon.org/misc/aarm01.htm.

9. Spurgeon, "Sovereign Grace and Man's Responsibility."

10. Carl Sagan, *The Demon-Haunted World* (New York: Ballantine Books, 1996), 9.

11. Bob Kertesz, *Survivor Stories: Finding Hope from an Unlikely Source,* Purple Pomegranate Productions, Jews for Jesus video, http://store.jewsforjesus.org/ppp/product.php?prodid=210.

27

The God Who Brings Good
Out of Bad

God explains a reason he permits evil—to glorify himself by demonstrating to his children the wonders of his character.

Paul writes, "What if God, choosing to show his wrath and make his power known, bore with great patience the objects of his wrath—prepared for destruction? What if he did this to make the riches of his glory known to the objects of his mercy, whom he prepared in advance for glory?" (Romans 9:22–23).

We cannot here address the difficult issue of some people being described as "objects of [God's] wrath, prepared for destruction." But that debate needn't distract us from the main point of this verse. God says he shows patience to those whom he will ultimately judge. He shows his wrath, power, and patience to unbelievers, "to make the riches of his glory known to the objects of his mercy, whom he prepared in advance for glory."

The objects of God's mercy are his redeemed people. By permitting evil to continue until the final judgment, God reveals to us his attributes. This passage parallels Ephesians 2:7, which adds that God's saving work in Christ, including his resurrection triumph, happened "in order that in the coming ages he might show the incomparable riches of his grace, expressed in his kindness to us in Christ Jesus."

God's glory is the highest good of the universe. We glorify him as his children when we see the wondrous realities of his character. God knows that permitting evil and suffering—and paying the price to end them, as well as patiently delaying judgment and then bringing it decisively—will all ultimately reveal his character and cause his people to worship him forever.

Satan and God intend the same suffering for entirely different purposes, but God's purpose triumphs.

Satan sought Job's ruin and loss of faith; God sought Job's refining and faith-building. The very thing Satan intended for Job's destruction, God intended for his betterment and ultimate reward (though certainly at a terrible cost).

Second Corinthians 12:7 gives us a striking picture. We see God sending a physical disability for his purposes and Satan sending the same disability for his. Paul says, "To keep me from being conceited because of these surpassingly great revelations, there was given to me a thorn in my flesh." If the text stopped here, it would be obvious who gave the thorn in the flesh—God, who wanted to keep Paul from becoming conceited. Certainly the devil would not lift a finger to prevent Paul from becoming conceited.

But Paul continues to describe the thorn in the flesh as "a messenger of Satan, to torment me." Two supernatural beings, adamantly opposed to each other, are said in a single verse to have distinct purposes in sending Paul a thorn in the flesh. God's purpose is not to torment him, but to keep him from becoming conceited; Satan's purpose is to torment him, likely in the hope of turning him from God. Whose purpose will be accomplished? Who will win?

Paul says, in the next verses, he asked God three times to remove the "thorn," but God refused. He did, however, reveal the purpose behind Paul's unanswered prayer: "My grace is sufficient for you, for my power is made perfect in weakness."

How did Paul respond? He said he rejoiced in his afflictions. Why? Because he knew God had a sovereign and loving purpose.

Joseph's brothers intended his suffering for evil; God intended it for good.

Satan intended Job's suffering for evil; God intended it for good.

Satan intended Jesus' suffering for evil; God intended it for good.

Satan intended Paul's suffering for evil; God intended it for good.

In each case, God's purpose prevailed.

Satan intends your suffering for evil; God intends it for good.

Whose purpose in your suffering will prevail? Whose purpose are you furthering?

Satan attempts to destroy your faith, while God invites you to draw near to him and draw upon his sovereign grace to sustain you.

If we recognize God's sovereignty even over Satan's work, it changes our perspective. Some Christians constantly assign this mishap to Satan, that one to evil people, another to themselves, still others to God. Sometimes they are right, but how can they be sure which is which? Second Corinthians 12 makes clear that God works through *everything* that comes our way, no matter whom it comes from. If God can use for good "a messenger of Satan," then surely he can use for good a car accident or your employer's unreasonable expectations.

You might not know whether demons, or human genetics under the Fall, or a doctor's poor decision, or God's direct hand have brought about your disease, but you know as much as you need to—that God is sovereign, and whether he heals your body now or waits until the resurrection to heal you, he desires to achieve his own good purpose in you.

Scripture uses a variety of terms to describe God's relationship to evil, including *permit* and *allow*.

An ax head flies from its handle and kills someone. So what does God say? "If [the man] does not do it intentionally, but God lets it happen, he is to flee to a place I will designate" (Exodus 21:13). Moses doesn't write that God causes the accident, but rather he "lets it happen."

We find similar language in Mark 5:12–13 where demons beg Jesus to send them into a herd of pigs and Jesus "gave them permission."

God says, "I let them become defiled…that I might fill them with horror so they would know that I am the LORD" (Ezekiel 20:26). God had a good purpose even in permitting terrible sin.

Sometimes God inhibits demonic and human choice by not permitting them to fulfill their evil desire. Jacob said of Laban, "God has not allowed him to harm me" (Genesis 31:7). God tells Abimelech, "I have kept you from sinning against me" (Genesis 20:6). When casting out demons, Jesus "would not allow them to speak" (Luke 4:41).

I have heard people argue against saying "God allows" because they think "God causes" is more accurate. But Scripture uses both kinds of language, and so should we.

I am deliberately focusing now on God's permission rather than God's decrees or ordination, because it is common ground for different theological persuasions. But my larger reason is that I want to make the rarely understood point that *divine permission is not passive and weak, but active and strong.* The more power someone has, the more significant permission-giving becomes. Randy Alcorn permitting a neighbor to cut down my tree blocking his view is one thing; the president permitting a general to move troops onto foreign soil is another.

Countless millions of choices and actions are contemplated every instant across this globe. Our all-knowing and all-powerful God chooses exactly which ones he will permit and not permit. Scripture suggests he does not permit evils arbitrarily, but with specific purposes in mind. Everything he permits matches up with his wisdom and ultimately serves both his holiness and his love.

God "permitting" something, then, describes what is far stronger than it may sound. After all, whatever God permits actually happens; what he doesn't permit doesn't happen. And as Joni Eareckson Tada puts it, "God permits what he hates to achieve what he loves."[1]

In the final chapter, the author of Job, inspired by the Holy Spirit, says Job's family and friends "comforted and consoled him over all the trouble the LORD had brought upon him" (42:11). The author told us from the beginning that Job's troubles were Satan's idea and the result of Satan's actions permitted by God. Yet he doesn't say Job's friends comforted Job over all the trouble they *supposed* the Lord had brought upon him. The inspired wording indicates that Satan's efforts were, indirectly by means of his sovereign permission, God's doing.

Many find this truth disturbing, but properly understood it should be comforting. What should be disturbing is the notion that God stands passively by while Satan, evildoers, diseases, and random accidents ruin the lives of his beloved children.

Human choices, real as they are, cannot thwart God's sovereign plan.

C. S. Lewis wrote, "Perhaps we do not realize the problem, so to call it, of enabling finite free wills to co-exist with Omnipotence. It seems to involve at every moment almost a sort of 'divine abdication.'"[2]

In one sense every murder, rape, and natural disaster confirms that God has permitted the world to violate his will, which could be called a "divine abdication." But what if this apparent abdication is not nearly so great as it appears, or is of a completely different nature than what we understand?

Scripture indicates that when an omnipotent God grants real and effectual choice, he does not lose power. He delegates power, which can be and regularly is abused. Yes, he can still overrule; he can perform miracles of intervention. But if he does this too often, he will take back the power he has delegated, thus minimizing the consequential dimension that makes choice meaningful.

Before sin, God gave people dominion over the world. In delegating this responsibility, God acted like a father who started a great business, then handed over the company to his children. Though he remains as owner, controller, and final decision maker, he has granted leadership powers to his children. Consequently he chooses to subject his company to their decisions, good or bad. If he intervenes to stop all the bad ones, he revokes his charge to them.

Now suppose the manager of the universe can do what a human father could never do—sovereignly use every decision, right or wrong, to accomplish an ultimate purpose. Could he not then be seen to maintain control even as he apparently abdicates it? This, I think, is what Scripture teaches.

Do we believe human agents who violate God's moral will can frustrate his ultimate intentions and plans? Do we believe that in the instant a teenager's CD gets stuck in his car player and he takes his eyes off the road, swerves, and hits someone's daughter while she waits for a school bus, that all the good things God had planned for that girl forever dissolve into nothingness? Or do we believe that God has a plan even in that dark moment?

One of Corrie ten Boom's favorite analogies was that God is weaving together a beautiful tapestry. While he sees from above the magnificence of his creation, we see the knots and tangles on the underside. But one day we will be with God and see the topside of the tapestry. This is an analogy for God decreeing, not only permitting, for a master weaver doesn't merely permit threads, he carefully chooses and weaves them. Corrie ten Boom never denied evil or suffering in the concentration camp, and neither should we. But God can weave the tapestry despite evil and suffering, and can even use them to create a finished work of startling beauty. One day we will behold it.

God sometimes uses evil spirits to accomplish his purpose.

Critics argue that the Bible contradicts itself because 2 Samuel 24:1 says God incited David to take a census of Israel, while 1 Chronicles 21:1 says Satan prompted David's decision. Which is correct? Both.

In fact, three times Scripture says God sent evil spirits: once to judge a murder (see Judges 9:23–24), once to torment King Saul (see 1 Samuel 16:14–23), and once to deceive evil King Ahab (see 1 Kings 22:19–23).

We're told of some rebellious people that "God sends them a strong delusion" through demons (2 Thessalonians 2:11–12). Here again God does no evil, but still uses evil demons, who are doing what they want, to bring judgment on evil people. I would never have come up with such an idea on my own and would not believe it—except for the fact that God's Word reveals it. I therefore submit to its authority and adjust my theology accordingly.

Even "random" occurrences can accomplish God's sovereign purpose.

In a fascinating passage, evil King Ahab assembles his troops for war. A brave prophet tells him, "The LORD has decreed disaster for you" (2 Chronicles 18:22). Ahab asks an allied king to go to battle in Ahab's royal attire, while Ahab dresses like a common soldier. That way, any enemy going after King Ahab will actually pursue someone else.

What happens? "But someone drew his bow at random and hit the king of Israel between the sections of his armor.... Then at sunset he died" (2 Chronicles 18:33–34). Scripture itself uses the term "random," but God's hand directed that shaft in its flight through the air. That "random" arrow had Ahab's name on it.

This passage doesn't prove God orchestrates or directs every random occurrence. Nonetheless, it demonstrates God has decreed that at least some "random" events accomplish eternal purposes, even if he alone understands them.

Can't God have a purpose and plan in a tragic "accident" or an "unlucky" fall just as he can in a "random" arrow? This should bring not resentment, but comfort to the family of a father who backs up his car at the exact moment his four-year-old son runs after a ball his brother kicked. Such terrible events, heartbreaking as they are, do not lie outside God's power, nor beyond God's purpose and plan.

The false notion of random events outside of God's control sets us up for a lifetime of "what ifs" and "if onlys."

No matter what we mean by *free will,* we should distinguish it from *autonomy.* Autonomy speaks of complete independence and self-governance. This does not square with God's sovereignty. None of our actions lie outside the reach of his governance. For this we should feel deeply grateful. Otherwise we could wonder, *What if the doctor had run the right tests or looked at the x-rays more carefully two years ago?* Or, *What if I'd stopped to make the phone call or if the line had been shorter at the grocery store, or if I hadn't had that five-minute conversation before leaving? Then I wouldn't have been at that intersection when the drunk driver ran the light and smashed my car, and then my wife wouldn't have died.*

If the world is as random as some theologians suggest, it would seem that people, demons, and luck determine our destinies. We can drive ourselves crazy with such thoughts—or embrace God's higher purpose in painful and even tragic events, thus affirming God's greatness.

God calls us not to victimization or to fatalism, but to faith in his character and promises.

ROMANS 8:28

Working all things together for our eternal good, including evil and suffering, sovereignly demonstrates God's love.

We need to take a closer look at a verse I've mentioned, one of the most treasured (and also maligned) in Scripture: "And we know that in all things God works for the good of those who love him, who have been called according to his purpose" (Romans 8:28).

The context shows that the Holy Spirit's main concern is conforming God's children to the image of Christ. He brings challenging circumstances into our lives so we may develop Christlikeness.

Paul's use of "we know" indicates that if you don't know this, you know less than God intends you to; and when times of evil and suffering come, you'll be ill-equipped to face them.

I believe that if God could not use something, in eternity, to contribute to the good of his child, then he will not permit it to happen. I know of no other way to interpret this passage, written in a context of profound evil and suffering. It does not say God causes *some* or *most* things to work for our good, but *all* things. And what does "all things" not include?

Romans 8:28 declares a cumulative and ultimate good, not an individual or immediate good.

Different translations of Romans 8:28 suggest different nuances: for those who love God, "all things work together for good" (ESV, KJV), "in all things God works for the good" (NIV), "God causes all things to work together for good" (NASB).

In each case there is an all-inclusiveness in "all things." Three of these translations use "together," emphasizing a focus not on isolated events in the believer's life, but on the sum of all events. It does not say "each thing by itself *is* good," but "all things work together *for* good," and not on their own, but under God's sovereign hand.

Before my mother made a cake, she used to lay each of the ingredients on the kitchen counter. One day, as only a boy can, I decided to experiment. I tasted all the individual ingredients for a chocolate cake. Baking powder. Baking soda. Raw eggs. Vanilla extract. I discovered that *almost everything that goes into a cake tastes terrible by itself.* But a remarkable metamorphosis took place when my mother mixed the ingredients in the right amounts and baked them together. The cake tasted delicious. Yet judging by the individual ingredients, I never would have believed cake could taste so good.

In a similar way, the individual ingredients of trials and apparent tragedies taste bitter to us. Romans 8:28 doesn't tell me I should say, "It is good," if my leg breaks, or my house burns down, or I am robbed and beaten, or my child dies.

But no matter how bitter the taste of the individual components, God can carefully measure out and mix all ingredients together, and raise the temperature in order to produce a wonderful final product.

When Paul says, "for good," he clearly implies final or ultimate good, not good subjectively felt in the midst of our sufferings. As his wife, Joy, underwent cancer treatments, C. S. Lewis wrote to a friend, "We are not necessarily doubting that God will do the best for us; we are wondering how painful the best will turn out to be."[3]

We define our good in terms of what brings us health and happiness now; God defines it in terms of what makes us more like Jesus.

In the next verse, Paul explains the basis on which he can claim that God works everything together for our good: "For those God foreknew he also predestined to be conformed to the likeness of his Son" (verse 29).

As a young Christian I believed that going to Heaven instead of Hell was all that mattered. But as I read the Bible, I saw that to be called according to God's purpose is to be conformed to the character of Christ. God's purpose for our suffering is Christlikeness. That is our highest calling. If God answered all our prayers to be delivered from evil and suffering, then he would be delivering us from Christlikeness. But Christlikeness is something to long for, not to be delivered from.

Ten months after his son was killed in a car accident, Greg Laurie told me, "What I wish is that I could have learned and grown and drawn close to the Lord *just like I have,* but that Christopher was still here." Greg captured it perfectly— I too wish I could have all the good God has brought me, and will bring me, through adversity, but without all that pain and loss. But it doesn't work that way, does it?

When a sovereign, all-powerful God predestines our conformity to Christ, all the evil and suffering that intrude upon our lives form part of that plan. Our doctrine of human free will must never lead us to believe that God cannot act unless we give him permission. Although we have a real ability to choose (for God has made it so), he will still accomplish his purposes.

Everything that comes into your life—yes, even evil and suffering—is Father-filtered. Whether suffering brings us to Christlikeness depends, to some degree, upon our willingness to submit to God and trust him and draw our strength from him. Suffering will come whether we allow it to make us Christlike or not—but if we don't our suffering is wasted.

God wondrously displays his greatness when he brings good out of bad.
We judge someone's greatness by the size of the obstacles he overcomes. Climbing
Mount Everest brings glory to the climber and testifies to his greatness precisely
because of the mountain's enormity. An athlete who pole-vaults ten feet does
nothing amazing. But one who pole-vaults twenty feet makes history. People still
celebrate the U.S. hockey team's "miracle on ice" in 1980 because of the greatness
of their Soviet opponent.

So it is with the drama of redemption. Sin and death, the Fall and the Curse,
Satan and his demons, the Hell we deserve—what powerful obstacles for God to
overcome. But the biggest obstacle was the satisfaction of his own holiness. For
God to demonstrate his greatness, he had to overcome all these obstacles.

The greater the obstacles, the greater the glory to God.

We see something remarkable about a person who can bring some good out
of bad. But most remarkable is to bring something incredibly good out of something desperately bad. To redeem what appears irredeemable magnifies the greatness of the Redeemer. If the universe exists to demonstrate God's infinite
greatness, then shouldn't we expect God to scale the highest redemptive mountain? The problems of death, evil, and suffering must be vast in order for God to
show his superior greatness.

Every time we ask God to remove some obstacle in our lives, we should realize we may be asking him to forgo one more opportunity to declare his greatness.
Certainly he sometimes graciously answers our prayers to relieve our suffering.
This too testifies to his greatness, and we should praise him for answering. But
when he answers no, we should recognize that he desires to demonstrate his
greater glory. May we then bend our knees and trust his sovereign grace.

Notes

1. Joni Eareckson Tada and Steven Estes, *When God Weeps* (Grand Rapids, MI:
   Zondervan, 1997), 83.
2. C. S. Lewis, "The Efficacy of Prayer" *The World's Last Night and Other Essays*,
   (Harvest Books, 2002), 7.
3. C. S. Lewis, *Letters of C. S. Lewis* (Orlando: Harcourt Books, 1966), 477.

The Two Eternal Solutions
to the Problem of Evil:
Heaven and Hell

28

Heaven: Eternal Grace to Unworthy but Grateful Children

Jesus said that when his followers hunger, weep, and are hated and insulted, we should rejoice. Why? "Because great is your reward in heaven" (Luke 6:23).

In contrast, he added, "But woe to you who are rich, for you have already received your comfort. Woe to you who are well fed now, for you will go hungry. Woe to you who laugh now, for you will mourn and weep" (verses 24–25).

His listeners would have immediately understood that he was addressing a fundamental problem of human existence, the same one that *If God Is Good* is all about. Christ's point? God has an eternal two-part solution to the problem of the righteous presently suffering and the wicked presently prospering: Heaven and Hell.

The life to come flows out of this one; hence the believer's present sufferings comprise only a tiny part of our total life experience, which will continue forever.

Paul wrote, "I consider that our present sufferings are not worth comparing with the glory that will be revealed in us" (Romans 8:18).

C. S. Lewis commented on this verse: "If this is so, a book on suffering which says nothing of heaven, is leaving out almost the whole of one side of the account. Scripture and tradition habitually put the joys of heaven into the scale against the sufferings of earth, and no solution of the problem of pain which does not do so can be called a Christian one."[1]

Many people believe this life is all there is: "You only go around once on this earth, so grab for whatever you can." But if you're a child of God, then you do *not* just "go around once"; you'll inhabit the New Earth forever! It's those in Hell who go around only once on Earth.

Here, we have bodies and we work, rest, play, and relate to one another—we call this *life*. Yet many have mistakenly redefined *eternal life* to mean an off-earth disembodied existence stripped of human life's defining properties. In fact, eternal life will mean enjoying forever, as resurrected (which means embodied) beings, what life on Earth at its finest offered us. We could more accurately call our present existence the *beforelife* rather than calling Heaven the *afterlife*. Life doesn't merely continue in Heaven, it emerges at last to its intended fullness.

Dinesh D'Souza writes,

> The only way for us to really triumph over evil and suffering is to live forever in a place where those things do not exist. It is the claim of Christianity that there is such a place and that it is available to all who seek it. No one can deny that, if this claim is true, then evil and suffering are exposed as temporary hardships and injustices. They are as transient as our brief, mortal lives. In that case God has shown us a way to prevail over evil and suffering, which are finally overcome in the life to come.[2]

The resurrection means that the best parts about this world will carry over to the next, with none of the bad; hence, what we forgo here will prove no great loss.

Only the resurrection can solve the gigantic problems of this world—and resurrection cannot come without death. Without Christ's resurrection and what it means—an eternal future for fully restored human beings, dwelling with Christ on a fully restored Earth—all the promises of Christianity vanish like smoke in a stiff wind. As Paul says, "If Christ has not been raised, your faith is futile; you are still in your sins.... We are to be pitied more than all men" (1 Corinthians 15:17, 19). Thankfully, our resurrection is certain because of Christ's.

Without this eternal perspective we assume that people who die young, who have handicaps, who suffer poor health, who don't get married or have children, or who don't do this or that will miss out on the best life has to offer. But the theology underlying those assumptions has a fatal flaw. It presumes that our present Earth, bodies, culture, relationships, and lives are all there is—or that they will somehow overshadow or negate those of the New Earth.

What are we thinking?

The stronger our concept of God and Heaven, the more we understand how Heaven resolves the problem of evil and suffering. The weaker our concept of God and Heaven, the stronger our doubt that Heaven will more than compensate for our present sufferings.

If Heaven did not exist, we could never solve the problem of evil and suffering, for we would never receive any lasting compensation for it.
Nanci read me letters written in 1920 by her grandmother, Ana Swanson, to her family in Sweden. Because Ana suffered severe health problems, she moved to Montana to be cared for by relatives. Her husband, Edwin, remained in Oregon, day and night working and caring for their seven children. Ana's letters tell how Edwin wore himself out, became sick, and died. Ana lacked the strength to raise her younger children, so they, including Nanci's mother, Adele, were placed for adoption. Ana's letters reflect her broken heart, her nagging guilt…and her faith in God.

Nanci and I wept as we read those letters. What inconsolable disappointment and pain! Ana and Edwin loved Jesus. Perhaps they asked a good God why he would allow such tragedy. That day, Nanci and I considered what God might give this broken family on the New Earth. Certainly they will be healthy—Ana won't live with illness, fatigue, grief, anxiety, and guilt. Edwin won't work himself to death, pining away for his dearest companion. Based on what I know of God, and the promises of Jesus about our earthly fortunes being reversed in Heaven, I believe that in the resurrection God may give this family wonderful times together that the old Earth denied them. Perhaps they'll travel together and God will grant them indescribably rich times with one another, parents and children.

How like God that would be!

God originally planned that human beings live unswervingly happy, fulfilled, righteous, and God-centered lives on Earth. If our current lives present the only opportunities for that, then God's plan has failed. But if we know the God revealed in Scripture, we realize his plans do *not* fail. His promises to resurrect both us and the earth itself guarantee his plan will forever succeed.

We want every chapter of our lives to feel good. It doesn't work that way. The current chapter may be terribly hard, but the story hasn't ended. God promises a final chapter in which he ties together all the story's loose ends and launches us into an eternal sequel of incredibly grand proportions.

Make no mistake—the promise of God is that *all* his children, including Ana and Edwin Swanson and each of us who know Jesus, will live happily ever after.

In order to share Christ's glory forever on the New Earth, we must share his sufferings temporarily on the fallen Earth.
When the New Testament discusses suffering, it repeatedly puts Heaven before the eyes of believers. Sadly, many churches fail to follow this example. When we say nothing, or put our hope in a health and wealth gospel, or hope only in medical advances, we rob God's people of an eternal perspective.

"Now if we are children, then we are heirs—heirs of God and co-heirs with Christ, if indeed we share in his sufferings in order that we may also share in his glory" (Romans 8:17). Paul says we will become Christ's heirs and share in his glory *if* we share in his sufferings. No suffering, no glory.

F. F. Bruce writes, "It is not merely that the glory is a compensation for the suffering; it actually grows out of the suffering. There is an organic relation between the two for the believer as surely as there was for his Lord."[3]

As Romans 8:18 emphasizes, our present sufferings are not worth comparing to the future glory that God and we and others will see in us.
Paul offers a one-word answer to the question, "Why suffering?" He replies, "Glory." Glory is a state of high honor, involving a brilliant, radiant beauty. Our glory is secondary, not primary. We are not its source, God is. He is the sun who shines upon us, bestowing an eternal glory rooted in himself, purchased for us by his suffering on the cross. God will be glorified by imparting his honor to us and sharing it with us.

God's promise of glory doesn't minimize our suffering, of course; Paul affirms we will experience great sufferings (see Romans 8). Only an immeasurably greater glory can eclipse our present suffering—and that is exactly what will happen. Romans 8:18 says God will not *create* that glory, but will *reveal* it. It's already there—just not yet manifested.

The treasures we'll enjoy won't lie only outside us, but, Paul says, "in us." God uses suffering to achieve the glorious transformation of our characters to prepare us for service and joy in the next life (see 2 Corinthians 4:17–18).

God will not simply wait for our deaths, then snap his fingers to make us what he wants us to be. He begins that process here and now, using our suffering to help us grow in Christlikeness. Phillips renders Romans 8:19, "The whole creation is on tiptoe to see the wonderful sight of the sons of God coming into their own." As a master artist's magnum opus awaits unveiling at an exhibit, so our Christlikeness, forged in suffering, awaits revealing at the Master's perfect time.

We can rejoice now because Christ promised that in Heaven he will replace our weeping with laughter; our poverty with wealth; our hunger with satisfaction; and hatred, insults, and rejection with eternal reward.
Luke, a physician, tells of many who came to Jesus "to hear him and to be healed of their diseases. Those troubled by evil spirits were cured, and the people all tried to touch him, because power was coming from him and healing them all" (Luke 6:18–19).

Christ knew that even those he healed would one day grow weak again and die, leaving their families wailing over their graves. What could Jesus say to offer them hope not just for the short term but the long term? Luke tells us: "Blessed are you who are poor, for *yours is the kingdom of God.* Blessed are you who hunger now, for *you will be satisfied.* Blessed are you who weep now, for *you will laugh.* Blessed are you when men hate you, when they exclude you and insult you and reject your name as evil, because of the Son of Man. Rejoice in that day and leap for joy, because *great is your reward in heaven*" (6:20–23).

Jesus promises the hungry that they'll find satisfaction. He assures those with eyes swollen from tears that they will laugh in Heaven. He tells the persecuted to leap for joy *now* because of their great reward *then*.

Most people think of Heaven as an otherworldly place, very unlike Earth. But in a parallel passage to Luke 6, Jesus says, "Blessed are the meek, for they will inherit *the earth*" (Matthew 5:5). We will inherit an Earth where righteousness dwells (see 2 Peter 3:13). On that New Earth God will reverse life's injustices and tragedies—and all the blessings Jesus promised will become ours.

In order to appreciate our eternal future, we will remember the sufferings of the present.

When Christ sets up his eternal kingdom, he will banish evil and suffering—yet we will remember both in a way that won't cause us pain, but will prompt our gratitude and worship. God told the Israelites to remember their bondage in Egypt, long after he had freed them, as they celebrated Passover each year (see Exodus 12:14). Likewise, I'm convinced that in Heaven we'll remember evil and suffering in order to provide the backdrop to better see God's holiness and grace.

Personality requires memory. "For the sins which so often made us tremble, are washed away in the blood of Jesus, and are, therefore, no longer a source of trouble. The remembrance of them rather intensifies our love for the God of mercy, and therefore increases our happiness."[4]

Isaiah 65:17 is often cited as proof that in eternity we won't remember our present lives: "Behold, I will create new heavens and a new earth. The former things will not be remembered, nor will they come to mind." We should, however, view this in context. In the previous verse God says, "The past troubles will be forgotten and hidden from my eyes" (parallel to God saying in Jeremiah 31:34, "I will…remember their sins no more").

Remember is a covenant word that includes acting upon what comes to mind. To not remember doesn't mean to forget. It means that though God could recall our past sins, he will never hold them against us because he sees that we are covered by Christ's blood and made righteous in him.

God doesn't have a mental lapse; he *chooses* not to bring up our sins. Likewise, Isaiah 65:17 suggests that our former sins and sorrows will not preoccupy or distract us in eternity. In other words, the evil and suffering we remember will have no hold on us (just as the martyrs of Revelation 6:9–11 remember they were killed for Christ, yet that memory in no way diminishes their experience in Heaven but enhances it).

Even though God will wipe away the tears attached to this world, he will *not* erase from our minds human history and Christ's intervention. We'll never forget that *our* sins nailed Jesus to the cross, for Christ's resurrection body has nail-scarred hands and feet (see John 20:24–29). But rather than causing us eternal grief, this will prompt us to eternal joy and worship of God for his grace.

Heaven's happiness won't be dependent on our ignorance of what happened on Earth—it will be enhanced by our changed *perspective* on it.

Jim, my friend dying of ALS, wrote me, "I hope I never lose the memory of this illness throughout eternity. Keeping the memory will help me worship Jesus in a much deeper way. Also, having the memory of my paralysis will make each day, each breath, and each movement more enjoyable and more fulfilling."

My children's book *Wait Until Then* tells the story of a boy in a wheelchair who loves baseball and dreams of running the bases. His grandfather, once a professional baseball player, now relies on a walker. On the final page I fast-forward to the New Earth, where Nathan runs the bases after a home run, with his family, including Grandpa, cheering him on. At the far left of the picture we see two relics—Nathan's wheelchair and Grandpa's walker—with flowers growing up through them.

We will enjoy the magnificence of our God and his Heaven, not merely *in spite of* all we suffered here. We will enjoy it all the more *because of* everything we suffered here.

God promises he will destroy death and forever remove the Curse upon us and upon Earth.

Christ guaranteed his final defeat of evil spirits (see Matthew 12:28; Luke 10:18–19; John 12:31; Colossians 1:13; 2:15). John said, "The reason the Son of God appeared was to destroy the devil's work" (1 John 3:8).

On the New Earth, "No longer will there be any curse" (Revelation 22:3). Christ's victory over the Curse will be total, not partial. Death won't limp away wounded. The King will annihilate it: "[God] will destroy the shroud that enfolds all peoples, the sheet that covers all nations; he will swallow up death forever" (Isaiah 25:7–8; see also Revelation 20:14; 21:4).

The magnificent hymn "Joy to the World" by Isaac Watts contains great theology:

> No more let sins and sorrows grow
> Nor thorns infest the ground;
> He comes to make His blessings flow
> Far as the curse is found.

If redemption failed to reach the farthest boundaries of the Curse, it would remain incomplete. The God who rules the world with truth and grace won't feel satisfied until he removes every sin, sorrow, and thorn. N. T. Wright says, "The evil that humans do is integrated with the enslavement of creation.... When humans are put back to rights, the world will be put back to rights."[5] The Curse is real, but *temporary.* Jesus will reverse the Curse. Earth won't merely be put out of its misery; Christ will infuse it with a far greater life. Then, at last, it will become all God intended it to be.

If the present Earth under the Curse can seem so beautiful and wonderful; if our bodies, so weakened by the Curse, at times feel overcome with a sense of the Earth's majesty and splendor—then *how magnificent will the New Earth be?* And what will it feel like to enjoy it in perfect bodies? God promises that every one of his children will one day experience the answers to those questions.

The assurance of Heaven's compensation for our present life should give us an eternal perspective.

Failing to grasp God's promises concerning the world to come sets us up for both discouragement and sin. We tell ourselves, *If I don't experience an intimate friendship now, I never will.* Or, *If I can't afford to travel to that beautiful place now, I never will.* We feel desperate to get what we *think* we want. So we're tempted toward fornication, indebtedness, or theft.

But if we understand both the negative truth that God will judge all sin and the positive truth that we'll actually live in a new universe full of new opportunities, then we can forgo certain pleasures and experiences *now,* knowing we can enjoy far greater ones *later.*

Jesus sees nothing wrong in looking forward to rewards—he assures those caring for the poor "you will be repaid at the resurrection" (see Luke 14:12–14).

But we should look for that reward from God in the next life rather than from people in this one. Jesus said we will enjoy forever in Heaven the treasures we lay up now (see Matthew 6:19–20).

What excites and interests you most? A new car? A chance to get rich? An attractive person? A vacation? Or being with God and his people on the New Earth?

Deep in our hearts, we don't desire a disembodied existence in a spiritual realm; we desire an embodied life on a righteous Earth—which is *exactly* what God promises.

"A ghost does not have flesh and bones, as you see I have," Jesus told his fearful disciples after his resurrection (Luke 24:39). Yet countless Christians imagine themselves as ghosts, disembodied spirits, in the eternal Heaven. The magnificent, cosmos-shaking victory of Christ's resurrection—by definition a physical triumph over physical death in a physical world—somehow escapes them.

If Jesus had become a ghost and did not physically rise from the dead, he would not have accomplished our redemption. When Jesus lived in his resurrection body, he demonstrated, in mostly normal ways—walking and eating and drinking and talking—*how* we would live as resurrected human beings. He also demonstrated *where* we would live—on Earth, where he lived for forty days after he rose.

"The Lord Jesus Christ...will transform our lowly bodies so that they will be like his glorious body" (Philippians 3:20–21). As Jesus rose again and lived in a physical body on Earth, so we too, in bodies like his, will rise again to live on a renewed Earth (see 1 Thessalonians 4:14; 1 John 3:2; Revelation 21:1–3).

On the cross Christ paid the qualitatively eternal punishment for our sins. Because he, due to his redemptive work, is forever scarred in his resurrection body (John 20:25–29), we will forever be without scars in ours.

Our bodily resurrection will return us to an earthly life, this time freed from sin and the Curse. Our resurrected bodies will have some essential connection to the bodies God created for us here, but will be flawless (see 1 Corinthians 15:49). We know the resurrected Christ looked like a man because Mary, in the morning dimness, through her tears mistook him for the gardener at the tomb and called him sir (see John 20:15). Jesus, in his raised body, didn't hover or float. He started a fire, cooked fish for his disciples, and said, "Come and have breakfast" (John 21:12).

One day Christ appeared in a locked room where the disciples had gathered (see John 20:19). They could touch him and cling to his body, and he could consume food; yet that same body could vanish and "materialize" as well. Might the molecules of our own resurrection bodies pass through what we think of as solid materials? We don't know yet, but won't it be fun to find out?

The wonders of our resurrected bodies and our future lives on the New Earth await us. But as we enjoy them, day after day, surely we'll look back to this life with profound gratitude for how God used everything, even evil and suffering, to prepare us for our eternal home.

You may not feel satisfied with your current body or mind, but your resurrection upgrade will never disappoint you.
Many of us look forward to Heaven more now than we did when our bodies (or minds) functioned better. Inside your body, even a broken or failing one, lies the blueprint for your resurrection body.

Joni Eareckson Tada says,

> I still can hardly believe it. I, with shriveled, bent fingers, atrophied muscles, gnarled knees, and no feeling from the shoulders down, will one day have a new body, light, bright, and clothed in righteousness—powerful and dazzling. Can you imagine the hope this gives someone spinal cord–injured like me? Or someone who is cerebral palsied, brain-injured, or who has multiple sclerosis? Imagine the hope this gives someone who is manic-depressive. No other religion, no other philosophy promises new bodies, hearts, and minds. Only in the Gospel of Christ do hurting people find such incredible hope.[6]

Joni once spoke to a class of mentally handicapped Christians. They smiled when she said that one day she would get a new body. But then she added, "And *you're* going to get new minds." The class erupted in cheers and applause. They knew what they most looked forward to!

As an insulin-dependent diabetic, I've seen both my body and my mind fail me. I suffer under the Curse enough to know just what I want—a new body and a new mind, a transformed heart without sin, no suffering or disability. Every passing year increases my longing to live on the resurrected Earth in my resurrected body, with my resurrected family and friends, worshiping and serving the resurrected Jesus. I get goose bumps just thinking about it!

Many disabled believers have heard others say about the resurrection, "You must look forward to walking and running." True enough, but one handicapped

Christian made a particularly revealing comment: "What I look forward to most is kneeling."

Our resurrected bodies will fulfill their highest function as we glorify God in our bodies, worshiping him without hindrance, fatigue, or distraction.

We're not past our peaks; the best is yet to come.

Many people look to cosmetic surgeries and other techniques to renovate crumbling bodies. We try to hold on to youthfulness with a white-knuckled grip, but all in vain.

Nanci and I both watched our dear mothers die, then saw our fathers grow old and frail. From a human perspective, it felt hopeless. They'd been at their physical and mental peaks years earlier, and all they could do was slide downhill.

But the last years of our lives before we die are, in fact, *not* the end of our lives. A moment after we die physically, a dramatic upward movement will take us immediately to Christ. We'll go right on living, just in another place. And one day, in the resurrection, we'll live again on Earth, a life so rich and joyful as to make this life seem utterly impoverished. Millions of years from now, we'll still look, feel, and *be* young. Our knowledge and skills and life experiences will apparently continue to develop. We will *never* pass our peak.

In the final months before Nanci's father died, I heard her say to a friend, "Life is closing in on him, but he's headed in the right direction." Nanci's dad now has a restored mind—and one day he'll have a body to match it. And both will far exceed what he had here even on his best days.

When hymn writer Fanny Crosby wrote the lines "His glory we shall see" and "When our eyes behold the city," she'd never seen anything past infancy. She'd tell people not to feel sorry about her blindness, because the first face she'd ever see would be Christ's. Fanny Crosby was miraculously healed—she received her sight in a dramatic moment in 1915...the moment she died.

I had the privilege of spending two hours alone with Campus Crusade founder, Bill Bright, six months before he died. As Bill sat there, tubes running to his oxygen tank, he almost jumped out of his chair as we talked about Heaven and the God he loved. Bill wasn't past his peak; he was leaning toward it. "The path of the righteous is like the first gleam of dawn, shining ever brighter till the full light of day" (Proverbs 4:18).

Bill Bright reminded me of those who "saw [the things promised] and welcomed them from a distance," and "admitted that they were aliens and strangers on earth," because "they are looking for a country of their own" and "they were longing for a better country—a heavenly one." We're told of these people, "Therefore God is not ashamed to be called their God, for he has prepared a city for them" (Hebrews 11:13–16).

We don't have to just admire such people. By God's grace, we can *be* such people!

God sometimes gives us foretastes of our future deliverance from this world of evil and suffering.

As a teenager held in a Japanese prison camp in China, Margaret Holder felt the almost unbearable pain of forced separation from her family. But as the war progressed, American planes dropped barrels of food and supplies. When Nanci and I spoke with her forty-five years later, Margaret recalled with delight "care packages falling from the sky."

One day an American plane flew low and dropped more of those wonderful food barrels. But as the barrels neared the ground, the captives realized something had changed. Her eyes bright, Margaret told us, "This time the barrels had legs!" The sky rained American soldiers, parachuting down to rescue them. Margaret and several hundred children rushed out of the camp past the Japanese guards, who offered no resistance. Free for the first time in six years, they ran to the soldiers, throwing themselves on their rescuers, hugging and kissing them.

Imagine the children's joy! Imagine the soldiers' joy!

Yes, I know those six years of confinement and separation from family caused great suffering for that young girl and her family. But I also know what I saw in the eyes and heard in the voice of Margaret Holder almost half a century later. She exuded sheer *joy*, a joy she never would have known without the suffering that preceded it.

In the sixty-five years since their dramatic rescue from that prison camp, most of those children have died. Those who loved Jesus are now with him. Imagine their joy in being reunited *yet again* with their parents and with some of their rescuers! But this time the reunion will never end. And this time they will live forever with Jesus, the source of all joy.

If the soldiers rejoiced in rescuing those children, think how God rejoices in rescuing us. Whether he returns in the sky to liberate us or draws us to himself through our deaths, he will indeed rescue us and unite us with him and loved ones. He'll liberate us from a world under the Curse and take us home—where evil and suffering can never touch us, his beloved children, again.

The New Earth will be an everlasting, righteous kingdom, which will compensate for all the evils of fallen kingdoms preceding it.

Daniel 7 gives a prophetic revelation of four earthly kingdoms, beginning with Nebuchadnezzar's Babylon, that will one day give way to an eternal, fifth kingdom. "There before me was one like a son of man, coming with the clouds of heaven. He approached the Ancient of Days and was led into his presence. He was given authority, glory and sovereign power; all peoples, nations and men of every language worshiped him. His dominion is an everlasting dominion that will not pass away, and his kingdom is one that will never be destroyed" (verses 13–14).

Because the four pagan kingdoms dominated Earth, the passage implies that this fifth kingdom—God's eternal kingdom—will also dominate Earth. We're told the Messiah's dominion will be "everlasting" and "will not pass away" and "will never be destroyed" (verse 14). Clearly, this cannot refer to the Millennium, because a thousand-year kingdom does not last forever. The kingdom with the everlasting dominion does not occupy a *different* realm but the *same* realm— Earth. Christ will not merely destroy the earth where fallen kings once ruled; rather, he will rule over that same earth, after it is resurrected and transformed.

At Daniel's request, an angel interprets his vision, then makes an extraordinary statement: "But the saints of the Most High will receive the kingdom and will possess it forever—yes, for ever and ever" (verse 18). Daniel 7 definitively teaches that the coming reign of God and his people will take place *on Earth,* replacing the corrupt reigns of prior kings. And the angel isn't content with saying that God's people will possess this magnificent earthly kingdom "forever"— lest it doesn't register that this is an eternal kingdom, he adds, "yes, for ever and ever."

The ongoing parade of Earth's unrighteous rulers should make us hunger for the day when our righteous God will rule, not just in Heaven but on Earth. God's will *shall* be done on Earth. It will be done for all eternity, under the reign of Christ and redeemed mankind, his servant kings.

Whom will we rule under in Christ's New Earth kingdom? I think it will be my privilege to serve under faithful, unassuming people, including those who endured great suffering. Or perhaps I'll serve under those who gave great amounts of time and money to help the needy and reach unbelievers with the gospel. When we meet these people, we will hear their stories. When we do, they'll cause us to look at this world's suffering much differently than we do today.

In Sudan, before Make Way Partners built dormitories, children rescued from the sex-slave trade slept outside. In only nine months, 278 orphans died from exposure or attacks by wild dogs or hyenas. What terror and heartbreak these children endured in their short lives! Knowing God's love for children and believing what Jesus taught about relieving the poor of their mourning—replacing it with laughter in Heaven—I believe that in Christ's kingdom, we may have the privilege to serve under such children.

How marvelous that we have the privilege to serve them today as well. Jesus said, "The King will reply, 'I tell you the truth, whatever you did for one of the least of these brothers of mine, you did for me'" (Matthew 25:40).

To resolve the problem of evil, humans must enjoy full continuity of their personal identities.

When I came to Christ, I became a new person. But I still had the same body, DNA, and overall personality. I was the old Randy, made new. I will undergo yet another change at death. And I will undergo still *another* change at the resurrection. But through all these changes, *I will remain who I was and who I am.* There will be continuity from this life to the next. I can say with Job, "I myself will see him with my own eyes—I, and not another" (19:27).

Despite the radical changes that occur through salvation, death, and resurrection, we remain the unique beings whom God created. We'll have the same history, appearance, memory, interests, and skills because of something we might call "redemptive continuity."

If we don't grasp the principle of redemptive continuity, we cannot understand the nature of resurrection. "There must be continuity," writes Anthony Hoekema, "for otherwise there would be little point in speaking about a resurrection at all. The calling into existence of a completely new set of people totally different from the present inhabitants of the earth would not be a resurrection."[7]

First Corinthians 15:53 says, "The perishable must clothe itself with the imperishable, and the mortal with immortality." It is *we,* the very same people who walk this Earth, who will walk the New Earth. "*We* will be with the Lord forever" (1 Thessalonians 4:17).

The empty tomb provides definitive proof that Christ's resurrection body was the same one that died on the cross. If resurrection meant the creation of a previously nonexistent body, then Christ's original body would have remained in the tomb. When Jesus said to his disciples after his resurrection, "It is I myself!" (Luke 24:39), he emphasized that he was the same person—in spirit *and* body—whom they'd accompanied the past three years. His disciples saw the marks of his crucifixion, unmistakable evidence that he had the same body.

If Job were not still Job in eternity, then Job's suffering on Earth would not have been worth it. If Ana Swanson were no longer who she was, then the Ana Swanson who suffered would not be the Ana Swanson relieved of suffering and made to rejoice and laugh. God does not merely promise that evil and suffering will disappear. He promises that his same children who endured evil and suffering will live in eternal joy.

Heaven will fulfill our greatest dreams and surpass our highest expectations.

Philip Yancey writes, "In any discussion of disappointment with God, heaven is the last word, the most important word of all."[8] In *The Lord of the Rings* Sam asks Gandalf,

> "Is everything sad going to come untrue? What's happened to the world?"
>
> "A great Shadow has departed," said Gandalf, and then he laughed, and the sound was like music, or like water in a parched land; and as he listened the thought came to him that he had not heard laughter, the pure sound of merriment, for days upon days without count.... It fell upon his ears like the echo of all the joys he had ever known. But he himself burst into tears. Then, as a sweet rain will pass down a wind of spring and the sun will shine out the clearer, his tears ceased, and his laughter welled up, and laughing he sprang from his bed.
>
> "How do I feel?" he cried. "Well, I don't know how to say it. I feel, I feel"—he waved his arms in the air—"I feel like spring after winter, and sun on the leaves; and like trumpets and harps and all the songs I have ever heard!"[9]

How will we feel when the great shadow departs forever? How will we feel when everything happy comes true, and everything sad comes untrue?

We will feel, perhaps, like it couldn't get any better than that.

But each new day will prove us wrong.

Notes

1. C. S. Lewis, *The Problem of Pain* (New York: Macmillan, 1962), 144.
2. Dinesh D'Souza, *What's So Great About Christianity* (Washington, D.C.: Regnery, 2007), 291.
3. F. F. Bruce, *The Epistle of Paul to the Romans* (Downers Grove, IL: InterVarsity, 1985), 168.

4. Father Boudreau, quoted in Randy Alcorn, *50 Days of Heaven* (Carol Stream, IL: Tyndale, 2006), 189–90.

5. N.T. Wright, *Evil and the Justice of God* (Downers Grove, IL: InterVarsity Press, 2006), 72.

6. Joni Eareckson Tada and Steven Estes, *When God Weeps* (Grand Rapids, MI: Zondervan, 1997), 216.

7. Anthony A. Hoekema, *The Bible and the Future* (Grand Rapids, MI: Eerdmans, 1979), 251.

8. Philip Yancey, *Disappointment with God* (Grand Rapids, MI: Zondervan, 1998), 244.

9. J. R. R. Tolkien, *The Return of the King* (New York: Random House, 1973), 247.

29

Hell: Eternal Sovereign Justice Exacted upon Evildoers

If there is no Hell, there is no justice.

When most people speak of what a terrible notion Hell is, they talk as if it involves the suffering of innocent people. That would indeed be terribly unjust—but nowhere does the Bible suggest the innocent will spend a single moment in Hell.

When I think of Hell, I recall a man I met on a train out of Kiev, whose mother was the only one of twelve children in her family to survive Stalin's enforced starvation in Ukraine. I think about Vek and Samoeun Taing, as they walked us through the Killing Fields, telling us of the atrocities committed against their families.

Without Hell, justice would never overtake the unrepentant tyrants responsible for murdering millions. Perpetrators of evil throughout the ages would get away with murder—and rape, and torture, and every evil.

Even if we may acknowledge Hell as a necessary and just punishment for evildoers, however, we rarely see *ourselves* as worthy of Hell. After all, we are not Hitler, Stalin, Pol Pot, Bundy, or Dahmer.

God responds, "There is no one righteous, not even one; there is no one who understands, no one who seeks God. All have turned away, they have together become worthless; there is no one who does good, not even one" (Romans 3:10–12).

As we saw in chapters 7–9, in our unredeemed state, we remain alienated from God, the source of all goodness. And while by his common grace some of his goodness leaks both onto us and into us, our predominant condition is far from good. In his book *The Nazi Doctors*, Robert Lifton coined the phrase "the normalcy of evil." Evil permeates the human condition. The Nazi doctors were respectable, educated people who loved their families yet thought nothing of performing sadistic experiments on Jewish children. They considered themselves good people. We consider ourselves good people.

We're wrong.

Guilty people can always rationalize sin. Hell exists because sin has no excuse.

After detailing a long list of human atrocities, Os Guinness asks the painful question, "What does it say of us as human beings that the people who do these things are the same species as we are?"[1]

To see the face of evil, we need only look in the mirror. If we don't see evil's reality in our lives, it's no surprise. Evil people typically don't.

Hell exists precisely because God has committed himself to solving the problem of evil.

Hell is not evil; it's a place where evil gets punished. Hell is not pleasant, appealing, or encouraging. But Hell is morally good, because a good God must punish evil.

Hell will not be a blot on the universe, but an eternal testimony to the ugliness of evil that will prompt wondrous appreciation of a good God's magnificence. That sounds like nonsense to Hell-hating moderns, but it makes perfect sense when we recognize and hate *evil* for what it is. We each have our preferred ways of sinning, whether as prostitutes, porn addicts, materialists, gossips, or the self-righteous. We all are sinners who deserve Hell.

We hate Hell precisely because we don't hate evil. We hate it also because we deserve it.

We cry out for true and lasting justice, then fault God for taking evil too seriously by administering eternal punishment. We can't have it both ways. Sin is evil; just punishment of sin is good. Hell is an eternal correction of and compensation for evil. It is justice. To fear and dread Hell is understandable, but to argue against Hell is to argue against justice.

Were this our only life, for there to be justice all evil would have to be judged here and all goodness rewarded here.

Christianity teaches that one's life in this fallen world will give way to an unending life, either in Heaven or Hell. *That* life, not this one, will bring perfect justice.

Atheists consider the world terribly unjust, for they think that only in this life can any retribution for good or evil take place. But the Bible teaches that God will exercise justice in a never-ending afterlife. At the end of this fallen world, just before the inauguration of the New Heaven and New Earth, God will at last bring ongoing justice to both unbelievers and believers (see Revelation 20).

Hell is the only just alternative to Heaven.

Fallen angels along with humans who haven't accepted God's gift of redemption in Christ will inhabit Hell (see 2 Peter 2:4; Revelation 20:12–15). After Christ returns, believers will be resurrected to eternal life in Heaven while unbelievers will be resurrected to an eternal existence in Hell. Jesus said, "Do not be amazed at this, for a time is coming when all who are in their graves will hear his voice and come out…and those who have done evil will rise to be condemned" (John 5:28–29).

God will judge the unsaved for their sins. Christ will say to those who don't know him, "Depart from me, you who are cursed, into the eternal fire prepared for the devil and his angels" (Matthew 25:41).

JESUS AND HELL

In the Bible, Jesus spoke more about Hell than anyone else did.

Jesus referred to Hell as a real place and described it in graphic terms (see Matthew 10:28; 13:40–42; Mark 9:43–48). He spoke of a fire that burns but doesn't consume, an undying worm that eats away at the damned, and a lonely and foreboding darkness.

Christ says the unsaved "will be thrown outside, into the darkness, where there will be weeping and gnashing of teeth" (Matthew 8:12). Jesus taught that an unbridgeable chasm separates the wicked in Hell from the righteous in paradise. The wicked suffer terribly, remain conscious, retain their desires and memories, long for relief, cannot find comfort, cannot leave their torment, and have no hope (see Luke 16:19–31).

Our Savior could not have painted a bleaker picture of Hell.

C. S. Lewis said, "I have met no people who fully disbelieved in Hell and also had a living and life-giving belief in Heaven."[2] The biblical teaching on both destinations stands or falls together. If the one is real, so is the other; if the one is a myth, so is the other. The best reason for believing in Hell is that Jesus said it exists.

It isn't just what Jesus said about Hell that matters. It is the fact that it was he who said it.

"There seems to be a kind of conspiracy," wrote Dorothy Sayers, "to forget, or to conceal, where the doctrine of hell comes from. The doctrine of hell is not 'mediaeval priestcraft' for frightening people into giving money to the church: it is Christ's deliberate judgment on sin.... We cannot repudiate hell without altogether repudiating Christ."[3]

Why do I believe in an eternal Hell? Because Jesus clearly and repeatedly affirmed its existence. As Sayers suggested, you cannot dismiss Hell without dismissing Jesus.

Atheist Bertrand Russell wrote, "There is one very serious defect to my mind in Christ's moral character, and that is that He believed in hell. I do not myself feel that any person who is really profoundly humane can believe in everlasting punishment."[4]

Shall we believe Jesus or Bertrand Russell? For me, it is not a difficult choice.

C. S. Lewis said of Hell, "There is no doctrine which I would more willingly remove from Christianity than this, if it lay in my power. But it has the full support of Scripture and, specially, of Our Lord's own words; it has always been held by Christendom; and it has the support of reason."[5]

We cannot make Hell go away simply because the thought of it makes us uncomfortable. If I were as holy as God, if I knew a fraction of what he knows, I would realize Hell is just and right. We should weep over Hell, but not deny it. If there isn't an eternal Hell, Jesus made a terrible mistake in affirming there is. And if we cannot trust Jesus in his teaching about Hell, why should we trust anything he said, including his offer of salvation?

We may pride ourselves in thinking we are too loving to believe in Hell. But in saying this, we blaspheme, for we claim to be more loving than Jesus—more loving than the One who with outrageous love took upon himself the full penalty for our sin.

Who are we to think we are better than Jesus?

Or that when it comes to Hell, or anything else, we know better than he does?

God determined he would rather endure the torment of the Cross on our behalf than live in Heaven without us.

Apart from Christ, we would all spend eternity in Hell. But God so much wants us not to go to Hell that he paid a horrible price on the cross so we wouldn't have to. This can be distorted into self-congratulation: if God paid such a great price for us, we must be extremely valuable. A better perspective is that if God had to pay such a great price for us, it emphasizes both the extent of his love *and* the extent of our evil.

Jesus asks a haunting question in Mark 8:36–37: "What good is it for a man to gain the whole world, yet forfeit his soul? Or what can a man give in exchange for his soul?"

The price has been paid, but we can't benefit from forgiveness unless we choose to receive it. A convicted criminal may be offered a pardon, but if he rejects it, he remains condemned.

By denying Hell's reality, we lower the stakes of redemption and minimize Christ's work on the cross.

If Christ's crucifixion and resurrection didn't deliver us from a real and eternal Hell, then his work on the cross is less heroic, less potent, less consequential, and less deserving of our worship and praise.

Theologian William Shedd put it this way: "The doctrine of Christ's vicarious atonement logically stands or falls with that of eternal punishment."[6]

ANNIHILATION

The Bible teaches Hell is a place of eternal punishment, not annihilation.

Jesus said, "Then they will go away to eternal punishment, but the righteous to eternal life" (Matthew 25:46). Here in the same sentence, Christ uses the word "eternal" *(aionos)* to describe the duration of both Heaven and Hell. Thus, according to our Lord, if some will consciously experience Heaven forever, then some must consciously experience Hell forever.

Despite the clarity of Matthew 25:46, even some evangelical Christians have affirmed that upon dying, or at the final judgment, those without Christ will cease to exist. Clark Pinnock writes, "It's time for evangelicals to come out and say that the biblical and morally appropriate doctrine of Hell is annihilation, not everlasting torment."[7] Pinnock makes a revealing statement:

> I was led to question the traditional belief in everlasting conscious torment because of moral revulsion and broader theological considerations, not first of all on scriptural grounds. It just does not make any sense to say that a God of love will torture people forever for sins done in the context of a finite life.[8]

Note that Pinnock admits he reached his conclusions about annihilation "not first of all on scriptural grounds." John Stott wrote about eternal conscious torment, "Emotionally, I find the concept intolerable and do not understand how people can live with it without either cauterizing their feelings or cracking under the strain.... Scripture points in the direction of annihilation."⁹

But would John Stott, whom I greatly respect and who is an advocate of the inspiration and authority of Scripture, have ever said Scripture points toward annihilation if it were not for the emotional strain put upon him by the passages that clearly appear to teach everlasting punishment?

Revelation 20:10 says not only that Satan, but also the beast and the false prophet, "will be tormented *for ever and ever.*" Revelation 19:20 shows the beast and false prophet are humans, put in Hell a thousand years earlier. Hence, we at least know that Hell for humans *cannot* mean immediate annihilation at death.

The most graphic New Testament statement of the eternal suffering of the unrepentant says simply, "The smoke of their torment goes up *for ever and ever,* and they have no rest, day or night" (Revelation 14:11). It's hard to imagine a more emphatic affirmation of eternal punishment.

If we are going to discard the doctrine of eternal punishment because it feels profoundly unpleasant to us, then it seems fair to ask what other biblical teachings we will also reject, because they too don't square with what we feel. And if we do this, are we not replacing the authority of Scripture with the authority of our feelings, or our limited understanding?

Annihilation makes no sense in light of Revelation 20.

One popular annihilationist position maintains that unbelievers cease to exist when they die. But if they no longer exist, then how can they be raised to stand at the Great White Throne Judgment of Revelation 20? Would God re-create them to stand before him in judgment? After this judgment, Revelation 20 says they will be cast into the lake of fire. Would this be a second annihilation?

Another view states that unbelievers are destroyed not at death, but sometime later. They suffer some punishment appropriate to their offenses (as the rich man experiences in Luke 16), some shorter and some longer, then are snuffed out of existence.

But as we've seen, two human beings, the antichrist and the false prophet, will be thrown into the lake of fire after a thousand years of suffering. If it is wrong for punishment to last forever, wouldn't it seem wrong to last over a thousand years? If there's an eventual end to people's suffering in Hell, where is that indicated in Scripture? Why Christ's emphasis on "eternal punishment" and fire that isn't quenched and a worm that doesn't die?

People believe in annihilation because it doesn't seem nearly so bad as eternity in Hell. The rich man of Luke 16 does not cease to exist when he dies. But will he one day cease to exist? If so, when he begs for relief, wouldn't we expect Abraham to say, "When your sins are paid for, then you will no longer suffer"? But Abraham offers him no hope for relief.

Annihilation is an attractive teaching compared to the alternative—I would gladly embrace it, were it taught in Scripture. But though I've tried, I just can't find it there.

Annihilation would not satisfy God's justice and solve the problem of evil. Do you believe that Stalin, Pol Pot, and Idi Amin got their just punishment in this life? Do you think the life imprisonment of Charles Manson—in which he receives food, clothes, reading material, television privileges, and protection from other inmates—supplies full justice for his arrogant, unrepentant slaughter of innocent human beings? Would eternal nonexistence be a just punishment for such men? In what sense does an annihilated person, who by definition experiences nothing, experience any punishment at all?

Can you imagine God saying to Hitler, Stalin, and Mao at the final judgment, "For all your evil rebellion against me and your unspeakable crimes against humanity, your punishment is to no longer be conscious"? The "pain" of nonexistence is no pain at all. To cease to exist is to not be held accountable for sin. How could God satisfy his justice if he responded to despicable sins against himself and humanity by merely flicking a switch into nothingness?

Annihilation is no solution to the injustice of evil and suffering. If it were true, annihilation might itself raise a serious moral problem, for it suggests that our sins are not so grievous and the consequences for committing them are painless, or at worst exist only for a limited time.

If, as the Bible teaches, Christ's redemptive work is so magnificent that it delivers us from an eternal Hell, then it should elicit maximum worship from us. But if it delivers us only from nonexistence—which is exactly the end atheists, naturalists, and materialists believe in—then we may feel grateful to God for what we are rescued to, Heaven, but not so grateful for what he rescued us from, mere nonexistence.

Although the doctrine of annihilation continues to gain ground among believers, Christians must realize that embracing this doctrine minimizes, or worse, eliminates altogether the horrors of Hell. This doctrine in its most popular form merely confirms what most unbelievers already think, that their lives will end at death, and therefore there's nothing to be concerned about. In contrast, the Bible speaks of an eternal Hell as something that should motivate unbelievers to turn to God, and motivate believers to share the gospel with urgency.

Is Hell a Problem or a Solution?

Many see Hell as the ultimate cruelty and injustice.

Jesus said God prepared Hell "for the devil and his angels" (Matthew 25:41). Humans go there only as they align themselves with that cosmic minority of fallen angels who reject God.

Clark Pinnock writes, "I consider the concept of hell as endless torment in body and mind an outrageous doctrine.... How can Christians possibly project a deity of such cruelty and vindictiveness whose ways include inflicting everlasting torture upon his creatures, however sinful they may have been? Surely a God who would do such a thing is more nearly like Satan than like God."[10]

It's hard to imagine a more serious accusation, since Jesus, the second member of the triune God, makes the clearest statements in Scripture about everlasting punishment. Can any Christian really believe that in doing so Jesus was saying God is "cruel" and "like Satan"?

Many atheists believe early Christians invented Hell as a doctrine to frighten people into conversion. But Christ's followers merely repeated their Lord's teaching. They didn't make them up.

Doesn't our main objection to Hell center in the belief that we are far better than we really are? We may accept in theory that we're sinners; we may even be able to list some of our sins (though we can give quite good reasons for many of them). But we do not even begin to see the extent of our evil in the sight of an all-holy God.

If we regard Hell as a divine overreaction to sin, we deny that God has the moral right to inflict ongoing punishment on any humans he created to exist forever. By denying Hell, we deny the extent of God's holiness and the extent of our evil. We deny the extreme seriousness of sin. And, worst of all, we deny the extreme magnificence of God's grace in Christ's blood, shed for us on the cross. For if the evils he died for aren't big enough to warrant eternal punishment, then perhaps the grace he showed us on the cross isn't big enough to warrant eternal praise.

Suppose that
- God is far more holy than we realize.
- We are far more sinful than we realize.

If these premises are true—and Scripture demonstrates they are—then why should it surprise us that God decisively and eternally punishes sin?

If we better understood both God's nature and our own, we would not feel shocked that some people go to Hell. (Where else could sinners go?) Rather, we would feel shocked—as perhaps the angels do—that any fallen human would be permitted into Heaven. Unholy as we are in ourselves, we are disqualified to claim that infinite holiness cannot demand everlasting punishment.

The more we believe in God's absolute holiness and justice, the more Hell will make sense to us.

Are you tired of all the evil and corruption in this world? Do you long for a world in which such things don't exist? Then you long for a Heaven without evildoers. And that requires either that God forces everyone to repent, come to Christ, and embrace his righteousness, or that God provides an alternative residence for those who do not. Hell is that place.

It saddens me to think of people suffering forever. But if there were no Hell, that would diminish the very attributes of God that make Hell necessary and Heaven available.

Should we want Hell eliminated if our righteous God determines it should exist? I believe we should leave Hell in God's hands, trust him, and submit to his judgment, not our own.

Just as most people in prison don't think they belong there, so most of us can't imagine we deserve Hell. But when at last we begin to grasp that we do deserve it, we praise God for his grace on a far deeper level.

Our opinion about Hell's existence holds no sway; God doesn't give us a vote.

Simone Weil wrote, "One can only excuse men for evil by accusing God of it."[11]

Some in ancient Israel claimed the way of the Lord was not just. God replied, "Is it not your ways that are unjust?" And then he reiterated that everyone will die for his own sin (see Ezekiel 18:25–29).

Just because I don't like the idea of Hell doesn't make Hell unjust. Of course, sinners oppose the idea that they deserve eternal punishment, just as a little boy opposes the idea that he deserves punishment because he hit his little sister.

Why do we have more difficulty accepting the doctrine of Hell than ancient people did? Perhaps because our tolerant, therapeutic, positive-thinking culture assumes our basic goodness.

In a day of television and Internet news polls that determine what percent of a population approves of certain issues or candidates, it's easy to think that our opinion about Hell carries weight. But God doesn't take opinion polls. He refuses to adjust his revelation about Hell to fit our modern sensibilities.

Hell will have degrees of punishment; each person's punishment will exactly correspond to his sins.

All whose names are not written in the Lamb's Book of Life will be judged by God in relation to their works, which have been recorded in the books of Heaven (see Revelation 20:12–15). The severity of punishment will vary with the amount of truth known, and the nature and number of the sins committed (see Luke 20:45–47; Romans 2:3–6).

Jesus said the Day of Judgment would be more bearable for some than for others (see Matthew 11:20–24). Some will be "beaten with many blows" and others "beaten with few blows" (Luke 12:47–48).

Hell is not one-size-fits-all. Revelation 20 explicitly says that God records all human works so that all punishment will be commensurate to the evil committed (verses 12–13, see also Matthew 5:21–28; 12:36; 1 John 3:15).

Eternal punishment is not disproportionate or infinite.

People commonly ask, "Why would God inflict infinite punishment for finite sins? Isn't that disproportionate punishment and therefore unjust?"

Scripture nowhere teaches infinite punishment; rather, it teaches punishment proportionate to the evil committed. The confusion comes in mistaking *eternal* for *infinite*. No one will bear in Hell an infinite number of offenses; they will bear only the sins they have committed (see Revelation 20:12–13).

The length of time spent committing a crime does not determine the length of the sentence for that crime. It may take five seconds to murder a child, but five seconds of punishment would hardly bring appropriate justice. Crimes committed against an infinitely holy God cannot be paid for in finite measures of time.

John Piper, agreeing with the viewpoint of Jonathan Edwards, says, "The length of your sin isn't what makes the length of suffering just, it's the height of your sin that makes the length of the suffering just."[12]

Since the absence of God is the absence of good, Hell is a place without the slightest trace of good.

In Luke 16 Abraham and Lazarus dwell together in paradise, but the rich man stands alone in Hell. Expect no comforting company in a place from which God has withdrawn. "They will be punished with everlasting destruction and shut out from the presence of the Lord and from the majesty of his power" (2 Thessalonians 1:9). Hell is horrible because it means being locked out from God's presence.

Since God is the source of all good, there can be no good where God is not. No wonder Dante, in the *Inferno*, envisioned this sign chiseled above Hell's gate: "Abandon all hope, you who enter here."[13]

The vast majority of those who believe in Hell do not believe they are going there.

Many more Americans believe in Heaven than believe in Hell. For everyone who believes he's going to Hell, a hundred and twenty believe they're going to Heaven.[14] This optimism stands in stark contrast to Christ's words in Matthew 7:13–14: "Enter through the narrow gate. For wide is the gate and broad is the road that leads to destruction, and many enter through it. But small is the gate and narrow the road that leads to life, and only a few find it."

Our culture considers Heaven the default destination (when did you last attend a funeral in which a speaker pictured the departed in Hell?). But since "all have sinned and fall short of the glory of God" (Romans 3:23) and "without holiness no one will see the Lord" (Hebrews 12:14), none of us will enter the presence of an infinitely holy God unless something in us radically changes. Until our sin problem gets resolved, Hell will remain our true destination.

Once this life ends, the unbeliever's sin nature becomes permanent, likely assuring future evildoing that demands future punishment.

At death, God will transform his children so that righteous men will be made perfect (see Hebrews 12:23). But he can do nothing more for those who have refused his grace. Hell isn't simply a sentence that falls upon us; it is the inevitable destination we choose with every sin and every refusal to repent and turn to God for grace.

When developing photographs, technicians immerse negatives in different solutions; so long as the photograph remains in the developing solution, it can change. But once it gets dropped into the "stop bath," it's permanently fixed. So will it be when we die and enter eternity; our lives on Earth will be fixed, never to be altered or revised.[15] "Man is destined to die once, and after that to face judgment" (Hebrews 9:27).

D. A. Carson argues that rebellion may continue eternally in Hell, and if so, then Hell is eternal precisely because the sinful rebellion is eternal. Hell would then be a place where "sinners go on sinning and receiving the recompense of their sin, refusing, always refusing, to bend the knee."[16] Hell would be ever-ongoing punishment for ever-ongoing sins.

This position makes perfect sense if we recognize death as forever sealing or making permanent our natures. The believer has been granted an eternal identity with the nature of Christ, and this identity allows him to enter Heaven. But at death the unregenerate person, the unrepentant sinner, forever remains unregenerate. There is no longer a possibility of transformation. Yes, he will acknowledge God's existence, but so do the demons even now, shuddering (see James 2:19). He will regret being punished, but that doesn't mean he will repent, nor will he cease to sin against God in thought and word (and action, if action is possible in Hell). Because his nature is unrepentant, and that nature cannot change after death, he can continue for all eternity not to trust God, not to value Christ's work, and to otherwise commit sins against God.

Hell's torment may be to unendingly experience lusts, greed, and other sinful desires with no hope of fulfillment, coupled with ongoing judgment for these ongoing sins.

Fairness doesn't demand that God give people a second chance after death, since he gives us thousands of chances before death.

God grants every person a lifetime to reform, to turn to him for grace and empowerment. For those who die young or otherwise lack the mental capacity to respond to Christ, many Christians throughout the ages have believed God may extend the atonement of Christ to cover them, as an act of grace. I agree.

God gives people on this fallen Earth adequate opportunity to turn to him in their "first chance." He has revealed himself to us in the creation and in our conscience so that "men are without excuse" (Romans 1:20). If people respond to God, I believe he will send them further revelation of himself through human agents, angels, direct intervention in dreams or visions, or however he chooses.

God gives us second chances and third and tenth and hundredth chances every day of our lives. The chance to respond to the message of creation that cries out, "There is a God," is repeated multiple times daily, over a lifetime. Every breath is an opportunity to respond to a conscience that convicts people of their guilt.

If God allowed everyone to die first and then decide whether to trust God, it would make faith irrelevant. In the end all people would submit to Christ by sight, not faith; instead of trusting, they would merely be acquiescing to his infinite power. He has no desire for this.

If a woman were given a choice between being buried alive in a swamp and marrying a certain man, she would choose to marry the man. But what man would want such a wife? God doesn't need our love, but he does want it. He doesn't want people who merely desire to escape Hell. He wants people who value and treasure him above all else, who long to be with him.

Because our choices in this life orient us for eternity, God-rejecters might be as miserable in Heaven as Hell.

C. S. Lewis spoke to those who questioned the doctrine of Hell:

> In the long run the answer to all those who object to the doctrine of hell is itself a question: "What are you asking God to do?" To wipe out their past sins and, at all costs, to give them a fresh start, smoothing every difficulty and offering every miraculous help? But He has done so, on Calvary. To forgive them? They will not be forgiven. To leave them alone? Alas, I am afraid that is what He does.[17]

Lewis said the doors of Hell are barred from the inside. If he means those in Hell refuse to give up their trust in themselves to turn to God, I think he's right. But if we imagine that people in Hell won't want to get out to avoid its sufferings, that's certainly false. The rich man in Luke 16 desperately desired to have his agony relieved; he even requested a drop of water from paradise. Wanting out of Hell, however, is not the same as wanting to be with God. And God desires us to be with him only if we want to be with him. Feeling sorry for the consequences of our sins is not the same as repenting of our sins.

The redeemed say, "In your presence there is fullness of joy; at your right hand are pleasures forevermore" (Psalm 16:11, ESV). But what do the unredeemed say when exposed to God's presence? "They called to the mountains and the rocks, 'Fall on us and hide us from the face of him who sits on the throne and from the wrath of the Lamb!'" (Revelation 6:16).

Heaven and Hell are places defined, respectively, by God's presence or absence, by God's grace or wrath. They're real places, but also conditions of relationship to God. Whose we are, not where we are, determines our misery or our joy. To bring a man from Hell to Heaven would bring him no joy unless he had a fundamentally transformed relationship with God.

Three times in the final two chapters of Scripture we're told that those still in their sins have no access to Heaven and never will (Revelation 21:8, 27; 22:15). The condition of the unbelieving heart remains unchangeable at death. God's grace, even if offered, would remain forever repugnant to such a rebellious heart.

To the person sealed forever in righteousness, God will remain forever wondrous; to the one sealed forever in sin, God will forever remain dreadful.

We live our present life between Heaven and Hell and so get foretastes of each, which prepare us for one or the other.

Just as God and Satan are not equal opposites, neither is Hell the equal opposite of Heaven. God has no equal as a person, and Heaven has no equal as a place.

Hell will be agonizingly dull, small, and insignificant, without company, purpose, or accomplishment. It will not have its own stories; it will be a mere footnote on history.

I don't believe Hell is a place where demons take delight in punishing people, since Hell was made to punish demons, not reward them, and there will be no delight in Hell. People will not take solace by commiserating, since there will be no solace. More likely, each person remains in solitary confinement (the rich man of Luke 16 appears to have no company in Hell).

Both Heaven and Hell touch Earth—an in-between world leading directly into one or the other. What tragedy that this present life is the closest nonbelievers will ever come to Heaven. What consolation that this present life is the closest believers will ever come to Hell.

Our present suffering warns against the suffering of Hell; for unbelievers, the fear of Hell serves as a merciful call to repentance.

Suffering can help the Heaven-bound fall out of love with this life and live in light of the coming one. The sufferings of the present give us a bittersweet reminder of the horrors from which God has delivered us.

For the Hell-bound, suffering can serve as a frightening foretaste of Hell. Suffering reminds us of our imminent death, the wages for our sin. In our suffering we should look at our own evils and failures and beg God for mercy.

Spurgeon said, "If sinners will be damned, at least let them leap to hell over our bodies; and if they will perish, let them perish with our arms about their knees, imploring them to stay.... If hell must be filled, at least let it be filled in the teeth of our exertions, and let not one go there unwarned or unprayed for."[18]

Imagine how much of Spurgeon's passion and urgency would have disappeared if he'd believed no one would suffer eternal, conscious punishment.

Many speak of the fear of Hell as something wrong, primitive, and cruel. But Jesus said we should fear both God and Hell: "Do not be afraid of those who kill the body but cannot kill the soul. Rather, be afraid of the One who can destroy both soul and body in hell" (Matthew 10:28).

Bart Ehrman makes an honest and chilling admission:

> When I fell away from my faith—not just in the Bible as God's inspired word, but in Christ as the only way of salvation, and eventually from the view that Christ was himself divine, and beyond that from the view that there is an all-powerful God in charge of this world—I still wondered, deep down inside: could I have been right after all? What if I was right then but wrong now? Will I burn in hell forever? The fear of death gripped me for years, and there are still moments when I wake up at night in a cold sweat.[19]

I think this is God's Spirit confirming a truth that Ehrman doesn't want to acknowledge. Every time he "suffers" these thoughts, it's another opportunity to bow to the God of holiness and grace, who in Christ offers him pardon from Hell and citizenship in Heaven.

If we reject the best gift that a holy and gracious God can offer us, purchased with his own blood, what remains, in the end, will be nothing but Hell.

Notes

1. Os Guinness, *Unspeakable* (San Francisco: HarperCollins, 2005), 24.
2. C. S. Lewis, *Letters to Malcolm* (Boston: Houghton Mifflin Harcourt, 2002), 76.
3. Dorothy Sayers, *Introductory Papers on Dante* (London: Methuen, 1954), 44.
4. Bertrand Russell, *Why I Am Not a Christian* (New York: Simon & Schuster, 1957), 17.
5. C. S. Lewis, *The Problem of Pain* (New York: Macmillan, 1962), 118.
6. William Shedd, *The Doctrine of Endless Punishment* (New York: Scribner, 1886), 153.
7. Clark Pinnock and Delwin Brown, *Theological Crossfire* (Grand Rapids, MI: Zondervan, 1990), 226–27.
8. Pinnock and Brown, *Theological Crossfire*, 226.
9. David L. Edwards and John R. W. Stott, *Essentials* (Downers Grove, IL: InterVarsity, 1988), 314.
10. Clark Pinnock, "The Destruction of the Family Impenitent," *Criswell Theological Review*, 4 (1990), 246–47.
11. Simone Weil, in Os Guinness, *Unspeakable*, 62.

12. John Piper, message entitled "The Echo and Insufficiency of Hell," Resolved Conference, June 16, 2008.

13. Dante Alighieri, *Inferno*, canto 3, line 9.

14. K. Connie Kang, "Next Stop, the Pearly Gates...or Hell?" *Los Angeles Times*, October 24, 2003.

15. Randy C. Alcorn, *Money, Possessions, and Eternity* (Carol Stream, IL: Tyndale, 2003), 120.

16. D. A. Carson, *How Long, O Lord?* (Grand Rapids, IL: Baker Academic, 2006), 92.

17. C. S. Lewis, *The Problem of Pain* (New York: Macmillan, 1962), 128.

18. Charles Haddon Spurgeon, "The Wailing of Risca" (sermon 349, New Park Street Pulpit, December 9, 1860), www.spurgeon.org/sermons/0349.htm.

19. Bart D. Ehrman, *God's Problem* (New York: HarperCollins, 2008), 127.

God's Allowance and Restraint of Evil and Suffering

30

Why Doesn't God Do More to Restrain Evil and Suffering?

God may already be restraining 99.99 percent of evil and suffering.

W hy does the chaos that breaks out in some corner of the world always prove the exception rather than the rule? Why haven't tyrants, with access to powerful weapons, destroyed this planet? What has kept infectious diseases and natural disasters from killing 99 percent of the world's population rather than less than 1 percent?

In the collapse of New York's Twin Towers, fifteen thousand people came out alive. While this doesn't remove the pain felt by families of the nearly three thousand who died, it shows that even on that terrible day, suffering was limited.

Nanci said to me, "Given the evil of the human heart, you'd think that there would be thousands of Jack the Rippers in every city." Her statement stopped me in my tracks. Might God be limiting sin all around us, all the time? Second Thessalonians 2:7 declares that God is in fact restraining lawlessness in this world. For this we should thank him daily.

If God permitted people to follow their every evil inclination all the time, life on this planet would screech to a halt. Sometimes God permits evil by giving people over to their sins (see Romans 1:24–32), and this itself leads to the deterioration and ultimate death of an evil culture, which is a mercy to surrounding cultures. The most morally corrupt ancient cultures no longer exist.

"But many children suffer; why doesn't God protect them?" We don't know the answer, but we also don't know how often God does protect children. The concept of guardian angels seems to be suggested by various passages (see, for example, Matthew 18:10).

God gives us a brief, dramatic look into the unseen world in which righteous angels battle evil ones, intervening on behalf of God's people (see Daniel

10:12–13, 20). How many angels has God sent to preserve the lives of children and shield them from harm?

My earliest memory is of falling into deep water and nearly drowning; someone my family didn't know rescued me. As a parent and a grandparent I have seen many "close calls" where it appears a child should have died or suffered a terrible injury, but somehow escaped both.

This thought, of course, doesn't keep a parent's heart from breaking when her child suffers or dies. Still, though I can't prove it, I'm convinced God prevents far more evil than he allows.

God may also be preventing 99.99 percent of tragedies.

Great though they may be, God actively restrains the tests and temptations that come our way so that we will not experience anything greater than we can bear (see 1 Corinthians 10:13).

Fatal car and airplane accidents bring awful devastation, but statistically these are rare. On January 15, 2009, what should have brought certain death to passengers aboard Flight 1549, and catastrophe to Manhattan, turned into what secular reporters labeled a "miracle." The pilot, Chesley Sullenberger, safely landed a crippled plane in New York's Hudson River, with no serious injuries.

While chunks of ice and busy ferries filled most of the river, the place where the plane came down remained clear of both ice and boats. It landed without breaking apart. Ferryboat captains rescued all 155 people from the frigid river within minutes. The *New York Times* suggested "more than luck" brought the plane down mere minutes from experts trained in water rescues. Passengers who said they hadn't believed in God nevertheless prayed to him on the plane, then publicly thanked him for sparing their lives.[1]

I tell this story to raise a question—isn't it likely that a kind and all-powerful God routinely prevents terrible tragedies in ways that we do not see and therefore do not credit as miracles?

While the miracle of Flight 1549 appears to be the exception, not the rule, we cannot know about most of the equally miraculous interventions of God that may have invisibly prevented other catastrophes. Perhaps one day we'll hear those stories and marvel at how often God intervened when we imagined him uninvolved in our world.

God exercises wisdom and purpose by not always intervening in miraculous ways.

As a young Christian, a teenager, I often asked God to show me signs. In the darkness of my room at night I would light a match and ask him to blow it out. What a simple miracle I requested! Nothing on the level of raising the dead, not even turning water to wine. But he never granted my request. And though I didn't understand why at the time, now I have a better idea. What would I have asked him to do once he blew out the match? Levitate the pool table? And then what would I ask him to do to top that? Where would it end?

How many magician's tricks would we call upon Jesus to do? As we share Christ with a neighbor who says, "I don't believe in God," we might say, "Oh yeah? Watch this." Then we'd call on God to torch the man's maple tree. Seeing the tree vaporize would get his attention! And surely it would generate faith-oriented conversion, right?

No. That's not how faith works, and it's not how God works.

God did bring down fire from Heaven on occasions (see Numbers 16:35; 1 Kings 18:38). He even opened the earth to swallow up his enemies (see Numbers 16:31–33). Did this result in people turning to him for the long run? No. Jesus fed the multitudes and many followed for a while, but they turned away recoiling from his demanding words (see John 6:1–66). Abraham told the rich man that his brothers "will not be convinced even if someone rises from the dead" (see Luke 16:27–31).

We say, "Show me a miracle and I'll believe," yet countless people who have seen miracles continue to disbelieve.

In our eagerness to see greater miracles, we regard "natural processes" as minor and secondary, missing God's marvelous daily interventions on our behalf.

Focusing on God's "big miracles"—like curing cancer and making brain tumors disappear—causes us to overlook his small, daily miracles of providence in which he holds the universe together, provides us with air to breathe and lungs to breathe it, and food to eat and stomachs to digest it.

Years ago when I became an insulin-dependent diabetic, it dawned on me that I had never once, in the fifteen years I'd known him, thanked God for a pancreas that had worked perfectly until then.

No matter how much God reduced world suffering, we'd still think he did too little.

Evil and suffering make up part of a world in which God allows fallen people to go on living. How much evil and suffering is too much? Could God reduce the amount without restricting meaningful human choice, or decreasing the urgency of the message that the world's gone desperately wrong and we need to turn to the Redeemer before we die?

Suppose we rated all pain on a scale of one to ten, with ten representing the worst and most intense pain, and one describing the unpleasant yet quite tolerable. Say "engulfed in flames" got a ten rating while "mild sunburn" received a one. If God eliminated level ten pain, then level nine pain would become the worst. God could reduce the worst suffering to level three, but then level three, now the worst, would seem unbearable. Any argument that judges God's goodness strictly by his elimination of pain will, in the end, not leave us satisfied if he permits any pain at all.

Severe suffering seems unacceptable to us precisely because we are unaccustomed to it.

Susanna Wesley had nineteen children; ten of them died before they reached the age of two. Puritan Cotton Mather had fifteen children and outlived all but two. Ironically, the problem of evil and suffering seems worse to us who live in affluent cultures precisely because we face less of it than many people have throughout history.

I heard an exasperated woman at a restaurant table loudly proclaim that her Porsche had to be taken in for repairs and now she had to drive her Audi. In contrast I have met devout Christians in Africa and Southeast Asia who have endured famine, genocide, and persecution, yet smile genuinely as they affirm God's goodness and grace.

C. S. Lewis wrote,

> Imagine a set of people all living in the same building. Half of them think
> it is a hotel, the other half think it is a prison. Those who think it is a
> hotel might regard it as quite intolerable, and those who thought it was a
> prison might decide that it was really surprisingly comfortable. So that
> what seems the ugly doctrine is one that comforts and strengthens you in
> the end. The people who try to hold an optimistic view of this world
> would become pessimists: the people who hold a pretty stern view of it
> become optimistic.[2]

People who ask why God allowed their house to burn down likely never thanked God for not letting their house burn down the previous ten thousand days of their lives. Why does God get blame when it burns, but no credit when it doesn't? Many pastors and church members have experienced church splits, feeling the agony of betrayal and disillusionment. But where were the prayers of gratitude back when the church was unified? Our suffering seems extreme in the present only because God has graciously minimized many of our past sufferings.

Dorothy Sayers wrote,

"Why doesn't God smite this dictator dead?" is a question a little remote from us. Why, madam, did he not strike you dumb and imbecile before you uttered that baseless and unkind slander the day before yesterday? Or me, before I behaved with such a cruel lack of consideration to that well-meaning friend? And why sir, did he not cause your hand to rot off at the wrist before you signed your name to that dirty bit of financial trickery? You did not quite mean that? But why not? Your misdeeds and mine are none the less repellent because our opportunities for doing damage are less spectacular than those of some other people. Do you suggest that your doings and mine are too trivial for God to bother about? That cuts both ways; for in that case, it would make precious little difference to his creation if he wiped us both out tomorrow.[3]

Our birthright does not include pain-free living. Only those who understand that this world languishes under a curse will marvel at its beauties despite that curse. C. S. Lewis's final article, published after his death, carried the title "We Have No Right to Happiness." Believing that we do have such a right sets us up for bitterness.

Fallen beings could not survive in a perfectly just world where God punished evil immediately.

What if every time I gave a hundred dollars to feed the hungry, two hundred dollars appeared in my wallet? Or when I spoke a kind word to a weary supermarket checker, I received a Starbucks gift card?

Suppose that every time a man yelled at a child or looked at a woman lustfully, a painful shock jolted his frontal lobe? Or when he lied, he got an instant toothache or was struck dead by lightning?

If we think we want all evil judged now, we're not thinking clearly.

Were such rewards and punishments built into our lives, the world would certainly be more just—but at what cost? We would base our obedience on instant payoffs or the avoidance of instant pain, not on loving God. Our behavior might improve, but our hearts wouldn't. Faith would fade, because faith means trusting God to eventually make right what is now wrong.

Do you believe the world would be a better place if people immediately paid the just penalty for every sin? In God's sight, every evil is a capital crime (see Romans 6:23). The woman who tells a "little white lie," the teenager who shoplifts, the greedy man, the gossiper, all would instantly die. D. A. Carson writes, "Do you really want nothing but totally effective, instantaneous justice? Then go to hell."[4]

God restrains suffering through our limited life spans—people don't endure eons, millennia, or centuries of suffering, but only decades, years, months, weeks, days, and hours.
Take the total number of years you believe human life has existed. Now, ask yourself what portion of that time any one human being has suffered.

Suppose God permitted evil and suffering, yet limited them to one ghastly year of human history. Would we consider that duration of evil and suffering acceptable? What about one month? If someone could prove that we would become greater and happier beings for all eternity as a result, would you think it right for God to allow ten seconds of intense suffering? Likely you would.

Once we make that admission, do you see where it puts us? If we could justify ten seconds, then why not ten hours, ten days, or ten years? And in eternity, as we look back, how much longer will ninety years seem than ninety minutes?

Who holds the record for suffering among all human beings alive today? As I write, the oldest person in the world is 114 years old. She hasn't suffered her whole life. But suppose she suffered significantly for a century. Most people, obviously, will endure much less. Some suffer severely for five days, weeks, months, or years; some, perhaps, for fifty years. However, *no one* in this world suffers for 10,000, 1,000, or even 130 years.

To say God takes too long to bring final judgment on evil and suffering imposes an artificial timetable on someone time cannot contain. God's Son entered time in his incarnation. Though he understands our impatience, he won't yield to it—and one day we'll be grateful that he didn't.

God allows substantial evil and suffering because he values our sense of neediness and trust as we turn to him for his grace.
Each year before Christmas we look forward to our church choir singing "Send the Messiah." The haunting lyrics and powerful presentation resonate within us:

The cry of generations echoes in the heart of heaven....

I need a Savior who will walk the earth down here with me....
Send the Messiah, I need his love to own me.[5]

God sent the Messiah once, but he will send him again to deliver us. Paul, likely within months of his death, said God will grant a special eternal reward "to all who have longed for his appearing" (2 Timothy 4:8). *What makes us long for our Lord? Isn't much of it because of the evil and suffering we face in this life?*

Thankfully, while the Messiah may not return to Earth as soon as we'd like, he promises, "Surely I am with you always, to the very end of the age" (Matthew 28:20). So while we long for and pray for God to send the Messiah to bring an end to this age of evil and suffering, we need not wait until then to enter his presence.

In light of the work done by Christ, our sympathetic high priest, we're told, "Let us then approach the throne of grace with confidence, so that we may receive mercy and find grace to help us in our time of need" (Hebrews 4:16).

Until God sends the Messiah to rescue this world, or he rescues us through our deaths, may we approach his throne confidently, seeking his fellowship, comfort, mercy, and grace in our time of need...today, this very hour.

Notes

1. Michael Wilson, "Flight 1549 Pilot Tells of Terror and Intense Focus," *New York Times,* February 9, 2009.
2. C. S. Lewis, *God in the Dock* (Grand Rapids, MI: Eerdmans, 1994), 52.
3. Dorothy L. Sayers, "The Triumph of Easter," in *Creed or Chaos* (London: Methuen, 1954).
4. D. A. Carson, *How Long, O Lord?* (Grand Rapids, MI: Baker Academic, 2006), 161.
5. Daniel Perrin, "Send the Messiah," https://www.cedarpark.org/resources/media/html.php?id=60.

31

Why Does God Delay Justice?

For many, the most difficult problem with evil is its persistence, prompting the question, "How long, O Lord?"

Scripture assures us justice is coming. "God will bring every deed into judgment, including every hidden thing, whether it is good or evil" (Ecclesiastes 12:14).

God "has set a day when he will judge the world with justice" (Acts 17:31).

But why a *future* day of judgment? Why doesn't God simply reward each good and punish each evil as it happens?

Barbara Brown Taylor phrased it, "What kind of God allows the innocent to suffer while the wicked pop their champagne corks and sing loud songs?"[1]

We may say, "Yes, Lord, we accept your wisdom in permitting evil and suffering for a season—but enough is enough. *Why do you let it continue?*"

The Bible echoes the same sentiment. Jeremiah said, "You are always righteous, O LORD, when I bring a case before you. Yet I would speak with you about your justice: Why does the way of the wicked prosper? Why do all the faithless live at ease?" (Jeremiah 12:1–2).

If you think it's wrong for God's people to ask him about why he withholds judgment, then consider what John witnessed when taken to Heaven:

> I saw under the altar the souls of those who had been slain because of the word of God and the testimony they had maintained. They called out in a loud voice, "How long, Sovereign Lord, holy and true, until you judge the inhabitants of the earth and avenge our blood?" Then each of them was given a white robe, and they were told to wait a little longer, until the number of their fellow servants and brothers who were to be killed as they had been was completed. (Revelation 6:9–11)

Even "righteous men made perfect" (Hebrews 12:23) don't fully understand why God postpones his judgment. God tells them to "wait a little longer" until the final martyr's murder.

Jesus said, "And will not God bring about justice for his chosen ones, who cry out to him day and night? Will he keep putting them off? I tell you, he will see that they get justice, and quickly" (Luke 18:7–8). Once God acts, he will act quickly. But Jesus spoke these words two thousand years ago. God's idea of quick justice certainly differs from ours.

The delay of reward and retribution never exceeds a life span.

God's is not a vending-machine justice in which a coin of righteousness immediately produces reward or a coin of evil yields swift retribution. Packaged theologies seek to neatly account for everything, but as Job, Psalms, and the prophets repeatedly demonstrate, that's not how life works.

Yet God doesn't delay justice for as long as we often imagine. The wheels of justice may seem to turn slowly, but they turn surely. Some rewards of goodness and punishments of evil come in this life. And though ultimate rewards and punishments await the final judgment, considerable justice, both reward and retribution, gets dispensed upon death, when God's children immediately experience the joy of his presence and the unrepentant suffer the first justice of Hell (see Luke 16:19–31). This means that the maximum duration of injustice experienced by any person cannot exceed his life span.

How long is a life span? Remarkably short. David says, "You have made my days a mere handbreadth; the span of my years is as nothing before you. Each man's life is but a breath" (Psalm 39:5).

What we consider too long is not too long by God's standards.

Second Peter 3:9 explains why God postpones his judgment upon sin, allowing evil and suffering to continue before he brings to an end this cursed world: "The Lord is not slow in keeping his promise, as some understand slowness. He is patient with you, not wanting anyone to perish, but everyone to come to repentance." Shall we willingly endure the suffering of further delay so that others may obtain the mercy God extended to us?

Immediately before telling us that God patiently gives us time to repent, Peter says, "But do not forget this one thing, dear friends: With the Lord a day is like a thousand years, and a thousand years are like a day" (verse 8). Presently, the average global life expectancy is 66.26 years. If a thousand years were a day, that average life span would be one hour and thirty-five minutes. The average U.S. life expectancy of 78.06 years would convert to one hour and fifty-two minutes—the length of a short motion picture and less than a ball game. For some it's a daily commute. Think how brief our lives—even all of human history—will seem when we look back at them a million years from now.

One day we'll see the answer to the age-old question "How long?" *Only long enough to accomplish the greatest eternal good.*

God delays justice not to make our lives miserable, but to make our lives possible.

Since sin demands death (see Romans 3:23), if people are to live, justice must wait.

Throughout history God has delayed justice, both upon believers and unbelievers, to give them time to come to him, grow in Christlikeness, and trust him more deeply.

Don't we give thanks for God's patience with Saul, the self-righteous killer who became Paul? Or John Newton, the evil slave trader who accepted God's amazing grace and preached and wrote the song that countless millions have sung? Are we grateful for God's patience with us? Think of those who endured many years of suffering before the day you came to faith in Christ. Aren't you thankful God did not deliver this planet from the Curse when millions asked for relief, before you heard the gospel? I came to Christ in 1969. What if Christ had returned and brought final judgment in 1968? Or in 1950, before I was born? If God had brought justice long ago, where would you and I be today? We would either not exist, or we would have been ushered into an eternity without Christ.

After the September 11, 2001 terrorist attacks, American politicians made sweeping promises: "We're going to rid the world of this evil!" *This* evil meant the evil that had hurt us. (And evil it surely was.) But no one can ask that the world be rid of evil without asking that the world be rid of himself.

Like Zebedee's sons, we would love to call down fire from Heaven to judge others' evil (see Luke 9:52–56). But we're slow to see our own evil. We want selective justice, not true justice. We cry out for justice when we really want vindication and special treatment—relief from injustices done *against* us, without being judged for injustices done *by* us. Since God is just, *he cannot always give us the justice we want without also giving us the justice we deserve.*

Human parents, with good reason, frequently delay justice for their children.

If your son disobeys when seated in the back of the car, you may postpone discipline thirty minutes until you get off the freeway and arrive home. If he's older, you may deprive him of a future privilege, such as attending a concert or staying overnight at a friend's. Likewise, if your child does an exceptional job on her homework or accomplishes something noteworthy in academics or athletics, you might let her choose something special to do during summer vacation.

In a sense, the anticipation of future joy and privilege—or future loss—brings the future event to the present, making us joyful (or disappointed) now.

God delays justice for greater durations and on a larger scale, but it's the same principle. So if we can rightfully delay rewards and punishments, why shouldn't God?

God's offer of grace requires that he postpone judgment against evil, to grant more time for people to respond to the gospel.

In the midst of Babylon's conquest of Israel, Jeremiah said, "Because of the LORD's great love we are not consumed, for his compassions never fail. They are new every morning; great is your faithfulness" (Lamentations 3:22–23). Each day, God's loving and compassionate delay of our judgment keeps us from destruction. Every morning he renews his grace, faithfully keeping us from the fate we all deserve, long enough for us to have the opportunity to repent and surrender our lives in dependence upon him.

In a world with immediate justice, Christ could not have accomplished his redemptive work. He couldn't have gone to the cross, because God would have stopped or enacted the death sentence on every evil act leading up to it. Who would have remained to crucify him? A world with quick justice could never put to death a perfect being.

It's said of Christ, "By your blood you ransomed people for God from every tribe and language and people and nation" (Revelation 5:9, ESV).

For more people of every tribe to come to Christ, God waits for the gospel to be proclaimed everywhere: "And the gospel must first be preached to all nations" (Mark 13:10).

Peter tells us, "You ought to live holy and godly lives as you look forward to the day of God and speed its coming" (2 Peter 3:11–12). Evangelizing and supporting world missions help speed the day of Christ's return, with final reward and retribution. Peter also encouraged people to repent so that Christ might sooner return, for "he must remain in heaven until the time comes for God to restore everything" (Acts 3:21).

The Bible's triumphant affirmations of joy in the face of difficulty usually come after a period of waiting and struggle.

God used Joseph, Moses, and David after all three suffered through many years of severe trial and hardship. We hear David wrestling and also claiming joy: "I waited patiently for the LORD; he turned to me and heard my cry. He lifted me out of the slimy pit, out of the mud and mire; he set my feet on a rock and gave me a firm place to stand. He put a new song in my mouth, a hymn of praise to our God" (Psalm 40:1–3).

God's people have endured dark nights of the soul. Though they felt abandoned by God, he will reward their patience and faith: "The LORD is good to those who wait for him, to the soul who seeks him" (Lamentations 3:25, ESV).

John Piper writes, "A Christian, no matter how dark the season of sadness, never is completely without joy in God. I mean that there remains in his heart the seed of joy in the form, perhaps of only a remembered taste of goodness and an unwillingness to let the goodness go."[2]

We should wait patiently and live godly lives, knowing a relatively short time remains until God will make everything right.

Many passages promise reward in Heaven. During the delay between now and then, we store up rewards. Paul says, "Command them to do good, to be rich in good deeds, and to be generous and willing to share. In this way they will *lay up treasure for themselves* as a firm foundation for the coming age" (1 Timothy 6:18–19).

God promises his eventual intervention as a reward for his people's patience: "From of old no one has heard or perceived by the ear, no eye has seen a God besides you, who acts for those who wait for him" (Isaiah 64:4, ESV).

James calls upon us to exercise the faith and patience of the farmer:

> Be patient, then, brothers, until the Lord's coming. See how the farmer
> waits for the land to yield its valuable crop and how patient he is for the
> autumn and spring rains. You too, be patient and stand firm, because the
> Lord's coming is near. Don't grumble against each other, brothers, or you
> will be judged. The Judge is standing at the door! (5:7–9)

Why does the call to patience about the Lord's coming justice immediately precede a warning not to sin? Because the same judgment that will bring us reward will also hold us accountable. Knowing that the Judge stands at the door should motivate us to repent now and live righteously until he comes through that door.

The duration of suffering in this world is temporary; the correction of evil and the relief of suffering will be permanent.

In 2 Corinthians 4:17–18 Paul speaks of relative weights. He calls our present evils and sufferings "light and momentary." To us they may feel heavy. But *light* is a relative term; if we see sin, Hell, and the glories of Christ's presence for what they are, then the greatest present suffering will seem light by comparison.

When we face a lengthy period of great adversity, though it hardly seems momentary, in fact it *is*. In eternity, people in God's presence will fully agree with Paul that their earthly sufferings were unworthy to be compared with eternal glory.

Everything in God's plan has a proper time; the gap between the present and that proper time tests and cultivates our faith.

Just after promising we will reap whatever we sow, Paul says, "Let us not become weary in doing good, for *at the proper time* we will reap a harvest if we do not give up" (Galatians 6:9). God knows the proper time. It's our job to trust him. When the time does come, the harvest will correspond to the work invested: "Whoever sows sparingly will also reap sparingly, and whoever sows bountifully will also reap bountifully" (2 Corinthians 9:6, ESV).

God says he will repay the wicked "in due time" (Deuteronomy 32:35), just as he will lift up the humble "in due time" (1 Peter 5:6). After centuries of his people's prayers for deliverance, God sent his Son into the world in "the fullness of time" (Galatians 4:4, ESV). Even demons recognize that their freedom to inflict suffering on people will expire and they will be severely judged at "the appointed time" (Matthew 8:29).

On various occasions people wanted to kill Jesus, but they didn't because "his time had not yet come" (John 7:30; 8:20). Likewise, God knows the proper time for Christ's triumphant return. God intends to "bring all things in heaven and on earth together under…Christ." That plan will "be put into effect *when the times will have reached their fulfillment*" (Ephesians 1:10).

Though we often wish he would move sooner, *God is always right on time.* While I've been writing this book, several dear friends have suffered one of life's greatest heartaches—children who've turned from God and are making terrible choices. The hardest test for our friends has been the length of their children's rebellion. Yet sometimes after all hope seems lost, the breakthrough comes. Parents and grandparents who have prayed for the breakthrough sometimes don't live to see it. God may use even their deaths to accomplish it. The length of time in which prayers seem to go unanswered tests and cultivates our trust in God.

The *ultimate* harvest comes only in the next life. The believer reaps eternal reward or loses that reward when he stands before Christ in judgment (see 1 Corinthians 3:11–15; 2 Corinthians 5:10; 2 John 8).

A composer's work gets praised for its long movements of depth, texture, and contrast, with transitions between major and minor keys.

Do we criticize a great composer whose symphony doesn't end in ten minutes or half an hour? Do we complain when he moves from a major key to a minor key and back to a major?[3] No, we celebrate his artistry. When we hear the dark and melancholic sections, we don't conclude he's made a mistake. Once we reach the ending, we recognize the symphony as a far greater work than one that consists of only bright melodies.

A concert may last three hours. God's concert has lasted thousands of years. What if the melody and harmony, major and minor keys all prove in the end to have contributed to the whole?

" 'I know the plans I have for you,' declares the LORD, 'plans to prosper you and not to harm you, plans to give you hope and a future'" (Jeremiah 29:11). God gave this promise to the Israelites when they lived in a minor key, during a period of melancholic dissonance.

When we view life through the eyes of faith, we can say, "Things appear one way, but my God is sovereign, loving, merciful, and kind. Through his grace and empowerment, I will cling to him. I will come out on the other side of this evil and suffering a deeper and more Christlike person, marked forever by Jesus' grace. And someday I will see that every minute was worth it."

The Bible never promises immediate justice, but ultimate justice; whatever we sow we will eventually reap.

Jesus said, "A time is coming when all who are in their graves will hear his voice and come out—those who have done good will rise to live, and those who have done evil will rise to be condemned" (John 5:28–29).

Charles Manson is the only member of the notorious "Manson Family" who has never expressed sorrow for his sins. (Four have professed faith in Christ.) Isn't it a shame he's gotten away with his terrible crimes?

God says that though final judgment for evil doesn't come here and now, he keeps track of all evil. One day he will judge it decisively (see Romans 2:5–6). Therefore, *no one* "gets away with" anything. Eternal punishment will come. No one beats the system, not Charles Manson or anyone else. Justice delayed is not justice denied.

"A man reaps what he sows" (Galatians 6:7). "What goes around comes around" means the same thing. The kind man receives kindness in turn. The generous man reaps generosity. The liar loses trust. The gossiper gets gossiped about. The one who gets his co-worker fired eventually gets fired himself.

Of course, "what goes around" doesn't always come around immediately. But the expression doesn't say *when* it will come around, just as Galatians 6:7 doesn't stipulate *when* a man will reap what he sows. Farmers know they have to wait for the harvest. Christ-followers know we have to wait for God to punish and reward.

Two men owned farms side by side. One was a bitter atheist, the other a devout Christian. Constantly annoyed at the Christian for trusting God, the atheist said to him one winter, "Let's plant our crops as usual this spring, each the same number of acres. You pray to your God, and I'll curse him. Then come October, let's see who has the bigger crop."

When October came the atheist was delighted because his crop was larger. "See, you fool," he taunted, "what do you have to say for your God now?"

"My God," the other farmer replied, "doesn't settle all his accounts in October."

Notes

1. Barbara Brown Taylor, "On Not Being God," *Review and Expositor* 99, no. 4 (Fall 2002): 611.
2. John Piper, *When I Don't Desire God* (Wheaton, IL: Crossway Books, 2004), 220.
3. Peg Rankin uses a similar symphony analogy in her book *Making Sense of Evil.*

32

Why Doesn't God Explain
His Reasons?

When I need a point-of-view adjustment, I read the last five chapters of Job. God's powerful self-revelation to this man who endured such terrible suffering offers great perspective. At the end of the book, the focus shifts from Job's suffering to God's majesty.

I never read those chapters without feeling that God has been put in his proper place and I've been put in mine.

WHAT JOB TEACHES US ABOUT GOD

Insisting on knowing the unknowable dooms us to frustration and resentment toward God.

When God takes the microphone in Job's final chapters, we might expect him to defend why he allows evil and suffering. He doesn't. He simply demonstrates the absurdity of making ourselves his judge.

We lack God's omniscience, omnipotence, wisdom, holiness, justice, and goodness. If we insist we have the right, or even assume we have the capacity, to understand the hidden purposes of God, we forfeit the comfort and perspective we could have had in kneeling before his vastly superior wisdom.

He is infinite; we are finite. He is the Creator; we're the creatures. Shouldn't that say it all?

Job had a better basis for complaint than nearly any of us ever will. Yet after listening to Job's grievances, God finally speaks to him: "Brace yourself like a man; I will question you, and you shall answer me" (38:3).

God is saying, "You are unhappy with me, Job. You have questioned me. You assume you know far more than you do. Now it's my turn to ask you some questions."

God never faults Job for being finite, only for failing to recognize that he has no right to pass judgment on the wisdom and goodness of an infinite Creator.

"Where were you when I laid the earth's foundation? Tell me, if you understand. Who marked off its dimensions? Surely you know!" (38:4–5).

God has always been; Job just showed up. In Hebrew culture, wisdom came with old age. God is eternally old, Job ridiculously young.

"Tell me, if you understand," God says. Job doesn't and can't.

Who marked off the dimensions of space, at least twenty-eight billion light-years and unceasingly expanding at fifty miles per second? Who assembled Earth and measured it? Who tells the ocean waves where to stop? Does Job give orders to the morning or show the dawn its place? Has he seen the gates of death? No. Well then, "Have you comprehended the vast expanses of the earth? Tell me, if you know all this" (verse 18). God informs Job, "I am infinitely big; you are incredibly small." Or to borrow the title of a theatrical musical, "Your Arm's Too Short to Box with God."

While this doesn't answer the question of evil and suffering, it does suggest God's answer is beyond our understanding. One day we'll know far better than now, but even in eternity, God will still be infinite and we'll still be finite.

A man saw me reading a book about evil and suffering as we traveled on a plane. Thoughtfully and humbly, he told me of losing his beloved wife three years earlier and his thirty-year-old son a year after that. He told me how, despite his pain, he had come to trust God more than ever. Time spent in suffering and in God's presence had made its mark on that man. I could see it.

God never tells Job to shut his mouth; but after seeing God's greatness, Job realizes he *must*.

After piling question upon question, God says to Job, with divine sarcasm, "Surely you know, for you were already born! *You have lived so many years!*" (38:21).

God asks Job if he can bind the beautiful Pleiades or loose the cords of Orion. Can he bring forth the constellations in their seasons or lead out "the Bear with its cubs" (verse 32), Ursa Major, with its Big Dipper? The night sky looked wondrous to Job. But he couldn't imagine what we've known for only decades—that in the bowl of that same Big Dipper, the Hubble Space Telescope photographed, in a tiny point 1/25,000 the size of the bowl's area, two thousand galaxies. That amounts to probably forty million *detectable* galaxies in the bowl, each galaxy averaging perhaps a hundred million stars, as well as untold planets. Billions and billions of worlds exist out there—and God made every one of them.

God speaks with artist's pride about his earthly creations, including the horse, hawk, and eagle (38:39–39:30). Then he says to Job, "Will the one who contends with the Almighty correct him? Let him who accuses God answer him!" (40:2).

Job responds, "I am unworthy—how can I reply to you? I put my hand over my mouth.… I have no answer…I will say no more" (verses 4–5).

But God isn't done with Job yet. It's fine to open our mouths and cry out in our distress and ask God questions. The book of Psalms shows us that. What isn't fine is to keep our mouths open and our eyes and ears closed in the face of God's self-revelation. Though he appeared to Job in a storm, God reveals himself to us first and most reliably in his Word, then in creation, conscience, people, and our personal experiences with him.

Job's humble response to God's self-disclosure gives us a timeless model for approaching the problem of evil.

After God makes his closing statement, a chagrined Job responds, "I know that you can do all things; no plan of yours can be thwarted. You asked, 'Who is this that obscures my counsel without knowledge?' Surely I spoke of things I did not understand, things too wonderful for me to know.… My ears had heard of you but now my eyes have seen you. Therefore I despise myself and repent in dust and ashes" (42:2–6).

Job quotes God's questions back to him, showing he got the message. He humbles himself before God, having seen the Almighty as he really is. Realizing his own smallness, Job says, "I repent."

Charles Spurgeon stated, "He who demands a reason from God is not in a fit state to receive one."[1] It is when Job surrenders himself to God that he at last, at the end of himself, finds comfort.

Bruce Waltke gives a helpful summary of Job:

In the prologue we observe Job as an idealist in elementary school (chaps. 1–2); in the dialogue, Job is a sophomore in college on the way to becoming wise (chaps. 3–31); finally the I AM speeches address him as a student in graduate school, where he is humbled and accepts that there are sufficient reasons to trust I AM without demanding of him rational explanations (37:1–42:6).[2]

God values Job's faith to the extent that he leaves out what to us seem critical parts of the explanation: God's wager with Satan, and the fact that God had defended Job as blameless. But the Creator knows what Job needed to know and what he didn't. He knows the same about us.

D. A. Carson puts it this way in *How Long, O Lord?*: "This is, at the end of the day, the ultimate test of our knowledge of God. Is it robust enough that, when faced with excruciating adversity, it may prompt us to lash out with hard questions, but will never permit us to turn away from God?"[3]

God grew angry at Job's friends for dispensing their smug, orderly theological answers in the face of their friend's suffering.

Job's friends came to conclusions that appeared theologically astute. "Since God is just," they deduced, "for Job to suffer so badly means God must be punishing him for his sin."

While they began with a true premise, they ended with a false conclusion. The theology of Job's friends, which later became the theology of the Pharisees (and still exists today), leaves no room for the possibility that the innocent can suffer. They couldn't accept that some suffering isn't God punishing specific sins.

God, after disclosing himself to Job, tells Eliphaz, "I am angry with you and your two friends, because you have not spoken of me what is right, as my servant Job has" (42:7). God tells Job to offer a sacrifice for his friends and to pray for them.

Job's friends made their theology consistent with itself, but not with reality. They said many wonderfully true things about God. But they drew dead-wrong conclusions about both Job and God. We, too, need to make sure our theology is both logical *and* biblical. Too many people begin with a biblical truth only to stray from it because of where they think it logically leads. God is loving or gracious, they affirm, but then they draw from these truths conclusions wildly inconsistent with Scripture. Like Job's friends, even when we begin with true premises, we may arrive at false conclusions.

I hope you are finding help from reading *If God Is Good*, but I also hope it's clear that I'm not proposing shrink-wrapped answers. There are none.

God's response to Job satisfies Job and therefore should satisfy us.

I used to believe, as many still do, that God's revelation of his greatness in Job 38–41 didn't answer Job's questions. Job's response has changed my mind. Philosophers and theologians may not be satisfied with God's answer, but Job was. And isn't the test of an answer how well it satisfies the questioner?

Bullet-point answers couldn't have satisfied a parent whose children died. God explaining his wager with Satan would have raised as many questions as it answered. Instead, in Job 38–41, God tells us he's unfathomably great (and we're not). Rather than explaining *why,* he reveals *who:* himself. His greatness is the only answer. When God shows himself to Job, lesser answers become unnecessary.

While writing this chapter, I received an e-mail from a dear friend of ours. Despite the horrors she endured as a child, God revealed himself to her profoundly:

> My dad raped me from age three to nine. He also raped my older sisters. Horrible, disgusting and repugnant. I had nightmares as a child, and into adulthood. But I also had two things God gave me during those times. One was a vivid picture of me lying in the palm of God's hand, where I slept peacefully. Another was of someone placing a star blanket over me as I slept, covering me in safety. This was early elementary age.
>
> I always remember that time of my life because even while the molestation happened, I knew God allowed it, but walked with me through it. I grew in an intimacy with God that is supernatural. It isn't about my own spirituality. But I have always pictured myself sitting securely in God's lap. I haven't ever struggled with why He allowed it. Statistics indicate a high percentage of abused kids have trouble relating to God as their Father. Not me.
>
> When I was in seventh grade, I prayed and asked God to use the garbage of my childhood to bring glory to Him. That was a GOD prayer…beyond my own vision. I can't count how many people I have been able to encourage who have similar backgrounds as mine. He has answered that prayer many times over. I became able to call on God right in the middle of dreams that used to scare me, and He would put His mighty arm between me and the danger.
>
> He has used my dark times for His glory and my blessing. He is such a personal God, isn't He? And I don't understand why He chose to reveal Himself to me so personally, but He did and still does. It is as if He cracks the door to Heaven open for me here on Earth, letting me know that He loves me and watches over me.
>
> Pain and suffering is not garbage when God uses it to show Himself through it.

WHY HASN'T GOD MADE HIS PURPOSES FOR EVIL AND SUFFERING CLEARER?

Our inability to understand all God's purposes in evil and suffering should not surprise us.
Sometimes we make the foolish assumption that our heavenly Father has no right to insist that we trust him unless he makes his infinite wisdom completely understandable to us. This lays an impossible demand upon God, not because of his limitations, but because of ours. A physicist father bears no blame because he can't explain quantum mechanics to his three-year-old.

Isaiah 55:8–9 says, "'For my thoughts are not your thoughts, neither are your ways my ways,' declares the LORD. 'As the heavens are higher than the earth, so are my ways higher than your ways and my thoughts than your thoughts.'"

Luke 2:41–51 gives us an interesting twist on the parent-child analogy. Although the boy Jesus stayed behind in Jerusalem, Mary and Joseph thought he had joined their larger group of family and friends. After a day's journey from Jerusalem, they realized their error. Panicking, they rushed back to look for him. After three days they found him in the temple courts, sitting among the teachers, listening and asking questions. His mother said, "Son, why have you treated us like this? Your father and I have been anxiously searching for you."

"Why were you searching for me?" the Messiah-child responded. "Didn't you know I had to be in my Father's house?"

Relieved as they felt to find Jesus, it didn't negate their three days of suffering. Jesus could have prevented their anguish by telling them his plans. But he didn't.

Scripture tells us, "They did not understand what he was saying to them." Luke adds, "His mother treasured all these things in her heart." She didn't merely toss and turn in perplexity, she *treasured* these things, *she ascribed value to the mystery of her Son's ways.* She contemplated the mystery and embraced it. She believed God's purposes to be right and good, even though they'd caused suffering.

What we call the problem of evil is often the problem of our finite and fallen understanding.
We assume God should answer our questions. But sometimes our questions can't be answered.

If the problem of evil were the only thing we didn't understand, our complaint might get sympathy. But we are veterans of not understanding, aren't we?

C. S. Lewis wrote, "Can a mortal ask questions which God finds unanswerable? Quite easily, I should think. All nonsense questions are unanswerable. How many hours are there in a mile? Is yellow square or round? Probably half the questions we ask—half our great theological and metaphysical problems—are like that."[4]

Sometimes we couldn't understand the answer even if God explained it. Or God may have explained it in Scripture, but we fail to notice it or refuse to believe it.

Children don't understand why their parents won't let them stay up late, eat cookies in bed, or feed chocolate to the dog. They don't understand why we discipline them, make them clean their rooms, or take them to the dentist. One day, when they grow up, they'll understand.

And so will we.

God's explanations probably wouldn't be as helpful or comforting as we imagine.

God doesn't explain the particular reasons we suffer, yet millions of people attest to the comfort he has brought them.

A friend told me recently of the deep and lasting impression the Willis family's loss of six children made on him when he saw their powerful interviews in 1994 as the story unfolded. Suppose God had appeared to Scott and Janet before the accident and said, "I'm about to take six of your children to Heaven, but I want to assure you that it will touch many people deeply." Would God's explanation have made their experience easier? I doubt it. Were God to explain why he permits us to experience each suffering and evil, sometimes we might feel even more troubled.

When a child falls off a bike, she doesn't need her father to say, "Sweetheart, here's why it happened—given your speed and the weight of this bike, it couldn't tolerate that sharp turn and…" No. The child simply wants comfort. We don't need explanations; we need "God, who comforts the downcast" (2 Corinthians 7:6).

If God offered constant explanations, our lives would not be free or normal, and would not allow for faith or trust.

While playing softball, my friend John Franklin, then a healthy thirty-nine-year-old, developed a headache and neck pain, so he took himself out of the game. By the time the game finished, he needed help walking.

Taken to the hospital, John became completely paralyzed and unable to speak. Soon he was breathing with a ventilator. John spent seven weeks in ICU and another four months in the hospital. He underwent speech therapy, then a few years of occupational and physical therapy. Now, twenty-two years later, John remains restricted to a wheelchair. Doctors never discovered why it happened.

John's youngest son, six years old when his father became disabled, wrote me, "I remember always being so mad that God did this to him. One day I asked my dad why he wasn't angry. He said, 'Why should I accept good from God and not evil?' I think my jaw dropped and at the time I was angry at him for saying that. But that experience has forever shaped my view of God and evil."

This wonderful family has certainly seen God at work. But they still have no clear explanation of his purpose for John's disability.

Consider what our lives would be like if God regularly explained to us why he allows everything that disappoints us.

Suppose you're a teenage girl, sick on prom day. God could whisper, *I let you get pneumonia so you wouldn't bond with that young man who wouldn't be right for you, and so your parents would go get you your favorite dessert, where they'll see a help-wanted poster and tell you so you apply and get the job, and meet the girl who will become your best friend and help you twenty years from now when your husband gets cancer, and...*

"Whoa! My husband? What's he like? And why would you let him get cancer?"

In order to make you more Christlike and help you become more of a servant and...

"But I don't want to be a servant. And cancer terrifies me!"

...and teach your husband to depend on me, and draw your children and grand-children closer to you, and...

"I'll have children and grandchildren? How many? Girls or boys? But how will they deal with their father's cancer?"

Do you see where this is going? And it's just one "simple" event. How could God explain his purposes without revealing to us the life he intends for us to live later, not now? And without imparting the grace that he will give us just when we need it, not in advance?

The God of providence weaves millions of details into our lives and into all the lives around us. Maybe he doesn't have one big reason for bringing a certain person or success or failure or disease or accident into our lives; in fact, he may have hundreds of little reasons. In order to understand God's explanations, we would have to be God.[5]

God has revealed just enough of himself to give us reasons for faith, but not enough to make faith unnecessary.

In Eden, God could have explained more to Adam and Eve. Certainly he could have enlightened Abraham more. But if God made himself so readily apparent in everyday life that we couldn't doubt him, it would change the nature of faith. We'd lack a vital element of character-building. God's daily intervention and appearance would overpower us. We would *have* to believe in him and thus faith would become impossible.

Paul Tournier said, "Where there is no longer any opportunity for doubt, there is no longer any opportunity for faith."[6]

God must give us room, not crowd in on us and micromanage us. Distance is necessary for faith to develop. If we can't help but be aware of him, there wouldn't be any spiritual growth.

God doesn't force himself on us. He invites us to take the initiative with him: "Draw near to God, and he will draw near to you" (James 4:8, ESV).

Frederick Buechner wrote, "Without somehow destroying me in the process, how could God reveal himself in a way that would leave no room for doubt? If there were no room for doubt, there would be no room for me."[7]

A friend experienced terrible childhood abuse, date rape, adultery, two divorces, and a life that she described as "forty-three years of hell." Yet, now in her fifties, she has experienced a deep sense of God's goodness and has a faith that one day she'll understand what eludes her now. She wrote, "I think in eternity I will be able to see how God comforted me during those times when I didn't know it. That God was ever present, weeping with me, angry at those who were victimizing me, working to move me forward toward life instead of death as Satan wished. I will see how God used it. How God transformed each thing. I see much of that transformation even now."

The no-see-um illustrates the mystery of evil and suffering under God's providence.

The no-see-um is a tiny midge with a huge bite. Alvin Plantinga points out that failing to see a no-see-um in your tent provides no evidence that it isn't there. Likewise, failing to see God's reason for evil and suffering provides no evidence that one doesn't exist.[8]

Let's take this further. Failure to see a no-see-um isn't merely the result of the insect's size, but our poor vision. After all, creatures with sharper eyes—a hawk, for instance—could see it.

We might assume God should make the reasons for suffering and evil easier to see than a no-see-um. But perhaps the reasons would be obvious to a sinless clear-sighted person. Maybe it's not that the reasons are invisible, but that we have a serious vision problem.

Spurgeon said,

> Providence is wonderfully intricate. Ah! you want always to see through Providence, do you not? You never will, I assure you. You have not eyes good enough. You want to see what good that affliction was to you; you must believe it. You want to see how it can bring good to the soul; you may be enabled in a little time; but you cannot see it now; you must believe it. Honor God by trusting him.[9]

Notes

1. Charles Spurgeon, sermon 1778, April 30, 1884, "A Heavenly Pattern for Our Earthly Life," www.spurgeon.org/sermons/1778.htm.
2. Bruce Waltke and Charles Yu, *An Old Testament Theology* (Grand Rapids, MI: Zondervan, 2007), 929–30.
3. D. A. Carson, *How Long, O Lord?* (Grand Rapids, MI: Baker Academic, 2006), 156.
4. C. S. Lewis, *A Grief Observed* (Whitstable, Kent, UK: Whitstable Litho, 1966), 55.
5. See John G. Stackhouse Jr., *Can God Be Trusted?* (Oxford: Oxford University Press, 1998), 90.
6. Paul Tournier, quoted in Douglas McKay, *Where Is God When Life Hurts?* (Grand Rapids, MI: Zondervan, 1992), 230.
7. Dale Brown, *The Book of Buechner* (Louisville, KY: Westminster John Knox, 2007), 152.
8. Alvin Plantinga, in *Christian Faith and the Problem of Evil,* ed. Peter van Inwagen (Grand Rapids, MI: Eerdmans, 2004), 4.
9. Charles Haddon Spurgeon, *God's Providence: A Sermon* (Choteau, MT: Gospel Mission Press, 1980), 19.

33

Understanding That God Is God and We Are Not

APPEARANCES VERSUS REALITY

Despite all appearances, God can act redemptively in the most terrible situations.

I f God had not made a world or if he'd made us machines, he could have prevented all tragedies. But he had higher purposes than merely avoiding what's bad.

Aquinas quoted Augustine as saying, "Since God is the highest good, He would not allow any evil to exist in His works unless His omnipotence and goodness were such as to bring good even out of evil."[1]

What possible good can come from that deranged man murdering my uncle with a meat cleaver? Or the terrible accident that killed my nineteen-year-old friend Greg? Or my family members and friends who've wasted away from diseases?

I can't say that a commensurate good has yet come out of those situations. But I can say I have seen *some* good come through each of them, enough to give me faith that there may exist countless goods I cannot see. That's even apart from the fact that God has promised these people, those who are redeemed, an eternal glory that far outweighs all their suffering.

Even many unbelievers look back at difficult and painful experiences and see that good came out of them. Since we know that happens *sometimes,* couldn't it happen far more often than we realize?

Gregory Boyd writes, "It's very difficult to see how some of the more horrendous episodes of evil in this world contribute to a higher good."[2] His conclusion is, therefore, that they don't.

I agree "it's very difficult to see." It may well be *impossible* to see. But the question isn't whether we can see it but whether God can do things we cannot see.

Both Scripture and human experience testify to the surprising good God can bring out of evil and suffering. God calls upon us to trust him, that he will work all evil and suffering in our lives for good. We can learn to trust God in the worst of circumstances, even for what we cannot currently see—indeed, that is the very nature of biblical faith (see Hebrews 11:8, 13, 27, 32–39).

Seeing good come out of suffering opens the door to the possibility that other suffering has meaning.

Lee Ezell grew up in an abusive, alcoholic home where domestic-violence calls were commonplace. One night she attended a Billy Graham Crusade "for a few laughs." But as she listened, Lee's heart softened and she eagerly received Christ. Lee felt God had given her a whole new life.

Then one terrifying night she was raped. She became pregnant. Everything fell apart.

After moving, Lee began attending a church. One morning a couple offered her a place to live. She accepted and decided to place her child for adoption. She didn't get to see or hold her baby girl, whom she came to think of as the "missing piece" in her life.

Eventually Lee married. One day, decades later, she received an unexpected call. Her daughter, Julie, had tracked her down. Julie told her she had two reasons for wanting to find her birth mother: first, to let her know she was a grandmother; and second, to tell her about Christ.

When they met, Julie handed her own daughter to Lee, introducing grandchild and grandma. When Julie's husband, Bob, greeted Lee, he said, "I want to shake your hand: Thank you for not aborting Julie. I can't imagine what my life would be like without Julie and our children."

Today, they remain in close contact. Julie speaks at pro-life meetings; mother and daughter delight in telling their story together.[3]

True, not every tragedy turns out so happily on this earth. Yet hearing such stories helps us conceive how one day we'll hear many more happy endings that we cannot imagine now.

Even in death camps, God is present, and suffering has meaning.

Reflecting on his experience in a concentration camp, Viktor Frankl wrote,

If there is a meaning in life at all, then there must be a meaning in suffer-ing. Suffering is an ineradicable part of life. I was struggling to find the *reason* for my sufferings, my slow dying. In a last violent protest against the hopelessness of imminent death, I sensed my spirit piercing through the enveloping gloom. I felt it transcend that hopeless, meaningless world, and from somewhere I heard a victorious "Yes" in answer to my question of the existence of an ultimate purpose.[4]

Christian Reger spent four years in Dachau, the notorious Nazi concentra-tion camp. In his first month he abandoned belief in a loving God. Yet even though God did not deliver him from the horrors, Reger began to realize God hadn't left him.

"God did not rescue me or make my suffering easier," he says. "He simply proved to me that He was still alive, and He still knew I was here.... I can only speak for myself. Others turned from God because of Dachau. Who am I to judge them? I simply know that God met me. For me, He was enough, even at Dachau."[5]

Is God enough for you, even where you are?

GOD'S WISDOM VERSUS OUR ARROGANCE

We are not positioned to know how much suffering is required to accomplish the best eternal purposes, nor how much it might hinder those purposes for God to make himself obvious.

Is it possible that all past, present, and future suffering is somehow necessary for God to accomplish the greater good his people will enjoy for all eternity? If you think this cannot be the case, why? And if you're certain it can't be, have you ever been wrong?

To people who say, "If I were God, I'd open the sky over New York City and announce to the world I truly do exist," philosopher Thomas Morris responds,

Many times these are people who don't have a clue as to what exactly they would do about the most pressing problems of their own city if they were mayor, or concerning the greatest difficulty facing their state if they were governor. They would probably be quite hesitant if asked how, precisely, they would solve the greatest national crises if they were president, but they have no hesitation whatsoever in venturing to declare how they would solve what may be the single most troubling cosmic religious problem if they were God.[6]

Part of being fallen is thinking we know more than we really do. Of all there is to know in the entire universe, how much do you know? Let's say you're the smartest human being who's ever lived and that you know 1 percent (of course, nobody knows nearly that much). Now, is it possible that in the 99 percent of all there is that you don't know, there exists or will exist enough goodness and happiness in the universe to outweigh all the evil and suffering?

Is it possible that in the 99 percent you don't know, a good God exists who has legitimate reasons for not making his purposes clearer and for not forcing people to recognize his existence? Is it possible that some rational explanation exists—if you were smart enough to understand it—for why this good God permits evil and suffering?

Is it possible that God's redemptive goodness will in the end utterly overshadow evil?

Joe Gibbs, the NFL Hall of Fame coach and NASCAR team owner, tells lots of great stories. One is about flying into Washington, D.C., when he worked as head coach of the Redskins. His cab driver had immigrated recently, and Joe had to explain to him how to get to the stadium. The driver suddenly recognized his passenger and, with a thick accent, asked if he was the coach. Joe nodded, feeling flattered and prepared to hear some affirmation. The cabbie gestured excitedly and exclaimed to Joe, "You should throw deep!"

Here was a cab driver who didn't even know how to get to the football stadium and probably knew next to nothing about American football, yet believed himself qualified to tell a Hall of Fame coach and winner of three Super Bowls how to run his team!

Even the most uninformed fans act as if they know more than the head coach.

And even the most clueless creatures act as if we know more than God.

We reveal a staggering arrogance in assuming God *owes* us an explanation for anything.

God understands our curiosity but owes us nothing. To demand an explanation is to hold God accountable to us. What arrogance to say, "If I cannot understand why a loving God would permit all this evil and suffering, then there cannot be a loving God!"

God gives us not the answers we want, but the answers we need. He calls upon us to trust him even when life seems to make no sense.

God occasionally gives us glimpses of his unseen reasons. One of my friends endured a serious accident and a painful recovery. But medical tests conducted because of the accident revealed an unrelated and hidden condition that needed immediate attention. His painful accident probably saved his life.

In that case, a compelling reason for the accident became clear. In other cases, we don't know the reasons. But given the height and depth and breadth of what we don't know, why would we assume that our ignorance of the reasons means there are no reasons?

As Creator, God has rights that we don't.

We tend to see God as a bigger, smarter version of ourselves. We say, "A good man wouldn't allow all this evil if he could stop it." If we had the power, we say, we'd stop it; therefore, so should God.

But God is *not* like us: "God is not a man, that he should lie, nor a son of man, that he should change his mind" (Numbers 23:19). God says, "You thought I was altogether like you" (Psalm 50:21). Whatever seems good to us, we think, should be good to God. Whatever we think is fair, God should do. We wouldn't permit murders and poverty, so neither should God.

Yet we have neither the qualifications nor the authority to exercise such judgment. Not only does God's character infinitely surpass our own, his thoughts and perspectives radically transcend ours (see Isaiah 55:8–9).

We should ask ourselves, "What sort of God does this argument prove doesn't exist?" *It proves the nonexistence of a god who does what we imagine we would do if we had his knowledge and power.* And that much is correct—such a god does not exist. The Bible makes that clear.

God is doing what it takes to create the greatest amount of ultimate good, even when, for now, that requires evil and suffering.

We see suffering as the central problem and evil as bad because it causes suffering; God sees evil as the central problem and suffering as a by-product he can use to prompt us to deal with our evil. The result of our coming to terms with our evil and turning to God for deliverance is a greater good.

Shouldn't a good God do everything possible to ensure the greatest and most lasting good to those he loves? If he knows that a limited amount of evil, lasting a limited amount of time, can result in far more eternal good, then wouldn't he be morally justified in allowing it? Instead of condemning God for a plan that includes evil and suffering, shouldn't we commend him for it in light of the greater redemptive good it will forever accomplish?

Ignorant beings often feel unhappy and confused because of decisions made by wiser and more powerful beings.

Likely my dog Moses thinks I don't "get it" when I hush him late at night. I'm cruel when I refuse to let him eat the steak he smells. Of course, he has no idea that his barking wakes up the neighbors, or that a whole steak wouldn't be good for him (he had one once, so this is not a theory), or that there are beings more important than he (perish the thought). Given his worldview, he may feel certain I'm not demonstrating goodness and love. But Moses is simply not in a position to grasp my reasons. They transcend his understanding.

Now, if you think comparing dogs to people is insulting, I will insult you further. We are, in fact, substantially closer to the level of our dog's intelligence than we are to God's. Of course, God created us in his image—making us far superior to dogs—but we share much in common with canines that we do not share with God. We are finite creatures, not infinite like our Creator. We have limited rather than unlimited knowledge, partial rather than total wisdom, limited rather than unlimited power, and fractional rather than endless goodness.

As I just signed a book for a teenage boy, I wrote, "Trust Jesus—He'll never let you down." I hope he didn't understand me to mean, "Your life will always go as you want it to." I meant that even when life doesn't go your way, Jesus remains faithful and works in your best interests. Life will bring countless disappointments, but that's very different than God letting you down.

If we keep before ourselves the big picture, we'll say with Paul in Romans 8, "If God is for us, who can be against us?" And we will proclaim, nothing "will be able to separate us from the love of Christ" (verses 31, 39).

If we have sufficient knowledge, wisdom, power, and goodness to put into effect a plan superior to God's, then we should create and manage our own universe.

"Imagine there is no evil...it's easy if you try," John Lennon wrote and sang. He celebrated a world without God: a secular utopia of free sex and drugs. But someone devastated by a partner's adultery or a father's sexual abuse or the crime-causing drug addiction of a loved one would picture a very different world: drugless and sexually pure.

That easily imagined world, if people like John Lennon and us were its architects, would in fact be filled with evil. And unlike God, we would lack the power to defeat the evil, bring good out of it, and guarantee by our righteous sacrifice that a goodness of cosmic proportions would one day eradicate the last remnant of evil.

When it comes to world-making, we might compare God's résumé with ours. Complainers should consider designing a better universe, creating it, then going to live in it.

If that's not practical, then maybe we should consider the possibility that God knows better than we do.

We who have not formed galaxies and fashioned worlds should not be so quick to tell God how to run his universe.

Notes

1. Thomas Aquinas, *Basic Writings of Saint Thomas Aquinas,* ed. Anton C. Pegis (New York: Random House, 1945), 23.
2. Gregory A. Boyd, *Is God to Blame?* (Downers Grove, IL: InterVarsity, 2003), 55.
3. Dan Wooding, "Lee Ezell's Story of Tragedy to Triumph," www.leeezell.com/aboutlee.htm.
4. Viktor E. Frankl, *Man's Search for Meaning* (New York: Simon & Schuster, 1985), 88.
5. Christian Reger, quoted in Philip Yancey, *Where Is God When It Hurts?* (Grand Rapids, MI: Zondervan, 1990), 160.
6. Thomas V. Morris, *Making Sense of It All* (Grand Rapids, MI: Eerdmans, 1992), 86.

Evil and Suffering

Used for God's Glory

34

Pain and Suffering in God's World

In the original perfect world, God created pain for humanity's good.

I magine Eden. Did God create finite human beings invulnerable, unable to
be affected by their environment? Or might they trip, fall, bruise, and bleed?
If Adam and Eve got too close to a fire, would they have felt pain as a warning to
draw back their hands?

Based on the design of the human body, I believe pain existed in Eden and
that it protected Adam and Eve from doing what could have injured them. Before
evil entered the world, the body's nervous system, including its ability to detect
pain, made up part of a creation God called "very good."

Emotional pain, as we know it, presumably did not exist in that world where
wrongdoing, bad motives, suspicions, and a history of damaged relationships did
not exist.

Under the Curse, physical pain, such as in childbirth, intensified. But even
now, post-Curse, pain often serves a good purpose. Imagine no chest pain before
a heart attack or no side ache before a burst appendix.

What is not a natural and original part of the human state is *suffering*—
relentless pain inflicted by people upon people, and the breakdown of body and
mind that leads us toward death.

Even today, though, we should acknowledge the body's astounding self-
healing properties. When people endure terrible trauma, physicians sometimes
say, "We have to wait for the body to heal itself." Shouldn't God get credit for
making our bodies with this capacity for self-healing, and not fully removing
that when the Curse fell upon us?

As leprosy proves, bodies that can't feel pain are terribly deprived.
Someone once asked Father Damien at his leper colony on Molokai what gift he
would pray for his patients to receive. Without pause, he answered, "Pain."

Leprosy prevents the body from feeling pain, with disastrous results. That's why leprosy specialist Dr. Paul Brand, with coauthor Philip Yancey, describes pain as an "ingenious invention."[1]

Leprosy, also called Hansen's disease, desensitizes nerve endings. The lack of pain allows the sufferer to do himself serious damage without realizing it, such as walking on a broken leg or not withdrawing his hand from a fire. The warning system of pain guards our health. Without it, we would either have to be made invulnerable to our environment or would have to be made inhuman in order to survive. Ironically, painlessness is one manifestation of the Curse.

Similarly, in this fallen world, if we felt no emotional pain, we would live as relational lepers, never understanding the harm we inflict upon others and ourselves. Without feeling the consequences of our evil and others' evil, we could not see our fallen nature and our desperate need for Christ's redemptive work.

God uses pain to get our attention and dissipate the illusion that all is well.

Job's friend Elihu says, God "speaks to them in their affliction" (36:15). C. S. Lewis called pain God's "megaphone to rouse a deaf world." He wrote,

> Until the evil man finds evil unmistakably present in his existence, in the form of pain, he is enclosed in illusion. Once pain has roused him, he knows that he is in some way or other "up against" the real universe....
> It gives the only opportunity the bad man can have for amendment. It removes the veil; it plants the flag of truth within the fortress of a rebel soul.[2]

Worse things can happen to us than dying young of a terrible disease. We could live in health and wealth, but if we die without Christ and go to Hell—or if we know Christ but fail to draw close to him—this is immeasurably worse than the disease that gets our attention and prompts us to look to him. Lewis writes,

> Now God, who has made us, knows what we are and that our happiness lies in Him. Yet we will not seek it in Him as long as He leaves us any other resort where it can even plausibly be looked for. While what we call "our own life" remains agreeable we will not surrender it to Him. What then can God do in our interests but make "our own life" less agreeable to us, and take away the plausible sources of false happiness?...

He stoops to conquer, He will have us even though we have shown that we prefer everything else to Him, and come to Him because there is "nothing better" now to be had.[3]

There is no sum of human misery, only individual misery.

The problem isn't the existence of pain, nor of brief and obviously purposeful suffering. The real problem is the extent and intensity of suffering, especially when we can't see its purpose.

One reason the problem of evil and suffering seems more acute to us is the cumulative weight we feel from media oversaturation. We see large-scale suffering the day it happens, wherever in the world that might be. At most, people used to bear the sufferings of their families and communities, or of their regions or nations. Now, through instant access to global events, we witness the sufferings of an entire world. While a tiny percentage of the world's inhabitants face a given crisis, the images each day of one disaster after another make it feel far more universal. This oversaturation desensitizes some to suffering, while overwhelming others.

Lewis provides help here as well:

We must never make the problem of pain worse than it is by vague talk about the "unimaginable sum of human misery." Suppose that I have a toothache of intensity x: and suppose that you, who are seated beside me, also begin to have a toothache of intensity x. You may, if you choose, say that the total amount of pain in the room is now $2x$. But you must remember that no one is suffering $2x$.[4]

Despite the horror of disasters, we must understand that suffering does not have a cumulative nature. The terrible suffering of six million people may seem six million times worse than the suffering of one. But no one, except God, can experience the suffering of six million people. All of us remain limited to our own suffering. While our suffering may include an emotional burden for others who suffer, it cannot grow larger than we are. The limits of our finite beings dictate the limits of our suffering.

Lewis concludes, "There is no such thing as a sum of suffering, for no one suffers it. When we have reached the maximum that a single person can suffer, we have, no doubt, reached something very horrible, but we have reached all the suffering there ever can be in the universe. The addition of a million fellow-sufferers adds no more pain."[5] In other words, "Suffering cannot really be quantified."[6]

Consider that while our suffering can rise only to the level we individually can suffer, Jesus suffered for all of us. All the evils and suffering that we tell him he never should have permitted, he willingly inflicted upon himself, for us.

True followers of Christ sometimes can't reconcile God's loving nature with their suffering.

Charles Spurgeon, who faced great adversity, said to the God whose love and sovereignty he exalted, "I could not bear to see my child suffer as Thou makest me suffer; and if I saw him tormented as I am now, I would do what I could to help him, and put my arms under him to sustain him."[7] Spurgeon felt God's comfort soon after this, yet sometimes went long periods without doing so. He affirmed God's loving presence even when he didn't feel it.

After C. S. Lewis's wife, Joy, died of cancer, his beliefs underwent a severe test. In *A Grief Observed,* written originally without intention of publication and only later published under a pseudonym, Lewis spoke these painful words:

> When you are happy, so happy that you have no sense of needing Him, so happy that you are tempted to feel His claims upon you as an interruption, if you remember yourself and turn to Him with gratitude and praise, you will be—or so it feels—welcomed with open arms. But go to Him when your need is desperate, when all other help is vain, and what do you find? A door slammed in your face, and a sound of bolting and double bolting on the inside. After that, silence. You may as well turn away. The longer you wait, the more emphatic the silence will become. There are no lights in the windows. It might be an empty house. Was it ever inhabited? It seemed so once. . . . Not that I am (I think) in much danger of ceasing to believe in God. The real danger is of coming to believe such dreadful things about Him. The conclusion I dread is not "So there's no God after all," but "So this is what God's really like. Deceive yourself no longer."[8]

Over time, tests can strengthen our faith and enhance our perspective.

Only a few dozen pages after the despairing passage I just quoted, C. S. Lewis said this:

> I have gradually been coming to feel that the door is no longer shut and bolted. Was it my own frantic need that slammed it in my face? The time when there is nothing at all in your soul except a cry for help may be just the time when God can't give it: you are like the drowning man who can't

be helped because he clutches and grabs. Perhaps your own reiterated cries deafen you to the voice you hoped to hear.... By praising I can still, in some degree, enjoy her, and already, in some degree, enjoy Him.[9]

Here you see Lewis's progress. Writers often quote only Lewis's darkest questions, leaving the impression that he lost his faith in God. But his blunt honesty with God parallels that of the psalmists, the prophets, and Job. Such eclipses of faith are real but temporary, so long as we hold fast to God and his promises in Scripture.

Trusting Christ doesn't mean we suffer less.

Nancy Guthrie's disabled daughter, Hope, died after living through 199 days of seizures and other complications. Nancy writes,

> The day after we buried Hope, my husband said to me, "You know, I think we expected our faith to make this hurt less, but it doesn't. Our faith gave us an incredible amount of strength and encouragement while we had Hope, and we are comforted by the knowledge that she is in heaven. Our faith keeps us from being swallowed by despair. But I don't think it makes our loss hurt any less."[10]

Their pain didn't decrease because they believed; rather, their faith kept their pain from incapacitating them. When I interviewed David and Nancy Guthrie, they said God stood with them *in* their pain, but God did not *remove* their pain. Those separated in death from their loved ones don't *want* the pain to go away entirely, because if it did, it would minimize the importance of their relationship. Nancy Guthrie says,

> It is only natural that people around me often ask searchingly, "How are you?" And for much of the first year after Hope's death, my answer was, "I'm deeply and profoundly sad." I've been blessed with many people who have been willing to share my sorrow, to just be sad with me. Others, however, seem to want to rush me through my sadness. They want to fix me. But I lost someone I loved dearly, and I'm sad.[11]

Jesus wept over the death of Lazarus and his bereaved sisters, Mary and Martha, not because he lost perspective, but because he *had* perspective. Death is an enemy, as is the suffering and disability that precedes death. God hates it. So should we. We are to rejoice for the coming day when God promises no more death and suffering. Such rejoicing can fully coexist with mourning great loss.

We should avoid spiritual-sounding comments that minimize suffering, such as, "God must have loved your son very much to take him home this young." Parents who hear this will say, "Then I wish God loved him less." A friend told me that when her child died, a well-meaning woman assured her it was "for the best." My friend, a committed believer, said, "I wanted to tell her to shut up."

Don't say to a person whose child has died, "I know what you're going through; my mom died." It may have been very difficult for you, it may help you empathize to a degree, but it's *not* the same. Those who suffer loss need our love and encouragement. They do not need us to minimize or erase their pain through comparison; they need to feel and express it fully.

On the worst day of his life, his ten children taken from him, Job worshiped God. On the worst day of his life, when a flood swept away his wife and four children, Robert Rogers turned to God in worship. He told me he did so, not because he didn't feel the loss; on the contrary, he felt it so deeply that he could not lose the one object he had left to grab on to: God. He couldn't function, couldn't go on living, without worshiping God.

We dare not wait for a time of crisis to learn how to worship God. Job and Robert both worshiped God *in* crisis because they worshiped God *before* the crisis. If we learn now the meaning of God's sovereignty and goodness, a biblical theology of suffering will sustain us when suffering comes.

Grief and weeping are common and healthy among God's people.
Paul wrote words of encouragement about our future with Christ and our loved ones who've died in Christ: "that you may not grieve as others do who have no hope" (1 Thessalonians 4:13, ESV).

Often we fail to realize that the biblical writers and their original readers were real people with deep emotions and genuine distress. We dismiss them as naive, idealistic, and out of touch with pain and suffering, when in fact they knew a great deal more about it than we do. We applaud Susanna Wesley, mother of Charles and John Wesley, as a great prayer warrior and mentor of her children. But remember, nine of her children died by age two. Even if we see the Curse or the devil as the reason for these deaths, God permitted and used her profound suffering to make her a champion of the faith.

Isaiah 53:3 portrays Jesus as "a man of sorrows." David wrote, "Record my lament; list my tears on your scroll—are they not in your record?" (Psalm 56:8).

Either David or another psalmist prayed, "My soul is weary with sorrow; strengthen me according to your word" (Psalm 119:28).

When Nanci and I passed through a particularly difficult period of our lives, we felt like we'd "done our time," as if we shouldn't have to face more difficulty for a while. But that's not how it works, is it? As everyone living with ongoing disabilities, diseases, and heartaches knows, in this life God does not parcel out a certain amount of suffering, so once it runs out we'll face no more. But the promise remains: "Though he brings grief, he will show compassion, so great is his unfailing love" (Lamentations 3:32).

To obtain God's help and healing, we must want it and ask for it.

At the pool of Bethesda, Jesus looked at a man paralyzed for thirty-eight years and asked him a remarkable question: "Do you want to be healed?" (John 5:6, ESV).

While sometimes we long to feel better, most of us who have faced depression know that times come when we simply don't want healing. Sometimes we find an odd comfort in living out of sync with the world. For one thing, it offers us excuses for not doing what we don't want to do. If healed, the paralyzed man would need to learn a trade and generate an income.

John Newton, the former slave-trader who wrote "Amazing Grace," endured the agony of watching cancer take his wife over a period of years. He wrote,

> I believe it was about two or three months before her death, when I was
> walking up and down the room, offering disjointed prayers from a heart
> torn with distress, that a thought suddenly struck me, with unusual force,
> to this effect—"The promises of God must be true; surely the Lord will
> help me, *if I am willing to be helped!*" It occurred to me, that we are often
> led…to indulge that unprofitable grief which both our duty and our peace
> require us to resist to the utmost of our power. I instantly said aloud,
> "Lord, I am helpless indeed, in myself, but I hope I am willing, without
> reserve, that thou shouldest help me."[12]

We also need to want others' help *and* to seek it. Many people are deeply hurt because church members don't reach out to them in their suffering. Yet often they didn't call for the help they needed. They've sat in a dark room, hoping the phone would ring, assuming others should have figured it out. But how often have they themselves failed to recognize when someone else was suffering? If possible, a person drowning should cry for help. Most often, those within earshot will respond.

It's unfair to blame people who "should have known" when we have failed to tell them.

Though evil cannot be good, it can serve good purposes when contrasted with the beauty of God's goodness.

The movie *Slumdog Millionaire,* despite the controversies surrounding it, won eight 2009 Academy Awards and gained popular acclaim. The story's poverty, violence, crime, and child exploitation provide a backdrop for a young man's pure, unwavering love for a girl he met in the slums. The pair is tragically separated for years, and after they see each other briefly, she's taken from him again. Yet he never stops trying to find her.

Against impossible odds, the boy and girl finally reunite. He pulls back her *dupatta*, revealing a long, captor-inflicted scar that disfigures her face. As she looks down in shame, the young man, his eyes full of tears, holds up her face and kisses her scar. Not first her lips, but her *scar.* It's as if the scar itself is at last redeemed, somehow made beautiful.

The extraordinary power of the story lies in the depth of their love, forged in a context of years of injustice, evil, suffering, and separation. That climactic, love-filled moment could not have happened without the story's disturbing setting. He could not have kissed her scar if she had no scar.

Likewise, the climax of Revelation 21:4, when God wipes away all tears from every eye, could not happen without the billions of tears shed because of the evil and suffering we've endured (and inflicted). It could not happen had Jesus not borne it on the cross for us.

Hasn't God in Christ kissed our scars? And when we look at the scars on the hands and feet of Jesus, might we not, with tear-filled eyes, wish to kiss them?

Put a diamond only in light, and you will see some of its wonders; but set it against something dark *then* shine a light on it, and you will see what otherwise would have remained invisible.

I fell in love with astronomy years before I fell in love with the Lord of the cosmos. Night after night I observed the marvels of planets, stars, nebulae, and galaxies. As every backyard astronomer knows, streetlights and bright moonlight obscure the wonders of the night sky. In order to see the full glory of the stars, I learned that you must stay out for hours in the cold darkness. I did this night after night because what I discovered was worth it.

As the Heavens declare God's glory in the absence of other light, so God shows himself against the backdrop of evil and suffering—if only we are willing to look…and to discover that seeing him is worth even the cold darkness.

Notes

1. See Philip Yancey and Paul Brand's *Fearfully and Wonderfully Made* (Grand Rapids, MI: Zondervan, 1997).
2. C. S. Lewis, *The Problem of Pain* (New York: Macmillan, 1962), 93, 95.
3. Lewis, *The Problem of Pain,* 96–97.
4. Lewis, *The Problem of Pain,* 115.
5. Lewis, *The Problem of Pain,* 116.
6. Dan G. McCartney, *Why Does It Have to Hurt?* (Phillipsburg, NJ: P & R Publishing, 1998), 36.
7. Charles Haddon Spurgeon, *The Autobiography of Charles H. Spurgeon* (Philadelphia: American Baptist Publication Society, 1899), 247.
8. C. S. Lewis, *A Grief Observed* (Whitstable, Kent, UK: Whitstable Litho, 1966), 9.
9. Lewis, *A Grief Observed,* 38.
10. Nancy Guthrie, *Holding On to Hope* (Carol Stream, IL: Tyndale, 2002), 9.
11. Guthrie, *Holding On to Hope,* 10.
12. John Newton, *The Works of John Newton* (Edinburgh, Scotland: Banner of Truth, 1985), 5:621–22.

35

Apparently Gratuitous Evil and Pointless Suffering

Life involves suffering that appears pointless.

Missionaries David and Svea Flood made great sacrifices to serve God in the Belgian Congo. They and another young couple, the Ericksons, felt God's leading back in 1921 to take the gospel to a remote area called N'dolera.

Because a tribal chief would not let them enter his village, they had contact only with a young boy who sold them food. Svea led the boy to Jesus. Then malaria struck and the Ericksons returned to the central mission station. The Floods remained alone near N'dolera. Within days of giving birth to a little girl, Svea died.

Stunned and disillusioned, David dug a crude grave where he buried his young wife. David gave his baby girl, Aina, to the Ericksons and returned to Sweden embittered, saying God had ruined his life. Soon thereafter, the Ericksons died. Aina again had no one to care for her.

Why did this happen? What possible good could have come from it?

Stories like this have led countless people to conclude that even noble sacrifices can have pointless endings.

Some believe the existence of gratuitous evil is fully compatible with God granting demons and people the capacity to choose.

Gratuitous evil, if it exists, is extreme, superfluous, and not outweighed by a greater good. *Pointless* evil serves no useful purpose.

Philosopher Michael Peterson argues, "Not only are real and potential gratuitous evils not a devastating problem for a theistic perspective, but, properly understood, they are a part of a world order which seems to be precisely the kind God *would* create to provide for certain goods."[1]

Peterson maintains that God has designed a natural order to serve as an arena in which free human beings can respond to real dangers and challenges. "Pointless" evils, though tragic, are a necessary part of that system. Hence, an evil could itself be pointless, while the natural order that permits it is not. In that sense, Peterson seems to be arguing that God may permit such evils to exist not *for* a greater good, but because of one.

God's goodness and sovereignty and his plan for the world, spoken of in Ephesians 1:8–9 and other passages, convince me that no evil is completely pointless. Yet, as Peterson states, even if you believe in pointless evil and suffering, its existence does not in itself disprove an all-powerful and all-loving God.

Even inscrutable evil does not have to be gratuitous.
Marilyn McCord Adams has written a book titled *Horrendous Evils and the Goodness of God.* Though I disagree with some of her conclusions—including that Hell doesn't exist—she makes a bold claim that I believe to be true:

> If postmortem, the individual is ushered into a relation of beatific intimacy
> with God and comes to recognize how past participation in horrors is thus
> defeated, and if his/her concrete well-being is guaranteed forever afterward
> so that concrete ills are balanced off, then God will have been good to that
> individual despite participation in horrors.[2]

Something can be tragic without being meaningless. Holocaust survivor Viktor Frankl said in *Man's Search for Meaning*, "There is nothing in the world...that would so effectively help one to survive even the worst conditions as the knowledge that there is meaning in one's life."[3] He added, "Despair is suffering without meaning." Frankl found meaning in his suffering and thereby avoided despair.

Inscrutable suffering is not necessarily *gratuitous. Inscrutable* is a more humble term. The word *gratuitous* assumes an absolute knowledge we don't possess.

Elisabeth Elliot wrote, "God is God. If He is God, He is worthy of my worship and my service. I will find rest nowhere but in His will, and that will is infinitely, immeasurably, unspeakably beyond my largest notions of what He is up to."[4]

While devastating experiences often produce eventual good, we normally cannot see this good when the difficulty falls upon us.
After serving in a ministry for fifteen years, Dan endured a ten-year spiritual drought. He told me, "I felt like God just wasn't there. My spiritual life became pointless."

Finally, Dan determined to draw near to God, hoping God would keep his promise to draw near to him (see James 4:8). Ten Saturdays in a row he took a chair into the woods and sat for hours at a time. He vowed he would keep coming until "God showed up." He brought pen and paper to write reflections. For the first nine weeks he sensed no contact with God and so had little to write.

On the tenth Saturday, suddenly Dan started writing. He felt God's presence like a wave, for the first time in ten years. Beginning that day, his life changed. He told me, "As miserable as those ten years were, I would not trade it for anything, because God showed me that my earlier fifteen years of Christian life and ministry had really been about me, not Him. I had lived on my terms, not His. At last I was seeing God."

Dan said, "After it was all over, I thanked God for those ten years." Yet during that dark time, Dan said he couldn't have imagined *ever* being grateful for it.

Dan now suffers from a combination of ailments resulting in severe insomnia, which has prevented normal sleep. This has worn him down physically and mentally. After surviving his lengthy ordeal of not sensing God in his life, how does Dan feel about this subsequent trial?

"Once again," he says, "I feel set on the shelf, but this time it's different. I don't resent God. As a result of what I learned in those dry years, I realize I serve at God's pleasure, not mine. If He wants me to serve Him at full capacity, that's up to Him. If not, I'm not indispensable. I'm willing to serve Him however He wants me to."

The argument that a good and all-powerful God shouldn't permit pointless suffering assumes—without proving—that "pointless suffering" exists.

Not *seeing* the point in extreme suffering doesn't prove there *is* no point. I put the term "pointless suffering" in quotes to emphasize it as a claim, not a proven reality.

Open theist John Sanders writes, "When a two-month-old child contracts a painful, incurable bone cancer that means suffering and death, it is pointless evil. The Holocaust is pointless evil. The rape and dismemberment of a young girl is pointless evil. The accident that caused the death of my brother was a tragedy. God does not have a specific purpose in mind for these occurrences."[5]

But how can he possibly know that? Each of these things is horrible, but horrible is not the same as pointless. No doubt John Sanders and his family suffered greatly from his brother's death. But does that mean God could not have a specific purpose, or multiple purposes, concerning it?

Some Christians believe God has specific purposes *for* suffering; others believe that he doesn't but still brings about certain good results *from* suffering. But if an all-knowing God determines in advance to bring about certain good results from suffering, doesn't that qualify as a purpose? And if God will not permit anything to happen that he can't use to glorify himself or bring ultimate good to his people, then even a terrible evil would not be gratuitous.

Evils such as rape and murder certainly *look* gratuitous. But are we qualified to say they really are? Didn't the violent, excruciating death of Jesus, when it happened, appear both gratuitous and pointless in the extreme? Didn't the terrible murders of five young missionaries in Ecuador in 1956 seem pointless? Yet in retrospect nearly every missionary in the world sees great and far-reaching good that came out of their deaths.

To label suffering as pointless, we must be able to see clearly that it lacks any point—but we can't.
Imagine an air traffic controller instructing a pilot to assume a certain altitude and to take a certain line of descent. The pilot might argue, "That doesn't make sense to me. It would be easier to make a different approach." But he doesn't argue because he knows hundreds of other flights come in and out each hour. Good pilots must know the limits of their understanding and trust those who have the big picture, who can see the potential consequences of each pilot's decisions.

What if knowing God and growing in faith and becoming more Christlike is the point of my existence? What if the universe is not about human comfort and happiness?

I coach high school tennis. I constantly call upon young athletes to run, bend their knees, get on their toes, step into their shots, move their feet, get enough sleep, avoid junk food before the match, and drink water even when they don't think they need to. Teenagers tend to assume that many of the things we coaches make them do are pointless. We know otherwise. Team members must choose either to trust their coaches, or not. When they do, it's better for everyone.

Solzhenitsyn spent eight years suffering in a hard-labor camp for criticizing Stalin in a private letter to a friend. What could seem more pointless? And yet, had it not happened, he might not have come to Christ and would not have emerged as one of the greatest figures of the twentieth century, a man who exposed the terror of atheistic communism and the Soviet regime.

Only God is in the position to determine what is and isn't pointless.
Suffering may cause us to long for God to complete his redemptive plan. It may

cause us to grieve for the human rebellion that caused suffering. If it does those things, it is not pointless.

Behind almost every expression of the problem of evil stands an assumption: we know what an omniscient, omnipotent, morally perfect being *should* do. But we lack omniscience, omnipotence, and moral perfection—so how could we know? We should recuse ourselves as judges. As finite and fallen individuals, we lack the necessary qualifications to assess what God should and should not do. Not only do we know very little, even what we think we know is often distorted.

Animal suffering is seen by many as particularly pointless.

Some say that even if a purpose for human suffering exists, no one can point to a purpose for animal suffering. Can an animal learn virtue, compassion, or trust in God through suffering?

Certainly higher animals suffer. Pet owners see the pained expressions and hear the cries of their animals. Although we know human suffering from the inside, we don't know animal suffering the same way. How much animal suffering is due to conscious self-awareness, and how much is only an instinctive, physical reaction to pain that doesn't involve self-awareness? No one knows. But I would never make light of animal suffering.

William Rowe writes about a hypothetical fawn as an example of pointless suffering: "In some distant forest lightning strikes a dead tree, resulting in a forest fire. In the fire a fawn is trapped, horribly burned, and lies in terrible agony for several days before death relieves its suffering."[6]

Rowe's illustration is heartbreaking. But he makes assumptions that can't be proven. For instance, what if God grieved over the fawn's suffering, drew near, and as it suffered comforted it in a way we couldn't possibly know? What if he did lessen its suffering? What if God determined he would create a New Earth on which animals, including perhaps that specific fawn, will exist and never again suffer pain, but instead frolic in eternal delight? To some this seems far-fetched, but significant biblical evidence from both the Old and New Testaments suggests this may well be the case.[7]

The entire creation, which clearly includes animals, groans as it awaits our resurrection (see Romans 8:19–21). Just as all creation, including animals, fell with Adam and suffered the painful effects of the Curse, so all creation will be renewed in the resurrection of a righteous humanity. Seen in this light, could not God's new creation compensate for past animal suffering? And might what appears to be pointless suffering actually serve to demonstrate the horrible consequences of human evil on all creation, as well as the greatness of Christ's redemptive work that encompasses the whole cosmos?

Usually we cannot know what God does to relieve horrible suffering.
If a man falls off a ship and drowns, we ask why God would allow him to go through such a horror. But what if God *did* relieve the man's horror? How would we know? If someone burns to death in a building, how do we know she didn't die of smoke inhalation before the fire touched her? Not all shocking and tragic deaths involve as much suffering as we sometimes suppose.

This we do know, according to God's Word: For the believer in Christ, this life's suffering, no matter how great, ends at death. Jesus paid a terrible price on the cross so that no person's suffering need continue beyond this life.

If God should eliminate any one evil, the result might be to permit ten other evils and prevent ten goods.
We might imagine that if we were God, we wouldn't allow a child to be born with a severe disability. But what if, without that child's disability, the parents would divorce? What if otherwise they would become self-absorbed rather than servant-hearted people? What if the child would not have grown up to love God, but because of his disability will come to Christ and spend eternity with his Savior and also with his parents? Since we're not God, we can't know.

A celebrated *Star Trek* episode depicts 1930s America. Historically, Edith Keeler, a peace advocate and social reformer, was killed when hit by a car. But Dr. McCoy, thrown back in time, saves her life, changing history. Keeler's peace movement flourishes, and America delays entering the war against Germany. Although this seems good—since war involves much suffering—catastrophe results. German scientists invent the atomic bomb before the Allies do, the world falls under the control of the Nazis, and millions more lives are lost than would have been had the one woman died. So the apparent good of saving a noble woman's life instead brings terrible evil and suffering to the world. Knowing this, Captain Kirk follows McCoy back in time to stop him from preventing the fatal accident—even though Kirk has fallen in love with the woman. She dies and the Allies win the war.

The moral of this story? Since detailed past, present, and future knowledge is unavailable to us, we sometimes consider accidents random and pointless. We do not see that God has and will accomplish good purposes through them. Some good actions may result in great evils, while one tragic death may save the world from tyranny. Who but God is in a position to know such things?

Some of the most meaningful accomplishments of our lives come in the context of our most difficult, seemingly pointless suffering.

I once asked Bryant Young what he considered his greatest achievement in fourteen years of playing professional football. He didn't say, "Coming in as an All-American from Notre Dame and winning the Super Bowl my rookie year." He didn't mention being a first-round draft choice, his selection as Defensive Rookie of the Year, having nearly ninety career sacks, going to four Pro Bowls, or being voted team MVP.

His greatest achievement, Bryant told me, came after a devastating broken leg in 1998, which appeared likely to end his career. Doctors inserted an eighteen-inch titanium rod into his leg. He suffered through a long and hard rehabilitation, but God used it to build his character. The following season he started every game and was voted the NFL's Comeback Player of the Year. Out of suffering and adversity, God brought the single most satisfying accomplishment of Bryant Young's career.

Suffering in the context of professional sports, of course, is nothing compared to the suffering many others have faced, including the single mom who works a second job to pay for medicine for her sick child. Still, whatever we have to do, we commonly find the greatest satisfaction in overcoming the hardest challenges.

Scripture puts it this way: "And we rejoice in the hope of the glory of God. Not only so, but we also rejoice in our sufferings, because we know that suffering produces perseverance; perseverance, character; and character, hope" (Romans 5:2–4).

Sometimes we get to hear the point behind "pointless" sacrifices and sufferings.

Remember how this chapter began? Missionary Svea Flood, in the Belgian Congo, died after giving birth to a little girl. The infant's father, David, left baby Aina with the couple's co-workers, the Ericksons, and then returned to Sweden. The embittered man said God had ruined his life.

Within eight months, both the Ericksons died. American missionaries brought Aina to the United States where she was adopted, becoming Aggie Hurst. Years later, a Swedish Christian magazine appeared in Aggie's mailbox. She didn't understand the words, but a photo inside shocked her—a grave with a white cross, marked with a name she recognized—that of her mother, Svea Flood.

A college professor translated the article for Aggie: Missionaries came to

N'dolera long ago… A white baby was born… The young mother died… One little African boy was led to Christ… The boy grew up and built a school in the village. Gradually he won his students to Christ… The children led their parents to Christ… Even the tribal chief became a Christian.

After decades of bitterness, one day an old and ill David Flood had a visitor— his daughter, Aina Flood, now Aggie Hurst. She told David the story recounted in the article. She informed her father, "Today there are six hundred African people serving Christ because you and mother were faithful to God's call in your life."

David felt stunned. His heart softened. He returned to God. Weeks later, he died.

Aggie eventually met that African boy, by then superintendent of a national church in Zaire (formerly the Belgian Congo), an association of 110,000 baptized believers.[8]

The great tragedy in the lives of David, Svea, and Aina Flood was undeniably heartbreaking. It appeared utterly cruel and pointless. But in time it yielded a great harvest of joy that will continue for eternity.

Notes

1. Michael L. Peterson, *Evil and the Christian God* (Grand Rapids, MI: Baker Book House, 1982), 117.
2. Marilyn McCord Adams, *Horrendous Evils and the Goodness of God* (Ithaca, NY: Cornell University Press, 2000), 168.
3. Viktor E. Frankl, *Man's Search for Meaning* (New York: Simon & Schuster, 1985), 126.
4. Elisabeth Elliot, *Through Gates of Splendor* (Wheaton, IL: Tyndale, 1986), 267.
5. John Sanders, *The God Who Risks* (Downers Grove, IL: InterVarsity, 1998), 262.
6. William Rowe, quoted in C. Stephen Evans, *Faith Beyond Reason* (Edinburgh, Scotland: Edinburgh University Press, 1998), 131.
7. See Randy C. Alcorn, *Heaven* (Carol Stream, IL: Tyndale, 2004), 387–405. The Old Testament passages include Isaiah 11, 60, and 65.
8. Aggie Hurst, "A Story of Eternal Perspective," Eternal Perspective Ministries, www.epm.org/artman2/publish/missions_true_stories/A_Story_of_Eternal_Perspective.shtml.

36

How the Health and Wealth
Gospel Perverts Our View
of Evil and Suffering

Prosperity theology teaches that God will bless with material abundance and good health those who obey him and lay claim to his promises. "We don't have to wait for God's blessing in the life to come," it promises. "He'll send it to us here and now."

This popular "name it and claim it" teaching—also called the health and wealth gospel—is not limited to certain congregations, but has worked its way into mainstream evangelical churches where it gets subtly woven into many Christians' worldviews.

The author of *Total Life Prosperity* writes, "Biblical prosperity is the ability to be in control of every circumstance and situation that occurs in your life. No matter what happens, whether financial, social, physical, marital, spiritual, or emotional, this type of prosperity enables you to maintain control in every situation."[1]

The author of another book writes, "Poverty is so unnecessary. Loss is so painful.... I hate pain. Your pain can stop. I want you *completely healed. That's why I wrote this book.*"[2]

This false worldview breeds superficiality, seriously misrepresents the gospel, and sets people up to believe, when evil and suffering come to them, that God has been untrue to his promises.

Prosperity theology has poisoned the church and undermined our ability to deal with evil and suffering.

Some churches today have no place for pain. Those who say God has healed them get the microphone, while those who continue to suffer are shamed into silence or ushered out the back door.

Paul had a much different viewpoint. "It has been granted to you on behalf of Christ not only to believe in him, but to suffer for his sake" (Philippians 1:29). "In the world you will have tribulation," Jesus pledged (John 16:33, ESV). We should count on these promises as surely as we count on John 3:16.

The first story of the post-Fall world is Cain's murder of Abel, a righteous man who pleased God and suffered as a direct result. Noah, Abraham, Joseph, Moses, David, Daniel, Shadrach, Meshach, Abednego, and nearly all the prophets weren't just righteous people who happened to suffer. Rather, they suffered *because* they were righteous.

This continues in the New Testament, with Jesus as the prime example. Jesus said John the Baptist was the greatest of men (see Luke 7:28). Soon thereafter evildoers imprisoned then murdered John and mockingly displayed his head on a platter (see Matthew 14:6–12). What could be more utterly contradictory to the health and wealth gospel?

The Holy Spirit had hardly descended before wicked men stoned Stephen to death. Herod Agrippa beheaded James; later, Nero beheaded Paul. Tradition says Peter and Andrew were crucified; Matthew died a martyr; a lance killed Thomas; and Pharisees threw James the son of Alpheus from the temple, then stoned him and dashed his brains out with a club. First Peter is an entire book devoted to Christians suffering injustices for the sake of Christ.

Larry Waters writes, "Blessing is promised and experienced, but suffering is never eliminated. In fact, the normal life of a person who follows the Lord involves both blessing and suffering."[3]

Even at its best, the ancient world offered a hard life. Christians *routinely* suffered.

They still do. Even Christians who don't suffer persecution still pull weeds, experience pain in childbirth, become ill and die, just like everyone else.

The health and wealth gospel's claims are so obviously opposed to countless biblical passages that it is difficult to imagine, apart from the deceptive powers of Satan, how so many Christians could actually believe them.

In some cases, pleasing God results in suffering.

God promises suffering to Christians in general and to those in particular who honor him. Consider one of the great, unclaimed promises of Scripture: "Anyone who wants to live all out for Christ is in for a lot of trouble; there's no getting around it" (2 Timothy 3:12, MSG).

The most notable early Christians "conquered [Satan] by the blood of the Lamb and by the word of their testimony; for they loved not their lives even unto death" (Revelation 12:11, ESV).

We overrate health and underrate holiness. If physical health is our primary value, then why endanger it for a higher cause? While earlier Christians risked their lives to serve those dying from the bubonic plague, prosperity theology tends to encourage believers to flee from threatening ministry opportunities so that they might cling to what they cannot preserve anyway.

Yes, we should steward wisely the bodies God has entrusted to us; yet he sometimes calls on us to sacrifice our preferences, sleep, careers, vacation plans, and health to say yes to him. Does this sound demanding? Christ's words leave no room for equivocation:

> Be on your guard against men; they will hand you over to the local coun-
> cils and flog you in their synagogues. On my account you will be brought
> before governors and kings as witnesses to them and to the Gentiles....
>
> Brother will betray brother to death, and a father his child; children
> will rebel against their parents and have them put to death. All men will
> hate you because of me, but he who stands firm to the end will be
> saved....
>
> Anyone who does not take his cross and follow me is not worthy of
> me. (Matthew 10:17–18, 21–22, 38)

Emmanuel Ndikumana explained why he returned home to Burundi when the Hutu-Tutsi conflict threatened his life. In revenge for atrocities, Tutsis already had killed his Hutu father and grandfather. Emmanuel told me, "I do not condemn those who fled; I understand. But I felt I should not treasure safety. The only way for me to prove to my people that I believed the gospel was to return and suffer with them. If I fear death as unbelievers do, I have nothing to offer unbelievers. Only when you are free from the fear of death are you really free."

We should see our suffering as God keeping his promises, not violating them.

"Dear friends, do not be surprised at the painful trial you are suffering, as though something strange were happening to you. But rejoice that you participate in the sufferings of Christ, so that you may be overjoyed when his glory is revealed" (1 Peter 4:12–13).

Suffering—whether from persecution, accidents, or illnesses—shouldn't surprise us. God has promised it. One of the great tragedies about the health and wealth gospel is that it makes God seem like a liar. When people believe that God promises to keep them from suffering, God appears untrustworthy when suffering comes.

A woman who had based her life on the health and wealth worldview lay dying of cancer. She looked into a camera during an interview and said, "I've lost my faith." She felt bitter that God had "broken his promises." She correctly realized that the god she'd followed does not exist. She incorrectly concluded that the God of the Bible had let her down. He hadn't; her church and its preachers had done that. God had never made the promises that she thought he'd broken.

When hard times come, people should lose their faith in false doctrine, not in God. In contrast to jewelry-flaunting televangelists, Paul said, "We must go through many hardships to enter the kingdom of God" (Acts 14:22).

If you are a Christian, God will deliver you from *eternal* suffering. And even now he will give you joyful foretastes of living in his presence. *That's* his promise.

Christians should expect to suffer more, not less, since they suffer under the Fall *and* as followers of Christ.

If your goal is to avoid suffering in this life, then following Christ will not help you. Jesus himself said, "If the world hates you, keep in mind that it hated me first.... If they persecuted me, they will persecute you also" (John 15:18, 20).

Josef Tson was once the best-known pastor in Romania. At a time when the Christian faith had become virtually illegal, he openly preached the gospel. Police threatened him repeatedly with imprisonment and arrest. In his sixties he studied at Oxford for his doctorate, writing a dissertation that became a book titled *Suffering, Martyrdom, and Rewards in Heaven*.

I first opened the Scriptures with Josef in 1988, with a group of theologians discussing eternal rewards. Twenty years later, writing this book, I remembered his stories and insights and called him again. Josef explained to me how the belief that God doesn't want his people to suffer once corrupted the Romanian church. In the interests of self-preservation, he said, they failed to speak out against injustice, tyranny, and the idolatry of turning men into gods. He recalls joining the crowd on the streets and crying, "Glory to Stalin."

God convicted Josef. As a pastor he refused to glorify communist leaders and started to speak out boldly for Christ. Interrogators threatened him with death every day for six months. Finally he told them, "Your supreme weapon is killing.

My supreme weapon is dying. My preaching will speak ten times louder after you kill me."

Finally, in 1981, the Romanian government exiled him.

HEALTH

Medical and scientific advancements and spiritual claims of healing may convince us that suffering can and will be eliminated.

In an "it's all about me" world, we don't accept answers that entail our inconvenience, much less our suffering and death. We assume faith healing or medical breakthroughs can eliminate suffering and cure all diseases.

According to prosperity theology, we can declare our way out of diseases. Pastor Joel Osteen writes, "Maybe Alzheimer's disease runs in your family genes, but don't succumb to it. Instead, say every day, 'My mind is alert. I have clarity of thought. I have a good memory. Every cell in my body is increasing and getting healthier.' If you'll rise up in your authority, you can be the one to put a stop to the negative things in your family line.... Start boldly declaring, 'God is restoring health unto me. I am getting better every day in every way.'"[4]

Of course we should seek to be healthy, both physically and mentally. But we miss out on a great deal if we fail to see God can also accomplish his purposes when we lose our health and he chooses not to heal us.

Julia was a powerful woman who flaunted her beauty and wealth. Her volatile temper and sharp tongue put people in their place and left a trail of damaged relationships.

Then, in her midforties, Julia was diagnosed with an aggressive cancer. Despite treatment, the disease progressed. Doctors said she had less than a year to live.

As this unfolded, Julia underwent a remarkable change. Her diagnosis frightened her; she sought spiritual counsel, started reading the New Testament, confessed her sins, and gave her life to Jesus Christ. She wrote letters, made phone calls, invited people for coffee, and sought forgiveness from the many she'd hurt. She did all she could to restore relationships with family and others. She made peace with her ex-husband, grew close to her children, and developed a loving circle of Christian friends.

Several weeks before she died, Julia told her pastor that she considered her cancer to be a love gift from God. She believed the Lord had used her disease to draw her to himself. Julia said she would gladly exchange all her years of beauty, wealth, and influence for the two years of illness that taught her the unspeakable joy of loving Jesus and loving others.[5]

In contrast to Julia, however, after a terminal diagnosis, many people spend all the remainder of their lives searching for a scientific cure or a spiritual healing, or both. I don't, of course, fault sick people for seeking a cure! But, like Julia, we should focus our energies not simply on *avoiding* death, but on investing our time in *preparing* for it—getting right with God and ministering to others.

Let me share some bad news: I have a fatal disease. I'm terminal. I'm going to die. But the news gets even worse. *You* have the same fatal disease—mortality. You're going to die too.

Nothing could be more obvious. Yet somehow we don't take it to heart, do we?

We do a disservice to ourselves and to others when we turn the avoidance of suffering and death into an idol.

Even if we don't end up dying from a particular disease or accident, all of us will die unless Christ comes within our lifetime. Have you noticed there are no 120-year-old faith healers?

It's healthy to think about death and prepare ourselves for it. Well-meaning people say to the terminally ill, "You're going to be fine," and, "You must have faith for God to heal you." This can divert the dying from the gift God gives them to spend their remaining days cultivating an eternal perspective, preparing to meet him, healing and building relationships, and redeeming the time to serve him wholeheartedly.

While resisting death and fighting for life can be virtuous, it can also degenerate into idolatry if staying alive here becomes more important than anything else. Paul had it right: "Christ will be exalted in my body, whether by life or by death. For to me, to live is Christ and to die is gain" (Philippians 1:20–21).

C. S. Lewis wrote about seeking safety from the harder edges of God's love:

> Of all arguments against love none makes so strong an appeal to my
> nature as "Careful! This might lead you to suffering." To my nature, my
> temperament, yes. Not to my conscience. When I respond to that appeal I
> seem to myself to be a thousand miles away from Christ. If I am sure of
> anything I am sure that His teaching was never meant to confirm my con-
> genital preference for safe investments and limited liabilities.[6]

In the early church, committed Christian leaders routinely endured diseases and other suffering.

If God has healed you, rejoice! God can and does heal, and we should celebrate his mercy. I have often prayed for healing and sometimes witnessed it. But if you've prayed for healing and not received it, take heart—you're in good company!

Paul had to leave his friend Trophimus behind because of sickness (see 2 Timothy 4:20). Another beloved friend, Epaphroditus, became gravely ill (see Philippians 2:25–30). Paul's spiritual son Timothy had frequent stomach disorders, for which Paul told him to drink a little wine for medicinal purposes (see 1 Timothy 5:23). Those who claim anyone with enough faith will be healed must believe they have greater faith than Paul and his fellow missionaries.

Like many of God's servants in the early church, Paul had neither constant health nor significant wealth. When soldiers took Paul in chains from his filthy Roman dungeon and beheaded him at the order of the opulent madman Nero, two representatives of humanity faced off, one of the best and one of the worst. One lived for prosperity on Earth. The other one now lives in prosperity in Heaven.

When I became insulin-dependent, I wondered who wanted me ill, Satan or God. The obvious answer? Satan. But I'm also convinced, as was Paul, that the ultimate answer is God. Paul, under the inspiration of the Holy Spirit, saw God's sovereignty, grace, and humbling purpose of his disease (see 2 Corinthians 12:7–10). I have clearly and repeatedly seen the same in my own life.

Upon learning of my disease, well-meaning people sometimes ask whether I have trusted God to heal me. I respond that when it first appeared in 1985, I and others did ask God to heal me. After a while, when God chose not to answer our prayers that way, I stopped asking. When I say this, I sometimes get looks of alarm and quotes about persevering in prayer and having faith as a mustard seed. I point out that Paul asked God to remove his disease *three* times, not a thousand times or a hundred or even a dozen. Just three times he asked—but God made it clear the affliction had come from his gracious hand. Paul had no desire to ask God to remove that which his Lord wanted to use to create in him greater Christlikeness and dependence upon God.

Of course, I'd rejoice if God suddenly healed my pancreas and I no longer needed to take insulin or deal with low and high blood sugar and the toll they take. I'd feel grateful if an ethical medical technology could heal my disease. Yet if I could snap my fingers and remove my disease—apart from some direct revelation from God that I should do so—I would not use that power. Why not? Because *God* has chosen not to.

Mental lapses that come from low blood sugar sometimes leave me with vivid memories of a confused state I suffered only fifteen minutes earlier. It's as if I have Alzheimer's, but a glass of orange juice cures me. For now, I suffer only temporary mental lapses; perhaps one day I will become like my friends who suffer from "permanent" dementia. Except, it's not permanent at all! The work of Christ on our behalf guarantees for us, *in the resurrection,* never-ending health of mind and body.

All healing in this world is temporary. Resurrection healing will be permanent. For that our hearts should overflow with praise to our gracious God.

We should not demand or claim healing, but humbly ask for it, recognizing our unworthiness.

A centurion wanted Jesus to heal his beloved servant. Some Jewish elders told Jesus, "*This man deserves* to have you do this, because he loves our nation and has built our synagogue" (Luke 7:4–5). The centurion, on the other hand, sent his friends to say, "Lord, don't trouble yourself, for *I do not deserve* to have you come under my roof. That is why I did not even consider myself worthy to come to you. But say the word, and my servant will be healed" (verses 6–7). The leaders argued that the centurion deserved Christ's favor; the centurion argued the opposite. Although he wanted Christ to heal his servant, he didn't think himself worthy of Christ's intervention.

The centurion understood God's power and believed that Christ could heal from a distance. Jesus said to the crowd, "I tell you, I have not found such great faith even in Israel." The centurion's representatives returned to find the servant well (see verses 9–10).

This is not a formula for healing; it's an example of humility. We deserve neither healing nor answered prayers. This understanding leaves no room for the bitterness and resentment that inevitably accompany a sense of entitlement.

"A man with leprosy came and knelt before [Jesus] and said, 'Lord, if you are willing, you can make me clean'" (Matthew 8:2). Jesus agreed and healed him. Note that the man did not think himself entitled to healing. Nor did he "claim" healing. Neither did he presume to take control of the situation. He humbly requested healing while leaving it to the will of Christ. We should do likewise.

Perspective and peace in facing crisis, not immunity to crisis, testify to God's goodness, grace, and power.

Jesus backed away from people who only followed him to be fed and get healed and enjoy benefits any atheist would enjoy. He said to the crowd who followed him after a miraculous feeding, "I tell you the truth, you are looking for me, not because you saw miraculous signs but because you ate the loaves and had your fill" (John 6:26).

Prosperity theology claims that God's love causes him to withhold suffering from his children. The Bible, on the other hand, insists that God's love empowers his children to live gracefully and gratefully *with* their suffering. We do not testify to the world that we suffer less; we testify that God empowers us to face suffering with perspective. Paul Tournier wrote, "If healing through faith is striking, how much more so are spiritual victories without healing."[7]

Hudson Taylor described his little daughter Gracie's heartfelt prayer for a Chinese man they saw making an idol. After the man expressed no interest in the gospel, they stopped under a tree and sang a hymn together, then prayed. Taylor wrote, "The dear child went on and on, pleading that God would have mercy upon the poor Chinese and would strengthen her father to preach to them. I was never so moved by any prayer.... Words fail to describe it."

Gracie Taylor died just after turning eight. That same month in 1867, her father wrote to a friend in England, "Beloved Brother, the Lord has taken our sweet little Gracie to bloom in the purer atmosphere of His own presence. Our hearts bleed; but 'Above the rest this note shall swell—Our Jesus has done all things well.' The Gardener came and plucked a rose."[8]

Some would argue that evil and the Curse and Satan (or demons), not God, killed Gracie, and to say God takes a child is to accuse him of evil. But Hudson Taylor saw things differently. Like Job, who said God had taken Job's children in death (1:18–22), Taylor believed that God reigns over all.

Asking God to always heal us and remove adversity is like asking him to afflict us with spiritual apathy.

Scripture's prayers deal far more with spiritual growth than with physical health. Notice the focus of Paul's prayer for the Colossians:

> And we pray this in order that you may live a life worthy of the Lord and may please him in every way: bearing fruit in every good work, growing in the knowledge of God, being strengthened with all power according to his glorious might so that you may have great endurance and patience, and joyfully giving thanks to the Father, who has qualified you to share in the inheritance of the saints in the kingdom of light. (Colossians 1:10–12)

It's striking what Paul *doesn't* pray for: an elder's bout with cancer, the flu bug going around Colossae, an Asia Minor recession, kidney stones, back problems, and good weather for the church picnic. Did they have these issues back then? Sure. They had diseases, discomforts, financial strains, and bad weather. And did they pray for them? No doubt. But Scripture's recorded prayers seldom concern such things. They involve intercession for people's love for God, knowledge of God, walk with God, and service to God.

We should pray *for* ourselves and our suffering loved ones, not simply try to *pray away* suffering. "God, please heal this cancer" is appropriate. "God, please use for your glory this cancer, so long as I have it" is equally appropriate.

When you pray *only* for healing, what are you praying to miss out on? Christlikeness? Shouldn't we learn to pray that our suffering causes growth, that God will give us little glimpses of Heaven as we seek to endure, and that he would use us? I've mentioned Jim Harrell, a friend and ALS sufferer. Jim wrote me,

> As I contemplate what it would be like to be healed of this disease, God has caused me to focus on my own sinfulness and human condition. If healed, I genuinely fear that within a year at the latest I would begin to forget what it was like to be in this condition. I would fall into the trap of allowing life's distractions to divert me. While I realize these distractions are not bad in and of themselves, a clear and distinct advantage of suffering is its ability to sharply focus one on what's important.... The wonder of being healed would be indescribable; however, I seriously question whether or not that would be the best for my soul. I don't have an answer, but I do know my own heart.

Disease, suffering, and death are part of the Curse; one day Jesus will reverse the Curse...but not yet.

Health and wealth preachers often say, "There is healing in the Atonement." Yes, Jesus came to reverse the Curse. Yes, Jesus will remove all disease, disability, and death from us—but in his time, not ours. He will rescue us from suffering when he returns to set up his kingdom or when we go to him in death.

He also promises that, one day, leopard and lion and lamb and goat will lie down together in safety (see Isaiah 11:6). If you fail to understand God's timing, however, you might feel tempted to put them all in the same pen now.

The Bible's first chapters have no curse. In the last chapter God promises, "No longer will there be any curse" (Revelation 22:3). *Today* we do not live in the first two chapters of the Bible or in the last two. We live in between, post-Eden but pre–New Earth. Life here and now, under the Curse, involves suffering.

To lay claim now to a complete healing or freedom from evil and suffering is to do an injustice to Scripture.

WEALTH

Prosperity theology encourages us to spend on ourselves the unprecedented wealth God has entrusted to us for relieving world suffering.
A reporter asked Mother Teresa, "When a baby dies alone in a Calcutta alley, where is God?" Her response? "God is there, suffering with that baby. The question really is where are *you*?"[9]

As God laments over the suffering child, so should we. God's heart is stirred to bring help to the needy—normally by providing his people with the means to help. The poverty-stricken Macedonian Christians considered it a privilege to give sacrificially to help the needy in Jerusalem (see 2 Corinthians 8:1–4). Paul called upon the Corinthians to give generously to the needy (see verses 13–14). And, he added, "You will be made rich in every way so that you can be generous on every occasion" (9:11).

God has entrusted us with wealth that we may voluntarily distribute to those who need it most. Never have so many been in need. Never has God showered such abundance on Christians. When will we learn that God doesn't give us more to increase our standard of living, but to increase our standard of giving?

When we stand in his presence, Christ can show the scars on his hands and feet and say, "Here's what *I* did about evil and suffering." What will we say when he asks, "What did *you* do?"

Some Christian leaders think living comfortably gives them credibility, but the Bible equates good leadership with perseverance in suffering.
In health and wealth circles, leadership credibility is measured by jets, jewelry, and invitations to the White House. In contrast to the prosperity preachers of his day, whom he mockingly called "super-apostles," Paul argued for his own credibility as God's servant based on his "troubles, hardships and distresses; in beatings, imprisonments and riots; in hard work, sleepless nights and hunger" (2 Corinthians 6:4–5).

Our national or familial financial struggles bring hardship but also give us the opportunity to repent of past greed and foolishness. Neither Christian leaders nor lay believers should expect God to continue making us affluent. If we do not follow God when he prospers us, he may take away our national and personal prosperity to bring us to repentance and dependence (see Deuteronomy 28:47–48).

We should not embrace a theology of triumph and healing without a theology of the Cross and suffering.

Fear of suffering motivates us to distance ourselves from Christ and his people. But unless we are willing to be hated for Christ, we are not his disciples (see Luke 9:23–24). How can one hear he should "take up his cross daily" and then present the gospel as promising short-term deliverance from suffering? To take up our crosses daily means to "suffer daily."

Paul understood this: "I die every day" (1 Corinthians 15:31). "I have been crucified with Christ" (Galatians 2:20). And he taught Timothy, "Do not be ashamed to testify about our Lord, or ashamed of me his prisoner. But join with me in suffering for the gospel" (2 Timothy 1:8).

Christ's followers should resist attempts to solve the problem of evil by misrepresenting God and redefining the gospel.

I don't like suffering. Nor am I called to seek it. But when we bend over backward to avoid it, and value comfort over commitment, we do not live as Christ's disciples. It's not our job to be popular. We exist solely to please an Audience of One.

In America, a sharp-looking businessman stands up at a luncheon to give his testimony: "Before I knew Christ, I had nothing. My business was in bankruptcy, my health was bad, I'd nearly lost my family. Then I accepted Christ. He took me out of bankruptcy, and my business has doubled its profits. My blood pressure has dropped to normal, and I feel great. Best of all, my wife and children have come back, and we're a family again. God is good—praise the Lord!"

In China, a disheveled former university professor gives his testimony: "Before I met Christ, I had everything. Then I came to Jesus as my Savior and Lord. As a result, I lost my post at the university, lost my house, and now work for a subsistence wage at a factory. My wife rejected me because of my conversion. She took my son away, and I haven't seen him for five years. I live with constant pain from injuries when police dragged me away from our unregistered church service. But God is good, and I praise Him for His faithfulness."

Both men are sincere Christians. One gives thanks because of what he's gained. The other gives thanks despite what he's lost.

We *should* give thanks for material blessings and restored families. The brother in China would enthusiastically thank God to have them again; indeed, he gives heartfelt thanks each day for the little he does have. And while the American brother certainly should give thanks, he and the rest of us must carefully sort out how much of what he has is part of the gospel and how much is not.

Any gospel that is more true in America than in China is not the true gospel.

Notes

1. Creflo A. Dollar Jr., *Total Life Prosperity* (Nashville, TN: Thomas Nelson, 1999), x.
2. Mike Murdock, *7 Keys to 1000 Times More* (Dallas: Wisdom International, 1998), 13.
3. Larry J. Waters, "Missio Dei in the Book of Job," *Bibliotheca Sacra* 166, no. 661 (January–March 2009): 32.
4. Joel Osteen, *Become a Better You* (New York: Free Press, 2007), 45, 114.
5. Adapted from Alice Gray, *Treasures for Women Who Hope* (Nashville: W Publishing, 2005), 51–52.
6. C. S. Lewis, *The Four Loves* (New York: Harcourt Books, 1960), 20.
7. Paul Tournier, *The Person Reborn* (New York: Harper and Row, 1966), 172.
8. Hudson Taylor, letter to William Thomas Berger, August 29, 1867, quoted in Frederick Howard Taylor, *Hudson Taylor and the China Inland Mission* (London: China Inland Mission, 1927), 118.
9. John G. Stackhouse Jr., *Can God Be Trusted?* (Oxford: Oxford University Press, 1998), 67.

Why Does God Allow Suffering?

37

How God Uses Suffering
for His Glory

Since God is the source of all goodness, his glory is the wellspring of all joy. What God does for his own sake benefits us. Therefore whatever glorifies him is good for us.

And that includes the suffering he allows or brings (biblically, either or both terms can apply) into our lives.

God refines us in our suffering and graciously explains why: "See, I have refined you, though not as silver; I have tested you in the furnace of affliction. For my own sake, *for my own sake,* I do this" (Isaiah 48:10). For emphasis, God repeats the reason.

If you don't understand that the universe is about God and his glory—and that whatever exalts God's glory also works for your ultimate good—then you will misunderstand this passage and countless others. Some consider God egotistical or cruel to test us for his sake. But the testing he does for *his* sake accrues to *our* eternal benefit.

How often have you heard people say, "I grew closest to God when my life was free from pain and suffering"?

THE REFINING PROCESS

Suffering can help us grow and mature.
John Hick writes,

> We have to recognize that the presence of pleasure and the absence of
> pain cannot be the supreme and overriding end for which the world exists.
> Rather, this world must be a place of soul-making. And its value is to be
> judged not, primarily, by the quantity of pleasure and pain occurring in it

at any particular moment, but by its fitness for its primary purpose, the purpose of soul-making.[1]

I prefer the term *character-building* to *soul-making*. And although Hick sometimes draws what I think are unbiblical conclusions, he correctly emphasizes human character above comfort.

Josef Tson, who faced much evil in communist Romania, told me, "This world, with all its evil, is God's deliberately chosen environment for people to grow in their characters. The character and trustworthiness we form here, we take with us there, to Heaven. Romans and 1 Peter 3:19 make clear that suffering is a grace from God. It is a grace given us now to prepare us for living forever."

Mountain climbers could save time and energy if they reached the summit in a helicopter, but their ultimate purpose is conquest, not efficiency. Sure, they want to reach a goal, but they want to do so the hard way by testing their character and resolve.

God could create scientists, mathematicians, athletes, and musicians. He doesn't. He creates children who take on those roles over a long process. We learn to excel by handling failure. Only in cultivating discipline, endurance, and patience do we find satisfaction and reward.

As dentists, physicians, parents, and pet owners regularly demonstrate, suffering may be lovingly inflicted for a higher good.
We think to "love" means to "do no harm," when it really means "to be willing to do short-term harm for a redemptive purpose." A physician who re-breaks an arm in order for it to heal properly harms his patient in order to heal him. C. S. Lewis wrote,

> But suppose that what you are up against is a surgeon whose intentions are wholly good. The kinder and more conscientious he is, the more inexorably he will go on cutting. If he yielded to your entreaties, if he stopped before the operation was complete, all the pain up to that point would have been useless.... What do people mean when they say "I am not afraid of God because I know He is good"? Have they never even been to a dentist?[2]

If cancer or paralysis or a car accident prompts us to draw on God's strength to become more conformed to Christ, then regardless of the human, demonic, or natural forces involved, God will be glorified in it. A friend whose husband died wrote,

One thing that I've become convinced of is that God has different definitions for words than I do. For example, He does work all things for my eternal good and His eternal glory. But his definition of good is different than mine. My "good" would never include cancer and young widowhood. My "good" would include healing and dying together in our sleep when we are in our nineties. But cancer was good because of what God did that He couldn't do any other way. Cancer was, in fact, necessary to make Bob and me look more like Jesus. So in love, God allowed what was best for us...in light of eternity.

God sometimes uses suffering to punish evil.

While personal suffering doesn't always come as punishment for sin, this doesn't mean it *never* does. God speaks of bringing judgment on his children for participating in the Lord's Supper in an unworthy manner (see 1 Corinthians 11:27–32). David knew he'd suffered because of his sin (see Psalm 32:3–4). Christ said, "Those whom I love I rebuke and discipline" (Revelation 3:19).

God struck Gehazi, Elisha's servant, with leprosy for lying and for accepting material gifts under false pretenses (see 2 Kings 5:20–27). God struck down Herod for his pride and arrogance, and for accepting praise that belongs to God alone (see Acts 12:19–23). God struck down Ananias and Sapphira because they lied to the Holy Spirit (see Acts 5:1–11).

God's *occasional* direct punishment in this life reminds us of judgment to come, just as his *occasional* direct rewards in this life remind us of coming reward. But we should never assume we know God's reasons when he hasn't made them plain.

God can use suffering to display his work in you.

When Christ's disciples asked whose sin lay behind a man born blind, Jesus said, "Neither this man nor his parents sinned" (John 9:3). Jesus then redirected his disciples from thinking about the *cause* of the man's disability to considering the *purpose* for it. He said, "This happened *so that* the work of God might be displayed in his life." Eugene Peterson paraphrases Christ's words this way: "You're asking the wrong question. You're looking for someone to blame. There is no such cause-effect here. Look instead for what God can do" (MSG).

Nick Vujicic entered this world without arms or legs. Both his mom and his dad, an Australian pastor, felt devastated by their firstborn son's condition. "If God is a God of love," they said, "then why would he let something like this happen, and especially to committed Christians?" But they chose to trust God despite their questions.

Nick struggled at school where other students bullied and rejected him. "At that stage in my childhood," he said, "I could understand His love to a point. But…I still got hung up on the fact that if God really loved me, why did He make me like this? I wondered if I'd done something wrong and began to feel certain that this must be true."

Thoughts of suicide plagued Nick until one day the fifteen-year-old read the story in John 9 about the man born blind: "but that the works of God should be revealed in him" (NKJV). He surrendered his life to Christ. Now, at age twenty-six, he's earned a bachelor's degree and encourages others as a motivational speaker.

"Due to the emotional struggles I had experienced with bullying, self-esteem and loneliness," Nick says, "God began to instill a passion of sharing my story and experiences to help others cope with whatever challenge they might have in their lives. Turning my struggles into something that would glorify God and bless others, I realized my purpose! The Lord was going to use me to encourage and inspire others to live to their fullest potential and not let anything get in the way of accomplishing their hopes and dreams. God's purpose became clearer to me and now I'm fully convinced and understand that His glory is revealed as He uses me just the way I am. And even more wonderful, He can use me in ways others can't be used."[3]

Suffering in this life is part of our God-given destiny.
God's people suffer a great deal. "[Don't] be unsettled by these trials. You know quite well that we *were destined* for them," wrote Paul (1 Thessalonians 3:2–3). Voice of the Martyrs reports that the twentieth century produced more Christian martyrs than the previous nineteen centuries combined. Nearly two hundred thousand believers in Christ are executed per year, while millions more languish in prisons and enforced servitude.

"Those who suffer *according to God's will* should commit themselves to their faithful Creator and continue to do good," Peter said (1 Peter 4:19). This verse explicitly contradicts the concept that suffering cannot be God's will for us. God does not expect us to pray away all suffering. When we can find a solution, by all means, let's. When we can't, we should submit to the suffering and commit ourselves to God. Indeed, we should serve him all the more as we walk through new doors of opportunity that he opens through our suffering.

Scott Peck stated in *The Road Less Traveled,* "Life is difficult.… Once we truly know that life is difficult—once we truly understand and accept it—then life is no longer difficult."[4]

Well, it's *less* difficult, anyway!

As Michelangelo used his chisel to form *David* from a marble block, so God may use suffering to form us into the image of Christ.

God used Christ's suffering, not just his death, to accomplish a purpose: "Although he [Jesus] was a son, he learned obedience from what he suffered" (Hebrews 5:8).

In the context of suffering, God says we are "predestined to be conformed to the likeness of his Son" (Romans 8:29).

When Nanci and I saw *David* in Florence, it took our breath away. To produce his masterpiece, Michelangelo chose a stone that all other artists had rejected. Seeing that huge marble block's hidden potential, he chipped away everything that wasn't David. The master worked daily to transform it into something surpassingly beautiful.

Now, if marble had feelings, it wouldn't like the chiseling process. It might resent the sculptor.

While Michelangelo may not have called upon the stone to cooperate with him, God has called us to yield ourselves by submitting to his chisel. Because we fail to see the person God intends to form through our adversity, we too may resent the chiseling. The Master Artist chose us, the flawed and unusable, to be crafted into the image of Christ to fulfill our destiny in displaying Jesus to the watching universe.

We ask God to remove the chisel because it hurts, but it's a means of transformation: "And we, who with unveiled faces all reflect the Lord's glory, are being transformed into his likeness with ever-increasing glory" (2 Corinthians 3:18).

Joni Eareckson Tada writes, "Before my paralysis, my hands reached for a lot of wrong things, and my feet took me into some bad places. After my paralysis, tempting choices were scaled down considerably. My particular affliction is divinely hand-tailored expressly for me. Nobody has to suffer 'transverse spinal lesion at the fourth-fifth cervical' exactly as I did to be conformed to his image."[5]

God uses suffering to purge sin from our lives, strengthen our commitment to him, force us to depend on his grace, bind us together with other believers, produce discernment, foster sensitivity, discipline our minds, impart wisdom, stretch our hope, cause us to know Christ better, make us long for truth, lead us to repentance of sin, teach us to give thanks in times of sorrow, increase our faith, and strengthen our character. And once he accomplishes such great things, often we can see that our suffering has been worth it.

God doesn't simply want us to *feel* good. He wants us to *be* good. And very often, the road to *being* good involves not *feeling* good.

SUSTAINING US WHILE WE'RE REFINED

God can bear the full weight of our pain and give us strength and life when we feel only weakness and death.
Here's an amazing truth: "Cast all your anxiety on him because he cares for you" (1 Peter 5:7). God, the Creator of the universe and fountainhead of all marvels, *cares* for you? Think about that for a few million years.

The Lord does not call us merely to release our anxiety to him, but to willingly cast it upon him—and not some of it, but *all* of it. God wants us to trust him in both the big things and the little things. Worry is momentary atheism crying out for correction by trust in a good and sovereign God. Paul, whom we seldom think of as vulnerable, wrote, "For we were so utterly burdened beyond our strength that we despaired of life itself. Indeed, we felt that we had received the sentence of death. But that was to make us rely not on ourselves but on God who raises the dead" (2 Corinthians 1:8–9, ESV). God uses suffering to break us of self-dependence and bring us to rely on him.

Jesus said, "Apart from me you can do nothing" (John 15:5) After her eighteen-month-old son's death, Ann Stump said, "I learned what it was like not to be able to do something on my own. I couldn't get up in the morning without the Lord's help."[6]

Based on what God has given us in Christ, we can be sure he will give us all we need to endure evil and suffering.
The child whose father steps in front of him to protect him from a hail of bullets can trust him not to poison his food or push him off a cliff. He can trust his father to catch him as he lets go of the monkey bars. And yes, he can trust him even when his father chooses to let him face something dreadful that he could have kept from him.

"He who did not spare his own Son, but gave him up for us all—how will he not also, along with him, graciously give us all things?" (Romans 8:32). When God has given us the greatest gift, the one that cost him everything, shouldn't we trust him to give us the good gifts that cost him nothing?

Nothing in this world or outside it will ever separate us from God's love.
"For I am convinced that neither death nor life, neither angels nor demons, neither the present nor the future, nor any powers, neither height nor depth, nor

anything else in all creation, will be able to separate us from the love of God that is in Christ Jesus our Lord" (Romans 8:38–39). Paul, the one convinced of all this, endured repeated suffering and evil. I have suffered far less trauma than Paul, but my experiences and interviews with many sufferers have convinced me of the same truth: nothing can separate us from Christ's love.

It helps to personalize "God so loved the world." Christ didn't die for the world or the church in general, but for people in particular. Each individual believer's name is written in the book of life, and he will wipe away every tear from the eyes of each of us, one by one (see Revelation 21:4). In your moment of crisis, when you are suffering most, he cares about you in particular. The Shepherd goes after the one lamb who's most in need (see Luke 15:4).

In his novel *Perelandra,* C. S. Lewis has an eldil (angel) explain, "When He died in the Wounded World [Earth] He died not for men, but for each man. If each man had been the only man made, He would have done no less."[7]

God already has proven his eternal love.

May he give us eyes to see how he demonstrates that love every day in hundreds of ways, most of which we take for granted. In our suffering, God shows us his goodness, grace, and compassion.

Faith means believing that God is good and that even if we can't see it today, *one day* we will look back and see clearly his goodness and kindness. Countless believers have attested to this truth as they neared the end of their difficult lives (see Isaiah 30:18).

"The LORD is compassionate and gracious, slow to anger, abounding in love.... As a father has compassion on his children, so the LORD has compassion on those who fear him; for he knows how we are formed, he remembers that we are dust" (Psalm 103:8, 13–14).

Solomon summarizes God's dealings with David: "You have shown great kindness to David my father" (2 Chronicles 1:8). David agreed (see Psalm 18:50). Yet these assessments stand in stark contrast to the terrible circumstances described in the psalms that prompted David to cry out to God.

Sometimes God intervenes by removing our suffering. Often he comforts us in our suffering. Sometimes he holds our hands as he brings us home to the perfect world he's made for us.

When someone survives an accident or gets a negative biopsy report, we sigh in relief and say, "God is good." We're right to give heartfelt thanks. But God remains just as good if the person dies or the biopsy report brings bad news. *God is good even when we can't see it.*

My friend, writer Ethel Herr, had a double mastectomy, then discovered two months later that the cancer had spread. She said that a shocked friend, fumbling for words, asked her, "And how do you feel about God now?" Ethel felt a flood well up within her and said, "Oh, let me tell you how I feel about God!" She told our group of writers:

> As I sought to explain what has happened in my spirit, it all came clearer and clearer to me. God has been preparing me for this moment. He has undergirded me in ways I've never known before. He has made Himself increasingly real and precious to me. He has given to me JOY such as I've never known before—and I've no need to work at it, it just comes, even amidst the tears. He has taught me that no matter how good my genes are or how well I take care of my diet and myself, He will lead me on whatever journey He chooses and will never leave me for a moment of that journey. And He planned it all in such a way that step by step, He prepared me for the moment when the doctor dropped the last shoe.... God is good, no matter what the diagnosis or the prognosis, or the fearfulness of the uncertainty of having neither. The key to knowing God is good is simply knowing Him.[8]

One of Ethel's statements, I think, provides the solution to understanding the joy God has given her: "I've no need to work at it, it just comes, even amidst the tears." Over the years, this woman has invested much time studying God and his attributes—which led to worshiping him. Every day that she had meditated on God in Scripture, every book she read about God, every poem she wrote about him, every conversation in which she had praised God, quietly prepared her for facing her disease. Ethel knows God is good simply *because she knows God.*

"God has been preparing me for this moment," she said. It's healthy to ask ourselves what we're doing today to help God prepare us for such moments.

We can give thanks in everything precisely because we have God's promise that in everything he works for our good.

If we have a big view of God, then we can see him at work all around us. We might thank any number of people for a particular thing; but ultimately we should thank our God of providence. When I thank my wife for making dinner, I also thank God for my wife and for bringing me his goodness through her.

A friend told me that his grown daughter, sometime after her sister's murder, had great difficulty sleeping. She asked her dad to pray that God would let her sleep. He read to her a passage about giving thanks in everything (see Philippians 4:6). "I know this sounds crazy," he said, "but rather than praying that you'd be healed of insomnia, I think you need to thank God that you have to face this insomnia. If you don't mean it, tell him you don't, but that you're going to keep saying it anyway—and ask him to help you mean it."

He understood that God had a purpose for her insomnia that might not be fulfilled if the Lord simply took it away. A few weeks later she told him that the process of thanking God—which she found very difficult—made her admit her anger at God for what happened to her sister. When she did this, she said, she'd immediately started weeping. Then, she added, "Something inside me broke." While she wept, she fell asleep and for the first time in ages slept through the night. She hasn't suffered from insomnia since.

This woman finally embraced her suffering, seeing it as God's way of speaking to her, instead of just trying to wish it or pray it away. God used her pain to heal her both of her primary problem, anger, and her secondary problem, insomnia.

God sovereignly decrees and uses the suffering and death of his children.

As a child, Steve Saint thought of Timbuktu as a made-up name for "the ends of the earth." In 1986, while traveling in western Africa for Missionary Aviation Fellowship, he found himself stranded in the real Timbuktu.[9]

Steve decided to rent a truck to travel elsewhere, despite warnings that if it broke down, he wouldn't survive in the Sahara Desert. Men armed with scimitars and knives watched him suspiciously. After he failed to find a truck, Steve's thoughts ran to his father, Nate Saint, a former missionary in Ecuador. When Steve was only five, natives speared to death his dad and four other missionaries. Now, thirty years later, Steve found himself questioning his father's death. "I couldn't help but think the murders were capricious, an accident of bad timing."

Steve asked for directions to a church. Some children led him to a tiny mud-brick house with a poster on the wall showing wounded hands covering a cross. A dark-skinned man in flowing robes approached and introduced himself as Nouh Af Infa Yatara.

Steve asked Nouh, through a translator, how he came to faith in Christ. Nouh said he had stolen vegetables from a missionary's garden. The missionary gave him the vegetables and promised him an ink pen if he memorized some verses from the Bible. Nouh believed the verses he learned and came to Christ. Nouh's parents threw him out of the home and pulled him out of school. Nouh's mother even put a sorcerer's poison in Nouh's food at a family feast. Nouh ate the food but suffered no ill effects.

Steve asked Nouh, "Why is your faith so important to you that you're willing to give up everything, even your life?"

"I know God loves me and I'll live with him forever."

"Where did your courage come from?" Steve asked.

"The missionary gave me books about Christians who'd suffered for their faith. My favorite was about five young men who risked their lives to take God's good news to stone-age Indians in the jungles of South America. The book said they let themselves be speared to death, even though they had guns and could have killed their attackers!"

Stunned at these words, Steve said, "One of those men was my father."

"Your father?" Now Nouh felt stunned.

Steve assured Nouh of the truth of the story. And then Nouh assured Steve that God had used his father's death, many years later, to help a young Muslim-turned-Christian hold on to his faith. Steve realized that if God could plan the death of his own Son, he could also plan and use the death of Steve's dad, Nate Saint, to accomplish his sovereign purpose—including reaching one young Muslim for Christ and orchestrating this God-ordained meeting of two men at the ends of the earth.

Stories like this don't apply only to the deaths of missionary martyrs. Over time, God has brought countless people to Christ through the lives and deaths of ordinary housewives, common laborers, farmers, factory workers, business people, teachers, and schoolchildren.

We won't all, in this life, meet someone whose story will suddenly shed light on God's purpose in our loved one's suffering or death. But I think most of us will have that very experience one day, beyond the ends of this Earth, on that New Earth, where we, eyes wide, will hear countless jaw-dropping stories of God's sovereign grace.

Notes

1. John Hick, *Evil and the God of Love* (New York: Macmillan, 1966), 259.
2. C. S. Lewis, *A Grief Observed* (Whitstable, Kent, UK: Whitstable Litho, 1966), 36.
3. Nick Vujicic, "A Remarkable Story of God's Grace," Life Without Limbs, www .lifewithoutlimbs.org/about-nick-vujicic.php.

4. M. Scott Peck, *The Road Less Traveled* (New York: Simon & Schuster, 2002), 15.

5. Joni Eareckson Tada and Steven Estes, *When God Weeps* (Grand Rapids, MI: Zondervan, 1997), 117.

6. Ann Stump, www.epm.org/annstump.html.

7. C. S. Lewis, *Perelandra* (New York: Simon & Schuster, 1996), 186.

8. Personal letter from Ethel Herr, used by permission.

9. Steve Saint, "To the Ends of the Earth," www.itecusa.org/document_ends_of_ the_earth.html.

38

How God Uses Suffering
for Our Sanctification

DRAWS US TO GOD

Broken hearts more readily recognize their need for God's grace.

Action International works with street children in the Philippines. One of them is Wendy. Her father died and her mom's boyfriend abused her, so Wendy ran away. She soon found herself forced into servitude. She ran away again and met a Christian woman who took her into her family. She attended Bible studies and a camp for street kids, where she gave her life to Christ. She was mentored, began teaching a children's Bible class, and soon will graduate from Bible college.

Lino was a drug addict who slept on sidewalks. At an Action International camp for street kids, he chose to follow Christ. The local church trained him in the Scriptures, hired him as a janitor, and then sponsored Lino through a five-year pastoral course. Now he serves as a pastor, Bible teacher, and counselor.

Enrico suffered abuse as a houseboy. Later, as a drug addict, he joined a gang heavily involved in crime and witchcraft. One day he went out to recruit for the gang. Instead, a Christian recruited him to attend a street-kids camp. Eventually his heart softened and Enrico trusted Christ. His life changed dramatically. Lino and others trained him in the Scriptures, gave him work, and helped him graduate from high school. Enrico now works on a farm as a true follower of Jesus Christ.

Society had cast off Wendy, Lino, and Enrico as unloved and abused street kids, hopeless victims—and probable future perpetrators—of evil and suffering. Finding themselves at the bottom, their hearts opened to God's offer of rescue.

Had they grown up in whole families, with lots of money and security, they might never have met those Christians who modeled for them the love of Jesus.

Sometimes God delivers us from suffering, and other times he sustains us through suffering. Sometimes God calms the storm, and sometimes he calms the heart. Both are acts of grace, and both should prompt us to praise him.

God sometimes uses others' deaths to get our attention, humble us, and turn us back to him.

Armies and hospitals have chaplains, while political victory parties and Academy Award celebrations don't. Why not? Because hospitals and battlefields offer a clear view of death, while celebrations obscure it.

Death serves to draw our attention to what really matters—the state of our souls, and the God and people who will outlast this life. Death is a wake-up call, a reminder that our time here is fleeting and everyone's going to die.

"When I fed them, they were satisfied; when they were satisfied, they became proud; then they forgot me" (Hosea 13:6). We forget God to our own detriment. Suffering and death remind us of him in ways that pleasure and prosperity don't.

A young mother who had rebelled against God and her Christian upbringing wrote these words: "On January 5, 2009, there by my daughter's gravesite, I asked Jesus into my heart. I prayed with a pastor of a local church we had never really been a part of. I had thought about God a lot since that day Taylor left this earth. The moment came at the burial, where I thought, this is it! I need God right now! At that moment it all came to me, Taylor was sent here from God, to change my life, my husband's life and my entire family's life."[1]

Suffering should draw our attention to the ugliness of sin and its poisonous effects.

We cannot understand evil and suffering without understanding creation, the Fall, and redemption.

While we often don't grasp the purposes of a particular event or affliction, we understand that suffering exists because evil exists. God promised death would follow disobedience, and a world of death means a world of suffering. In Romans 6:23, we must understand the phrase "The wages of sin is death" to appreciate the one that follows: "But the gift of God is eternal life in Christ Jesus our Lord." To grasp redemption's meaning, we must see the devastation of the sin from which God redeems us.

Suffering, as sin's consequence, points us back to sin's ugliness. How horrible should we expect suffering to be? As horrible as sin. No less.

People's suffering from natural disasters, diseases, wars, and accidents demonstrates sin's horrors. If life in a fallen world didn't sometimes show us such dreadful consequences of sin and its curse, we might look at sin and wonder, "What's the big deal?" Without a sense of the misery it produces, we'd have no motive to turn from it.

Suffering should prompt us to see our sin as a greater horror than the suffering sin causes.

While sin does not directly cause all our suffering, *if we were not sinners, our world would not know suffering.* Therefore, regardless of its reasons, both our suffering and that of others should always cause us to *hate sin.*

Though God tells us the wages of sin is death, he graciously delays sin's payday, giving us time to repent and turn to him for eternal life. But that very delay can allow us to live under the illusion that we are not such great sinners or that sin will go unpunished. The pornography addict will tell himself nothing is wrong until he ends up losing his job, his wife, and his children. He cannot gain freedom until he faces the horrific consequences of his sin. To hate suffering is easy; to hate sin is not.

When natural disasters kill people, when cancer ravages a loved one, instead of getting mad at God, we should feel anger toward the sin that lies at the root of all suffering. For God's discipline to have its intended effect, our hatred of suffering must become a hatred of sin.

Martyn Lloyd-Jones wrote in 1939, as the Holocaust was in its early stages,

> God permits war in order that men may see through it, more clearly than
> they have ever done before, what sin really is. In times of peace we tend to
> think lightly of sin, and to hold optimistic views of human nature. War
> reveals man and the possibilities within man's nature. The First World War
> shattered that optimistic view of man which had held sway for so many
> years, and revealed something of the essential sinfulness of human
> nature.... It forces us to examine the very foundations of life. It makes us
> face the direct questions as to what it is in human nature that leads to such
> calamities.[2]

Evil alienates us from God, cutting us off from the Source of all goodness. Suffering serves as the hard, cold wake-up call that tells us how wretched we are without God. Though it does not *seem* a grace, suffering leads us to repentance and humility and trust in God.

Deepens Our Faith

Satan wishes to destroy our faith through suffering; God desires to refine it.

Suffering in a life spent pleasing God often looks indistinguishable from persecution. Paul juxtaposed sickness and sleepless nights with beatings and scourgings. He linked shipwreck and shivering to being stoned for the gospel (see 2 Corinthians 11:23–28).

The point is not the degree of evil intended against us, but our faithfulness in suffering. So regardless of why we suffer, God can use it to deepen our faith: "Rejoice that you participate in the sufferings of Christ, so that you may be overjoyed when his glory is revealed.... Those who suffer according to God's will should commit themselves to their faithful Creator and continue to do good" (1 Peter 4:13, 19).

David Guthrie, reflecting on the death of his disabled daughter, told me, "I spent my life waiting for the other shoe to drop. The shoe has dropped. I had thought I was invulnerable. Now I know better. I thought, 'Our child has died. How much worse can it get?' There's less to fear. God will be enough for us. Now we say it out of experience."

Modern writers cite the unprecedented horrors of the twentieth century as a reason to reject "superstitions" about God. Yes, modern weapons aided Hitler, and a modern train system took Jews to the death camps. Yet hunger, war, and natural disasters proliferated among ancients, with few defenses against them. The people commonly suffered wholesale slaughters, much shorter life spans, and acute vulnerability to disease. A cold virus could kill.

Still, the great majority of the ancients believed in God. Even most modern people don't resonate with the atheistic argument that suffering should keep them from God.

In 2005 the *Washington Post* conducted a major survey of Hurricane Katrina survivors who wound up as refugees in Houston. Asked about their faith in God, "Remarkably, 81 percent said the ordeal has strengthened their belief, while only 4 percent said it weakened it."[3]

Bertrand Russell claimed that no one could sit at the bedside of a dying child and still believe in God.[4] He was wrong—countless people, including ones I spoke with while researching this book, *have* sat at the bedside of their own dying children and *do* still believe in God. And while they don't believe the false promise that this life always goes well for believers, many have found their trust in God go deeper than ever.

Instead of blaming doctors, drunk drivers, and criminals for our suffering, we should look for what God can accomplish through it.

Fanny Crosby, blinded by an incompetent doctor at the age of six weeks, penned more than eight thousand hymns. She expressed delight that Jesus' face would be the first she would ever see. If she'd thought, "I'll never be able to see," she would have been profoundly sad. Instead, she could say with Job, "After my skin has been destroyed, yet in my flesh I will see God;... I, and not another" (Job 19:26–27).

Concerning her blindness, Fanny said, "It seemed intended by the blessed providence of God that I should be blind all my life, and I thank him for the dispensation.... If perfect earthly sight were offered me tomorrow I would not accept it.... I verily believe it was His intention that I should live my days in physical darkness, so as to be better prepared to sing His praises and incite others so to do."[5]

When you see God at work, you don't look to blame someone; you look to credit him.

Faithful believers who have endured intense suffering say, "Hang on to God and don't let go."

While it's not always easy to trust God in suffering, it's always possible.

On September 11, 2001, Lisa Beamer's husband, Todd, died on United Airlines Flight 93. Lisa says, "I can't see all the reasons [God] might have allowed this when I know he could have stopped it.... I don't like how his plan looks from my perspective right now, but knowing that he loves me and can see the world from start to finish helps me say, 'It's OK.'"[6]

John Greenleaf Whittier, in his poem "The Eternal Goodness," wrote of life's great sufferings. He said,

> Yet, in the maddening maze of things,
> And tossed by storm and flood,
> To one fixed trust my spirit clings;
> I know that God is good![7]

Suffering produces in us qualities that otherwise would never develop.

As many accident victims know, rehabilitation can be long and excruciating. People commonly get angry at their physical therapist, though she's acting in their best interests. Sometimes we may resent God for imposing unwanted difficulties on us. If we see through the lens of eternity, however, that resentment changes to thanksgiving for making us better and ultimately happier people, even if it costs us temporary pain and extreme inconvenience.

A woman whose husband's addictions ravaged their marriage wrote to me,

> I spent a number of years lukewarm in my faith. It was my husband's alco-
> holism that caused me to grab the foot of the cross and hold on tight until
> I could feel slivers in the palms of my hands. I asked God, "Why me?"
> And the answer I heard was, "Why not you?" Why should I expect to be
> exempt from pain?
>
> There was so much heartbreak in my marriage, but I came to a place
> of being able to thank God for those years because He taught me so much
> through the pain. There are still moments when I wish I could change the
> past, but I always return to thanksgiving for His faithfulness. I can say
> with complete confidence that nothing enters my life that isn't first filtered
> through the loving hands of my Father, caused or allowed for the purpose
> of refining me so that I become more like His Son.

George MacDonald wrote that Christ "suffered unto the death, not that men might not suffer, but that their suffering might be like his." [8]

TEACHES US TO TRUST

Seeing positive outcomes of *some* suffering should lead us to trust that God can bring good from all suffering.

Consider three people who through suffering became extraordinary:

Doctors once thought that Joseph Merrick, "The Elephant Man," had ele-phantiasis, though now they believe he suffered from Proteus syndrome, which causes abnormal growth of bones, skin, and other systems. Joseph was born in England in 1862 and appeared normal until age three. By age eleven, his deformities had grown severe; at that time his mother died, and later his new stepmother kicked him out.

He became a door-to-door salesman but suffered constant harassment. His condition worsened: protruding, cauliflower-like growths appeared on his head and body, and his right hand and forearm became useless. No longer able to do physical work, he took a job as a curiosity attraction. After a promoter robbed and abandoned him, he returned to London and visited Dr. Treves at the London Hospital, where he received permanent living quarters. Despite his adversities, Joseph Merrick remained cheerful and gentle, and never grew bitter. He found comfort in writing, including poetry. He died at age twenty-seven.

Merrick often ended his letters of thanks with a poem by hymn-writing theologian Isaac Watts: "'Tis true my form is something odd; / But blaming me, is blaming God.... / I would be measured by the soul; / The mind is the standard of the man."

Helen Keller was born in Alabama in 1880. A year later, illness took her vision and hearing. At age seven, her parents hired Anne Sullivan, whose innovative tutoring transformed Helen's life. Helen learned to speak at ten, and though listeners had trouble understanding her, she never gave up. She attended college and wrote several books, including *The Story of My Life.* She devoted herself to research, speaking, and raising money for organizations such as the American Foundation for the Blind. Helen traveled the world on behalf of the blind and visited thirty-five countries. At age seventy-five, she embarked on a five-month-long, forty-thousand-mile tour through Asia, bringing encouragement to millions.

Christy Brown was born in Dublin in 1932. His cerebral palsy caused everyone to consider him mentally handicapped until he used his left foot to grab a piece of chalk from his sister. His mother taught him to read and write. Well into adolescence, he could not speak intelligibly. He wrote an autobiography titled *My Left Foot* as well as several other novels and poetry collections. He typed using only his left foot. People loved Christy Brown for his warm and cheerful personality.

These stories don't prove that God always brings good out of evil in this life. But they do prove that he *sometimes* does. Shouldn't that give everyone hope?

A new depth of character emerges from trust developed in suffering.

A Viennese music professor said about one of his students, "She is a magnificent singer, and yet there is something missing. Life has been too kind to her. But if one day it happened that someone broke her heart, she would be the finest singer in Europe!"[9]

A woman wrote me,

When our son was diagnosed with Fragile X Syndrome, I thought (1) Did I do something to deserve this? (it's all about me, after all) and; (2) Why would a good God allow this? My husband and I didn't think we needed the kind of character-adjustment such a challenge brings.

Our son is profoundly mentally retarded—but with a normal life expectancy. So who will care for him when we no longer can?

Our son reminds me this life isn't about me. Following Christ is about serving God and others. Not about what this world should bring us. God has given me an opportunity to serve my son every day.

I've felt God's love when my husband's patience outlasts mine. I've seen it in my son's smile, and in a growing understanding of loving unconditionally.

If I'd been given the choice about whether or not to have Fragile X in my life, I would have chosen my son's health. But the truth is Fragile X has taught me more than any other challenges I've had in my life.

Suffering brings us into deeper intimacy with God.

My wife, Nanci, suffered through what she calls her "year of fear and free-floating anxiety that made me fall in love with God." Nanci knew God from childhood and trusted him all through my lawsuits, arrests, and job loss, then through her mother's death and other losses (and threatened ones). But that inexplicable year of her life, unrelated to any outside traumatic event, changed her. She coped by telling God, morning and night, how much she loved him.

She has continued her habit of praise and intimacy with God that developed when daily fear and dread fell upon her. The crushing emotions of that time have departed; the sense of intimacy with her Savior remains. To this day Nanci rejoices in God's love for her and her love for him in ways she never would have known without that year she otherwise could describe as hellish.

It was in the midst of extreme suffering that Job saw a remarkable vision of his Redeemer and expressed his certainty that after his death, in a redeemed body, he would see God with his own eyes (see Job 19:25–27). He cried, "How my heart yearns within me!"

In the midst of our suffering too, God makes some of his most profound and precious self-revelations. Perhaps he does so because only then are we ready to hear them.

Josef Tson writes, "During the time I was expecting to be crushed by the Romanian secret police interrogators, God became more real to me than ever before or after in my life. It is difficult to put into words the experience I had with God at that time. It was like a rapture into a sweet and total communion with the Beloved. God's test for me then became the pathway to a special knowledge of the reality of God."

Josef continues, "God achieves great things in the world through the one who accepts His way of suffering and self-sacrifice. In the end, however, it turns out that the greatest things are achieved in the sufferer himself. The one who sacrificially accepts to be a blessing for others discovers that, in the final analysis, he is the one who has harvested the greatest blessings."[10] Suffering can help us know God and prepare us to trade a shallow life not worth keeping for a deeper life we'll never lose.

Paul said, "I consider everything a loss compared to the surpassing greatness of knowing Christ Jesus my Lord, for whose sake I have lost all things. I consider them rubbish, that I may gain Christ" (Philippians 3:8). David Livingstone, the physician, spent most of his life in Africa, dying in 1873 after suffering greatly. His wife died; a lion bit him and maimed his hand; he contracted fevers and dysentery; the house he built burned down.

Someone once made the obvious remark to Livingstone that the missionary had sacrificed much for the gospel. Livingstone responded, "Sacrifice? The only sacrifice is to live outside the will of God."[11]

When someone else asked what helped him go on despite such hardship, Livingstone replied that, even on his worst days, he heard the words of Christ ringing in his ears: "Lo, I am with you always, even unto the end of the world" (Matthew 28:20, KJV). If we would turn off the television and read stories like these, we'd shut out a lot of nonsense and gain godly perspective in exchange. We would be richer people to learn about those who have suffered, often joyfully, for the gospel.

In Heaven, God will forever destroy the barriers of sin between redeemed human beings and himself. We will look into his eyes and see what we've always longed to see: the person who made us for his own good pleasure. In seeing God, we will clearly see everything else for the first time.

"Without Christ not one step," David Livingstone declared, "with Him anywhere."

Notes

1. Author's private correspondence.
2. Martyn Lloyd-Jones, *Why Does God Allow Suffering?* (Wheaton, IL: Crossway Books, 1994), 98–99.
3. Richard Morin and Lisa Rein, "Some of the Uprooted Won't Go Home Again," *Washington Post,* September 16, 2005, A01.
4. J. P. Moreland and Tim Muehlhoff, *The God Conversation* (Downers Grove, IL: InterVarsity, 2007), 35.

5. Fanny Crosby, *Fanny Crosby's Life-Story* (New York: Every Where, 1903), 13–14.

6. Lisa Beamer, "Finding Hope Beyond the Ruins: An Interview with Lisa Beamer," *Modern Reformation* 11, no. 5 (September–October 2002): 25.

7. John Greenleaf Whittier, "The Eternal Goodness," www.bartleby.com/42/792 .html.

8. George MacDonald, *Unspoken Sermons* (NuVision Publications, 2009), 21.

9. James S. Stewart, "Wearing the Thorns as a Crown," in *Classic Sermons on Suffering,* comp. Warren W. Wiersbe (Grand Rapids, MI: Kregel, 1984), 92.

10. Josef Ton, *Suffering, Martyrdom, and Rewards in Heaven* (Lanham, MD: University Press of America, 1997), 429.

11. Ajith Fernando, *A Call to Joy and Pain* (Wheaton, IL: Crossway Books, 2007), 77–78.

39

How God Uses Suffering to Build Our Character

Gratitude and Humility

It seems counterintuitive to give thanks in suffering, but God commands it and countless people have benefited from it.

Getting in touch every day with God's grace, learning to thank him for the small things, serves us well when we lose big things. It deepens our reservoir and gives us eyes to see God's faithfulness and blessings at a time when we most need clear vision.

Elisabeth Elliot, one of my heroes, writes, "On one of those terrible days during my husband's cancer, when he could hardly bear the pain or the thought of yet another treatment, and I could hardly bear to bear it with him, we remarked on how wonderful it would be to have just a single ordinary day."[1]

How many of us fail to express gratitude for those ordinary days, wishing instead for something better? If you've had a single ordinary day recently, why not thank God for it? Don't wait for an extraordinary day when you feel wonderful and everything goes your way. That day may not come. And if it does, God's hand will be no more in it than in all your other days.

Now that Bart Ehrman disbelieves in God, he says, tragically, "The problem is this: I have such a fantastic life that I feel an overwhelming sense of gratitude for it; I am fortunate beyond words. But I don't have anyone to express my gratitude to. This is a void deep inside me, a void of wanting someone to thank, and I don't see any plausible way of filling it."[2]

In contrast, Puritan pastor Richard Baxter wrote, "Resolve to spend most of your time in thanksgiving and praising God. If you cannot do it with the joy that you should, yet do it as you can.... Doing it as you can is the way to be able to do it better. Thanksgiving stirreth up thankfulness in the heart."[3]

Baxter is right—expressing gratitude makes a grateful heart. Children who learn to say thanks become more thankful. Gratitude is a wonderful perspective-shaping habit.

Cultivating thankfulness today will allow us to cling to God's goodness and mercy in our darkest hours. Those hours lie ahead of us—but beyond them stretch unending millennia of inexpressible joy that we will appreciate more deeply because of these fleeting days of darkness.

God uses suffering to make us thankful.

Psalm 107 begins, "Give thanks to the LORD, for he is good; his love endures forever. Let the redeemed of the LORD say this." The psalmist details the sufferings of God's people, wandering in desert wastelands, without homes, hungry, and thirsty. "Then they cried out to the LORD in their trouble, and he delivered them from their distress" (verse 6). For their deliverance he says, "Let them give thanks to the LORD for his unfailing love and his wonderful deeds for men, for he satisfies the thirsty and fills the hungry with good things" (verses 8–9).

Gratitude never comes from avoiding difficulty, but from finding yourself sustained through it. The degree of joy rises to the degree of gratitude, and the level of gratitude corresponds to the level of suffering. God's sustaining providence always brings relief, even when life grows especially difficult.

During the Civil War, in a time of great national suffering, Abraham Lincoln called upon the nation to come to God in thanksgiving. He wrote,

> The year that is drawing toward its close has been filled with the blessings of fruitful fields and healthful skies. To these bounties, which are so constantly enjoyed that we are prone to forget the source from which they come, others have been added which are of so extraordinary a nature that they cannot fail to penetrate and soften even the heart which is habitually insensible to the ever-watchful providence of Almighty God.
>
> In the midst of a civil war of unequaled magnitude and severity... peace has been preserved with all nations, order has been maintained, the laws have been respected and obeyed, and harmony has prevailed everywhere, except in the theater of military conflict.[4]

Lincoln pointed out that farming, textiles, shipping, lumber, and other aspects of the economy were flourishing, and iron, coal, and precious metals "have yielded even more abundantly than heretofore." He encouraged people to thank God that, despite the casualties, the population increased due to childbirth. He said to rejoice in the nation's strength and the promise of increased freedom. "No human counsel hath devised nor hath any mortal hand worked out these great things. They are the gracious gifts of the Most High God, who, while dealing with us in anger for our sins, hath nevertheless remembered mercy."

Hence, Lincoln continued, "It has seemed to me fit and proper that they should be solemnly, reverently, and gratefully acknowledged, as with one heart and one voice, by the whole American people." So he called upon the nation "to set apart and observe the last Thursday of November next as a day of thanksgiving and praise to our beneficent Father who dwelleth in the heavens."

How remarkable that the annual celebration of Thanksgiving began in the middle of what was arguably the most terrible period in all of the nation's history! Even in those darkest days, Lincoln could point to many reasons to thank God for his goodness and grace.

Once in God's presence, we'll find it staggering how little gratitude we in the Shadowlands expressed for the vastness of God's goodness and grace.

Though a providential clerical error finally won Corrie ten Boom's release, her father, sister, brother, and nephew all died in concentration camps. "I knew again," she said, "that in darkness God's truth shines most clear."

Corrie's sister, Betsie, in light of the command "Give thanks in all circumstances" (1 Thessalonians 5:18), insisted they should thank God even for the fleas and lice in their barracks. Corrie resisted until she realized that the fleas and lice made it possible for her to open the Bible and teach it unhindered to other prisoners. Guards could have confiscated her forbidden Bible, but they refused to enter because of the vermin.[5]

"Give thanks to the LORD, call on his name; make known among the nations what he has done" (Psalm 105:1).

Right now we may understand God's magnificence in the same way a child understands the sky is big. But the astronomer knows the bigness of the sky far beyond the child's wildest imagination. In fact, he knows it far exceeds his own ability to grasp.

Suffering cultivates humility.

Happy are the humble! Humility begins with recognition of our own evil. When speaking of the human condition, we generalize easily: "All people are sinners."

415

We even admit, "I am a sinner." Yet we excel as exception-finders: "What I did just *looked* bad; I had a good reason for doing it. Let me explain…"

The question is, will we trade our rationalizations for his scars—wounds that should have been inflicted upon you and me?

Charles Spurgeon wrote, "I venture to say that the greatest earthly blessing that God can give to any of us is health, with the possible exception of sickness.… If some men that I know of could only be favoured with a month of rheumatism, it would, by God's grace, mellow them marvelously."

Though he sought to avoid suffering, Spurgeon said, "I am afraid that all the grace that I have got of my comfortable and easy times and happy hours, might almost lie on a penny. But the good that I have received from my sorrows, and pains, and griefs, is altogether incalculable.… Affliction is the best bit of furniture in my house. It is the best book in a minister's library."

You may think, *I refuse to accept that suffering can prove worthwhile,* but your rejection of God's goodness will not make you better or happier; it will only bring resentment and greater pain. Accept health as God's blessing and its absence as God's severe mercy. Samuel Rutherford wrote these profound words in the seventeenth century:

> If God had told me some time ago that he was about to make me
> as happy as I could be in this world, and then had told me that he
> should begin by crippling me in arm or limb, and removing me from
> all my usual sources of enjoyment, I should have thought it a very
> strange mode of accomplishing his purpose. And yet, how is his wis-
> dom manifest even in this! For if you should see a man shut up in a
> closed room, idolizing a set of lamps and rejoicing in their light, and
> you wished to make him truly happy, you would begin by blowing
> out all his lamps; and then throw open the shutters to let in the light
> of heaven.[6]

The prodigal son left in pride and returned in humility. After he lost every-thing, he decided to go back and say to his father, "I am no longer worthy to be called your son; make me like one of your hired men" (Luke 15:19). His father ran to him and threw his arms around him. That's how God responds to humility.

"God opposes the proud but gives grace to the humble" (1 Peter 5:5).

Which do we want, God's opposition or his grace?

GODLINESS

Suffering can get our attention and lead us to repentance and transformation.

C. S. Lewis said, "God whispers to us in our pleasures, speaks in our conscience, but shouts in our pains: it is His megaphone to rouse a deaf world."[7]

Jim Harrell, reflecting on how his slow death from ALS was helping him to discover real life, wrote me, "Suffering is the icy cold splash that wakes us up from the complacency of living this life. We truly don't see God and his purpose and strength without suffering, because we just become too comfortable."

Paul wrote, "I see that my letter hurt you, but only for a little while—yet now I am happy, not because you were made sorry, but because your sorrow led you to repentance. For you became sorrowful as God intended and so were not harmed" (2 Corinthians 7:8–9). God intended to help these erring believers by drawing them back to him *through their pain.*

Jesus said, "It is not the healthy who need a doctor, but the sick. I have not come to call the righteous, but sinners to repentance" (Luke 5:31). We need a cure, and that may require nasty-tasting medicine, painful surgery, and rigorous physical therapy.

Richard Baxter wrote, "Suffering so unbolts the door of the heart, that the Word hath easier entrance."[8] God uses suffering to bring us to the end of ourselves and back to Christ. And that is worth any cost.

Suffering exposes idols in our lives.

Suffering uncovers our trust in God-substitutes and declares our need to transfer our trust to the only One who can bear its weight. God laments, "My people have committed two sins: They have forsaken me, the spring of living water, and have dug their own cisterns, broken cisterns that cannot hold water" (Jeremiah 2:13).

We may imagine God as our genie who comes to do our bidding. Suffering wakes us up to the fact that we serve him, not he us.

"The name of the LORD is a strong tower; the righteous run to it and are safe. The wealth of the rich is their fortified city; they imagine it an unscalable wall" (Proverbs 18:10–11). God uses any means necessary to tear down whatever we hide behind. Your job, reputation, athletic or artistic or musical accomplishments, house, prize roses, best-in-show spaniel, or material possessions may be your fortified city or your imaginary, unscalable wall. But anything less than God himself will come up short. By his grace you can discover this now, instead of after you die when it's too late to turn to him.

Paul wrote, "Watch your life and doctrine closely" (1 Timothy 4:16). To have solid footing for our lives, we need sound doctrine. We should be grateful when God uses suffering, including material losses, to topple idols and dismantle false beliefs (including prosperity theology).

Suffering reminds us of our inability to control life.

Joan Didion discovered after her husband's death, "I had myself for most of my life shared the same core belief in my ability to control events."[9]

We must relinquish our belief that we can prevent all bad things from happening. In a crisis we should lose our trust in the world and in ourselves, and cultivate our trust in God.

A childless Christian couple was unable to conceive or adopt. The woman loves children. She told me, "When I was young I used to dream about having children and what they would look like and what we would do as a family." She says God took away those dreams but replaced them by becoming her delight.

Diseases, accidents, and natural disasters remind us of our extreme vulnerability; life is out of our control.

God reminds us, "The earth is the LORD's, and everything in it, the world, and all who live in it" (Psalm 24:1). What we think belongs to us really doesn't: "'The silver is mine and the gold is mine,' declares the LORD Almighty" (Haggai 2:8). We don't even belong to ourselves: "You are not your own; you were bought at a price" (1 Corinthians 6:19–20).

We should repeatedly tell our Lord, "This house is yours. The money, this body, and these children belong to you. You own the title deed, you own the rights, you have the power of life and death."

It becomes much easier to trust God when we understand that what he takes away belonged to him in the first place (see Job 1:21).

Suffering draws independent people to faith and teaches them dependence on Christ.

We come into this world needy, and we leave it the same way. Without suffering we would forget our neediness. If suffering seems too high a price for faith, it's because we underestimate faith's value.

In the West, with our conspicuous prosperity and ease, Christianity's popularity continues to shrink. In Africa, Asia, and South America, with much greater adversity and suffering, it continues to grow. Josef Tson, nearly martyred in Ceauşescu's Romania, told me that 95 percent of Christians pass the test of adversity, while 95 percent fail the test of prosperity.

J. B. Phillips translates James 1:2–4, "When all kinds of trials and temptations crowd into your lives, my brothers, don't resent them as intruders, but welcome them as friends! Realise that they come to test your faith and to produce in you the quality of endurance. But let the process go on until that endurance is fully developed, and you will find you have become men of mature character, men of integrity with no weak spots."

How can we possibly obey this command to welcome difficulties instead of resenting them? By trusting that God tells the truth when he says these make us better people, increase our endurance, expand our ministry, and prepare us for eternal joy. If learning to trust God is good for us and God loves us enough to act for our good, why are we surprised when difficulties come?

My father, a Great Depression survivor, was a physically powerful and fiercely independent man. As he got older his strength faded. This opened his life to help from others, first from me, later from God. I took him shopping and helped him in ways he'd never have accepted before. Age, weakness, and incapacity humbled this proud man—and his eternity will be dramatically better because of it.

C. S. Lewis said in *The Problem of Pain,* "The human spirit will not even begin to try to surrender self-will as long as all seems to be well with it."[10] Our self-will deceives us; in loss, tragedy, and suffering we may finally come to terms with our need for help.

Why do God's children undergo pressures, suffering, and deadly peril? Paul answers clearly: "that we might not rely on ourselves but on God" (2 Corinthians 1:11).

Suffering shows us who we are so we can see what we need to become.

Lepers shipped to Molokai were cast from their boats just offshore, since the men bringing them to the island feared getting any closer. Father Damien came to Molokai to lead a ministry to help these lepers. Damien eventually contracted leprosy himself, as did other Christians serving with him. Many lepers, seeing the sacrifice of their caregivers, came to faith in Christ.

Robert Louis Stevenson visited the island and saw the work. At first, the suffering shook his faith. Yet in time, as he mingled among the lepers—despite warnings not to do so—his faith grew. Before he left, he wrote a poem in the hospital guest book to the Christian sisters who gave their lives to care for the lepers:

To see the infinite pit of this place,
The mangled limb, the devastated face,
The innocent sufferer smiling at the rod—
A fool were tempted to deny his God.
He sees, he shrinks. But if he gaze again,
Lo, beauty springing from the breast of pain!
He marks the sisters on the mournful shores;
And even a fool is silent, and adores.[11]

Suffering can prepare us for eternity.

Jim Harrell said, "I've seen more accomplished in the time I've had ALS than in the first fifty years of my life. This illness is a blessing because God is really working on my soul. I'm going into eternity with my soul in a lot better shape than if I hadn't gotten ALS."[12]

Does this glorify ALS or imply that a disease is the only way God can work in our lives? Of course not. Jim simply recognized God's work through his disease.

What if the highest good in life is to draw close to Jesus? And what if suffering will help us achieve that good?

Puritan Thomas Manton said, "While all things are quiet and comfortable, we live by sense rather than faith. But the worth of a soldier is never known in times of peace."[13]

Rather than taking us out of the game, suffering can put us into it. If we grasp this, we can see our suffering as the training required to win not an Olympic medal, but an eternal reward. As the training gets more demanding, we must keep our eyes on the prize (see 1 Corinthians 9:24–27).

STRENGTH

Faithful endurance builds Christlikeness.

David and Nancy Guthrie told me, "It troubles us that the church's one response to suffering is to pray that it will be taken away. Nobody's first prayer is 'Use this to help us become Christlike.'"

Paul, in contrast, wrote, "I want to know Christ and the power of his resurrection and the fellowship of sharing in his sufferings, *becoming like him in his death,* and so, somehow, to attain to the resurrection from the dead" (Philippians 3:10–11). God uses suffering as an instrument to make us better.

In missions work, suffering sometimes results in a short life culminating in martyrdom, sometimes in a long life of daily dying to self and living for Christ.

January 2006 marked the fiftieth anniversary of the martyrdom of the five missionaries in Ecuador. In our church services I interviewed Steve Saint, son of martyr Nate Saint; Steve McCully, son of martyr Ed McCully; and Mincaye, one of the tribal warriors who killed the missionaries and later came to faith in Christ. Afterward we joined some of Jim Elliot's family for dinner at Jim's childhood home.

There we met Jim's older brother, Bert, and his wife, Colleen. In 1949, years before Jim went to Ecuador, they became missionaries to Peru. When we discussed their ministry, Bert smiled and said, "I can't wait to get back from furlough." Now in their eighties, they're in their sixtieth year as missionaries, joyfully reaching people for Christ. Until that weekend I didn't know anything about them. Bert and Colleen Elliot may enter eternity under the radar of the church at large, but not under God's.

Bert said something to me that day I'll never forget: "Jim and I both served Christ, but differently. Jim was a great meteor, streaking through the sky."

Bert didn't go on to describe himself, but I will. Unlike his brother Jim, Bert is a faint star that rises night after night, faithfully crossing the same path in the sky, to God's glory. I believe Jim Elliot's reward is considerable, but it wouldn't surprise me to discover that Bert and Colleen's will be greater still.

"Those who are wise will shine like the brightness of the heavens, and those who lead many to righteousness, like the stars for ever and ever" (Daniel 12:3).

When our lives here end, what will we wish we had done less of? And what will we wish we had done more of in order to honor God and build our characters? Why not spend the rest of our lives closing the gap between what we've done for Christ and what we'll wish we had done?

The evils and suffering we face are steep hills that increase our spiritual lung capacity; resistance builds our endurance.

In our side yard a tree has survived ice storms, heavy snows, and howling winds. Several times in the thirty years we've lived here, I thought it would fall. Now I expect it to long outlast me. I've taken pictures of my preschool daughters in that tree, and now of their children, my grandsons. It has lost many thick limbs, but others have grown, and harsh circumstances have made it stronger. In contrast, many protected and untested trees have long since fallen.

This tree has another secret. It lies at the lower part of our property, where the water sinks deep into the soil. This tree has all the nourishment it needs. The

Bible says of the righteous man, "He is like a tree planted by streams of water, which yields its fruit in season and whose leaf does not wither. Whatever he does prospers" (Psalm 1:3).

Every athletic champion will tell you that excellence comes out of disciplined training—and all training centers on resistance. Without obstacles, we cannot build strength, whether in the physical or spiritual realms. Whatever costs nothing is worthless, but whatever is worthwhile costs a great deal.

The apostle wrote, "I, John, your brother and companion in the suffering and kingdom and patient endurance that are ours in Jesus, was on the island of Patmos because of the word of God and the testimony of Jesus" (Revelation 1:9). He considered three things inseparable: suffering, kingdom, and patient endurance in Christ. No suffering, no kingdom. No suffering, no endurance.

Let's be honest: virtually everyone who has suffered little in life is shallow, unmotivated, self-absorbed, and lacking in character. You know it and so do I. And yet we do everything we can to avoid challenges, both to our children and to ourselves. If we succeed in our avoidance, we'll develop in ourselves and our children the sort of character we least admire.

God's parenting method doesn't shield us from adversity and the character it builds. We would do well to learn from him.

God uses disappointments and suffering to train us to share his holiness and righteousness.

Not all discipline is designed to correct sin. Its purpose may be to cultivate righteousness. An athlete doesn't train just to fix a problem; he trains *to improve his condition.*

> Endure hardship as discipline; God is treating you as sons. For what son is not disciplined by his father? If you are not disciplined (and everyone undergoes discipline), then you are illegitimate children and not true sons. Moreover, we have all had human fathers who disciplined us and we respected them for it. How much more should we submit to the Father of our spirits and live! Our fathers disciplined us for a little while as they thought best; but God disciplines us for our good, that we may share in his holiness. *No discipline seems pleasant at the time, but painful.* Later on, however, it produces a harvest of righteousness and peace for those who have been trained by it." (Hebrews 12:7–11)

God gives us a clear reason for disciplining us: "that we may share in his holiness." This discipline helps us to turn from sin. Knowing that God is working to "later on" make us more Christlike can help us to endure the pain.

The farmer works long, hard hours each day, anticipating the eventual harvest. This coming harvest motivates him and brings him joy. Looking at our suffering is like looking at row after row of crops that need weeding and watering. It seems like endless work. Yet God calls upon us to look beyond the day's and season's work to the coming harvest.

Scripture promises, "God disciplines us *for our good.*" He doesn't miscalculate, doesn't make mistakes, and will never look back at what he brings and allows in our lives and say, "If I had it to do over again, I wouldn't do *that.*"

As athletes look to the crown and farmers to the harvest, so we who suffer should look to our eternal rewards from God's good hand.

Suffering can make us less fearful.

In my novel *Safely Home,* set in China, Li Quan voices what some Chinese Christians actually say: *True gold does not fear the fire.*

Job says of God, "He knows the way that I take; when he has tried me, I shall come out as gold" (Job 23:10, ESV). Fire strengthens those it refines. They do not seek the fire, but neither do they shrink from it.

A victim of a great evil told me, "I discovered in myself the spirit of entitlement. I learned that God was not going to go down my checklist of happiness and fulfill it. I learned what it meant to surrender to His will. Before, I wanted certain gifts from Him. Now I want Him."

Near the end of our conversation she said something just as powerful: "I have thought, if this was going to happen to someone, it was better for it to happen to me, with my faith in God, than to happen to a twelve-year-old or an elderly person, or to anyone without Christ." She continued, "I have come through this with an absolute confidence in God. I know He will walk with me through the rest of my life. I have been through the valley of the shadow of death, and He was with me. Because He's been faithful in all I've gone through, I have less to be afraid of now."

Notes

1. Elisabeth Elliot, *A Path Through Suffering* (Ann Arbor, MI: Servant Publications, 1990), 154–55.
2. Bart D. Ehrman, *God's Problem* (New York: HarperCollins, 2008), 128.

3. Richard Baxter, "The Cure of Melancholy and Overmuch Sorrow, by Faith," Puritan Sermons, www.puritansermons.com/baxter/baxter25.htm.

4. Abraham Lincoln's Thanksgiving Proclamation, signed October 3, 1863 in Washington, D.C.

5. Corrie ten Boom, *The Hiding Place* (Grand Rapids, MI: Chosen Books, 2006), 210, 220.

6. Samuel Rutherford, *Letters of Samuel Rutherford,* quoted in Joni Eareckson Tada and Steven Estes, *A Step Further* (Grand Rapids, MI: Zondervan, 1990), 179.

7. C. S. Lewis, *The Problem of Pain* (New York: Macmillan, 1962), 93.

8. Richard Baxter, *The Saints' Everlasting Rest,* ed. John Thomas Wilkinson (Grand Rapids, MI: Baker Book House, 1978), 246.

9. Joan Didion, *The Year of Magical Thinking* (New York: Knopf, 2005), 98.

10. Lewis, *The Problem of Pain,* 92.

11. John Tayman, The Colony (New York: Simon & Schuster, 2007), 367.

12. Jim Harrell, interview video, www.epm.org/artman2/publish/Christian_living_ suffering/Perspectives_in_Suffering_part_<1 or 2>.shtml.

13. Thomas Manton, quoted in John MacArthur, *The Power of Suffering* (Colorado Springs, CO: David C. Cook, 1995), 39.

40

Suffering Can Give Birth to Joy, Compassion, and Hope

Joy

People who choose resentment, distrust, and bitterness against God adopt a cause doomed to fail.

If Satan can't dethrone God, we certainly can't. What does our rebellion accomplish? Whose interests does it serve?

Christ will one day say to his children, "Enter into the joy of your master" (Matthew 25:21, ESV). Joy is in God alone. We can find no joy outside of him, for all secondary joys flow from the primary joy of his presence.

God permits rebellion while guaranteeing its failure. And what will rebellion buy in the meantime? A loss of joy—and for those who do not surrender to him, a *permanent* loss of joy in the world to come.

We harm no one through bitterness as much as we harm ourselves. Someone told me, "Bitterness is like drinking poison and waiting for the other person to die." In the face of evil and suffering, responding to God or others with bitterness, distrust, and accusations bears no good fruit. Responding in honest brokenness and turning to God in submission, faith, and trust yields untold riches of peace and comfort.

Suffering causes us to worship and brings inexplicable joy.
Christian slaves in nineteenth-century America sometimes were forbidden to sing. So when they went to the river for their chores, they would hang wet blankets around themselves, then fill water pots and sing into them to absorb the sound.

They couldn't hold inside their songs of praise. The slave songs reflected deep sorrow and deep joy at the same time.

One day you could face evil or suffering to such a degree that you may wonder if the God you love has turned his back on you. Your trial may last a day, a week, a year, a decade, or more. But I doubt your life will look worse than that of those Christian slaves, stripped of liberty and dignity, with families routinely torn apart, yet who couldn't refrain from singing praises to God.

We would do well to spend our days preparing to worship God in hard times—those who have long lived in those times testify of a joy in their midst, as surely as slaves found joy in times of great adversity.

Linda, after losing her father, her health, and her job, spoke of her suffering this way: "Worshiping God is a First Thing.... My health, my work, my family are all second things and should take second place. But how to put God first? How to give him his rightful place in my heart? I believe that comes through the dark nights of suffering. It is a lesson I am slowly learning."

Scripture commands us to rejoice in suffering because of the perseverance it produces in us.

Like James (in 1:2–3), Paul said, "We also rejoice in our sufferings, because we know that suffering produces perseverance" (Romans 5:3). Paul and James both claim we should rejoice in suffering because of what it produces: *perseverance.*

Adversity itself doesn't cause our joy. Rather, our joy comes in the expectation of adversity's by-product, the development of godly character. God doesn't ask us to cheer because we lose our job, or a loved one contracts cancer, or a child has an incurable birth defect. He tells us to rejoice because he will produce in us something money can't buy and ease will never produce—the precious quality of Christ-exalting perseverance.

Persevering is holding steady to a belief or course of action. It's steadfastness in completing a commitment. Jesus said, "If you hold to my teaching, you are really my disciples" (John 8:31). At the end of his life, Paul said, "I have fought the good fight, I have finished the race, I have kept the faith. Now there is in store for me the crown of righteousness" (2 Timothy 4:7–8).

God gives each of us a race to run. To finish well we must develop perseverance. The Christian life is not a hundred-meter dash, but a marathon. Those who lack patience, endurance, and discipline will drop out of the race.

We rejoice in suffering in the same way that Olympic athletes rejoice in their workouts—not because we find them easy, but because we know they will one day produce great reward.

When the Lion's claw rips away our dragon nature, we feel great pain; yet when we see the results, we feel great pleasure.

In C. S. Lewis's *The Voyage of the Dawn Treader,* Eustace Clarence Scrubb describes to Edmund how terrible it felt when Aslan, the Lion and Christ-figure, changed him from the dragon he'd become to the boy he was intended to be.

> "The very first tear he made was so deep that I thought it had gone right into my heart. And when he began pulling the skin off, it hurt worse than anything I've ever felt. The only thing that made me able to bear it was just the pleasure of feeling the stuff peel off. You know—if you've ever picked the scab off a sore place. It hurts like billy-oh but it *is* such fun to see it coming away."
>
> "I know exactly what you mean," said Edmund.
>
> "Well, he peeled the beastly stuff right off—just as I thought I'd done it myself the other three times, only they hadn't hurt—and there it was lying on the grass: only ever so much thicker, and darker, and more knobbly-looking than the others had been. And there was I as smooth and soft as a peeled switch and smaller than I had been. Then he caught hold of me— I didn't like that much for I was very tender underneath now that I'd no skin on—and threw me into the water. It smarted like anything but only for a moment. After that it became perfectly delicious and as soon as I started swimming and splashing I found that all the pain had gone from my arm. And then I saw why. I'd turned into a boy again."[1]

Eustace ends up loving the Lion who inflicted the pain. Through his anguish, the boy came to trust Aslan's good intentions and love. So will we, in the end. But let's not wait. The sooner we come to trust his goodness, the lighter the pain— no matter how great—we bear.

COMPASSION

Suffering makes hearts tender and gives us greater love for others.

Our suffering increases our mercy toward others. Many physicians and nurses testify to this phenomenon when they return to their vocations after long periods of personal suffering. When they've been the patient, they grow far more sensitive to patients' needs.

My friend John Kohlenberger, a gifted scholar, has written many biblical language reference works. Seven years ago doctors diagnosed John with an advanced cancer; he wasn't expected to live more than a few years. He told me that he'd kept himself away from people in the past, but suddenly he found himself constantly in doctors' offices, hospitals, experimental treatment programs, and support groups, and gathering with people at his church.

John tells me all this has transformed his relationships. He enjoys church in a way he never did. He's developed deep relationships instead of superficial ones. "My only regret," he said, "is that it took me fifty years to get here, and that it took cancer to open my eyes."

By dealing with his cancer, John told me he's learned to be authentic and honest. "It's much easier for me now to touch someone I don't know and pray for them," he said. When I walked with him for hours at a cancer-cure fundraising event, I saw repeatedly his warm interactions with many people he's come to know through his disease. John has reached out to others in need and found it rewarding. And though years earlier he could never have imagined such a thing, this lifelong scholar said to me, "You know, I'd really enjoy becoming a chaplain, helping people deal with cancer."

I've witnessed how God has touched John and used him powerfully. That doesn't minimize or glorify my friend's pain, or his family's, but it does show some of God's purpose in it (see 2 Corinthians 1:3–7).

Suffering gives us an ability to touch people's lives in ways that healing might never afford.

A remarkable Thornton Wilder play called *The Angel That Troubled the Waters* is based loosely on John 5:1–4. A physician comes periodically to the pool of Bethesda, hoping to be the first in the moving water and so healed of his depression. All the others at the pool also hope to jump first into the pool.

One day the angel blocks the doctor from stepping into the water. "Draw back, physician," he commands, "this moment is not for you."

The man responds, "I pray thee, listen to my prayer."

"Healing is not for you," the angel insists.

The physician argues. "Surely, O Prince, you are not deceived by my apparent wholeness." He points out the terrible burden of his depression.

The angel assures him he knows of his affliction, then says to him, "Without your wound, where would your power be? It is your very remorse that makes your low voice tremble into the hearts of men. The very angels themselves cannot persuade the wretched and blundering children on earth as can one human being broken on the wheels of living. In Love's service only the wounded soldiers can serve. Draw back."

Later, the person who enters the pool first is healed and rejoices. He then turns to the physician and begs him to come to his home: "My son is lost in dark thoughts. I—I do not understand him, and only you have ever lifted his mood.... My daughter, since her child has died, sits in the shadow. She will not listen to us but she will listen to you."

Some people talk to diseases and demons and say, "Be gone!" Shouldn't we begin by talking to God and asking him to take away our afflictions *unless* he has a higher purpose for them, even if it remains a hidden one? In my disease, lawsuits, job loss, and other experiences, I think God has a number of times graciously held me back from the pool of Bethesda.

Only the wounded can serve.

The comfort God gives us in our suffering prepares us to comfort others who suffer as we have.

One of God's purposes in our suffering is to prepare us to serve others, especially those who suffer as we have—for instance, from an addiction, miscarriage, abortion, infertility, divorce, or the loss of a spouse or child. Paul says, "The God of all comfort...comforts us in all our troubles, so that we can comfort those in any trouble with the comfort we ourselves have received from God" (2 Corinthians 1:3–4). The common ground of suffering breaks down barriers of wealth, education, vocation, and age. People in hospital waiting rooms often take an interest in one another's suffering and loved ones. They sail together on the same ship, riding the same rough waters.

A woman wrote me,

> At five years old, I was sexually assaulted repeatedly by some neighborhood boys. My home life was chaotic, full of drugs, dealing, and unsafe, neglectful parents. I worried incessantly about death, and shivered in my bed. When I shared my story, a mom and two of her adopted girls listened, and they'd experienced a similar home life. One girl asked her sister why God allowed me to go through all those things. The older sister said, "God allowed it so that she could understand and help girls like us." Hearing this, I cried. I realized God used all my horror to touch other girls who had endured trauma. It was the full-circle beauty of redemption. It's possible to be violated, then healed by a Sovereign God, in order to become an agent of redemption and change.

A novelist friend told me that her severe depression, which she suffered for years, became the source of a new depth in her stories. One of them deals with clinical depression. Readers have told her, "Your book saved my life."

How many saved lives does it take to make our struggles worthwhile?

We can comfort others in suffering even when our own suffering lies in different areas.

Joni Eareckson Tada pointed out to me the phrase in 2 Corinthians 1:4, "We can comfort those in *any* trouble," and said, "You don't have to be quadriplegic to comfort me."

You don't have to see your child die, get an abortion, or endure a divorce to offer comfort to someone who's suffered in any of those ways. You *must* have suffered, however. The résumé of every encourager and every counselor will contain suffering.

God uses suffering to call us to new ministry.

Robertson McQuilkin, at the peak of his career, resigned as president of Columbia Bible College in 1990 to become the full-time caregiver for his wife, Muriel, who had Alzheimer's. Robertson did this, he said, because Muriel was much happier when he was with her. Years later in a radio interview, Dennis Rainey asked if he had any regrets about the transition from college president to caregiver. McQuilkin said,

> I never think about "what if." I don't think "what if" is in God's vocabulary. So I don't even think about what I might be doing instead of changing her diaper or what I might be doing instead of spending two hours feeding her. It's the grace of God, I'm sure.

Rainey asked a follow-up question: "But do you ever think about what you may have given up to care for her?" McQuilkin responded,

> I don't feel like I've given anything up. Our life is not the way we plot it or plan it.... All along I've just accepted whatever assignment the Lord gave me. This was his assignment. I know I'm not supposed to have that kind of reaction, but you asked me, and I have to be honest. I never went to a support group. I had enough of my own burdens without taking on everybody else's. Sometimes I have accepted an invitation to speak at one of

these. A lot of angry people. They're angry at God for letting this happen—
"Why me?" They're angry at the one they care for, and then they feel
guilty about it because they can't explain why they're angry at them.....
I say, in acceptance there's peace.[2]

Suffering draws us close to others, deepening friendships.

At a publishers' dinner with two of her children, Karen Kingsbury received a call
saying her father, a few thousand miles away, had suffered a heart attack and
would likely die. When Karen's daughter came to my table and informed me, I
looked for someone to join me in praying with Karen. My eyes fell on Vonette
Bright, co-founder of Campus Crusade for Christ. When Vonette prayed over
Karen and her family, we sensed the very presence of Christ. I'm convinced that
no one on the planet could have prayed more effectively with Karen and her children that night. Now, Vonette Bright won't always be in the room, but I believe
our sovereign God will put just the right person within reach, even if by phone.

"Carry each other's burdens, and in this way you will fulfill the law of Christ"
(Galatians 6:2). We serve people best when we point them to their greatest source
of help, Jesus: "Since he himself has gone through suffering and testing, he is able
to help us when we are being tested" (Hebrews 2:18, NLT).

A dying young woman exhibited a genuine joy in Christ despite her suffering. One particularly difficult day, she asked her pastor why God hadn't let her die.
He didn't know what to say, until a few days later when he met an unfamiliar
young couple at church. They told him that they'd visited this woman in the hospital earlier that week. They spoke of how she had touched them on the deepest
level. The young man said, "We went home and decided that we want to become
Christians."[3]

And so came an answer to this dying woman's question: God had kept her
alive to bring these people to Christ. Many other answers for God's delay might
exist—but if this were the only one, the suffering woman knew it would have
been enough.

First Corinthians 12:26 speaks of the body of Christ: "If one part suffers,
every part suffers." Sometimes God wraps his arms around us in the form of
another person.

Though grief sometimes robs words of their power, it never robs actions of
their power. Recently someone reminded me of a night we'd spent together thirty
years ago, bailing out his flooding basement. That triggered a memory of a friend

who spent half a night outdoors, in bitter cold, helping me fix our burst water pipes. I don't remember anything he said to me that night. But I'll never forget those six hours of friendship and how God spoke to me through his cheerful service.

Fixing a car, mowing a lawn, trimming a hedge, or cleaning someone's gutters may touch a person at a far deeper level than saying the right words. A visit, meal, plate of cookies, book, or movie may be exactly what they need. People will remember your phone call or card less for the words said than the act done.

Suffering can help us move forward with a sense of focused devotion and service.

David Guthrie, after the deaths of two of his children, said, "We found our suffering has taught us life isn't easy, and it has toughened us for the next battle. We don't want our greatest spiritual landmarks to be behind us. Following Christ comes with struggle, not ease."

Because I've written books about Heaven, almost weekly I receive letters from those whose loved ones have died. One man wrote, "We lost our three little girls in an airplane accident ten months ago.... My wife and I decided to pursue God through this tragedy. We had to choose Life or Death and God has been faithful to comfort and change our lives from the inside out. After suffering this loss, we know that the only important things now are the ones that will last for eternity."

One pastor and Bible teacher made this interesting observation:

> The most cheerful people I have met, with few exceptions, have been those who had the least sunshine and the most pain and suffering in their lives. The most grateful people I have met were not those who had traveled a pathway of roses all their lives through, but those who were confined, because of circumstances, to their homes, often to their beds, and had learned to depend upon God as only such Christians know how to do. The "gripers" are usually, I have observed, those who enjoy excellent health. The complainers are those who have the least to complain about.[4]

HOPE

Our suffering can be a source of hope to others.

We are no substitute for God. But we do serve as his ambassadors. I heard Christian counselor David Powlison say that although God alone is the blazing sun, we can be 3-watt night-lights. In darkness even a tiny light can bring hope.

That we've come through suffering may comfort those who don't know us; indeed, it may help someone long after we've died. After I posted a blog about Charles Spurgeon and Martin Luther and the suffering they endured, I received this note: "Wow. I was depressed because once again I was not feeling well. It's amazing to realize these great leaders suffered so much. It gives me hope, as I suffer from near constant pain. Thanks. This really encouraged me—I needed it!"

Would Luther or Spurgeon have guessed that centuries later their suffering would be a source of comfort to God's people? Who is being, and will be, touched by your suffering that you won't know about until eternity?

Evil and suffering overwhelm us when we focus on the immediate, but our perspective improves when we focus on the eternal.

Jesus calls his followers citizens of Heaven. When we think more about dinner out tomorrow than the banquet on the New Earth with Abraham, Isaac, and Jacob, we lose sight of Heaven and surrender the present joy that comes in anticipating it.

Scripture tells us we should see our present sufferings in light of future glory. We must fix our eyes on things that, for the present, remain invisible (see 2 Corinthians 4:18).

Minnie Broas lay dying of cancer; within weeks her decimated body would stop working and she would have to leave behind her husband and son. They gave much thought to eternity, speaking openly of God's sovereign purposes. Minnie wrote online, "We can't forget this is about His glory and we will see and have seen His glory. He is faithful! We are never without hope. We have a very big God. His plans and purposes are still perfect and will forever be perfect no matter the number of our days. To Him be all glory, honor and praise!"

Minnie's husband, Daniel, signed off his wife's blog update with Psalm 30:11–12: "You turned my wailing into dancing; you removed my sackcloth and clothed me with joy, that my heart may sing to you and not be silent. O LORD my God, I will give you thanks forever."

It's precisely because they knew they will give thanks to God forever that they could give thanks to God during their suffering.

Six weeks after Minnie posted her letter, she departed to a better world.

Present suffering paints boldly across our lives the hope of promised resurrection, encouraging us to wait patiently, knowing it will come at just the right time.

In reference to the coming resurrection, Paul wrote, "For in this hope [of the redemption of our bodies] we were saved. But hope that is seen is no hope at all.

Who hopes for what he already has? But if we hope for what we do not yet have, we wait for it patiently" (Romans 8:24–25).

To many of us, "hope" sounds wishful and tentative, but biblical hope means *to anticipate with trust.* We expect a sure thing, purchased on the Cross, accomplished and promised by an all-knowing God.

I spoke with a friend whose beloved wife died three hours after we talked, leaving him and three teenage children behind. Weeping, he thanked God for his goodness in giving him an extra few months with his wife, painful as they were. Broken, he spoke to me of how he held on to the promise of resurrection. Wishful thinking? No. According to Scripture, his hope issues from a solidly grounded truth.

Dustin Shramek wrote about his son's death and how it affected him and his wife:

> My mother died when I was sixteen, two years after I had become a believer.... Having endured through her death I had come out on the other end with my faith intact and I again had hope that God was for me. After Owen died, my wife, who had not experienced the death of one so close, never believed that she would be able to have joy again. And while I certainly didn't feel joy, I knew that one day I would. The suffering I had endured through my mother's death had indeed produced hope. Even though my firstborn was dead I believed that I would again have joy. I had experienced God's faithfulness and I knew that he would be faithful again.[5]

God remains faithful, of course, even when circumstances seem to say otherwise. Hope endures because God's promises remain true, no matter what.

In Tolkien's *Return of the King,* Aragorn says, "Dawn is ever the hope of men." King David wrote, "Weeping may last for the night, but a shout of joy comes in the morning" (Psalm 30:5, NASB).

The night may seem long, but the truth is this: once it comes, the morning will never end.

Neither will the joy.

Notes

1. C. S. Lewis, *The Voyage of the Dawn Treader* (New York: HarperCollins, 1994), 115–16.

2. "A Promise Kept," interview with Robertson McQuilkin, Family Life Today, August 14, 2008.

3. Jon Tal Murphee, *A Loving God and a Suffering World* (Downers Grove, IL: InterVarsity Press, 1981), 115.

4. M. R. DeHaan, *Broken Things* (Grand Rapids, MI: Zondervan, 1948), 21.

5. Doug Wolter, "Justin, Dustin, and God's Lessons on Suffering," September 21, 2007. http://life2getherblog.com/2007/09/.

41

How God Uses Our Suffering
for the Good of Others

SPREADING THE GOSPEL

Through suffering we become powerless so that we might reach the powerless.

We like to serve from the power position. We'd rather be healthy, wealthy, and wise as we minister to the sick, poor, and ignorant. When those preaching God's Word have little personal familiarity with suffering, the credibility gap makes it difficult for them to speak into others' lives. But our suffering levels the playing field.

People hear the gospel best when it comes from those who have known difficulty. Paul says, "To the weak I became weak, to win the weak" (1 Corinthians 9:22).

Our suffering makes Jesus visible to the world.
Graham Staines left his home in Australia to minister to lepers in India for thirty-four years. He and his wife, Gladys, served Christ by serving the poorest of the poor.

At midnight on January 23, 1999—a year and a half before my wife, daughters, and I met Gladys and her daughter, Esther—a mob of militant Hindus murdered Graham and his two sons, Phillip, age eleven, and Timothy, age six. The killers invaded a Christian camp in the jungle, where Graham had ministered, and set fire to the Jeep in which Graham and his sons slept. When the fire finally cooled, believers found the charred body of Graham Staines with his arms around the bodies of his sons.

In the most appalling way, Gladys and Esther found themselves alone. Their response to the tragedy appeared on the front page of every newspaper in India.

"I have only one message for the people of India," Gladys said. "I'm not bitter. Neither am I angry. But I have one great desire: That each citizen of this country should establish a personal relationship with Jesus Christ who gave his life for their sins.... Let us burn hatred and spread the flame of Christ's love."

When asked how she felt about the murder of her dad, thirteen-year-old Esther said (in words that sound straight off the pages of the book of Acts), "I praise the Lord that He found my father worthy to die for Him."

Gladys stunned a nation by saying that God had called her and Esther to stay in India for that season. "My husband and our children have sacrificed their lives for this nation; India is my home. I hope to be here and continue to serve the needy."

At the funeral, masses of people filled the streets—Hindus, Muslims, and Christians. They came to show respect for the Staines family and demonstrate solidarity against the killers. Although persecution of Christians had recently increased, the president of India stated, "That someone who spent years caring for patients of leprosy, instead of being thanked and appreciated as a role model should be done to death in this manner is...a crime that belongs to the world's inventory of black deeds."

At the conference where we met them, after Gladys and Esther spoke, an Indian national leader told us about the impact of their response to the murders. He said the people of India asked, "Why would a man leave his wealthy country and serve lepers in India for thirty-four years? Why would his wife and daughter forgive the killers of their family? Why would they choose to stay and serve the poor? Who is this God they believe in? Could it be that all we've been told about Christians has been lies? Could it be that Jesus really is the truth?" He stated that many Hindus had come to Christ through their witness.

The Staines carried on a long tradition of God's people: "Others were tortured and refused to be released, so that they might gain a better resurrection. Some faced jeers and flogging, while still others were chained and put in prison. They were stoned; they were sawed in two; they were put to death by the sword. They went about in sheepskins and goatskins, destitute, persecuted and mistreated—*the world was not worthy of them*" (Hebrews 11:35–38).

Our faithful suffering gives others courage to speak up for Jesus.
Paul wrote of his imprisonment,

> Now I want you to know, brothers, that what has happened to me has really served to advance the gospel. As a result, it has become clear

throughout the whole palace guard and to everyone else that I am in chains for Christ. Because of my chains, most of the brothers in the Lord have been encouraged to speak the word of God more courageously and fearlessly. (Philippians 1:12–14)

Paul clearly saw God at work through his suffering. Just as boldness in imprisonment advances the gospel, so does boldness in disability, disease, or disaster.

Dispersion and persecution results in the gospel's spread.

Luke chooses an interesting word in Acts 8 and 11 to describe the scattering of the church through persecution: *diaspeiro,* used for scattering seeds. In Luke's eyes, these early Christians didn't leave as evacuees or refugees; they went as missionaries. The death of Stephen and the ensuing wave of persecution enabled the church to grow in new and exciting ways. What Satan intended for evil, God used for good. As Tertullian said, "The blood of the martyrs is the seed of the church."

Comfort, affluence, safety, and freedom often hinder the church.

Christ warned, "The cares of the world, and *the delight in riches,* and *the desire for other things* enter in and choke the word and it proves unfruitful" (Mark 4:19, RSV). Sometimes those who profess to preach the word choke it and make it unfruitful because of their obsession with this world and its riches. The very things that we imagine would help spread the gospel often produce apathy, self-centeredness, and a preoccupation with security.

God uses the suffering we try to avoid to spread the gospel and build his kingdom. Jesus said, "I tell you the truth, unless a kernel of wheat falls to the ground and dies, it remains only a single seed. But if it dies, it produces many seeds" (John 12:24).

Suffering creates a sphere of influence for Christ that we couldn't otherwise have.

E. Stanley Jones wrote, "Don't bear trouble, use it. Take whatever happens—justice and injustice, pleasure and pain, compliment and criticism—take it up into the purpose of your life and make something out of it. Turn it into testimony."[1]

Paul said, "It was because of an illness that I first preached the gospel to you" (Galatians 4:13). Some think this means that he changed his itinerary to recuperate in Galatia. But whatever the case, God specifically used Paul's illness to give him a new sphere of influence that brought the gospel to Galatia.

Ron and Carol Speer, whose nine-year-old son, Kyle, died of leukemia, spent hundreds of hours in hospitals, faithfully ministering to people they never would have met without their terrible suffering. Their son's illness opened a door to ministry, and God used him and them to reach many.

A man with a terminal illness told me he invited the fathers of five of his son's friends to meet with him. Explaining that he didn't have long to live, he shared the gospel, touching them deeply.

Suffering in persecution ministers to the persecutors.

Richard Wurmbrand's *Tortured for Christ* influenced me profoundly as a young Christian. In Romania, guards tied prisoners to crosses and smeared them with human excrement. From a human standpoint, the perpetrators seemed beyond redemption; yet some of the guards who did these unspeakable acts saw the inexplicable love, devotion, and faith of the Christians they tortured.

Wurmbrand wrote, "I have seen Christians in Communist prisons with fifty pounds of chains on their feet, tortured with red-hot iron pokers, in whose throats spoonfuls of salt had been forced, being kept afterward from water, starving, whipped, suffering from cold—and praying with fervor for the Communists."[2]

He told of guards coming to Christ while beating Christian prisoners, then confessing their faith and being imprisoned and tortured themselves.

Romanian pastor Josef Tson told me, "The gospel will *never* be spread without someone suffering."

Jesus saw our suffering as an opportunity to bring the gospel: "They will lay their hands on you and persecute you, delivering you up to the synagogues and prisons, and you will be brought before kings and governors for my name's sake. This will be your opportunity to bear witness" (Luke 21:12–13, ESV).

Suffering gives us a way to credibly demonstrate the love of Christ.

Larry Waters says, "How the believer deals with undeserved suffering may be the primary witness of God's goodness, justice, grace and love not only to the sufferer, but to a nonbelieving world."[3]

When an African named Joseph heard about Jesus in a roadside conversation, he turned to him as his Savior. Filled with excitement and joy, he went door to door, telling his whole village about Jesus. To his amazement, his neighbors became violent. They beat him with strands of barbed wire and left him to die in the bush.

After days of passing in and out of consciousness, Joseph found the strength to get up. He decided he must have left something out of the good news or surely they wouldn't have rejected it. After rehearsing the message, Joseph limped back to the circle of huts and proclaimed Jesus.

Again they beat him, reopening his wounds. Joseph awoke in the wilderness, bruised, scarred—and determined to go back.

This time, they attacked him even before he opened his mouth. As they flogged him, he spoke to them of Jesus. Before he passed out, he saw some of his female assailants begin to weep. When Joseph awoke, the ones who had so severely beaten him were trying to save his life and nurse him back to health. While he lay unconscious, the entire village had come to Christ.[4]

ACTS OF SERVICE

Suffering leads us to a fresh spiritual life and an expanded ministry to others.

Joni Eareckson Tada spoke of a woman, pregnant with a disabled child, who cried out in desperation to her husband, "Things will never be the same." His response? "Maybe God doesn't *want* them to be the same."[5]

I received a note from my friend Jerry Tobias who describes the ministry God has given him and his wife as a result of his cancer. He writes,

> I am constantly amazed by God's never-ending grace, the many "silver lin-ings" and the incredible purpose that my wife and I have experienced throughout this journey. So many encounters, relationships, and opportu-nities to encourage, briefly open windows through which to share God's great message of salvation. And all with people I would never have even met if I'd been healthy these last few years. I have connected very deeply with many medical personnel, urologists, oncologists, ENT surgeons, and neurologists. They are caring people who need Jesus. What an honor to have been allowed to intersect their lives. I don't want to waste my cancer. It really is all about Jesus. All that to say, we would not have wanted to miss this journey.[6]

Our suffering gives family and friends who become caregivers an opportunity for character growth.

In some cases it's not the sufferers but those around them who benefit most. My mother and I agreed together, and prayed to that end, that we would gladly suf-fer any loss that could bring my father to faith in Christ. Nine years after my mother died, my father came to Christ. But the two events had an unmistakable connection. The day my father turned to Christ I sensed my mother rejoicing with me.

None of us wants to "burden" our families. But we should have the humility to serve God even if it means serving him from disability, incontinence, and dementia. Hard as it is for us to embrace this as a calling, it may be what God wants to use in our families. And if our weakness can be used of God to bring them spiritual strength, it's a price we should be willing to pay.

When I consider how both of my parents and my wife's parents deteriorated at the end of their lives, I might argue that it wasn't worth it. Although at times I saw a clear spiritual impact in each situation, still, it didn't seem like the upside outweighed the downside. But *seem* is the operative word. What *seems* and what *is* are often different.

Through our parents' weakness, my wife and I and other family members grew in character, compassion, and love. Suppose we could ask our parents now, in the presence of Christ, "Were your suffering and your final years of indignity worth the character growth it brought about in you and your children and grandchildren and friends, and worth your and your family's spiritual impact on others, including caregivers?" I can picture them, in the universe next door, smiling and nodding emphatically.

Hardship and suffering have inspired powerful songs that have touched countless lives.

Joseph Scriven wrote "What a Friend We Have in Jesus" after his fiancée drowned. George Matheson wrote "O Love That Wilt Not Let Me Go" after his fiancée rejected him because he was going blind.

Horatio Spafford, a prosperous lawyer, real estate investor, and devout Presbyterian elder, lived comfortably in Chicago with his wife, Anna, and their four young daughters. Knowing that his friend D. L. Moody would preach in England in 1873, Spafford's family decided to vacation in Europe. Last-minute business detained Horatio, so Anna and the girls sailed on the ocean liner *S.S. Ville du Havre*. En route, a British vessel rammed the ship, and it sank within minutes. Rescuers picked up an unconscious Anna on a floating spar, but all four daughters drowned. When Anna arrived in England, she sent a telegram to Horatio with the words, "Saved alone."

Horatio immediately left Chicago to bring his wife home. On the Atlantic crossing, the captain called Horatio to his cabin to tell him that they had nearly reached the spot where his four daughters had perished. As he passed over their watery grave, Spafford wrote a hymn of profound depth that has touched millions: "It Is Well with My Soul."

Viewed from an eternal perspective, many tragedies are not what they seem.

If we can look at other tragedies and see some divine purpose in them, it can help us believe that there is purpose in our tragedies too.

Eric Liddell, "The Flying Scotsman" of the movie *Chariots of Fire,* shocked everyone by refusing to run the one-hundred meters in the 1924 Paris Olympics, a race experts favored him to win. He withdrew because the qualifying heat took place on a Sunday, and he refused to "violate the Sabbath." Liddell went on to win a gold medal—and break the world record—in the four-hundred meters, not his strongest event.

For a number of years Liddell served as a missionary in China, but when the Japanese occupation made life dangerous, he sent his pregnant wife and two daughters to Canada. Japanese invaders delivered him to a squalid prison camp where he lived several years before dying at age forty-three of a brain tumor, a few months before the war ended. Liddell never saw his family again in this life and never got to see the youngest of his three daughters.

Why did God withhold from this great man of faith a long life, years of fruitful service, the companionship of his wife, and the joy of raising those beloved children? It makes no sense.

And yet...

There is another way to look at the Eric Liddell story. Nanci and I discovered this firsthand some years ago while spending a day in England with Phil and Margaret Holder. Margaret was born in China to missionary parents. In 1939, when Japan took control of eastern China, soldiers separated thirteen-year-old Margaret from her parents and imprisoned her for six years.

Margaret told us many stories that day, several about a godly man who tutored her and the other children, organized sporting events, and brought God's Word to them. All the children in the camp loved him deeply. He was their inspiration. Margaret then told us this man's name: Eric Liddell.

Through fresh tears, Margaret said, "It was a cold February day when Uncle Eric died." If all Scotland mourned Liddell's death, no one mourned like the children in that camp. Only five months later, paratroopers rescued the camp's survivors, so the children were at last reunited with their families.

Eric Liddell's presence in that camp broke the hearts of his family. But for years, nearly to the war's end, God used him as a lifeline to hundreds of children, including Margaret Holder.

Viewed from that perspective, the apparent tragedy of Liddell's presence in that camp makes more sense, doesn't it? I'm convinced Liddell and his family would tell us—and one day *will* tell us—that the sufferings of that time are not worthy to be compared with the glory they now know…and will know forever.

God called Christ to suffer for our atonement; he calls us to suffer for service and growth.

God doesn't call us to repeat Christ's atonement, but to accept it. He does call us, however, to deny ourselves, take up our cross daily, and follow him (see Luke 9:23). That involves saying no to present desires and plans in order to say yes to God and others. The good Samaritan cheerfully took up his cross by setting aside his schedule and commitments, giving his time and money to help the beaten man lying in the ditch (see Luke 10:25–37).

Elisabeth Elliot writes, "It is an unsettling business, this being made conformable to His death, and it cannot be accomplished without knocking out the props. If we understand that God is at work even when He knocks out the small props, it will not be so difficult for us to take when He knocks out bigger ones."[7]

We want deliverance from suffering. We don't want our loved ones to die. We don't want economic crises, job losses, car accidents, or cancer. Our prayers and often our expectations boil down to this: Jesus should make our lives go smoothly. That's what we want in a Messiah.

But it is not what *God* wants. Jesus is not our personal assistant charged with granting our wishes. While he sometimes does not give us what we want, he *always* gives us what we need.

Only when we regard suffering servanthood as our calling, as Jesus did, will we have the ability to face it as he did: "Consider him who endured such opposition from sinful men, so that you will not grow weary and lose heart" (Hebrews 12:3). "To this [suffering] you were called, because Christ suffered for you, leaving you an example, that you should follow in his steps" (1 Peter 2:21).

God often uses people in direct proportion to their suffering.

While my hurts have been far less than those of many, I find that any ministry I've been able to have is inseparable from what God has done in my life through afflictions. God graciously used a lawsuit with an unjust verdict to open doors of fruitful ministry for Nanci and me that we otherwise never would have pursued.

To put your sufferings in perspective, read the biographies of missionaries and reformers, of people such as Martin Luther, John Calvin, William Carey, John Wesley, Charles Spurgeon, Harriet Tubman, William Wilberforce, Hudson Taylor, and countless others. You'll find the pages riddled with suffering, all of which God used to build their characters and expand their ministries. Rather than depressing us, these stories inspire and challenge us to say no to time-wasting trivia, seize the day and invest it in what matters. As Robert Moffat said, "We have all eternity to celebrate our victories, but only one short hour before sunset in which to win them."[8]

Suffering for the gospel inspires passion for reaching those without Christ.

John G. Paton served as a missionary in the South Pacific's New Hebrides islands. Less than twenty-five years earlier, natives clubbed to death the first two missionaries to visit the island, just fifteen minutes after they landed on the beach. The natives then cooked and ate the murdered men in sight of the ship that brought them there. No one dared return to the islands, until Paton did. His first weeks there, illness took his young wife; one week later, their infant died. He suffered intensely. But note Paton's perspective as he looked back on this years later:

> Oftentimes, while passing through the perils and defeats of my first years in the Mission field on Tanna, I wondered, and perhaps the reader hereof has wondered, why God permitted such things. But on looking back now, I already clearly perceive…that the Lord was thereby preparing me for doing…the best work of all my life: the kindling of the heart of Australian Presbyterianism with a living affection for these Islanders of their own Southern Seas…and in being the instrument under God of sending out missionary after missionary to the New Hebrides, to claim another island and still another for Jesus. That work, and all that may spring from it in time and Eternity, never could have been accomplished by me, but for first the sufferings and then the story of my Tanna enterprise![9]

Because of Paton's story, nearly one in six Presbyterian ministers in Australia left to serve God as missionaries. Only in eternity will we know the full effect of his sufferings.

Years earlier, as a successful young Scottish preacher, Paton determined to leave Glasgow to minister to this unreached people group. But most of his Christian friends urged him to do something more sensible with his life. Paton wrote,

> Amongst many who sought to deter me, was one dear old Christian gentleman, whose crowning argument always was, "The Cannibals! You will be eaten by Cannibals!" At last I replied, "Mr. Dickson, you are advanced in years now, and your own prospect is soon to be laid in the grave, there to be eaten by worms; I confess to you, that if I can but live and die serving and honoring the Lord Jesus, it will make no difference to me whether I am eaten by Cannibals or by worms; and in the Great Day my resurrection body will arise as fair as yours in the likeness of our risen Redeemer.[10]

Paton suffered much in his forty-three years in the New Hebrides, where he buried his wife and child, and endured grave illnesses, shipwreck, the betrayal of friends and some converts, and grief over martyred co-workers. On the other hand, John Paton lived to see Christ transform an entire culture, and to witness hundreds of missionaries follow behind him.

When he died, Paton could anticipate hearing words that would compensate for every evil and suffering he endured, words spoken by Jesus in Matthew 25:21: "Well done, good and faithful servant! You have been faithful with a few things; I will put you in charge of many things. Come and share your master's happiness!"

Notes

1. E. Stanley Jones, *A Song of Ascents* (Nashville: Abingdon, 1968), 180.
2. Richard Wurmbrand, *Tortured for Christ* (Bartlesville, OK: Living Sacrifice Book, 1990), 57.
3. Larry Waters, "Defining the Missio Dei," March 3, 2009, www.dts.edu/media/play/?MediaItemID=80e938f6-fc00-4c1b-bee2-2cbde5015202.
4. Michael Card, "Wounded in the House of Friends," *Virtue*, March–April 1991, 28–29, 69.
5. Joni Eareckson Tada, True Women Conference, October 10, 2008.
6. Jerry Tobias, e-mail, November 12, 2008.
7. Elisabeth Elliot, *A Path Through Suffering* (Ann Arbor, MI: Servant Publications, 1990), 151–52.

8. Robert Moffat, quoted in *Eternities: Webster's Quotations, Facts and Phrases* (San Diego: ICON Group, 2008), 3.
9. John Gibson Paton, *John G. Paton, Missionary to the New Hebrides* (Grand Rapids, MI: Fleming H. Revell, 1898) 359–60.
10. Paton, *John G. Paton*, 91.

Living Meaningfully in Suffering

42

Finding God in Suffering

Finding Comfort in His Promises

Evil is temporary; God's goodness and our joy will be eternal.

David cried out, "How long, O LORD? Will you forget me forever? How long will you hide your face from me? How long must I wrestle with my thoughts and every day have sorrow in my heart?" (Psalm 13:1–2). Still, he determined not to bury himself in his sorrows: "But I trust in your unfailing love; my heart rejoices in your salvation. I will sing to the LORD, for he has been good to me" (verses 5–6).

Jesus' tears in the presence of grieving Mary and Martha and his anguish in Gethsemane give us permission and encouragement to cry out to God for deliverance. Jesus didn't want to suffer on the cross, but said, "Father, if you are willing, take this cup from me; yet not my will, but yours be done" (Luke 22:42). Elisabeth Elliot, no stranger to suffering, wrote, "When our souls lie barren in a winter which seems hopeless and endless, God has not abandoned us. His work goes on. He asks our acceptance of the painful process and our trust that He will indeed give resurrection life."[1]

One day, evil will end. Forever. Suffering and weeping are real and profound, but for God's children, they are temporary. Eternal joy is on its way.

God's Word brings life-giving promises to us in our suffering.
Psalm 119 repeatedly connects God's Word to our afflictions. It is the longest psalm, and nearly all its 176 verses mention God's Word in one form or another. It's remarkable how many of the verses speak of affliction, including these:

> I am laid low in the dust;
>> preserve my life according to your word. (verse 25)

My soul is weary with sorrow;
>   strengthen me according to your word. (verse 28)

My comfort in my suffering is this:
>   Your promise preserves my life. (verse 50)

Before I was afflicted I went astray,
>   but now I obey your word. (verse 67)

It was good for me to be afflicted
>   so that I might learn your decrees. (verse 71)

I know, O LORD, that your laws are righteous,
>   and in faithfulness you have afflicted me. (verse 75)

If your law had not been my delight,
>   I would have perished in my affliction. (verse 92)

I have suffered much; preserve my life, O LORD,
>   according to your word. (verse 107)

Trouble and distress have come upon me,
>   but your commands are my delight. (verse 143)

Look upon my suffering and deliver me,
>   for I have not forgotten your law. (verse 153)

Earlier I mentioned Minnie Broas, who faced her terminal illness with grace and perspective. A few months before she died, Minnie posted the following online. Her letter drips with biblical language, reflecting the time she'd spent in God's Word:

> We want to make the most of each day God gives us.... Even though we are in the valley of the shadow of death we fear no evil. We have a very big God who is sovereign and mighty. His love is better than life. Yes, we still believe and will forever believe this truth. Our circumstances do not determine God's character. He is unchanging. He is our great and mighty God whose love knows no bounds.

In the midst of this dark valley, He blesses so abundantly.... No matter what or where God leads us in this journey we are going to praise and thank Him for He is God. He deserves our praise, worship, and thanksgiving.

In the midst of our pain, God showed up. He carried us and loved on us. All we can do is rest in God's truths and promises. We have to rest in who He is. He never promised easy—what He promised is He's never going to leave our side. We experienced the warmth of His tender embrace and His most amazing love and grace. While it would be nice for things to go away, we know God is more concerned with our souls and character than our comfort and happiness....We have a very big God.[2]

Clinging to Scripture sustains us through suffering.

A woman self-consciously told one of our pastors that before going to sleep each night she reads her Bible, then hugs it as she falls asleep. "Is that weird?" she asked. While it may be unusual, it's not weird. This woman has known suffering, and as she clings to his promises, she clings to God. Any father would be moved to hear that his daughter falls asleep with his written words held close to her. Surely God treasures such an act of childlike love.

In a time of dark suffering and dread, David affirmed, "The LORD is my light and my salvation—whom shall I fear? The LORD is the stronghold of my life—of whom shall I be afraid?... Though an army besiege me, my heart will not fear; though war break out against me, even then will I be confident.... Though my father and mother forsake me, the LORD will receive me.... I will see the goodness of the LORD in the land of the living. Wait for the LORD; be strong and take heart and wait for the LORD" (Psalm 27:1, 3, 10, 13–14).

Notice how David talks to himself about God's faithfulness and goodness, encouraging himself to wait on God. It's worth listening to self-talk *if* it involves speaking God's Word.

Years ago I turned off talk radio when I drive, to listen to the Bible instead. Scripture on audio accompanies me as I travel. I never regret investing my time this way—why listen to one more human voice when you can listen to God's? It prepares me to face whatever lies ahead. "Man does not live on bread alone but on every word that comes from the mouth of the LORD" (Deuteronomy 8:3).

J. C. Ryle wrote,

There is nothing which shows our ignorance so much as our impatience under trouble. We forget that every cross is a message from God, and intended to do us good in the end. Trials are intended to make us think—to wean us from the world—to send us to the Bible—to drive us to our knees. Health is a good thing but sickness is far better if it leads us to God. Prosperity is a great mercy; but adversity is a greater one if it brings us to Christ. Anything, anything is better than living in carelessness and dying in sin.[3]

God doesn't only promise to replace our grief *with* joy, but to *turn it into* joy.

Jesus said "I tell you the truth, you will weep and mourn while the world rejoices. You will grieve, but your grief will turn to joy. A woman giving birth to a child has pain because her time has come; but when her baby is born she forgets the anguish because of her joy that a child is born into the world. So with you: Now is your time of grief, but I will see you again and you will rejoice, and no one will take away your joy" (John 16:20–22).

Jesus could have said, "Your grief will end and joy will begin," or, "Joy will replace your grief." But these would separate the grief from the joy. Christ's words connect them: your sorrow will *turn into* joy (verse 20, ESV). It could be translated "your grief will *become* joy." The Message puts it, "You'll be sad, very sad, but your sadness will *develop into* gladness." (Similarly, sorrow turns into joy in Esther 9:22, wailing turns into dancing in Psalm 30:11, and mourning turns into gladness in Jeremiah 31:13.)

A woman giving birth suffers in a way directly connected to her impending joy. The child comes through suffering, and therefore the joy of having the child flows out of suffering. God transforms suffering into joy. Joy both eclipses and redeems the suffering.

Moffatt translates Romans 8:22, "The entire creation sighs and throbs in pain." There's a radical difference between death pangs, which anticipate an ending and look backward, and birth pangs, which anticipate a beginning and look forward. The old, fallen, cursed Earth, convulsing and groaning in the final pains of childbearing, will birth a New Earth. Earth will not merely survive, it will live forever, in ever-increasing wonder and glory—as will we, its caretakers, redeemed and birthed through the pains of this present time.

God sovereignly rules over our greatest adversities and heartaches, and pledges to be with us while we endure them.

The Lord says to us, "When you pass through the waters, I will be with you; and when you pass through the rivers, they will not sweep over you. When you walk through the fire, you will not be burned; the flames will not set you ablaze" (Isaiah 43:2).

In Psalm 16:8 David says, "I have set the LORD always before me. Because he is at my right hand, I will not be shaken." To set the Lord before me is to recognize his presence and his constant help.

God promises in Hebrews 13:5, "Never will I leave you; never will I forsake you." This unusual Greek sentence contains five negatives. Kenneth Wuest translates it, "I will not, I will not cease to sustain and uphold you. I will not, I will not, I will not let you down."[4]

The Bible models honesty with God concerning the problem of evil and suffering.

Job candidly expressed his doubts as he questioned God about his suffering: "I will not keep silent; I will speak out in the anguish of my spirit, I will complain in the bitterness of my soul.... I despise my life.... If I have sinned, what have I done to you, O watcher of men? Why have you made me your target? Have I become a burden to you?" (Job 7:11, 16, 20).

Just as God knew exactly how Job felt before he said a word, so God knows how you feel and what you're thinking. You can't hide it, so don't bother trying. When you pretend you don't feel hurt or angry or devastated, you're not fooling God. Be honest! Naomi cried, "The Almighty has made my life very bitter" (Ruth 1:20). David asked God, "Why have you forsaken me?" (Psalm 22:1). Jesus repeated the same question on the cross.

Don't misunderstand; I am *not* encouraging you to be angry at God or to blame him. He deserves no blame. Rather, I am encouraging you to honestly confess to God your feelings of hurt, resentment, and anger.

Psalm 13 begins, "How long, O LORD? Will you forget me forever? How long will you hide your face from me?" It ends, "But I trust in your unfailing love; my heart rejoices in your salvation. I will sing to the LORD, for he has been good to me" (verses 5–6). David travels a vast distance in a mere three verses. Like him, we can feel the pain of Psalm 13's first four verses, while affirming the truths of its last two.

Asaph struggled with the prosperity of the wicked and the suffering of the righteous...until he understood their final destiny.

"My feet had almost slipped; I had nearly lost my foothold. I envied the arrogant when I saw the prosperity of the wicked." In Psalm 73 Asaph notes the very opposite of prosperity theology: the wicked get health and wealth at the expense of the righteous. He feels frustrated because dishonesty, cheating, and embezzlement brought these wicked men riches. Today he might write about drug dealing, money laundering, insider trading, and corrupt politicians. But Asaph's lament turns dramatically midway through:

> When I tried to understand all this
> it was oppressive to me
> till I entered the sanctuary of God;
> then I understood their final destiny.
>
> Surely you place them on slippery ground;
> you cast them down to ruin. (verses 16–18)

Asaph went into the sanctuary, and there God opened his eyes. God will make right all evil when we reach our "final destiny," which for the wicked means ruin. Pondering final destinies gives Asaph an eternal perspective. So he turns the corner in his thinking:

> Yet I am always with you;
> you hold me by my right hand.
> You guide me with your counsel,
> and afterward you will take me into glory.
> Whom have I in heaven but you?
> And earth has nothing I desire besides you.
> My flesh and my heart may fail,
> but God is the strength of my heart
> and my portion forever.
>
> Those who are far from you will perish;
> you destroy all who are unfaithful to you.
> But as for me, it is good to be near God.
> I have made the Sovereign LORD my refuge;
> I will tell of all your deeds. (verses 23–28)

Habakkuk agonized over why God would use a wicked nation to judge his people...until he surrendered to God's sovereign and just purposes. Habakkuk didn't ask why the righteous suffered, but why the wicked didn't suffer more. Why don't bad things always happen to bad people? Habakkuk had called upon God to judge Israel for her sins, and God said he would. Habakkuk then wrestled with why God would use Babylon—a nation worse than Israel—as his instrument of punishment.

In the face of God's greatness, Habakkuk finally acquiesces: "The LORD is in his holy temple; let all the earth be silent before him" (2:20). In the end, he waits for God's judgment to fall on the wicked: "I heard and my heart pounded, my lips quivered at the sound; decay crept into my bones, and my legs trembled. Yet I will wait patiently for the day of calamity to come on the nation invading us" (3:16).

The prophet can accept injustice in the short term only by clinging to the promises of God that justice will prevail in the long term.

Habakkuk sounds like Alexander Solzhenitsyn, Corrie ten Boom, and other sufferers who have turned to God and found in him an inexpressible source of peace—as Paul called it, the "peace of God, which transcends all understanding" (Philippians 4:7). Habakkuk credited God with giving him the strength he needed to endure: "The Sovereign LORD is my strength; he makes my feet like the feet of a deer, he enables me to go on the heights" (3:19).

Through Job's story, God offers paradigm-shifting insights to face suffering.

Job has taught me many valuable lessons, including these:

- Life is not predictable or formulaic.
- Most of life's expectations and suffering's explanations are simplistic and naive, waiting to be toppled.
- When the day of crisis comes, we should pour out our hearts to God, who can handle our grief and even our anger.
- We should not turn from God and internalize our anger, allowing it to become bitterness.
- We should weigh and measure the words of friends, authors, teachers, and counselors, finding whatever truth they might speak without embracing their errors or getting derailed by their insensitivities.
- We should not insist on taking control by demanding a rational explanation for the evils and suffering that befall us.
- We should look to God and ask him to reveal himself to us; in contemplating his greatness we will come to see him as the Answer above all answers.
- We should trust that God is working behind the scenes and that our suffering has hidden purposes that one day, even if not in this life, we will see.

- We should cry out to Jesus, the mediator and friend whom Job could only glimpse, but who indwells us by grace.

LOOKING FORWARD TO HIS REWARDS

Properly responding to suffering brings eternal reward.

Moses "chose to be mistreated along with the people of God rather than to enjoy the pleasures of sin for a short time. He regarded disgrace for the sake of Christ as of greater value than the treasures of Egypt, *because he was looking ahead to his reward*" (Hebrews 11:25–26).

The believers described in Faith's Hall of Fame (see Hebrews 11) all endured severe tests. None of them had an easy life. Yet they all clung to their belief in God's promises, trusting his goodness, and believing "that He is a rewarder of those who seek Him" (verse 6, NASB).

Sadly, the doctrine of eternal reward is one of the most neglected teachings in the Western church today, partly explaining our failure to face suffering with greater perspective and to anticipate what awaits us in Heaven.[5]

"Do you not know that in a race all the runners run, but only one gets the prize? Run in such a way as to get the prize" (1 Corinthians 9:24). Paul commands us to "endure hardship" and then gives the examples of soldiers, athletes, and farmers, each of whom has a goal in mind as he endures—victory, a crown, and a harvest (see 2 Timothy 2:3–7).

Jesus told suffering believers to "rejoice…and leap for joy, because great is your reward in heaven" (Luke 6:23). Greater suffering for Christ will bring us greater eternal rewards.

Suffering while trusting God gives us eternal benefits that otherwise couldn't be ours, enlarging our capacity for eternal joy.

Trusting God to achieve something worthwhile through our suffering can become our greatest source of encouragement:

> Though outwardly we are wasting away, yet inwardly we are being renewed day by day. For our light and momentary troubles are achieving for us an eternal glory that far outweighs them all. So we fix our eyes not on what is seen, but on what is unseen. For what is seen is temporary, but what is unseen is eternal. (2 Corinthians 4:16–18)

These verses, as do Matthew 5:11–12, affirm an essential connection between present suffering and future glory. You can't have the second without the first.

When Darrell Scott looked back at his daughter's murder at Columbine High School, he said that years before, God had brought to him one of the most helpful preparations for this tragedy. Author Norman Grubb spoke of the eye of faith that allows us to see through our worst circumstances to God's purpose. Most people, Darrell told me, are *look-atters*. We should learn to become *see-throughers*.

Because Darrell had learned to think this way, he could, despite his incredible pain, see through Rachel's death to a sovereign, purposeful God. Simply looking *at* the horror and apparent senselessness of Columbine would have paralyzed him, while seeing *through* it prompted him before God to carry on Rachel's heart of ministry in reaching out to others.

God counts as precious our faithfulness in suffering for him, and he will never forget it.

Often we look at suffering from our perspective and forget that God sees from another vantage point. Our friend Patti Franklin wrote of life during the early years of her husband John's paralysis. Try to look at her words from God's perspective, imagining what they mean to him:

> I never once saw myself as strong, but weak and bewildered and afraid. But I remembered that God was strong and He was able, so I hung on to Him for dear life. Some of my prayers were along the line of "God, help me. Help John. Help our children." I would talk to Him as I drove back and forth to the hospital and at night and basically all the time.
>
> The worse things got for us, the more clearly we could see His beauty and goodness. The better we could see how worthy He was of our worship and how tenderly He cared for us and helped us.[6]

David asked God, "Record my lament; list my tears on your scroll—are they not in your record?" (Psalm 56:8). David believed his suffering mattered, that God counted it as precious, so precious that the Lord kept an account of every tear.

This gives special meaning to the promise that God will wipe away every tear from his children's eyes (see Revelation 21:4). Our tears are all recorded in Heaven's books. God is keeping track of the pain behind each and will deal with them one by one.

When he wipes away all our tears with his gentle, omnipotent hand, I believe our eyes will fall on the scars that made our suffering his, so that his eternal joy could become ours.

Notes

1. Elisabeth Elliot, *A Path Through Suffering* (Ann Arbor, MI: Servant Publications, 1990), 43.
2. The Web site that I copied Minnie Broas's words from no longer appears online.
3. J. C. Ryle, *Ryle's Expository Thoughts on the Gospels* (New York: R. Carter & Brothers, 1879), 180.
4. Kenneth Samuel Wuest, *Word Studies in the Greek New Testament* (Grand Rapids, MI: Eerdmans, 1980), 235.
5. See Randy Alcorn, *The Law of Rewards* (Carol Stream, IL: Tyndale, 2003).
6. Patti Franklin, "Ordinary People in Extraordinary Times," www.emp.org/pattifranklin.html.

43

Finding Help in Dark Times

Knowing that suffering will one day end gives us strength to endure this day.

Researchers conducted a study on stress with Israeli soldiers. They assured one group that the march would end at a certain point, but kept the other group in the dark. Although both groups marched an identical distance, those who didn't know how long they would march registered a much higher level of stress. Why? Because they had no hope, no tangible assurance that the forced march would end. They felt helpless, wondering when, or if, they could ever rest.

Hope points to the light at the end of life's tunnel. It not only makes the tunnel endurable, it fills the heart with anticipation of a world alive, fresh, beautiful, without pain, suffering, or war. A world without disease, without accident, without tragedy. A world without dictators or madmen.

A world ruled by the only One worthy of ruling (see Revelation 5:12).

Though we don't know exactly *when*, we do know for sure that either by our deaths or by Christ's return, our suffering will end. From before the beginning, God drew the line in eternity's sand to say for his children, "*This much and no more*, then endless joy."

When the lights go out, we should cling to Jesus.
Corrie ten Boom, from the depths of a concentration camp, recorded her sister Betsie's words: "There is no pit so deep that He is not deeper still."[1]

Suffering is God's invitation to look to Jesus and look forward to Heaven.

The answer to the problem of evil is a person and a place. Jesus is the person. Heaven is the place. No one else and nowhere else will satisfy.

Seek the Holy Spirit's guidance and comfort, meditating on his Word.
The Bible tells us to "live by the Spirit" and to "keep in step with the Spirit" (Galatians 5:25). It also says, "Let the word of Christ dwell in you richly" (Colossians 3:16).

I love to look at the books on people's shelves. One night when Nanci and I were at Ken and Joni Tada's home, I looked through the bookshelves, lined with classic works by great theologians and preachers, including many of my favorites, such as Charles Spurgeon. The books Joni reads are rich and deep, centered in God's Word, food for her soul. No wonder both the life she lives and the books she writes share those same qualities.

Before difficult times come your way, develop habits of studying God's Word, listening to Christ-centered teaching and music, and reading soul-nourishing literature, both nonfiction and fiction. Daily fill the reservoir from which you can draw when facing difficult times—and helping others face theirs.

SHEDDING LIGHT ON DEPRESSION AND SUICIDE

Depression isn't always wrong.
Some depression comes from simply feeling the crushing weight of pain and brokenness in one's life and the lives of others around the globe. Of course, self-preoccupied woe-is-me depression quickly becomes deeply unhealthy. But sometimes when we feel burdened, we may simply be joining the whole creation in groaning because of a world of suffering. In that case, we're in good company, for "the Spirit himself intercedes for us with groans that words cannot express" (Romans 8:26).

It's no sin to feel that burden, and sometimes it's a sin *not* to. Some of what passes for Christian contentment is, in fact, indifference to the evil and suffering around us. It's apathy toward the plight of God's image-bearers, demonstrated by the fact that we do so little and give so little to help them. Our lives should reflect a groaning that gives way to joy, celebrating what God has done for us in Christ, and thanking him that he will rescue us once and for all from evil and suffering.

I feel a profound sadness and mourning for human brokenness, for children exploited by the sex trade, killed by abortion, and dying of diseases and disasters. Still, my confidence in an all-good and all-powerful God allows me to simultaneously feel happiness even in this world of evil and suffering. When I ponder the scars on his hands and feet I say, "Yet will I trust him," then I seek to be his hands and feet to a needy world.

While I don't suffer chronic depression, I've had a few several month periods of depression that have awakened me to its reality and the hold it can have. A novelist friend wrote me:

> I went through a long spell of clinical depression. I was even hospitalized for a short time. I felt bereft and hopeless. I pleaded with God for healing and understanding. Why am I going through this emotional pain? I thought if I could just understand it, I'd somehow solve it.
>
> Never, in all my years of being a Christian, did I cling to God so closely. Never had I talked to Him so honestly. Those weeks, months, and even years of questioning and searching drew me nearer to Him. Walking through my discontent led me to a life so much richer than the one I'd been living. God used my depression and pain for something so much greater than I could envision. I've learned that there is purpose in struggle…even when we can't see it.

During her depression my friend couldn't see anything good. Now, looking back, the good seems obvious.

When I posted a blog about a time of depression I was experiencing, a few people expressed shock that someone who had written about subjects such as grace and Heaven could ever be depressed! I had to laugh, since far better people than I have experienced far worse depression, including Charles Spurgeon, Martin Luther, John Owen, and William Cowper, to name a few.

When I wrote about what I was learning from the depression, someone brought me a "prophetic word" that I was depressed because I wasn't trusting God. Ironically, I had come to trust God deeper in the midst of the depression than I had before it. God used that four-month period of depression to enrich my life. I hope I don't ever experience it again—but if I do, I pray he will enrich me through it again.

Sadness, grief, and times of depression are part of life under the Curse; God gives us the resources, including his people, to move forward.
Hurting Christians increasingly complain about the treatment they've received from church people. If you've had a bad experience, write out a list of what you wish church people had done for you and what you wish they hadn't done. Then use it as a guideline to reach out today and minister to others who need *your* wisdom and encouragement.

Don't grumble about others. Change yourself. Look closely inside the church and you'll find many believers way ahead of you in their care and compassion. Perhaps you haven't seen the church helping the suffering because you haven't stayed with the suffering enough to see what the church *is* doing. Many hurting people have told me amazing stories of faithful love shown by God's people in Christ's body. In hard times, Nanci and I have experienced the same. Imperfect as it is, we thank God for the church.

"The LORD is close to the brokenhearted and saves those who are crushed in spirit" (Psalm 34:18). Reaching out to others in need is one of the greatest cures for loneliness and depression. "In humility consider others better than yourselves. Each of you should look not only to your own interests, but also to the interests of others" (Philippians 2:3–4).

Helen Keller, blind and deaf since a toddler, wrote, "Although the world is full of suffering it is also full of the overcoming of it.... Believe, when you are most unhappy, that there is something for you to do in the world. So long as you can sweeten another's pain, life is not in vain."[2]

Suicide is from the devil, who is a murderer and lies to tempt us to self-murder.

I must mention suicide because the idea seduces some suffering people. God commands us not to murder (see Exodus 20:13). Suicide is self-murder. God calls us to "endure hardship...like a good soldier of Christ Jesus" (2 Timothy 2:3). To take your life is to go absent without leave.

Trust God's purpose for your life even when you can't grasp what it is. Value the life he has given you, even when it doesn't *seem* worth living. Reach out to others and get help. Talk with someone trustworthy who will stand with you and help you hold on to what's right and good, including the preservation of the life God has entrusted to you.

Even in the midst of suffering we can embrace the gift of laughter and a happiness that speaks to others of Christ's reality.

A close friend once told me, "I always know when you're hurting. You joke and laugh more."

For Nanci and for me, laughter is therapy. We love to laugh. As people instinctively blink to get something out of their eye, we laugh to lighten our hearts. "[God] will yet fill your mouth with laughter and your lips with shouts of joy" (Job 8:21).

I spent three hours with Carol King, a godly woman in her fifties who was dying of cancer. She'd read a few of my books and wanted to talk about Heaven. What struck me that day was the gift of laughter.

"I need some new clothes," Carol said, "but why buy them? I used to get jumbo-sized shampoo, but now it's a waste. I don't even buy green bananas, because by the time they ripen I'll probably be gone!" Carol said it not morbidly, but with heartfelt peace and joy. She anticipated a better world. Carol had already suffered great pain and had no romantic notions about death. But she faced death with quiet joy and contagious laughter.

I left, encouraged by a dying woman I'll always consider my friend. She went to her Savior soon after. I look forward to laughing with Carol in the world where Jesus promised those now weeping, "You will laugh" (Luke 6:21).

Puritan Matthew Henry, who knew considerable suffering, embraced a theology that made its way to his heart. Henry was said to have "possessed the desirable disposition and power of looking on the bright side of everything.... There was a loveliness in his spirit and a gladness in his heart, which caused others to feel 'how happy a thing it must be to be a Christian.'... This cheerfulness pervaded his entire life. One reason of the great power of his life over many who were not religious men, lay in the constancy of that happy spirit which they saw and coveted."[3]

LIGHTENING THE LOAD THROUGH PRAYER

Even if God doesn't grant deliverance, we can pray persistently, with humble acceptance of God's will.

We should ask God to deliver us from Satan's attacks of unbelief and discouragement. We should learn to resist them, in the power of Christ (see James 4:7). Trusting God for the grace to endure adversity is as much an act of faith as trusting him for deliverance from it.

This does not mean God will always answer our prayers as we would like him to. Jesus pleaded three times for God to "Take this cup from me," yet God didn't. Three times Paul asked God to remove the thorn in his flesh, yet God didn't. Jesus and Paul both recognized God had higher purposes and willingly submitted to them.

Pray in light of God's sovereign grace and unfailing love, and your anxiety will eventually give way to peace.

"Rejoice in the Lord always. I will say it again: Rejoice! Let your gentleness be evident to all. The Lord is near. Do not be anxious about anything, but in everything, by prayer and petition, with thanksgiving, present your requests to God. And the peace of God, which transcends all understanding, will guard your hearts and your minds in Christ Jesus" (Philippians 4:4–7).

Great peace comes in meditating on the attributes of our God and his care for us. Spurgeon said, "It would be a very sharp and trying experience to me to think that I have an affliction which God never sent me, that the bitter cup was never filled by his hand, that my trials were never measured out by him, nor sent to me by his arrangement of their weight and quantity."[4]

God hears the desires of the afflicted and promises to listen to them and strengthen their hearts.
"You hear, O LORD, the desire of the afflicted; you encourage them, and you listen to their cry" (Psalm 10:17).

Joni Eareckson Tada writes,

"O God," I often pray in the morning, "God, I cannot do this. I cannot do this thing called quadriplegia. I have no resources for this. I have no strength for this—but you do. You've got resources. You've got strength. I can't do quadriplegia, but I can do all things through you as you strengthen me [Phil. 4:13]. I have no smile for this woman who's going to walk into my bedroom in a moment. She could be having coffee with another friend, but she's chosen to come here to help me get up. O God, please may I borrow your smile?"[5]

Joni then speaks of the humble and afflicted:

They are people who are humiliated by their weaknesses. Catheterized people whose leg bags spring leaks on somebody else's brand-new carpet. Immobilized people who must be fed, cleansed, dressed, and taken care of like infants. Once-active people crippled by chronic aches and pains. God opposes the proud but gives grace to the humble, so then submit yourselves to God.

It is when your soul has been blasted bare, when you feel raw and undone, that you can be better bonded to the Savior. And then you not only meet suffering on God's terms, but you meet joy on God's terms. And then God—as he does every morning at 7:30 when I cry out to him out of my affliction—happily shares his gladness, his joy flooding over heaven's walls filling my heart in a waterfall of delight, which then in turn always streams out to others in a flood of encouragement, and then erupts back to God in an ecstatic fountain of praise. He gets your heart pumping for heaven. He injects his peace, power, and perspective into your spiritual being. He imparts a new way of looking at your hardships. He puts a song in your heart.[6]

LOOKING FORWARD TO BRIGHTER DAYS

God does not want to merely get us out of the pain to the joy; he desires to walk with us *in* the pain.

This verse bears repeating: "Weeping may remain for a night, but rejoicing comes in the morning" (Psalm 30:5). God focuses not only on the morning, but *he stays with us in the night when we can do nothing but weep.* When we languish in the deepest pit and darkness weighs on our souls and we wonder if God even exists, this psalm reminds us that he remains there with us.

For God's children, weeping is often healthy and always temporary. David and his men wept when enemies took their wives and children captive (see 1 Samuel 30:3–4). Jesus wept (see John 11:35). So should we.

We can trust God even though we can't see God.

God's presence remains with his children whether we recognize it or not. In periods of darkness, God calls upon us to trust him until the light returns.

"But if I go to the east, he is not there; if I go to the west, I do not find him. When he is at work in the north, I do not see him; when he turns to the south, I catch no glimpse of him. But *he knows the way that I take;* when he has tested me, I will come forth as gold" (Job 23:8–10).

God sets a limit on evil and suffering in your life. In Job's life, Satan could do only so much for so long. God determined the limits. If you are God's child, then your suffering cannot outlast your lifetime. And since life continues after death, your suffering can last only the tiniest fraction of your true eternal lifetime. Rest in this knowledge. He offers you comfort before death and—one day—rescue *by* death or his return, whichever comes first.

Trusting God in suffering involves obeying God even if he chooses not to rescue us.

Shadrach, Meshach, and Abednego refused to worship an idol even though King Nebuchadnezzar threatened to throw them into a blazing furnace. The three young men answered, "If we are thrown into the blazing furnace, the God we serve is able to save us from it, and he will rescue us from your hand, O king. *But even if he does not,* we want you to know, O king, that we will not serve your gods or worship the image of gold you have set up" (Daniel 3:16–18).

Some people hold tenaciously to a faith that their child will not die, that their cancer will disappear, that their spouse will recover from a stroke. Do they have faith in God or is their faith in what they desperately want God to do?

The three young Hebrew men trusted and obeyed God, knowing he could deliver them from the fire and asking him to do so, but realizing he might not. God sometimes chooses to heal in supernatural answer to prayer. Still, all who pray for healing should affirm, like Daniel's friends, that they will worship and honor and obey God "even if he does not."

We cannot have the right perspective in facing evil and suffering without a picture of the love-driven agony of Jesus on our behalf.

If the hands and feet of Jesus had not bled for me, I would not follow him. Since they did, by his grace I will follow him anywhere.

Jesus faced the problem of evil by undergoing the only suffering that would ultimately kill death. The carpenter of Nazareth, first crying in a wooden manger, then with splinters in his hands, and finally nails in his hands, has forever won my heart.

We could never pay the penalty for our sins even by suffering eternal punishment; God's wrath against our evil would never be quenched. Yet Christ bore God's complete wrath for us, and he did it in a matter of hours—because he loved us.

God's people have always put their own suffering in perspective by looking at Christ's. Martin Luther said, "When I consider my crosses, tribulations, and temptations, I shame myself almost to death, thinking what they are in comparison of the sufferings of my blessed Savior Christ Jesus."[7]

Christ rescues Hell-bound people, changing both their destination and their characters.

"And they sang a new song: 'You are worthy to take the scroll and to open its seals, because you were slain, and with your blood you purchased men for God from every tribe and language and people and nation. You have made them to be a kingdom and priests to serve our God, and they will reign on the earth'" (Revelation 5:9–10).

This passage lauds Christ as the ultimate hero for two reasons: first for the suffering and death he endured for us, out of love; and second, for what he accomplished through it. Christ's suffering and death reversed the Curse so God's original design for our world would prevail.

Martyn Lloyd-Jones tells of how God spoke to John Wesley in a crisis at sea:

> John Wesley, prior to his conversion…knew all about religion, but while crossing the Atlantic, and in a terrible storm that seemed to be leading to certain death, he felt that he had nothing. He was afraid to die and afraid of everything. And what struck him was the contrast presented by the Moravian Brethren who were in the same ship. They were in comparison with Wesley ignorant men, but their religion meant something real and vital to them. It held them in the storm, and gave them peace and calmness, and indeed joy, even face to face with death. Wesley's religion appeared to be excellent. He gave all his goods to the poor, he preached in prisons, and he had crossed the Atlantic to preach to pagans in Georgia. He was a man of immense knowledge of things religious. And yet the trial revealed to him and to others the nature of his religion, and showed it to be worthless.[8]

Wesley's realization that he desperately feared death, yet the Christians on that ship did not, made him reevaluate whether he really believed. Ultimately it helped lead him to true faith in Jesus.

Although death is the last enemy, the ghastly result of the Fall and the Curse, Christ made death a passageway into the loving presence of God, "so that by his death he might destroy him who holds the power of death—that is, the devil—and free those who all their lives were held in slavery by their fear of death" (Hebrews 2:14–15).

Christ has liberated us from the need to fear death!

Emmanuel Ndikumana was nineteen years old when he heard that a group of young men in Burundi had planned to murder him in two weeks. He chose to stay where he was and survived the attempted murder through God's amazing providence. When telling his story, Emmanuel made this enlightening comment: "You Americans have a strange attitude toward death; you act as if it is the end."

Notes

1. Corrie ten Boom, *The Hiding Place* (Grand Rapids, MI: Chosen Books, 2006), 227.

2. First part of quote from Helen Keller, *The World I Live In* (New York: New York Review of Books, 2004), 130; second part "Believe…" from Helen Keller, *We Bereaved* (New York: L. Fulenwider, 1929).

3. Charles Chapman, *Matthew Henry* (London: Arthur Hall, Virtue, 1859), 114–17.

4. Charles Haddon Spurgeon, *Christian History* 10, no. 1 (1991): 29.

5. Joni Eareckson Tada, "Hope…the Best of Things," in John Piper and Justin Taylor, *Suffering and the Sovereignty of God* (Wheaton, IL: Crossway Books, 2006), 195.

6. Joni Earecksdon Tada and Steve Estes, *When God Weeps,* (Grand Rapids, MI: Zondervan, 1997), 196–97.

7. *The Table Talk or Familiar Discourse of Martin Luther,* 86.

8. Martyn Lloyd-Jones, *Why Does God Allow Suffering?* (Wheaton, IL: Crossway Books, 1994), 42–43.

44

Finding Grace to Ease Others' Suffering and to Endure Our Own

To teach us how to mourn, God includes many laments in his inspired Word.

Laments make up more than one-third of the psalms. The contrast between Israel's hymnbook and the church's says a great deal about our failure to acknowledge suffering. If we don't sing about suffering and struggle, why shouldn't our people feel surprised when it comes?

Read Psalm 88, arguably the most discouraging portion of the Bible: "My soul is full of trouble and my life draws near the grave.... You have put me in the lowest pit, in the darkest depths. Your wrath lies heavily upon me; you have overwhelmed me with all your waves.... My eyes are dim with grief.... Why, O LORD, do you reject me and hide your face from me?" Not exactly a sunny day! And listen to how it ends: "You have taken my companions and loved ones from me; the darkness is my closest friend."

Yet even then the psalmist cries out to "the God who saves me" (verse 1).

The psalms of lament grant us permission to express to God our honest questions, doubts, griefs and despair. That our heavenly Father chose to include these as inspired Scripture suggests that parents should encourage emotional honesty in their children. They should learn to voice to God and to us their disappointments, fears, and frustrations along with their dreams, happiness, and gratitude. Certainly we should resist whining and self-pity, both in ourselves and our children. But we should also guard against pretense and the silent seeds of disillusionment and bitterness.

Musician Michael Card writes,

My experience with lament and with the living God occurred several years ago, when I was diagnosed with a degenerative liver disease. My father had died when I was seventeen, and now faced with the possibility that I might die, leaving behind my seventeen-year-old son and fourteen-year-old daughter, I was overwhelmed with feelings of anger and confusion and pain. When I finally let go and cried out to God, it was in fury and frustration that I unleashed on Him, accusing Him, questioning Him. It did not make any sense to me. How could a loving God allow my children to go through the pain that I had? I had done all that He had asked of me. I had been a faithful servant and made the right choices and sacrifices. Why was He doing this to me? How dare He? I was certain that I had pushed Him too far, that I was now going to experience His wrath and condemnation for my ranting and unbelief. But what I found instead was great mercy and tenderness. I experienced His loving-kindness in a way that I never had before. He had been waiting all along for me to come to the end of myself and fall on my knees before Him. He had been waiting for me to be completely honest with who I was, instead of who I thought I should be. And I realized that it was in my brokenness and weakness that I was truly able to know the tremendous love that my great God has for me. He could take anything that I hurled at Him. He was not going to let me go.[1]

GIVING COMFORT

People need to feel loved.

A hurting child needs to feel his father's arms around him. When the father is away, he may leave written words of love, as God has in his Word. But he may also call on the child's older brothers and sisters to express his love to his child.

To ignore someone's pain is to add to that pain. Instead of fearing we'll say the wrong thing, we should reach out to hurting people. Many times it's better just to put our arms around someone and cry with them; people almost always appreciate it when you acknowledge their loss. Yet so long as your heart is right, saying *something* is nearly always better than saying nothing.

There is a time for silence, to just sit and listen and weep with those who weep.

We often condemn Job's friends, but we should remember that they started well. When they saw his misery, they wept aloud. And then for seven days and nights they sat with him, in silence, wordlessly expressing their concern for him (see Job 2:11–13).

If we don't know what to say to a friend in crisis, remember that so long as Job's friends remained quiet, they helped him bear his grief. Later, when they began giving unsolicited advice and rebuke, Job not only had to deal with his suffering, but with his friends' smug responses, which *added* to his suffering.

When someone in pain expresses raw emotions, we shouldn't scold them. Friends let friends share honest feelings. When the premature and misguided correction of Job's friends hurt Job, they didn't have sense enough to say, "I'm sorry," and then shut up. They went right on hurting him. So Job said to them, "Miserable comforters are you all!" (16:2).

Darrell Scott told me that after his daughter Rachel was murdered at Columbine, people often quoted Romans 8:28 to him. He wasn't ready to hear it. How sad that such a powerful verse, cited carelessly or prematurely, becomes a source of pain when it should offer great comfort. Think of God's truths like tools. Don't use a hammer when you need a wrench. And don't use either when you need to give someone a hug, a blanket, or a meal—or just weep with them.

On the other hand, Nancy Guthrie says sufferers should extend grace to the insensitive comforters who hurt them. The last thing a grieving person needs is to take on the burden of resentment. "Be kind and compassionate to one another, forgiving each other, just as in Christ God forgave you" (Ephesians 4:32).

Don't disappear or avoid your friend who needs you now more than ever.

My mother died in 1981, when I was a young pastor. Ten years earlier, not long after I'd become a Christian, I had the joy of leading Mom to Christ. We grew together, reading and discussing Scripture and great books, praying and laughing together, and later fussing over my children, her granddaughters, Karina and Angela. When she died, I mourned my loss, my wife's, and above all my children's. I felt like part of me had been taken away.

As I walked into church that first Sunday after Mom's death, I felt as though my presence parted the Red Sea. Instead of greeting me warmly in their usual way, people stepped aside. I knew they did it because they didn't know what to say, yet it magnified my loneliness.

Most of us have seen friends disappear when we most needed them—and without meaning to, we've done the same to others. If you find yourself not wanting to make a phone call when you hear about someone's crisis, remind yourself that any expression of concern is better than none. When people lose a loved one, they don't want to "move on" as if the person never existed. Even if doing so makes them cry, usually they want and need to talk about them.

"Rejoice with those who rejoice; mourn with those who mourn" (Romans 12:15). We tend to do better at rejoicing. Because we don't like to feel pain, we tend to ignore others' pain. But they need us to become the arms of Christ to them.

If we're not there for them, who will be?

Allow the dying to come to terms with it and seek dying grace from God.

While reading one chapter a day from my book *Heaven,* a man and his dying wife spent her last forty-six days talking openly about her eternal future. This allowed them to cry and laugh together. After reading the final chapter, they prayed and then she died. He called their final days together precious.

Think of how that time might have played out, if one of them had refused to accept her impending death. We associate fighting death with courage, and sometimes that's true. At other times there is greater courage in accepting and facing death and preparing for it.

"Jesus began to show to His disciples that He must…suffer many things… and be killed, and be raised the third day" (Matthew 16:21, NKJV). Peter, instead of accepting Christ's death, fought it: "Then Peter took Him aside and began to rebuke Him, saying, 'Far be it from You, Lord; this shall not happen to You!'" (16:22, NKJV). In the very next verse Jesus said to Peter, "Get behind me, Satan! You are a stumbling block to me; you do not have in mind the things of God, but the things of men."

Some things in life are hard to accept. Denying, arguing, and complaining will not help. Worse, those responses keep us from seeing what God is doing, and from trusting him and drawing near in the hour we need him most.

COMFORT IN THE BODY OF CHRIST

To serve God in suffering, we need the companionship of faithful brothers and sisters in Christ.

Relational tension, anger, broken hearts, and lack of forgiveness can cause great suffering. We have a friend who found it easier to accept her beloved mother's death than the rejection of her estranged sister.

Regardless of the cause, those who suffer should seek companionship and encouragement, rather than withdraw. "Two are better than one.… For if either of them falls, the one will lift up his companion. But woe to the one who falls where there is not another to lift him up" (Ecclesiastes 4:9–10, NASB).

One Sunday morning at John Franklin's church, they called the leaders up to the platform to pray. John rolled up in his wheelchair. A disabled person came to him after the service, saying, "I've been to a number of churches and I've never once seen a church leader with a disability!" John, just being who he is, encouraged her. Neither he nor the church lets his condition sideline him from serving Christ.

Paul wrote, "Now when I went to Troas to preach the gospel of Christ and found that the Lord had opened a door for me, I still had no peace of mind, because I did not find my brother Titus there. So I said good-by to them and went on to Macedonia" (2 Corinthians 2:12–13). Paul needed a brother to help him face his ministry difficulties. When he didn't find Titus, even the great apostle lacked the support he needed to go through the door God had opened for him.

God eased Paul's distress through sending Titus at last: "For even when we came into Macedonia our flesh had no rest, but we were afflicted on every side: conflicts without, fears within. But God, who comforts the depressed, comforted us by the coming of Titus" (2 Corinthians 7:5–6, NASB). Paul acknowledged his depression, and God comforted him through the presence of a beloved brother.

Some time after the death of his son, Owen, Dustin Shramek wrote,

> During the first months after Owen's death we felt very little comfort from God.... On the six month anniversary I was reading through all the e-mails and cards we had received from God's people and I was reflecting on the help we had received from his people in the Middle East and in Istanbul where he was born. Then…it dawned on me. God was and is comforting us by the coming of countless brothers and sisters in Christ. Often we don't feel the warm presence of the Lord in our suffering, but that does not mean he has left us alone. We are a part of the body of Christ and it is through this body that he ministers to us in our darkest days.[2]

SUFFERING WELL

When suffering comes, we should ask God to use it for his glory.
Josef Tson told me our first question in suffering should not be, "Why?" but, "God, what do you want to do in the world through my suffering?"

When interrogators worked Josef into exhaustion for ten hours a day, one of his persecutors made a strange statement: "Pastor Tson, when I interrogate people

I am used to feeling their hatred for me. But you do not hate me. It has become a delight for me to be with you."

Josef viewed his suffering as God's means to accomplish God's purpose. As a result, the gospel his persecutors tried to dismiss touched them instead.

Blaming God and others keeps us from suffering's redemptive aspects.

Our impatience with life's struggles and adverse circumstances becomes impatience with God. In Job 40:8 God asks, "Would you condemn me to justify yourself?"

Countless people have let themselves fall into the black hole of blame. Blaming God is a dead-end street, because in doing so you turn away from your greatest source of comfort. Blaming others doesn't work either. Those who throw themselves into vindictive lawsuits never find joy. Others seek comfort in the execution of their loved one's killer. True and lasting comfort eludes them.

Anger harbored in our hearts gives "the devil a foothold" (Ephesians 4:27). Bitterness metastasizes and consumes our passion for serving God. Refuse to engage in thoughts and conversations that feed bitterness. Instead, delight yourself in God, his Word, his people, and the privilege of being a forgiven and Heaven-bound child of God.

Recognizing that suffering has meaning helps us learn not to waste it.

Shortly after speaking together at a conference on suffering, John Piper and David Powlison both learned they had cancer. They formulated ten points under the exhortation, "Don't waste your cancer." They said, "You will waste your cancer if you

1. do not believe it is designed for you by God
2. believe it is a curse and not a gift
3. seek comfort from your odds rather than from God
4. refuse to think about death
5. think that "beating" cancer means staying alive rather than cherishing Christ
6. spend too much time reading about cancer and not enough time reading about God
7. let it drive you into solitude instead of deepen your relationships with manifest affection
8. grieve as those who have no hope

9. treat sin as casually as before

10. fail to use it as a means of witness to the truth and glory of Christ."[3]

How you handle suffering tells your life story.

At memorial services no one says, "When Dad got that big promotion and was voted man of the year, he maintained a cheerful attitude." They say, "Dad faced his disability and his job loss and cancer and Mom's death with a faithful trust in God, never bitter and always kind, even when his heart ached."

Twenty-five years ago, my friend Roger Huntington was a successful Alaskan businessman, bank director, and chairman of the board of a $200 million corporation.

"As I became an adult," he says, "I aspired to be a tall tree. Roger was at the top." He and Carole "realized that even with our earthly abundance, we didn't have any joy."

In 1988 Roger crashed his plane. The fuel-tank cover dislodged and gasoline poured on his head. A fire burned 60 percent of his body, permanently marring his face.

The first time Roger saw himself sideways in a mirror, he wept. He asked God why. He contemplated suicide but refused to do it because eleven of his family members had killed themselves. He knew the pain it inflicted on others.

Roger realized that all he had depended on had disappeared. "My tree was cut down," he said. He turned to Jesus. As Roger put it, "I got a new tree, with Jesus Christ at the top."

Since then, Roger and Carole have dedicated their lives to helping native young people and their families follow Christ. He has developed character and touched lives through his response to great suffering. Roger considers his scars a tribute to human weakness. But he says those scars are also "a testimony to God's healing power."

Learn to find your identity in God, not your illness.

We live in a time when we are defined as disabled, bipolar, alcoholic, ADHD, victims of lupus, cancer, Parkinson's disease, and nearly everything else. Our condition easily becomes our primary reference point.

I am an insulin-dependent diabetic, but my disease doesn't define me. I learn what's necessary, take care of myself, and live. I shouldn't become preoccupied with a disease any more than with a career, a hobby, possessions, or a retirement program. I want Jesus Christ first, and my family second, and then my church and ministry to define my life.

David Powlison wrote,

People will often express their care and concern by inquiring about your health. That's good, but the conversation easily gets stuck there. So tell them openly about your sickness, seeking their prayers and counsel, but then change the direction of the conversation by telling them what your God is faithfully doing to sustain you with ten thousand mercies. Robert Murray McCheyne wisely said, "For every one look at your sins, take ten looks at Christ."... For every one sentence you say to others about your cancer, say ten sentences about your God, and your hope, and what he is teaching you, and the small blessings of each day. For every hour you spend researching or discussing your cancer, spend ten hours researching and discussing and serving your Lord.[4]

We should view our God-permitted suffering as his specific calling to us, and not resent it if he calls others to suffer less.

Sufferers commonly ask, "Why me? Why not someone else? Why haven't my friends lost a child or their husband? Why can they walk and ride bikes while I'm in a wheelchair? Why have you treated me differently, God?"

The resurrected Jesus told Peter that one day he'd be taken "where you do not want to go" (John 21:18). Verse 19 reads, "Jesus said this to indicate the kind of death by which Peter would glorify God. Then he said to him, 'Follow me!'"

On hearing this, Peter immediately looked at John and asked, "Lord, what about him?" Instinctively he wanted to compare God's difficult calling on his life with his plans for John. Jesus answered, "If I want him to remain alive until I return, what is that to you? You must follow me" (John 21:21–22).

Now, Jesus did *not* want John to remain alive until his return. He wanted Peter to get his point: *John's time and manner of death are none of your business.* He was saying, "Regardless of when and how my other disciples will suffer and die, you are to trust and follow me in my plan for you, including your death."

Comparison is poison. We shouldn't resent but rejoice for those who don't have our diseases or losses. We should thank God he knows exactly what suffering and death he's called each of us to endure. Early tradition says that when Peter was about to be crucified, he asked to be turned upside down, judging himself unworthy to die upright like his Lord.

As Jesus knew the details of Peter's death, he knows all about yours and mine. Whatever death God has in view for us, it should likewise be *a death by which we will glorify God.*

God knows how much we can bear; he knows how to relieve suffering and how to strengthen us to endure it.

"No test or temptation that comes your way is beyond the course of what others have had to face. All you need to remember is that God will never let you down; he'll never let you be pushed past your limit; he'll always be there to help you come through it" (1 Corinthians 10:13, MSG). This truth applies to every aspect of our lives, including the manner, timing, and duration of our dying.

As a young Christian, I loved the writings of Joseph Bayly. Joe and his wife lost three of their children—one at eighteen days, after surgery; another at five years, from leukemia; and a third at eighteen years, in a sledding accident complicated by hemophilia. Joe spoke honestly and from his heart. He grieved for his children and stood strong for his Lord.

In 1969, the year I came to Christ, Joe wrote a little book called *Psalms of My Life.* It contained a poem that a few years later I typed and placed on the wall by my desk in our first apartment. Forty years later, it still touches me. It's called "A Psalm While Packing Books."

This cardboard box
Lord
see it says
Bursting limit
100 lbs. per square inch.
The box maker knew
how much strain
the box would take
what weight
would crush it.
You are wiser
than the box maker
maker of my spirit
my mind
my body.
Does the box know
when pressure increases close to
the limit?
No
It knows nothing.
But I know

when my breaking point
Is near.
And so I pray
Maker of my soul
Determiner of the pressure
within
upon
me
Stop it
lest I be broken
Or else
change the pressure rating
of this fragile container
of your grace
so that I may bear more.[5]

Notes

1. Michael Card, *A Sacred Sorrow* (Colorado Springs: NavPress, 2005), 9.
2. Doug Wolter, "Justin, Dustin, and God's Lessons on Suffering," September 21, 2007. http://life2getherblog.com/2007/09/.
3. John Piper and Justin Taylor, eds., *Suffering and the Sovereignty of God*, (Wheaton, IL: Crossway Books, 2006), 207–16.
4. John Piper and Justin Taylor, eds., *Suffering and the Sovereignty of God*, 212–213.
5. Joseph Bayly, *Psalms of My Life* (Colorado Springs: David C. Cook, 2002). Copyright © 2002 Cook Communications Ministries. Used with permission. May not be further reproduced. All rights reserved.

45

Discovering Death's Curse and Blessing

Death is life's greatest certainty.

No exercise program, diet, or therapy prevents death. Corpses don't undertake cosmetic surgery. Even the young die from overdoses, accidents, and diseases. Famous athletes and Hollywood stars alike wind up in nursing homes. Suffering and old age are the great equalizers.

David wrote,

> Show me, O LORD, my life's end
>> and the number of my days;
>> let me know how fleeting is my life.
> You have made my days a mere handbreadth;
>> the span of my years is as nothing before you.
>> Each man's life is but a breath.
> Man is a mere phantom as he goes to and fro:
>> He bustles about, but only in vain;
>> he heaps up wealth, not knowing who will get it.
> But now, Lord, what do I look for?
>> My hope is in you. (Psalm 39:4–7)

We shouldn't obsess over death. Neither should we follow our culture's lead in denying death until it thrusts itself upon us. When we fail to face death, we remain unprepared for what awaits us on the other side.

We should live our short todays in light of what A. W. Tozer called "the long tomorrow." Many who receive a terminal diagnosis experience for the first time the bittersweet blessing of coming to terms with their mortality.

When our friend Leona Bryant discovered she had a short time to live, she told me of her radical change in perspective. "The most striking thing," she said, "is that I find myself totally uninterested in all the conversations about material things. Things used to matter to me, but now I find my thoughts are never on possessions, but always on Christ and people. I consider it a privilege to live each day knowing I'll die soon. What a difference it makes!"

We can deny death, but we can't avoid it.

An old story concerns a slave who traveled with his master to Baghdad. Early one morning, milling through the marketplace, the slave saw Death in human form. The slave recoiled in terror, convinced Death's threatening look meant he intended to take him that day.

The slave ran to his master. "I've seen Death," he wailed. "Please let me flee on my camel so tonight I can reach Samarra where Death cannot find me." His master agreed and the terrified servant took off on the fifteen-hour journey.

A few hours later, the master himself saw Death among Baghdad's throngs. He boldly approached Death and asked him, "Why did you give my servant a threatening look?"

"That was not a threatening look," Death replied. "That was a look of surprise. I was amazed to see your servant today in Baghdad, for I have an appointment with him tonight in Samarra."

Of course, it's our righteous Master, not Death, who has the power to call us home at his appointed time. But the story teaches a valid point: None of us knows the time or place of our death. Neither can we know its manner. And there's nothing we can do to escape it: "No man has power over the wind to contain it; so no one has power over the day of his death" (Ecclesiastes 8:8).

The statistic never wavers: 100 percent of people die.

Wise people live in light of death's certainty.

The last thing most people want to think about is the last thing they'll do: die.

In the oldest psalm, Moses wrote, "The length of our days is seventy years—or eighty, if we have the strength; yet their span is but trouble and sorrow, for they quickly pass, and we fly away.... Teach us to number our days aright, that we may gain a heart of wisdom" (90:10, 12).

Christians get two opportunities to live on Earth. This first one begins and ends. It is but a dot. The second opportunity will be an infinite line, extending on forever. We all live *in* the dot. If we're wise, we'll live *for* the line. "In keeping with his [God's] promise we are looking forward to a new heaven and a new earth, the home of righteousness" (2 Peter 3:13).

Two things stand between where we live now and that marvelous world where we'll live forever: death and resurrection. If we never died, we'd never be resurrected. We'd never enjoy a glorious eternity with Christ and our spiritual family.

So while death is an enemy and part of sin's curse, because of Christ's death and resurrection, it's the dark passage through which we enter the brilliance of never-ending life.

Death isn't the worst that can happen to us; for God's children, it leads to the best.

To die apart from Christ is terrible because it ends all opportunity and hope. To die loving Christ means spending eternity with God. That's what Justin Martyr meant when he wrote to persecutors in AD 150, "You can kill us, but you can't hurt us."[1]

Dying is far better for the Christian than doing evil. It's much worse to deny Christ than to die. At death our sin will end and we'll be with Christ forever. Meanwhile, these words from a hymn make an excellent prayer: "O let me never, never outlive my love for Thee."

Our grief at death is real and deep, yet knowing Christ transforms it.

The Bible everywhere assumes that people will grieve. Job grieved unbearably at the loss of his ten children (Job 1:20; 2:13); so did the widow of Nain, who lost her son and received Jesus' compassion (see Luke 7:11–13).

Men stoned Stephen to death. Before dying, he beheld Jesus at the Father's right hand. Remarkably, Luke tells us, "Godly men buried Stephen and mourned deeply for him" (Acts 8:2). They mourned a brother who had died righteously and who in dying had seen his beloved Jesus! Knowing that Stephen was far better off with the Lord didn't keep his friends from mourning their loss.

Death is not a "natural" part of life as God intended it. It is the unnatural result of evil. And yet, God has removed the ultimate sting of death, which explains the appropriate sense of peace and triumph that accompanies grief at a Christian's memorial service.

"Brothers, we do not want you to be ignorant about those who fall asleep, or to grieve like the rest of men, who have no hope" (1 Thessalonians 4:13). We grieve differently, yet honestly and openly, precisely because we look forward to a New Heaven and New Earth (see 2 Peter 3:13).

I've conducted funerals for both Christians and non-Christians. As I look into the audience, the tears are just as real for Christians, but I also see hope, perspective, and peace in the midst of mourning. The promise of God over-shadows everything: "He will wipe every tear from their eyes. There will be no more death or mourning or crying or pain, for the old order of things has passed away" (Revelation 21:4).

We haven't "lost" our believing loved ones, because we know where they are. And we know in the resurrection we will live with God and with them on a New Earth. We shouldn't restrict our vision to the narrow horizons of this world (see 1 Corinthians 15:19).

For Christians, death is not a wall but a doorway.
Death is not a last good-bye, but a "See you later." When my mother died, it felt like part of me went to Heaven with her. Just a few hours before Mom died in 1981, Nanci prayed with our two-and-a-half-year-old. Karina asked Nanci, "When Gramma Alcorn dies and Jesus takes her to Heaven, will he take her bed with her?"

My wife told her no. Karina nodded and said, "She won't need her bed in Heaven because she can lay in Jesus' lap!"

After Mom's death that night, I returned from my parents' house at 3:00 a.m. and woke Karina to tell her. "Do you know where Grandma Alcorn is right now?" I asked my groggy daughter.

Karina smiled and said, "Yes, Daddy—*she's in Heaven.*"

I stared at her, stunned. Her grandmother, to whom Karina was very close, had been in bed at her own house for the previous two months. How did my daughter know she'd gone to Heaven? I'm convinced God told her as she slept.

While we should never pray to our loved ones, only to God, I've often asked God to give my mom a hug or tell her I love her. It's part of anticipating our reunion.

We do a disservice to ourselves and to others when we turn death-avoidance into an idol.
"Death is the destiny of every man; the living should take this to heart" (Ecclesiastes 7:2).

Speak openly of death with your dying family members. If you're the one dying, talk about it directly. Read Philippians 1:20–23. Read aloud Revelation 21–22, as I did regularly to my mother in the final months of her life. Read Psalm

23: "Even though I walk through the valley of the shadow of death, I will fear no evil, for you are with me; your rod and your staff, they comfort me.... My cup overflows. Surely goodness and love will follow me all the days of my life, and I will dwell in the house of the LORD forever" (verses 4–6).

Don't let discomfort or denial keep you from walking hand in hand with your family through the valley of death's shadow, where God can comfort and calm fears, where cups can overflow, and where you can celebrate and anticipate God's eternal goodness and love.

Many people later regret not conversing directly and praying about death and Heaven during their loved ones' last days here. Don't be one of them.

We should use every day of our lives to prepare for the day of our death.

Shortly before a crazed gunman murdered her, Virginia Tech student Lauren McCain wrote in her diary, "Show me your purpose for me at Tech, and on this earth. But, if you choose not to, I will still praise you and walk where you lead, not because I am selfless, or holy, or 'determined to sacrifice myself to do what is right' but because you are the delight of my heart and I cannot live without you."[2]

Lauren's great passion for Christ touched even more people after her death. She's an example of using the time we have to prepare for whatever God has next for us, including our deaths. Lauren's mother, Sherry, wrote, "We have only one thing to mourn—that Lauren isn't with us. We miss her so much, but we don't mourn for Lauren because she is with Jesus. She has lost nothing compared to what she has gained and we wouldn't bring her back. We only mourn our loss. And in our mourning he still comforts us."[3]

Matthew Henry wrote, "It ought to be the business of every day to prepare for our last day."[4]

My father showed more hostility to the gospel than anyone I've ever known. At age eighty-four, when he had a gun in hand, ready to take his life, God intervened. At last, in a hospital room before getting wheeled into surgery—suffering and desperate—he listened to the gospel I had tried to share with him over the years. I read to him from Romans 3, 6, and 10. God used his Word to break through to Dad's heart. Stunned but joyful, I heard my father repent, confess, pray, and entrust himself to Jesus as his Savior.[5]

Four years later, Nanci and I, our high school daughters, Karina and Angela, and my brother, Lance, stood at Dad's bedside. We watched as his pulse monitor dropped from one hundred beats per minute, to ninety, then eighty, then steadily down to twenty, then went blank. My dad had departed the room, leaving his body behind.

Yet, because he had given his life to Jesus four years earlier—after God had used his suffering to bring him spiritual clarity—we said good-bye knowing we would see him again. That moment I'd dreaded for so many years—my father's death—brought me not only pain but an overshadowing peace and joy.

Death isn't easy to accept, but God remains sovereign over it.

Steve Saint told me about the day he and his wife, Ginny, eagerly waited to meet their daughter, twenty-year-old Stephenie, at the Orlando airport after she returned from a long trip. With the Saints stood Mincaye, one of the tribal warriors who, in 1956, murdered the five missionaries in Ecuador, including Steve's father, Nate. Eventually the gospel his victims had brought to him transformed him. Mincaye became part of the Saint family, with the children calling him Grandfather. At the airport, Grandfather Mincaye waved a sign (upside down) reading *Welcome Home, Stephenie.*

That night, in the midst of their celebration, Stephenie developed a headache and asked Steve to pray for her. Ginny sat on the bed and held Stephenie, while Steve put his arms around both of them and started praying. While he prayed, Stephenie suffered a massive cerebral hemorrhage. They rushed her to the hospital, where Mincaye saw his beloved Stephenie, whom he called Star, lying on a gurney with a tube down her throat and needles in her arm. He grabbed Steve and said, "Who did this to her?"

"I don't know, Mincaye. Nobody is doing this."

Mincaye grabbed Steve again and said, "Babae, don't you see? *God Himself is doing this.*"

Excitedly, Mincaye addressed all the people in the emergency room: "Don't you see? God loving Star, He's taking her to live with Him."

Then he told them, "Look at me, I'm an old man; pretty soon I'm going to die, too, and I'm going there."

Finally, with a pleading look on his face, Mincaye exhorted these bystanders, "Please, please, won't you follow God's trail, too? Coming to God's place, Star and I will be waiting there to welcome you."

Within a few hours, Stephenie died. I'm confident that when she left this world a celebration erupted in another world where others, including her Lord and her Grandfather Nate Saint, who she'd never met, stretched out their arms and said, "Welcome home, Stephenie."

Notes

1. Justin Martyr, *First Apology,* ed. Alexander Roberts and James Donaldson (Grand Rapids, MI: Eerdmans, 1973).
2. Lauren McCain, journal entry December 22, 2006; Beth J. Lueders, *Lifting Our Eyes* (New York: Berkely Publishing, 2007), 165.
3. Lauren McCain, 182.
4. Matthew Henry, quoted in Rick Warren, *The Purpose Driven Life* (Grand Rapids, MI: Zondervan, 2002), 40.
5. I tell the full story in my book *In Light of Eternity* (Colorado Springs: WaterBrook, 1999), 102–7.

Conclusion

Final Thoughts About God, Goodness, Evil, and Suffering

If you're considering whether you should believe in God, the problem of evil and suffering is only one issue—don't overlook the others.

A great deal of evidence argues for God's existence. Though it's beyond the scope of this book to present in detail these arguments, allow me to summarize just a few of them.

The cosmological argument cites the world's existence as evidence of an uncaused, eternal being who created and sustains it. Either something comes from nothing (an unscientific notion), or a first cause or "prime mover" existed prior to everything else. Francis Schaeffer argued that a personal first cause, God, could account for both the material and personal elements of life, while a material first cause could only account for the material.[1]

The transcendental argument says that no part of human experience and knowledge has meaning apart from God's existence. Without God, we have no basis for or explanation of order, logic, reason, intelligence, or rationality. Since Christians and atheists agree there is order and basis for reasoning, this is evidence for God.

The moral argument claims the existence of universal moral values—what humans generally recognize as right and wrong—has no explanation or objectivity without God.

The design argument looks at the universe, noting its clear organizational structures that indicate an intentional complex plan. This argument warrants a broader summary.

How can such high level design exist without a designer? To claim that chance accounts for the world's order and extreme complexity is irrational.

While the design argument has ancient roots, modern science has infused it with stunningly persuasive implications. Atheist Richard Dawkins admits, "There is enough information capacity in a single human cell to store the *Encyclopedia Britannica,* all 30 volumes of it, three or four times over."[2]

We now know what Darwin couldn't imagine, nor could his theory have begun to explain: DNA stores information in the form of a four-character digital code, with strings of precisely sequenced chemicals that transmit detailed assembly instructions. DNA builds protein molecules, the intricate machinery that allows cells to survive.

Consider the most complex software program you've ever used. Could it have developed on its own, without an intelligent designer? Of course not. How much more ridiculous is it to suppose that time, chance, and natural forces—on their own—produced the far more complex DNA?

Scientists once likened the components of living cells to simple LEGO blocks. Now they know that "cells have complex circuits, sliding clamps, energy-generating turbines, rotors, stators, O-rings, U-joints, and drive shafts."[3] None of those tiny engines work unless all parts are present. Hence, they must have coexisted from the beginning. That's what biochemist Michael Behe calls "irreducible complexity."[4]

Non-Christian physicist Paul Davies writes, "We now know that the secret of life lies not with the chemical ingredients as such, but with the logical structure and organizational arrangement of the molecules.... Like a supercomputer, life is an information processing system.... It is the software of the living cell that is the real mystery, not the hardware.... How did stupid atoms spontaneously write their own software?... Nobody knows."[5]

I think there's a better answer than "Nobody knows"; namely, *the atoms didn't write their own software. God did.*

Readers who wish to explore the compelling arguments for intelligent design should take advantage of many excellent resources.[6]

Again, *no truth-seeker should reduce his consideration of God's existence to the single question of evil and suffering.* Though it's one of the most difficult issues, it's not the only one.

The future will fully vindicate God's righteous integrity and the wisdom of his plan.

As God culminates his plan of the ages, Heaven's inhabitants will cry out, "Great and marvelous are your deeds, Lord God Almighty. Just and true are your ways, King of the ages. Who will not fear you, O Lord, and bring glory to your name? For you alone are holy. All nations will come and worship before you, for your righteous acts have been revealed" (Revelation 15:3–4).

In Revelation 16, bowls of wrath are poured out on Earth and an angel declares, "You are just in these judgments" (verse 5). The afflicted rebels curse God "because of their pains and their sores, but they refused to repent of what they had done" (verse 11).

That God's righteous acts will be revealed, that his ways will be shown as just and true, means that God *will* vindicate his character. When he does and eternal judgment falls upon those who refuse to repent, no clear-thinking being will ever again view evil and suffering as evidence against his existence, omnipotence, omniscience, goodness, or love. When we see God for who he is, we will credit him with all goodness and will blame him for no evil. As we kneel in his presence, the "problem of evil and suffering" will vanish like a shadow in the noonday sun.

Telling yourself the truth about suffering can help you deal with it.

Suffering is limited. It could be far worse.

Suffering is temporary. It could last far longer.

Suffering, as we've seen, produces some desirable good. It can make us better people, and it can reveal God's character in ways that bring him glory and bring us good.

God can see all the ultimate results of suffering; we can see only some. When we see more, in his presence, we will forever praise him for it. He calls upon us to trust him and begin that praise now.

The Christian worldview best answers the problem of evil and suffering, but God doesn't force faith on anyone.

As a young Christian I heard the story of a railroad switch operator who brought his beloved son to work with him. At one point he saw two trains coming from opposite directions on the same track. He could avoid the collision only by throwing a switch so one train moved to other tracks—but he looked up to see his boy playing on those very tracks. If he didn't pull the switch, hundreds of people would die. If he did pull the switch, just one would die—his only son.

The train operator pulled the switch. As he saw his son crushed, through his tears he watched hundreds of people pass, clueless to the sacrifice he just made on their behalf.

Likewise, many of us remain oblivious of or indifferent to God's sacrifice of his only Son to preserve us from destruction and to purchase for us eternal life.

In Dostoevsky's *Brothers Karamazov,* Ivan, despite the eloquence of his arguments against God, cannot refute the Christian response. Still, he stubbornly rejects God, saying, "I would rather remain with my unavenged suffering and unsatisfied indignation, *even if I were wrong.*"[7] Ivan's anger and resentment of the true God became his false god.

If you insist on rejecting God, then what can I or anyone else say that will make a difference? You feel angry with a God you claim doesn't exist. Denying him is your revenge—but you are the one who will end up suffering for it. Whether you bow to him now in love or later in judgment, every knee *will* bow to him (see Philippians 2:10–11).

Set aside all other arguments and study the person of Christ. Read of his life in the gospels, the books of Matthew, Mark, Luke, and John. Listen to his words. Can you look at Jesus and not be broken? Can you gaze on the crucified Christ and still resent God for not doing enough to show his love?

Make sure you have received God's gift of eternal life that will deliver you from all evil and suffering after you die.

We *can* know for sure we'll go to Heaven when we die: "I write these things to you who believe in the name of the Son of God so *that you may know* that you have eternal life" (1 John 5:13). Here's a summary of what God calls "the Good News":

To sin means to fail to meet God's holy standards. "All have sinned and fall short of the glory of God" (Romans 3:23). Sin separates us from a relationship with God (see Isaiah 59:2). Sin has terrible consequences, but God has provided a solution: "The wages of sin is death, but the gift of God is eternal life in Christ Jesus our Lord" (Romans 6:23).

Jesus Christ, God's Son, loved us so much that he became a man to deliver us (see John 3:16). Jesus lived a sinless life (see Hebrews 2:17–18; 4:15–16). He died to pay the penalty for our sins (see 2 Corinthians 5:21). On the cross, he took upon himself the Hell we deserve, in order to purchase for us the Heaven we don't deserve. When he died, he said, "It is finished" (John 19:30), using the Greek word for cancelling certificates of debt; it meant "paid in full." Jesus then rose from the grave, defeating sin and conquering death (see 1 Corinthians 15:3–4, 54–57).

How many routes can take us to the Father in Heaven? Peter preached, "Salvation is found in no one else [but Jesus], for there is no other name under heaven given to men by which we must be saved" (Acts 4:12).

"Jesus answered, 'I am *the* way and *the* truth and *the* life. No one comes to the Father *except through me*'" (John 14:6). That's an exclusive statement, but Jesus made it. Do you believe him?

God freely offers us forgiveness in Christ: "He does not treat us as our sins deserve or repay us according to our iniquities.... As far as the east is from the west, so far has he removed our transgressions from us" (Psalm 103:10, 12). To be forgiven, we must repent: "If we confess our sins, he is faithful and just and will forgive us our sins and purify us from all unrighteousness" (1 John 1:9).

"If you confess with your mouth, 'Jesus is Lord,' and believe in your heart that God raised him from the dead, you will be saved" (Romans 10:9).

Righteous deeds will not earn us a place in Heaven (see Titus 3:5). We can take no credit for salvation: "For it is by grace you have been saved, through faith—and this not from yourselves, it is the gift of God—not by works, so that no one can boast" (Ephesians 2:8–9).

Christ offers to everyone the gift of forgiveness and eternal life: "Whoever is thirsty, let him come; and whoever wishes, let him take the free gift of the water of life" (Revelation 22:17).

If you have not accepted this gift offered by Christ at such a great price to him, what's stopping you?

The more we store up our treasures in Heaven, the better we'll prepare ourselves for death.

Jesus said that treasures we store up on Earth won't last. Treasures we store up in Heaven await us and will last forever (see Matthew 6:19–21).

Our choice of where to store up treasures *dramatically* affects how we face death and the afterlife. If someone lays up treasures on Earth, every day he gets closer to death, he moves *away* from his treasures. To him, death is loss.

He who lays up treasures in Heaven, however, looks forward to eternity. He moves daily *toward* his treasures. Since his heart lies with his treasures in Heaven, to him, death is gain, for it will bring him at last to what he most treasures.

When you leave this world, will you be remembered as one who accumulated treasures on Earth that you couldn't keep? Or will you be recalled as one who invested treasures in Heaven that you can never lose?[8]

We should teach our families and churches a theology of suffering.

Read with your children the whole Bible, including its many accounts of evil and suffering (the age appropriate ones). Talk with them about troubling news stories and sick people you know. Prepare your children for life and death. Pass on to them a great gift: a biblical worldview.

Those without a biblically grounded theology of suffering are always just one accident, disease, disability, natural disaster, or combat fatality away from losing their faith. Children absorb their parents' worldview. If they haven't seen a durable, realistic, and biblical response to suffering in their parents—or if they lack the worldview framework to interpret evil and suffering—then during college or before, they will ultimately slide into other worldviews, such as naturalism, materialism, atheism, agnosticism, or false religion.

Reading and discussing biographies of faithful believers can give both children and adults footprints to follow through our suffering.

To suffer and die well, your eyes must lock on the invisible God. When they do, God will make himself visible to you and to others through you.

God considers precious our faith in him to fulfill his promises of future deliverance from evil and suffering.

In Malachi 3, God says to his people, "You have said harsh things against me" (verse 13). They had said it was futile to serve God, since it didn't pay off and the wicked often prospered (see verses 14–15).

But then, we're told, "Those who feared the LORD talked with each other, and the LORD listened and heard. A scroll of remembrance was written in his presence concerning those who feared the LORD and honored his name" (verse 16).

Heaven contains books with detailed historical records of all earthly lives (see Revelation 20:12). Each of us has a place in these records. Obscure events and words originally heard or known by only a handful of people will become public: "What you have whispered in private rooms shall be proclaimed on the housetops" (Luke 12:3, ESV). Your acts of faithfulness and kindness, your private conversations affirming your faith in God in the midst of suffering find full documentation in God's books. He will reward you for them in Heaven. Jesus said he will never forget even our smallest acts of faith (see Mark 9:41).

Although our full reward awaits, the delay will make the reward all the richer when it comes—and it will cultivate our faith as we wait patiently for God to fulfill his promises.

Biblical faith in God is informed by the past and focuses on the future.

Those who question God fixate on the present and past: "It *is* futile to serve God. What *did* we gain?" But God speaks of the future: "They *will* be mine.... I *will* spare them.... You *will* again see the distinction.... Surely the day *is coming*.... The sun of righteousness *will* rise.... You *will* go out and leap like calves" (Malachi 3:17–4:2).

Faith means believing God for the future, that he will deal with evil and suffering, judge the wicked, and reward the righteous (see Hebrews 11:6). We are to live by faith (see Galatians 2:20), stand in faith (see Romans 11:20), walk by faith (see Romans 4:12), take up the shield of faith (see Ephesians 6:16), and hold on to faith (see 1 Timothy 1:19). We must call upon God to empower our faith. We cultivate faith by reverently studying and meditating on God's Word (see John 20:31; Romans 10:17).

We should view the deaths of Christian loved ones not as an end but only an interruption, followed by a grand reunion.

Jerry Hardin was my best friend from childhood. We played sports together, sang in choir, went to carnivals, and spent nights under the stars in our sleeping bags in my backyard. We served as each other's best man at our weddings.

At age thirty-eight, after doctors diagnosed him with terminal cancer, Jerry and I talked about suffering, healing, and Heaven. I picked out books for him, and he read them all. When it appeared God wasn't choosing to heal him, we talked about God's grace in giving him time to prepare for what awaits every one of us. We prayed together for his wife, Carol, and their children, Bryan and Natalie. He'd lived well and didn't have to make many changes to be ready to die and meet his Creator.

Only a month before Jerry died, we played tennis together one last time. When I lost a point, he'd accuse me of going easy on him. When I won, he'd accuse me of taking advantage of a man dying of cancer. We laughed and kidded until we cried.

In our final coherent conversation, after I'd read him many scriptures, I said to Jerry, "We were made for another world, not this one." He smiled and said with a weak voice, full of conviction, "Amen."

Jerry got steadily worse. His family brought him home from the hospital, as he requested. As I needed to head to the airport one Thursday morning, I decided to leave home an hour early to see Jerry.

While Nanci sat with Carol in another room, I visited Jerry alone. I hunkered up close to him and read him the last two chapters of the Bible, the same passage I'd read to my mother many times when she lay dying. (She'd died eleven years earlier, to the day.) As I read Revelation 21:4, God "will wipe every tear from their eyes," I looked up and saw tears falling from one of Jerry's eyes. I wiped them away.

I continued to read through my own tears, looking at Jerry between verses, right until Revelation 22:17: "The Spirit and the bride say, 'Come!' And let him who hears say, 'Come!' Whoever is thirsty, let him come; and whoever wishes, let him take the free gift of the water of life."

As I read the word *life*, I looked up, startled by what I saw. Jerry's body was vacant. Between the time I started reading that verse and the time I finished, my old friend had died.

The fact that the last words Jerry heard in this world were God's words, and a specific invitation to come to Heaven (what a verse to go out on), heightened my sense of honor in being with him as his death in one world gave birth to his life in another.

The moment Jerry left, the room seemed utterly vacant. His body had served as a temple in which his spirit and God's Spirit had dwelt together. The moment he died, that temple lay deserted. The glory had departed. Jerry's wasted body was not what was left of him. It was simply what he left.

Looking at Jerry's empty form I sensed exactly what Scripture says is true—death dissolves the union between spirit and body. The body dies but the person lives on.

Jerry and I had attended our grade school and high school graduations together, celebrating afterward. I'd been with him again at his greatest graduation, from this life to the next.

In my final act of friendship in this world, I conducted Jerry's memorial service, a tear-filled, laughter-filled, Christ-centered celebration of his life.

Make no mistake. *Jerry* didn't come to an end. My old friend simply left his temporary residence, relocating to a better place. One moment he labored to breathe the stale air of Earth, the next he effortlessly inhaled the fresh air of Heaven. His death didn't end our friendship; it only interrupted it. The friendship that began on Earth will resume and thrive in a far better world, the world for which God made us, a world of wonders beyond our wildest dreams.

I miss you, Jer. How I *long* for the great reunion!

Thank you, King Jesus, for the price you paid to assure it will happen.

In the end, Jesus Christ is the only satisfying answer to the problem of evil and suffering.

I've tried in this book to avoid putting too much weight on any single argument. But about this I am certain: the best answer to the problem of evil is a person—Jesus Christ. In fact, I'm convinced he is the *only* answer.

In this world of suffering and evil, I have a profound and abiding hope, and faith for the future. Not because I follow a set of religious rules to make me better. But because for forty years I've known a real person, and today I know him better than ever. Through inconceivable self-sacrifice he has touched me deeply, given me a new heart, and utterly transformed my life.

Because he willingly entered this world of evil and suffering and didn't spare himself, but took on the worst of it for my sake and yours, he has earned my trust even for what I can't understand. I and countless others, many of whom have suffered profoundly, have found him to be trustworthy.

He is "the Alpha and the Omega...the Beginning and the End" (Revelation 22:13).

When it comes to goodness and evil, present suffering and eternal joy, the first Word and the last is Jesus.

Notes

1. See Francis A. Schaeffer, *He Is There and He Is Not Silent* (Carol Stream, IL: Tyndale, 1972).
2. Richard Dawkins, *The Blind Watchmaker* (New York: Norton, 1996), 115–16.
3. Marvin Olasky, "Dialogue with Darwinists," *World Magazine,* February 14, 2009.
4. Michael J. Behe, *Darwin's Black Box* (New York: Simon & Schuster, 1998).
5. Paul Davies, "Life Force," in *New Scientist* 163 (September 18, 1999): 27–30.
6. See www.epm.org/intelligentdesign.html.
7. Fyodor Dostoevsky, *The Brothers Karamazov,* (New York: Modern Library, 1995), 272.
8. These concepts are developed in my book *The Treasure Principle* (Sisters, OR: Multnomah, 2001).

About the Author

RANDY ALCORN is the founder and director of Eternal Perspective Ministries (EPM). Prior to 1990, when he started EPM, he served as a pastor for fourteen years. He has spoken around the world and has taught on the adjunct faculties of Multnomah University and Western Seminary in Portland, Oregon.

Randy is the best-selling author of over thirty books with more than four million in print. Randy has written for many magazines and produces the popular periodical *Eternal Perspectives*. He's been a guest on over six hundred radio and television programs including *Focus on the Family, The Bible Answer Man, Family Life Today, Revive Our Hearts, Truths that Transform,* and *Faith Under Fire.*

The father of two married daughters, Karina Franklin and Angela Stump, Randy lives in Gresham, Oregon, with his wife and best friend, Nanci. They are the proud grandparents of four grandsons: Jake, Matt, Ty, and Jack. Randy enjoys hanging out with his family, biking, tennis, research, and reading.

You may contact Eternal Perspective Ministries by e-mail through their Web site at www.epm.org or at 39085 Pioneer Blvd., Suite 206, Sandy, OR 97055 (503) 668-5200.

Visit Randy Alcorn's blog at www.randyalcorn.blogspot.com.
Connect with Randy also at www.facebook.com/randyalcorn and
www.twitter.com/randyalcorn.

Scripture Index

Topical Index